Early Praise for *High Performance PostgreSQL for Rails*

Wow, what an incredible learning experience! This book will provide Rails developers with the knowledge and confidence to adeptly manage projects as their data scales. The book not only instills best practices but also equips developers to counter the instinctive reactions advocating for a transition to microservices, serverless architectures, or alternative technologies like MongoDB, Kafka, and more. It's a valuable resource that not only addresses performance challenges but empowers developers to make informed decisions about their application architecture in the face of growing data demands.

➤ **Daniela Baron**
Software Engineer https://danielabaron.me/

This book is the missing link. Andrew has written the most valuable resource for Rails application developers looking to optimize database performance and scale with ease.

➤ **Nate Berkopec**
Ruby on Rails performance consultant

This is the PostgreSQL manual for Ruby on Rails we've been missing. Andrew's combined PostgreSQL and Rails knowledge in this book will give you more confidence working with SQL and Active Record. This is without a doubt one of my recommended resources moving forward.

➤ **Jason Charnes**
Staff Software Developer, Co-Host of the Remote Ruby podcast

I love that this book lives in two worlds, Rails and Postgres, which are tightly coupled together when running a production application, but are typically separated in terms of knowledge communities. This book brings together a body of knowledge from two different focus areas, Rails and Postgres, to strengthen the application and data relationship. This book is a key resource for anyone running Rails in production at scale.

➤ **Elizabeth Christensen**
    Crunchy Data

A book with this information in it would've allowed me to shortcut several years off of learning Postgres the hard way.

➤ **David Bryant Copeland**

A veritable PostgreSQL "cheat sheet" for the busy application developer, I wish this book existed earlier. Filled front to back with practical, useful examples of common database problems and their solutions, it serves as a killer resource for any dev interested in solving pressing, challenging PostgreSQL problems they may face.

➤ **Brian Davis**

With this book Andrew has demystified DBA concepts so you can go beyond Rails and into PostgreSQL, when scaling starts to hit. The ideas and recommendations on building a performance database, optimizing with bulk upserts, and ensuring data integrity will be particularly handy to gain insight into how your app's data is evolving. The book's expert advice is explained clearly throughout — it's useful to any Rails developer that's wondering if they need to pay their PaaS more, or if there's an alternative through gaining more insight into how their app is scaling.

➤ **Kasper Timm Hansen**
  ex-Rails core and Rails consultant

This book gave me the confidence and the motivation to elevate the performance of my Rails apps in a way I couldn't quite unlock before.

➤ **Ifat Ribon**
  Principal Architect, LaunchPad Lab

High Performance PostgreSQL for Rails

Reliable, Scalable, Maintainable Database Applications

Andrew Atkinson

The Pragmatic Bookshelf

Dallas, Texas

For our complete catalog of hands-on, practical, and Pragmatic content for software developers, please visit *https://pragprog.com*.

Contact *support@pragprog.com* for sales, volume licensing, and support.

For international rights, please contact *rights@pragprog.com*.

The team that produced this book includes:

Publisher:	Dave Thomas
COO:	Janet Furlow
Executive Editor:	Susannah Davidson
Development Editor:	Don N. Hagist
Copy Editor:	Karen Galle
Indexing:	Potomac Indexing, LLC
Layout:	Gilson Graphics

ISBN-13: 979-8-88865-038-7
Book version: P1.0—June 2024

Contents

Part III — Operate and Grow

Part IV — Optimize and Scale

Part V — Advanced Usages

Preface

If you're looking to expand your knowledge and build new skills with Postgre-SQL and Ruby on Rails, you've come to the right place. This book is loaded with practical examples and exercises and is inspired by real-world challenges. Completing them will help you build the skills needed to squeeze out[1] all the performance possible.

Maybe the use of your application has grown, and your team is facing performance problems. Maybe your data has ballooned in size, and you're wondering how to preserve good performance despite high growth. You may be wondering how to make changes to indexes, parameters, or your schema design to improve overall performance while making your operations more predictable. You'll get the context you need while building confidence in your skills.

While the traditional database administrator (DBA) role has declined in popularity,[2] there are more database-backed web applications than ever. Relational databases are the system of record,[3] simultaneously safeguarding irreplaceable company data while serving it to thousands of clients.

Businesses expect that database systems store data safely and reliably and are scalable and cost-efficient. Companies, from small startups to huge corporations, choose PostgreSQL. This means it can grow with your organization, but there isn't a one-size-fits-all configuration. A lot of pressure is placed on databases as data and query volumes grow. That's where you come in! Maybe you'll be the hero who can fix problems and design solutions that sidestep them entirely.

The skills you'll develop as you complete exercises are portable and practical. You'll use modern versions of PostgreSQL and Ruby on Rails, which have the freshest features. You'll start from an existing Rails application and begin

---

1. https://blog.danslimmon.com/2023/08/11/squeeze-the-hell-out-of-the-system-you-have
2. https://builtin.com/software-engineering-perspectives/database-administrator
3. https://en.wikipedia.org/wiki/System_of_record

iterating on it, learning how to make database operations faster, more reliable, and more resilient.

The Rails application and databases are the test lab that you'll use to develop your skills. You'll work with millions of rows of data to help simulate a production environment with slow queries and maintenance operations. Besides core PostgreSQL and Ruby on Rails functionality, you'll add more than 40 Ruby gems and PostgreSQL extensions from the open source ecosystem.

Who Is This Book For?

Topics are chosen for back-end engineers looking to deepen their knowledge and skills with PostgreSQL and Ruby on Rails. Whether you're working on consumer scale Internet applications or enterprise B2B Software as a Service (SaaS), scaling PostgreSQL and Rails application codebases is mission critical for the success of your business. Your team expects to build on and operate these technologies while managing huge data growth amidst shifting business priorities.

If your job responsibilities or career aspirations include any of the following descriptions, this book will help you grow:

- Ruby on Rails application developers sharpening their database skills
- PostgreSQL database administrators (DBAs) learning Ruby on Rails
- Infrastructure and DevOps engineers learning Ruby on Rails
- Database reliability engineers (DBRE) learning how to perform sharding, replication, and table partitioning
- Developers coming from other relational databases
- Web developers with experience in frameworks like Laravel[4] or Django,[5] learning Ruby on Rails
- Data engineers learning PostgreSQL, replication, and change data capture (CDC)

Two major categories of database work are transactional work, also called *online transaction processing* (OLTP), and analytical, also called *online analytical processing* (OLAP).

---

4. https://laravel.com
5. https://www.djangoproject.com

Here, we're focused on OLTP. OLTP has short-duration queries running in high volume, with high concurrency. The result set sizes are small. Wikipedia defines online transaction processing as follows:[6]

> Such systems are expected to respond to user requests and process them in real time.

Now that you've seen a bit about what is covered, what's not covered?

What's Not Covered in This Book?

This book is designed for intermediate professional programmers and isn't an introduction to relational database systems, the Ruby on Rails framework, or the Ruby programming language. Readers are expected to have familiarity with PostgreSQL, Ruby on Rails, or comparable technologies. Readers are also assumed to be familiar with SQL basics, shell scripting, and Docker containers.

If you're new to PostgreSQL, consider *PostgreSQL: Up and Running*[7] as an introduction to PostgreSQL.

If you're new to Ruby on Rails, consider books like *Agile Web Development with Rails 7*[8] for a broader overview of Ruby on Rails beyond the more narrow focus here on Active Record.

If you're new to the Ruby language, consider *Programming Ruby 3.3 (5th Edition)*.[9]

The internals of PostgreSQL, like storage and data layout, are outside the scope of this book, although high-level information is provided. Concepts like multiversion concurrency control (MVCC) and transaction isolation levels are covered at a high level. Readers are directed to PostgreSQL documentation for further information. The online document, "The Internals of PostgreSQL for Database Administrators and System Developers,"[10] is highly regarded.

While PostgreSQL administration and authorization concepts are outside the scope, there are scripted configurations that readers use and can learn from. Concepts like roles and users, grants, and privileges are not covered deeply. The post, "PostgreSQL Basics: Roles and Privileges,"[11] is a great starting point. Concepts like row-level security (RLS) and policies[12] are not covered.

---

6. https://en.wikipedia.org/wiki/Online_transaction_processing
7. https://www.oreilly.com/library/view/postgresql-up-and/9781491963401/
8. https://pragprog.com/titles/rails7/agile-web-development-with-rails-7/
9. https://pragprog.com/titles/ruby5/programming-ruby-3-3-5th-edition/
10. https://www.interdb.jp/pg/
11. https://www.red-gate.com/simple-talk/databases/postgresql/postgresql-basics-roles-and-privileges/
12. https://www.postgresql.org/docs/current/ddl-rowsecurity.html

In later chapters, readers set up multiple types of replication using multiple PostgreSQL instances with Docker. Concepts like high availability (HA) and automatic failover are mentioned but not covered deeply. Consider the book *Database Reliability Engineering*[13] for more on those topics.

Collecting and testing database backups is *critical*. Make sure to collect them automatically and periodically verify their integrity. With that said, backups are outside the scope. They fall more into the realm of infrastructure DBA topics, as compared with application-focused topics. Backups also depend on how PostgreSQL has been deployed. For general information, check out the PostgreSQL documentation chapter, "Backup and Restore."[14]

Finally, we're focused here on the traditional "single primary" (or "single writer") form of PostgreSQL. This is the default open source community distribution. Other types of distributed PostgreSQL variations are outside the scope.

Extra software that readers will work with is open source, permissively licensed, and noncommercial. This allows readers to install all the software locally for hands-on exercises.

Ruby on Rails Skills Are in Demand

In the post, "Big Transitions in the Tech Industry" from Hired's "2023 State of Software Engineers Survey,"[15] Ruby on Rails was the most sought-after skill.

> Ruby on Rails surfaced as the most in-demand skill for software engineering roles, creating 1.64x more interview requests for the developers proficient in it.

Combining Ruby on Rails and PostgreSQL is a great way to build database-backed web applications. Rails Guides even have a page dedicated to "Active Record with PostgreSQL."[16]

Active Record continues to add support for PostgreSQL capabilities in new versions. For example, generated columns from PostgreSQL 12 was added to Active Record as virtual columns.[17] Common table expressions (CTE) were added to Active Record in version 7.1.

Native support for multiple databases[18] in Active Record was added in version 6, providing developers with powerful ways to leverage multiple PostgreSQL

---

13. https://www.oreilly.com/library/view/database-reliability-engineering/9781491925935/
14. https://www.postgresql.org/docs/current/backup.html
15. https://hired.com/state-of-software-engineers/2023/
16. https://guides.rubyonrails.org/active_record_postgresql.html
17. https://blog.saeloun.com/2022/01/25/rails-7-postgres-support-for-generated-columns.html
18. https://guides.rubyonrails.org/active_record_multiple_databases.html

instances to scale out their workload. With multiple databases, Postgre-SQL instances can support read and write splitting, application-level sharding, and horizontal sharding. Readers will implement these capabilities with PostgreSQL and Active Record in upcoming chapters.

PostgreSQL Is a Popular Award Winner

You've made a great choice to invest your time learning PostgreSQL. Postgre-SQL is praised for reliability, SQL standards conformance,[19] and having a high bar for features and documentation quality.

PostgreSQL was the #1 most popular database in use with Rails according to the "2022 Ruby on Rails Community Survey,"[20] with data spanning 13 years, from 2009 through 2022.

PostgreSQL was a three-time #1 Winner in 2017, 2018, and 2020 in "DB-Engines Ranking,"[21] an annual ranking of the most popular databases in the world.

In 2022, PostgreSQL was the third most popular database behind Snowflake[22] and Google BigQuery,[23] which are both primarily OLAP databases.

The 2022 "Stack Overflow Developer Survey"[24] gathered input from nearly 50,000 professional developers. When the developers were asked what database they used most, PostgreSQL was the #1 answer.

Both technologies have vibrant, international communities, helping improve their core features and documentation year after year. Ruby on Rails 7.1 had more than 800 contributors,[25] while the PostgreSQL 16 Release Notes[26] acknowledged more than 350 people.

PostgreSQL and Ruby on Rails are vibrant today and will be for years to come!

---

19. https://www.postgresql.org/docs/current/features.html
20. https://rails-hosting.com/2022/#databases
21. https://db-engines.com/en/ranking
22. https://www.snowflake.com
23. https://cloud.google.com/bigquery
24. https://survey.stackoverflow.co/2022/#most-popular-technologies-database-prof
25. https://rubyonrails.org/2023/10/5/Rails-7-1-0-has-been-released
26. https://www.postgresql.org/docs/current/release-16.html#RELEASE-16-ACKNOWLEDGEMENTS

Acknowledgments

The following people all contributed to the content, accuracy, style, or quality of this book. I deeply appreciate their contributions.

Thank you to these fine folks for your mentorship over the years: Paul Barry, Jamie Gaskins, Andrew Kane, David Rowley, Haki Benita, Craig Kerstiens, and Ryan Booz.

Thank you to Jonathan Gennick for providing the initial spark for this book. Thanks to Brian Hogan for sharing your enthusiasm for education and the Pragmatic Bookshelf.

Thanks to Nate Kadlac for the cover illustration and promotional advice.

Thanks to the following individuals who provided excellent technical feedback: Nate Berkopec, Jason Charnes, Elizabeth Christensen, Michael Christofides, David Bryant Copeland, Andy Croll, Brian Davis, Lukas Fittl, Michael Harris, Greg Navis, Franck Pachot, Ifat Ribon, Gabrielle Roth, and Robert Treat.

Thank you to beta readers who provided detailed feedback: Daniela Baron, Henrietta Dombrovskaya, Kevin Murphy, Xavier Noria, Steve Hill, and Ben Sheldon.

Thanks to Michael Christofides and Nikolay Samokhvalov for the Postgres.fm podcast. Not only did I learn a lot, the weekly cadence provided steady motivation to write!

A huge thank you to the Pragmatic Bookshelf team for your support: Tammy Coron, Erica Sadun, Margaret Eldridge, and especially Don N. Hagist.

To my family, especially my partner Sara: thank you for your generous support that allowed me to pursue this endeavor. Without you, this wouldn't have been possible!

Part I

Getting Started

## CHAPTER 1

An App to Get You Started

Welcome! Glad to have you here! PostgreSQL and Ruby on Rails are powerful open source technologies that you probably love working with.

This book covers many PostgreSQL database concepts that will be new for programmers who have only worked with their relational database in a basic way. While reading about new topics is important, you'll get the most value from hands-on practice, reading examples, running through exercises, and creating your own experiments.

To help you get started, you'll set up a Rails app and a PostgreSQL database that you'll use throughout the book. Each chapter focuses on a broad theme, which is covered in a series of related sections. Within the chapters, you'll find terminology guides, examples, and hands-on exercises. You'll set up your local development environment from scratch, get PostgreSQL up and running, and then connect the Rails app to it. Instructions are provided at publication time for macOS, although other platforms may be supported in the future. Check GitHub for the latest code and documentation.

The Ruby on Rails app you'll work with is called *Rideshare*.

What's it all about?

What Is Rideshare?

Rideshare is a back-end Rails API app that you can imagine powering a fictional ridesharing service. Think of popular ridesharing services like Uber or Lyft. Imagine that a small fraction of their codebase, around ten models (backed by database tables), was extracted. What you'd have is something like the Rideshare codebase.

Despite being a small Rails app, you'll use it to explore advanced topics like replication, sharding, and partitioning.

The core Active Record models in Rideshare are Driver, Rider, Trip, and TripRequest.

If you've picked up this book and you're less experienced with Rails, you'll need to know some basics about Active Record.

Active Record is the default *Object Relational Mapping* (ORM) layer for Ruby on Rails. Active Record allows developers to work with Ruby objects and Ruby code, written as Ruby classes, that manage persistence with PostgreSQL.

Active Record objects are initialized from database data by issuing SELECT queries to PostgreSQL, which happen from Active Record methods like .find() or .where(). When Active Record objects are saved or updated, INSERT and UPDATE SQL statements are issued. Active Record can be used outside of Ruby on Rails in other Ruby web frameworks like Sinatra.[1]

Active Record uses "Convention over Configuration"[2] as a design principle. This means that Active Record models have far less configuration compared with other frameworks.

For example, Active Record models use singular names like Driver or TripRequest, with corresponding plural database table names like drivers or trip_requests.

Rideshare includes a diagram you can use to explore the models and their relationships visually. Navigate to https://github.com/andyatkinson/rideshare to find the application. In the root directory, there's an *Entity Relationship Diagram* (ERD) PDF file erd.pdf.[3] Click the ERD PDF to view it. The ERD is kept up-to-date automatically when Active Record migrations are run.

Besides persistence, Active Record is used for schema evolution. How does that work?

Active Record Schema Management Refresher

Active Record is used by Rails developers to evolve their database schema design. Each change is represented as a *migration*. The schema design is dumped (or *serialized*) into a file that's committed to version control. The schema file can use a Ruby format or a SQL format. Rideshare uses the SQL format, which means the file is db/structure.sql.

---

1.   https://sinatrarb.com
2.   https://rubyonrails.org/doctrine#convention-over-configuration
3.   https://github.com/andyatkinson/rideshare/blob/main/erd.pdf

If you've used schema management tools like Flyway[4] or Liquibase,[5] you'll find similarities to Active Record migrations.

Let's look at migration files. Migrations are versioned Ruby files in the db/migrate directory. They contain Active Record code that generates SQL *Data Definition Language* (DDL) statements like CREATE TABLE or CREATE INDEX. Migrations are generated using a Rails command-line generator. Each file gets a unique version number. Rails compares the files and the versions that have been applied to determine whether there are pending migrations to apply. Active Record manages a table called schema_migrations to do that, which is a table that's added to all Rails app databases.

Active Record Schema Evolution

 Developers generate migrations, which are versioned files that describe changes to the database structure. Versions are added to schema_migrations when they've been applied. This happens when a developer runs bin/rails db:migrate connected to their local database. Behind the scenes, pg_dump runs (for PostgreSQL), dumping the structure of the database into the file db/structure.sql. Versions from schema_migrations are dumped as INSERT statements, which makes them ready to run on another database. These are the basics of how two or more database structures are kept in sync.

Besides DDL, developers can place *Data Modification Language* (DML) statements like INSERT, UPDATE, and DELETE into migrations. While possible, a good practice is to perform data modifications separately from migrations. Since migrations run during code deployment, they should run quickly and reliably to minimize their impact during new releases.

While db/structure.sql contains mostly structural information, it can also contain data. For example, the schema_migrations versions are dumped as INSERT statements into the file, along with column data.

Remember that db/structure.sql is generated by developers from their local databases. This means unrelated changes can creep in. Make sure that changes being proposed to db/structure.sql are only related to the code that's changing. db/structure.sql is meant to be in sync with what's deployed in production.

With that refresher in place, you're ready to proceed. Let's look at the development environment dependencies for Rideshare.

---

4.   https://flywaydb.org
5.   https://www.liquibase.com

Exploring Rideshare Dependencies

To run Rideshare on your local macOS machine, you'll need Ruby, PostgreSQL, and other software dependencies. Rideshare has been tested on macOS Sonoma, which was released in late 2023. Refer to GitHub, where you may find instructions for other platforms besides macOS.

Review the following list of software and versions that you'll need:

	Version	Year
PostgreSQL	16.0	2023
Homebrew	4.1.20	2023
Git	2.42.0	2023
rbenv (Ruby version manager)	1.2.0	2023
Ruby	3.2.2	2023

Rideshare uses a specific version of Ruby that may not match the version you've got installed. Let's use a Ruby version manager to install Ruby. The recommended one is rbenv.[6]

Bundler[7] is included with Ruby, and you'll use it to install Ruby gems the project needs.

Another tool you'll need is Homebrew.[8] Install Homebrew by following the instructions at https://brew.sh. For new macOS installs, you may be prompted to install the Xcode Command Line Tools. Once Homebrew is installed, run brew --version and confirm it's 4.1.20 or higher.

Let's begin installing the development environment.

Installing Application Dependencies

To clone the repo and work with source code, you'll need Git. Run git --version in your terminal. Verify that you're running 2.42.0 or greater. Otherwise, install it with Homebrew.

Run the following command in your terminal to install the packages needed for Rideshare:

---

6. https://github.com/rbenv/rbenv
7. https://bundler.io
8. https://brew.sh

```
sh/intro_brew_install_steps.sh
brew install git \
  rbenv \
  graphviz
```

Run rbenv --version and confirm that version 1.2.0 or greater is installed.

Graphviz[9] is a program that's used to generate new versions of the ERD mentioned earlier. You need to install it now before running migrations since it's called when migrations are applied.

With those packages installed, let's get PostgreSQL up and running.

Installing PostgreSQL on macOS

PostgreSQL can be installed in a variety of ways on macOS. The recommended way is to install *Postgres.app.*[10]

You may prefer to install PostgreSQL 16 via Homebrew, which is another popular method. If you're comfortable with your Homebrew PostgreSQL 16 installation, review the following note and skip the remainder of this section.

PostgreSQL Homebrew Installation

If you installed PostgreSQL via Homebrew, you may be missing configuration compared to how PostgreSQL is installed when using the recommended method of Postgres.app. For example, you'll need a PostgreSQL user called postgres with a password. If you don't have this user, create it by running createuser -s postgres --pwprompt, then type postgres for the password.

The exercises also expect that you've got a database and a superuser that both have the same name as your OS user. For example, if your OS user is named "andy" and you need to add this database and superuser, type: createdb -O andy andy to do that. This command creates a "andy" database that's owned by the "andy" user created in the preceding sentence.

To install Postgres.app, visit https://postgresapp.com in your browser and navigate to the "Downloads" section. Choose the "Universal" version, which supports both Intel and ARM processors, if you're not sure which version you need.

---

9.   https://graphviz.org

10. https://www.postgresql.org/download/macosx/

Double-click the .dmg file and follow the instructions. If you get stuck, refer to the documentation at https://postgresapp.com/documentation/, or review troubleshooting information in the appendix *Getting Help*.

Once installed, launch Postgres.app. The app runs as a menu bar app in the upper top right area of macOS. Look for an elephant icon! When you find it, open it and choose "Open Postgres".

From there, the left column shows the PostgreSQL server versions that are installed. It will be empty to start. Choose the plus icon, then "Create new Server." Review the version 16 default settings and choose "Create Server".

Once you've done that, PostgreSQL will be ready to use but will not be running. Choose "Start". PostgreSQL is now running on the default port 5432.

By default, Postgres.app adds a database that has the same name as your macOS user, which is what you see when you run the whoami command in your terminal.

When you run psql without any arguments, you connect to this database by default.

Before closing the Postgres.app window, explore the "Server Settings" area. Take note of the Data Directory, Config File, and Log Directory. You'll work with these later on.

Now that PostgreSQL is running, you will need a client to connect to it. You will use the built-in command-line program to do that. Before connecting, you'll need to configure your terminal.

Let's make sure PATH is configured properly so it works with psql. Run the following command from your terminal to create the paths.d directory and place the Postgres.app configuration there:

```
sh/postgres_app_setup.sh
#
# Configure your $PATH
# https://postgresapp.com/documentation/cli-tools.html
#
sudo mkdir -p /etc/paths.d &&
  echo \
  /Applications/Postgres.app/Contents/Versions/latest/bin \
  | sudo tee /etc/paths.d/postgresapp
```

After doing that, restart your terminal or close your current one and open a new one. Let's test that psql and pg_dump client programs work as expected.

Run the following commands from your terminal:

```
sh/postgresql_cli_programs_test.sh
psql --version

pg_dump --version

pg_config
```

Verify psql and pg_dump use version 16.0 or greater. Run pg_config and verify the last line shows VERSION = PostgreSQL 16.0 (or greater). The point here is that you don't want to use older client versions that might have been installed and are incompatible with your server version.

With the client programs installed and the terminal configured, let's continue with verifying the connection.

Run psql from your terminal without any arguments. If your username is andy, and you've configured your psql prompt similarly, you'd see the following information:

```
psql (16.0)
Type "help" for help.

andy@[local]:5432 andy#
```

Your prompt may be slightly different. If you'd like to configure an equivalent prompt, refer to the .psqlrc.sample file in the postgresql directory of Rideshare.

Let's break down the parts we're seeing here in the prompt. The psql client version is 16.0, which matches the server version. We've connected as user andy (in PostgreSQL, users are "roles" that can log in) which is visible as the left-most part of andy@[local]:5432 andy#. We also see localhost for the host, port 5432, and the database name is andy. No password was needed or supplied.

Later on, you'll connect to PostgreSQL with a required password for authentication, but you'll configure a special file to store the password so that you don't have to supply it.

To verify the database you're connected to, connect with psql from your terminal and run this:

```
SELECT CURRENT_DATABASE();
```

Note that SQL keywords and functions are shown in uppercase throughout to identify them more easily. However, they aren't case sensitive and work the same in lowercase.

If that ran correctly, you should see the andy database returned (or your default database name). Great! Type the meta-command (you'll learn about those later) \q to quit psql. You're now back in your terminal.

With PostgreSQL configured, you're ready to shift your focus to setting up Rideshare.

Installing Rideshare

First, you'll need a copy of the Rideshare source code.

From your terminal, cd into the directory where you normally store your source code. For example, you might use a Projects directory in your home directory. To go there, run cd /Users/andy/Projects. Once there, run the following command to clone the Rideshare repo:

```
git clone https://github.com/andyatkinson/rideshare.git
```

Once cloned, cd into the rideshare directory. This is the main directory that all examples will be based on. Explore some of the important top-level directories like db and postgresql. Besides the top-level README.md, each of those directories has its own README.md. Check those out to get familiar with their content.

Rideshare Installation

 While these instructions are intended to be accurate, they are limited to macOS only and may become outdated as time passes.

For the latest instructions, visit Rideshare on GitHub at https://github.com/andyatkinson/rideshare.

The .ruby-version file in the root directory lists the exact version of Ruby that's used.

Run cat .ruby-version to see the version. Currently, that's version 3.2.2. To install it, run rbenv install 3.2.2. Compiling Ruby may take a few minutes!

Once that's complete, run ruby --version from the Rideshare directory and confirm the correct version is set. Running rbenv versions shows all installed Ruby versions. You should see output similar to this:

```
  system
* 3.2.2 (set by /Users/andy/.rbenv/version)
```

The system Ruby version displayed previously is installed but is not in active use. Version 3.2.2 is the active version, indicated by the asterisk. If you see something different, refer to the section "Learn how to load rbenv in your shell" from the rbenv documentation.[11]

---

11. https://github.com/rbenv/rbenv#using-package-managers

Selecting the Correct Ruby Version Automatically

 Make sure the required Ruby version is selected automatically when you cd into the Rideshare directory.

From this point forward, we'll assume Ruby version 3.2.2 (or the version listed in .ruby-version) is installed and active.

You're ready to continue with the installation of Rideshare Ruby gems. To do that you'll use Bundler, which is included with your installation of Ruby. Confirm that by running bundler --version from your terminal and verify that version 2.3.6 or greater is displayed.

After verifying Bundler is installed, run the following command from the Rideshare directory in your terminal:

```
bundle install
```

If you run into Ruby gem installation issues, refer to the troubleshooting information in the appendix *Getting Help*.

We'll assume you installed the gems successfully and are ready to proceed.

Let's recap what you've done so far. The application source code is in place, and the Ruby gems and dependencies are installed, which means you're ready to connect the application and database.

Configuring PostgreSQL for Rideshare

Normally, in Rails apps, you run bin/rails db:create to create their databases. To set up the databases for Rideshare, you'll use a custom shell script. The reason is because the script is much more opinionated about how the users, privileges, schemas, and grants should be configured compared with what would be done by default.

Here's an overview of what the script does:

- Creates users owner, app, and app_readonly with secure passwords
- Creates the rideshare_development database
- Creates the rideshare schema
- Grants the required privileges to the schema and users
- Alters the default privileges following PostgreSQL best practices
- Removes the public schema

In PostgreSQL, users are *roles* that have the LOGIN privilege.[12]

Each user has a password that's set, which is a generated, unique value. To generate the password, the script uses openssl on macOS, which is a program that's installed by default, although you may generate a secure password using a different mechanism.

To avoid placing a secure value into your shell history, the generated password is assigned to the environment variable RIDESHARE_DB_PASSWORD within the script. The hex option for openssl is used to avoid generating slash characters, which can break password parsing.

Run the following command from your terminal to set RIDESHARE_DB_PASSWORD:

```
sh/set_database_password_variable.sh
export RIDESHARE_DB_PASSWORD=$(openssl rand -hex 12)
```

Review the value that was set by running echo $RIDESHARE_DB_PASSWORD. Now that it's set, you'll be using this password to authenticate with a PostgreSQL user. You won't need to supply the password in connection strings, though. Instead, the password is stored in a special file called ~/.pgpass that command-line clients are configured to read automatically.

If you aren't familiar with ~/.pgpass, refer to a sample file in the postgresql directory of Rideshare.

The file has a line for each credential that's stored, and it uses a specific colon-separated format to describe the different parts of a connection string for users connecting to PostgreSQL.

A line like the following is created when you run the script. The HSnDDgFtyW9fyFI password is the generated password and is set for RIDESHARE_DB_PASSWORD. It will be a different value when you run it, but we'll keep using it here in examples.

```
localhost:5432:rideshare_development:owner:HSnDDgFtyW9fyFI
```

More details on ~/.pgpass are covered later on. For now, it's enough to know the file provides the password. In the previous example, the owner user authenticates to PostgreSQL using the password value that it reads from the file.

There's another environment variable you'll need to set before running sh db/setup.sh. Set DB_URL by running the following in your terminal:

```
export DB_URL="postgres://postgres:@localhost:5432/postgres"
```

This variable creates a connection to the postgres database using the postgres superuser. This is needed mainly for the initial connection to the server so that the connection can then be used to run commands for other databases.

We're still getting you up to speed on what db/setup.sh does, and you're just about ready to run it. Let's do one more pre-run check. Run the following commands to make sure each of the following environment variables are set:

- echo $DB_URL
- echo $RIDESHARE_DB_PASSWORD

The main command you'll run from your terminal is sh db/setup.sh. Let's use a variation that captures the command output into a file called output.log file. You can then review the file later and make sure there are no errors listed.

Alright, you're ready to run it. cd to the Rideshare root directory in your terminal, and run the following command:

```
sh/db_setup.sh
#
# The portion '2>&1 | tee -a output.log'
# captures output to `output.log`
#
sh db/setup.sh 2>&1 | tee -a output.log
```

Tearing Down

 If you see errors in output.log and are happy to reset, there's a corollary db/teardown.sh script that removes all Rideshare databases and objects. To use it, run sh db/teardown.sh and then try sh db/setup.sh again.

This will only take a few moments to run. If sh db/setup.sh ran successfully, the Rideshare schema, users, database, and other objects are fully configured.

Check output.log for any mentions of ERROR. For troubleshooting, refer to the appendix *Getting Help* or the Rideshare README.md on GitHub.

Great! You're all set. Before moving on, since this is a book about PostgreSQL, after all, let's review some more technical details about what you've just configured.

Configuring Database Access

As you saw in the script, you configured the owner role to connect using a password supplied from the ~/.pgpass file. The owner role connects to the rideshare_development database and is the owner of objects like tables within the schema. Now that db/setup.sh has run, you've got the user in place. Let's test that out.

Reference the .env file in the root directory of Rideshare for the DATABASE_URL environment variable. You'll want to set that variable in your local shell, or even better, have it set automatically any time you open a new shell.

To get you going, the db/setup.sh prints out instructions showing you how to export DATABASE_URL using the value in the .env file. In your same terminal, you should be able to connect right away by running psql $DATABASE_URL. Try it and make sure you can do that since you'll be running that a lot in upcoming chapters.

What about configuring that automatically for new shells? You have got a few options. You could run export every time you open a new shell, but that's a pain.

A better option is to add DATABASE_URL to the shell file for your system, which is loaded when new shells open. The specific file depends on which shell you use. For example, in Z shell, which is the default on macOS, you'd place the export line you saw printed out or ran earlier into the file ~/.zshrc on your system. When you open new shells, the content in that file runs, and the variable is set.

Once DATABASE_URL is set for all new shells, you'll always be able to connect to it using psql by running psql $DATABASE_URL.

You'll know you've connected correctly when you see the rideshare_development database and owner user listed in your psql prompt (see prompt customization in Rideshare postgresql directory and the ~/.psqlrc file).

Let's check the prompt. Run psql $DATABASE_URL and verify it looks like this:

```
psql (16.1, server 16.1)
Type "help" for help.

owner@localhost:5432 rideshare_development#
```

Great. You're able to quickly connect to the PostgreSQL Rideshare database using the correct user and with their credentials.

How can you set up quick access for Rails?

For Rails, Rideshare reads the .env file in the root directory. That file supplies a value for DATABASE_URL. The dotenv[13] Ruby on Rails gem reads that file and uses it for Rails commands like rails db or rails console. Since the variable doesn't contain sensitive parts like the password, the file was added to Git.

---

13. https://github.com/bkeepers/dotenv

Try running bin/rails db and verify that a psql prompt is launched for the correct user and database that you saw earlier. Running bin/rails console should use the same approach.

Great! You've now verified that you can connect from psql and Rails console.

Let's make sure the Rideshare database schema is up to date. Run bin/rails db:migrate in your terminal to be sure.

Which Rails Executable?

 Ruby on Rails may be installed on your system as a Ruby gem and as a rails executable. To avoid using the incorrect one, commands will use bin/rails.

If migrations run without errors, you've completed the final required step of setting up your development environment for Rideshare. Nice!

Let's recap. PostgreSQL is up and running, and Rideshare is connected to it. Any pending migrations have been applied, so your database structure is up to date.

As you move into new chapters, you'll explore a lot of concepts with PostgreSQL, Ruby on Rails, and SQL.

Let's preview some of the terminology you'll work with.

Learning PostgreSQL Terminology

PostgreSQL is an *Object Relational Database*. If you're a programmer who's familiar with object-oriented programming (OOP) in software, you might be wondering what objects are in PostgreSQL.

In PostgreSQL, objects are things like tables, indexes, schemas, column defaults, or constraints. Objects in PostgreSQL can have dependencies and participate in inheritance hierarchies, too.

Databases have a lot of unique terminology. Terminology guides with simplified definitions are included in every chapter. For authoritative definitions, refer to official sources like the "PostgreSQL Glossary."[14]

If you haven't worked with relational databases or PostgreSQL deeply, you might see terms like *relations*, *tuples*, *bloat*, or something called the *optimizer*. What do they mean? Let's cover some basics.

---

14. https://www.postgresql.org/docs/current/glossary.html

In PostgreSQL, the documentation describes a *relation* as "essentially a mathematical term."[15] Most of the time, when you see relation used, it's probably referring to a table.[16] *Tuples* are another concept you'll see. What are they?

Rows in database tables that users see are actually presenting hidden versions of rows. Changes to rows are captured as immutable row versions and are not actually changed in place.

These row versions are called tuples. The basic idea is that PostgreSQL supports multiple tuples (row versions) for a row that can exist at the same time for different concurrent access. Tuples can be live or dead, which you'll learn more about later.

You'll also see the term *bloat* and work with it in upcoming chapters. Bloat relates to extra allocated space that's not used in the file system and those old row versions that aren't needed that you saw in the last paragraph. High amounts of bloat create inefficient data storage or fragmented storage, which contributes to more latency when data is accessed.

In PostgreSQL, data is stored in *pages* (which is a term that's mostly interchangeable with "blocks" here). Each page has a fixed size of 8 KB by default. Data that's stored in PostgreSQL must fit into a page. Pages have pre-allocated space and are filled from inserts, updates, and deletes for table rows or index entries. Some space is left unused to allow for additional updates.

These pages (or blocks) are stored in regular files you're familiar with inside the data directory. You'll work with that later on.

With basics for PostgreSQL covered, let's review some SQL terminology.

Learning SQL Terminology

SQL is a *declarative* paradigm,[17] which refers to how the programmer and client application interact with the server. As the programmer, you write SQL queries sent using your client to the server. The queries describe the data you're looking for. PostgreSQL gets to choose the method used to find it. The programmer describes "what" is needed and PostgreSQL chooses "how." The separation is intentional in this model.

---

15. https://www.postgresql.org/docs/current/tutorial-concepts.html
16. https://www.postgresql.org/docs/current/tutorial-concepts.html
17. https://en.wikipedia.org/wiki/Declarative_programming

To figure out how to perform the requested task, PostgreSQL parses the SQL query or command it receives. When it's a query to read data, PostgreSQL determines an optimal retrieval algorithm. The tables, indexes, estimates, data distribution, and computational costs are all considered on the fly to generate one or more alternative query plans.

PostgreSQL shows you the query plan it selected, with a wealth of information about it. PostgreSQL compares alternative plans using statistics that it continually collects, along with estimates like the cost of various operations.

While PostgreSQL doesn't allow you to control the exact plan that's selected, you'll learn how you can strongly influence the selected plan.

The planner uses a *cost-based algorithm* to compare the costs of various alternative plans. The planner is also called the *optimizer*.

In upcoming chapters, you'll write a lot of SQL. Besides SQL statements, you'll run commands, develop and call *functions*, and write and execute *procedures*.

What are functions and procedures? Functions enhance your database. You can use built-in functions or even create your own as *user-defined functions*. Functions can be written in SQL or a procedural language. Procedures expand on functions, providing more capabilities such as *transactional control.*[18]

What are *transactions*?

PostgreSQL is a *transactional* database. A database transaction in PostgreSQL is a critically important concept that's fundamental to how operations are performed and how concurrency works. Concurrency in PostgreSQL uses mechanisms to support thousands of clients being connected simultaneously to PostgreSQL, performing different operations, including ones that conflict and will be canceled. That's normal!

The term transaction is overloaded and can also refer to how multiple operations can be performed as one unit of work.

To do that, transactions have an "isolated" view of the data at a point in time based on their configurable *isolation level.*[19] To explore transactions in greater depth, you'll create explicit transactions in upcoming chapters and deliberately cause conflicts to see what happens.

---

18. https://www.postgresql.org/docs/current/plpgsql-transactions.html
19. https://www.postgresql.org/docs/current/transaction-iso.html

Let's recap some of the terminology you've seen in this section:

Glossary of Database Terms

- Declarative model—In this model, users write SQL to declare the results they want, but not how to get them.

- Relation or relname—Usually, a relation refers to a table, but it's a general mathematical term.

- Data Manipulation Language (DML)—This is a category covering INSERT, UPDATE, and DELETE statements.

- Data Definition Language (DDL)—This category of statements covers ALTER TABLE or CREATE INDEX, which are structural changes.

- Transaction—A unit of work that occurs as one, and an isolated view of the data

- Query execution plan—The plan PostgreSQL selects to perform an action

With PostgreSQL and SQL terminology behind you, let's look at Ruby on Rails and Active Record.

Ruby on Rails Terminology

You'll primarily work with the Object Relational Mapping (ORM) layer in Ruby on Rails called Active Record.[20]

While having features in common with other ORM systems, Active Record goes beyond basic persistence. Migrations provide a schema evolution mechanism. Active Record provides programmers with expressive data modeling and validation capabilities.

Active Record *associations*, like has_many() and belongs_to(), appear like documentation but are callable Ruby methods.

Active Record *validations* document and enforce correctness and consistency at the application layer. They can hook into lifecycle events that are triggered when models are created, saved, updated, or deleted.

---

20. https://guides.rubyonrails.org/active_record_basics.html

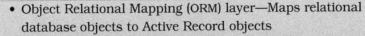

Active Record Terminology

- Object Relational Mapping (ORM) layer—Maps relational database objects to Active Record objects

- Migrations—Ruby classes with versions that generate SQL statements to change the database

- Associations—Active Record model methods like has_many() or belongs_to() that describe model relationships

- Validations—Active Record model methods that describe and enforce data correctness

Now that we've covered PostgreSQL, SQL, Ruby on Rails, and Active Record, let's preview some of the writing conventions you'll see throughout.

Conventions Used in This Book

Most of the code snippets are placed in external files with an extension that helps describe their type and provides syntax highlighting. Some of the files are shell scripts, SQL, or Ruby. For code snippets in exercises, copy and paste them from these files instead of trying to type them in to save yourself time and avoid mistakes.

Shell script files (.sh) may start with a "shebang" line like #!/usr/bin/env bash. When that's included, it means the script can be run from your terminal.

When there's no shebang line, the intention is to run those commands individually. The commands were placed in a .sh file in those cases to make it easier to copy and paste them and for syntax highlighting.

For CLI programs that support short and long versions of option names, for example, -v and --version, the long version is used. When commands are too long for the page width, they'll be split across multiple lines using a backslash to end a line.

For psql meta-commands, like \q, the expanded form of the abbreviation is usually written out to help reinforce their purpose. For example, the \du meta-command might be written as *describe user*.

You'll be doing a lot of work in your terminal. On macOS, use the built-in terminal application or a third-party option like iTerm2.[21]

---

21. https://iterm2.com

When you encounter a shell script like load_data.sh that's in Rideshare, cd to the directory where the script is located, then type sh load_data.sh to run it.

Units like KB, MB, and GB will be in monospace and separated from their number with a space to match how they're formatted by the PG_SIZE_PRETTY() function.

Let's preview some SQL formatting conventions.

SQL Formatting Conventions

SQL keywords and functions are capitalized and in monospace, for example SELECT, WHERE, LIMIT, or SELECT CURRENT_USER;. However, the capitalization is not necessary for SQL. It's used here to differentiate functions and keywords from other types of query text.

You may also encounter fragments of queries or specific clauses. These aren't runnable on their own and that will be called out.

Proper nouns in PostgreSQL like *System Views*[22] will be presented using the format from official documentation.

Let's look at conventions for Ruby on Rails.

Ruby and Rails Formatting Conventions

When Ruby or Ruby on Rails keywords are listed, they'll match official documentation like "Ruby on Rails Guides."[23] Ruby on Rails layers like Active Record or Active Job use multiple words separated by a space.

Ruby methods in code samples generally start with a dot and are in lowercase with explicit parentheses. For example: .average(). The dot, lowercase, and explicit parentheses help distinguish Ruby code from SQL functions or keywords. Note that this same format is used without regard for whether the method is a class or instance method.

You're Ready

With Rideshare installed and configured, the conventions in the book, and some new terminology behind you, you're ready to move forward and face new challenges.

---

22. https://www.postgresql.org/docs/current/views.html
23. https://guides.rubyonrails.org

For many Rails developers, database administration tasks are unfamiliar. They may not ever connect directly to PostgreSQL or perform administration tasks. This lack of familiarity can prevent Rails developers from gaining access to valuable observability information and system administration functions, which is limiting when troubleshooting issues.

Let's fix that! To improve your administration skills, you'll start connecting directly to your Rideshare database and exploring new areas.

See you in the next chapter!

Part II

Design and Build

## CHAPTER 2

Administration Basics

In this chapter, you'll begin performing administration tasks to grow your operational knowledge with PostgreSQL.

In the last chapter, you installed and configured the Rideshare Rails app connected to a PostgreSQL database. If you skipped the introduction and aren't familiar with Rideshare, consider going back and setting it up before proceeding since you'll be using the database for exercises.

You'll use new terminology like meta-commands, the psql client, observability in PostgreSQL, locks, database parameters, and extensions.

Let's get started.

Touring psql Features

When connecting to PostgreSQL, you'll need a client application. While there are great graphical (GUI) clients,[1] in this book, you'll work from your terminal using the command-line (CLI) client psql.

psql is recommended for several reasons. psql ships with PostgreSQL, so it's always available. psql can be used on remote hosts and offers low latency. As the native client for PostgreSQL, it's well-tested and supported.

To learn more about why psql is recommended, and to expand on the meta-commands and tips and tricks you'll use in this chapter, visit the appendix *Why psql?* in the back of this book.

With that said, let's begin using it.

---

1. https://wiki.postgresql.org/wiki/PostgreSQL_Clients

In the last chapter, you configured DATABASE_URL, which specified a database name and user. Run echo $DATABASE_URL to make sure it's set. If needed, reference the value in the Rideshare .env file.

With that set, run psql $DATABASE_URL from your terminal:

```
sh/psql_dbname.sh
export DATABASE_URL="postgres://owner:@localhost:5432/rideshare_development"

psql $DATABASE_URL
```

With this method, you should be able to connect quickly and easily using psql.

Let's imagine that you're new to psql. You're now connected, but you're staring at a blank prompt. What can you do from here?

Let's explore. A backend process ID was started up for your psql session. Run SELECT PG_BACKEND_PID(); to see the pid value. You'll learn more about backends and pid values in upcoming sections.

While still in psql, type \s and press return. This is a *meta-command* and it might be the first one you've used. psql has loads of meta-commands. The post, "17 Practical psql Commands,"[2] lists many of them, and you'll be using some of them in this chapter.

The \s meta-command lists the history of commands you've run. They're listed in chronological order, which means the oldest commands are at the top, and the newest commands are at the bottom.

If you run a statement like SELECT 1; and then run \s again, you'll see the statement is now in your history at the bottom. If Vim is configured to be your editor, typing G brings you to the bottom of the file.

Let's continue this tour and move to a new topic.

You'll begin working with PostgreSQL extensions and *system catalogs*,[3] or more simply a "catalog." What are those? From psql, run SELECT * FROM pg_extension; to see installed extensions. What is pg_extension here? pg_extension is one of the many system catalogs that PostgreSQL provides. PostgreSQL has these for "internal bookkeeping," and they're some of the tools you'll use to get visibility into what's happening. System catalogs start with pg_*.

---

2.   https://www.postgresqltutorial.com/postgresql-administration/psql-commands/
3.   https://www.postgresql.org/docs/current/catalogs-overview.html

---

Administration Terminology

- Meta-commands—psql commands that start with a backslash
- Backends—A backend process with a pid and query
- System catalog—A PostgreSQL table or view that tracks internal information

---

As you begin typing many commands in psql, you'll want to search back through them.

If you've used the history command in your terminal, psql can support a similar "reverse search" by typing "ctrl-r". This requires adding bind "^R" em-inc-search-prev to a file ~/.editrc.[4] Once that is present and you've launched psql, type ctrl-r, then SEL to match any SELECT statements you've run before.

When you wish to run the previous statement again, psql supports \g to do that.

Let's look further at the history file. The commands history is stored in the file ~/.psql_history by default. While the history file is a plain text file that can be opened in an editor, it's not readable and is meant to be used within psql.[5]

To add space to store more commands, increase the HISTSIZE option value. Review the HISTFILE and HISTSIZE options in the psql documentation at https://www.postgresql.org/docs/current/app-psql.html if you want to customize these.

psql customizations can be added to your ~/.psqlrc file. The ~/.psqlrc file is read when psql starts up. The Thoughtbot post "An Explained psqlrc"[6] shows various ways to customize it, with lots of great tips.

You may also want to edit SQL queries directly in a text editor launched from psql. How can that be set up? To do that, use the \e meta-command.

This meta-command launches the text editor you've configured or a default one. From there, type out SQL queries, wrapping lines and doing formatting as you like. When you save your changes, you're returned to your psql prompt where your query runs.

To save your SQL query output to a file, use the \o meta-command. For example, type \o file.txt. This doesn't return anything. The next query you run, though, will send results to file.txt.

---

4. https://github.com/andyatkinson/dotfiles
5. https://stackoverflow.com/a/31649807
6. https://thoughtbot.com/blog/an-explained-psqlrc

Output will continue to go into that file until you've toggled it back. Do that by typing \o again, without a filename. You should now see query results again in psql.

To exit psql, type \q. View the query result contents of the output file you just created by running cat file.txt from your terminal.

Let's recap some of the meta-commands you've seen in this section in the following table.

Command	Description
\q	Quit psql
\s	See history of commands
\e	Launch a text editor from psql
\o	Toggle output between psql and a file

That concludes this basic tour of psql. Hopefully, you've picked up some tips and have gotten more comfortable using it.

Next, let's dive into your PostgreSQL configuration.

Modifying Your PostgreSQL Config File

Modifying your local PostgreSQL configuration is a way to practice changes that you might want to perform in your production PostgreSQL instance. With cloud providers, you may use a web UI or CLI program to modify parameters and not edit a config file directly, but the parameter names, values, and change process are about the same. Depending on which parameters you are changing, either you will be able to reload the configuration without restarting PostgreSQL, or you'll need to restart PostgreSQL for the changes to be applied.

First, you'll need to find the config file. From psql, run the following statement to find the path:

sql/show_config_file.sql
```
-- Connected as `postgres`
-- Connect as `owner`, which was granted `pg_read_all_data`
SHOW config_file;
```

Paths with Spaces

 If you installed PostgreSQL using Postgres.app on macOS, and your installation path has the directory Application Support with a space separating the words, add double quotes around the path (or "escape" the space character).

Open the file with your text editor and take a look at the content.

```
sh/edit_postgresql.conf.sh
vim "/Users/andy/Library/\
  Application Support/Postgres/\
  var-16/postgresql.conf"

# ----------------------------
# PostgreSQL configuration file
# ----------------------------
#
# This file consists of lines of the form:
#
#   name = value
#
# (The "=" is optional.)  Whitespace may be used.
# Comments are introduced with "#" anywhere on a line.
# The complete list of parameter names and allowed
# values can be found in the PostgreSQL documentation.
#
# (continued...)
```

Within postgresql.conf, you will see lots of parameters. It's a long file. Search within the file for the section called shared_preload_libraries. Most parameters will be commented out, meaning they're not being used.

The default value might be an assignment to an empty string:

```
shared_preload_libraries = ''
```

You will remove the comments for this line and assign a value to shared_preload_libraries. Before doing that, make a backup of the file you can use, if needed, to revert the changes. Rideshare also has sample PostgreSQL configuration files you can refer to in the project's postgresql directory.

The change you'll make configures the pg_stat_statements[7] extension, by adding that value as the right-hand-side assignment within the single quotes. You're adding one value here, but this value can also be a comma-separated list of extensions. There will still be one more step after this, which is running CREATE EXTENSION, which you haven't seen yet. What does that do?

Loading an extension essentially amounts to running the extension's script file.[8]

---

7.   https://www.postgresql.org/docs/current/pgstatstatements.html
8.   https://www.postgresql.org/docs/current/sql-createextension.html

---

PostgreSQL Extensions Management for Rails Devs

For Rails developers familiar with managing Ruby gems, it might aid learning to manage PostgreSQL extensions to roughly equate the steps.

Adding extensions (when required) to shared_preload_libraries is roughly similar to adding gems to your Gemfile with require: false, then running bundle install.

The second step in PostgreSQL, running CREATE EXTENSION, could be roughly thought of as an initializer file for a Ruby gem that requires (loads) the gem code.

Let's get back to pg_stat_statements. This extension collects statistics from queries running in your database with a minimal amount of overhead. Since you'll work with this extension a lot, it will be abbreviated as PGSS going forward. This is a good extension for nearly all PostgreSQL installations, which is why it's being introduced here early.

To add it to postgresql.conf, add the string 'pg_stat_statements' inside the single quotes to the right-side assignment of shared_preload_libraries. After making a backup copy of postgresql.conf, edit the original file as follows:

sh/shared_preload_libraries.sh
```
shared_preload_libraries = 'pg_stat_statements'
```

Whenever you change shared_preload_libraries, you will need to restart PostgreSQL for the changes to take effect. In your production database server, a restart needs to be carefully planned out since it will disrupt live traffic. Configuration changes that require only a "reload" are much better because they don't interrupt live traffic.

Since you're working locally and are the sole user of the database, restarting is no big deal. If you're using Postgres.app on macOS, you can restart PostgreSQL by clicking "Stop" and "Start" from the menu bar app.

To restart PostgreSQL from your terminal, use the pg_ctl program and restart argument. This command expects PGDATA to be set either as an environment variable or as a command argument. If you haven't done this before, you might be wondering where your PostgreSQL data directory (PGDATA) is located.

To find it, from the following command from psql, connect as postgres or owner:

sql/show_data_directory.sql
```
-- Connected as `postgres`
-- Or connect as `owner`, which was granted `pg_read_all_data`
SHOW data_directory;
```

This might be something like /Users/andy/Library/Application Support/Postgres/var-16.

Copy and paste this path to your clipboard. Type \q to exit psql and return to your terminal.

You can now run pg_ctl restart and use the --pgdata or -D (they are equivalent) option, then paste the file path as the value.

The full command with the path is shown here:

```
sh/pg_ctl_restart.sh
pg_ctl restart \
  --pgdata "/Users/andy/Library/Application Support/Postgres/var-16"
```

To make this less complex going forward, you can set PGDATA in your terminal (see Set PGDATA for pg_ctl, on page 406). With that set, you won't need an explicit data directory option.

Once PostgreSQL is restarted, connect again from psql. PGSS is running "cluster wide," meaning for all databases, but you'll need to enable the system view for each database where you want to see the data it provides. To do that, run the CREATE EXTENSION command.

Run CREATE EXTENSION as a different user from owner, which is how you normally connect. This time connect as the postgres superuser.

The following command shows how to connect to the rideshare_development database as the postgres user. Run the following command from your terminal:

```
psql -U postgres -d rideshare_development
```

Once connected as postgres, run the following statement:

```
sql/create_extension_pg_stat_statements.sql
CREATE EXTENSION IF NOT EXISTS pg_stat_statements
WITH SCHEMA rideshare;
```

Disconnect as the superuser by running \q. Connect again normally by running psql $DATABASE_URL as the owner role. List the enabled extensions by running the following query or the \dx meta-command, confirming 'pg_stat_statements' is listed:

```
sql/select_pg_extension.sql
SELECT * FROM pg_extension;
```

Great! You've now configured and enabled a very useful extension that you'll use in upcoming chapters.

Next, you'll continue to explore what's currently happening in your database. What other kinds of observability capabilities are there?

Getting Started with Observability

When you begin working with a new database and application, take a look at the schema (or the "structure"), tables, table relationships, constraints, and indexes. You'll develop a general sense of what the data looks like. Since you're looking at static data, what you're not seeing is current activity in your database. How can you see that?

PostgreSQL exposes the current activity from a catalog called pg_stat_activity. Let's explore it. From psql, run the following query:

sql/pg_stat_activity.sql
```
SELECT * FROM pg_stat_activity;
```

Try toggling \x (another meta-command) to make the output appear vertically, which can be easier to read. Even with no application queries running, you might see results like autovacuum launcher or logical replication launcher, which are running background processes.

To inspect details about your psql session, query pg_stat_activity using the pid for your current backend process. This uses the query you saw earlier to find your backend pid.

sql/select_pg_backend_pid.sql
```
SELECT * FROM pg_stat_activity
WHERE pid = (SELECT PG_BACKEND_PID());
```

Explore the fields from the pg_stat_activity result row about your current session.

Querying pg_stat_activity in your production database is safe to do, although it may produce an overwhelming amount of information.

If you see INSUFFICIENT PRIVILEGES, you'll need to connect and run the statement with a higher-privileged user.

Take a look at the pid Process ID field.[9] If you have a query that's running too long and you want to stop it, you'll need the pid value and can cancel or terminate the backend process associated with the query.

These capabilities are part of the PostgreSQL System Administration functions.[10] The following example shows the format where you'd replace pid with the pid value.

```
-- Find the "pid" value, pass it in

SELECT PG_CANCEL_BACKEND(pid);
```

---

9. https://www.postgresql.org/docs/current/monitoring-stats.html#MONITORING-PG-STAT-ACTIVITY-VIEW
10. https://www.postgresql.org/docs/current/functions-admin.html

This statement tries to cancel the query by sending a SIGINT signal, a more graceful shutdown attempt.

If that doesn't work, terminate the query by sending a SIGTERM signal using the following command. Terminating a running query may cause data loss.

Multiple queries may be in progress with the backend process. Only use this option when it's really needed.

```
SELECT PG_TERMINATE_BACKEND(pid);
```

Later, you'll learn about safeguards you can add to reduce the likelihood of needing to manually cancel or terminate a query.

Queries in a blocked state are another type of query error. One of the key design features of PostgreSQL is how it locks and unlocks resources to handle a lot of concurrent writing and reading activity. The trade-off is that a query can become blocked while waiting to acquire a lock.

In the next section, you'll peek into some of the details of lock activity.

Glancing at Current Lock Behavior

PostgreSQL generally uses pessimistic locking (although it's also possible to use optimistic locking), which means lockable resources like tables or rows are locked upfront before they're modified. When queries try to access lockable resources, depending on the query type, it will require either a *shared* lock or *exclusive* lock.

Although a deep dive into lock types and lock conflicts is beyond the scope of this chapter, we'll cover some basics to help you get started.

Exclusive locks are the more disruptive kind and should be minimized because they block all queries trying to access the same resource. In upcoming chapters, you'll learn how to troubleshoot lock conflicts and how to add lock-related safeguards.

For locked tables with high row counts, locks are in effect for longer lengths of time. This is an issue when making table definition changes, where every row needs to be modified. If a table that's changing is being queried while locked, those queries will be blocked and possibly canceled, resulting in application errors.

Although locks can be created explicitly, usually resources are locked "implicitly" based on the statement. You'll learn how to map SQL statements to lock types in future chapters.

If you want to get a jump start on that, Hussein Nasser did the heavy lifting, creating the PostgreSQL Lock Conflicts tool available at https://pglocks.org. This tool shows all the lock types and maps specific SQL commands to the lock types they acquire. Another resource is PostgreSQL documentation showing lock modes and conflicts on the "Explicit Locking"[11] page.

One of the lock problems faced is *deadlocks*. Deadlocks happen when two processes block each other permanently.[12]

For live information about locking activity, query the pg_locks catalog from psql as follows:

sql/view_pg_locks.sql
```
SELECT * FROM pg_locks;
```

To recap, pg_stat_activity and pg_locks are system catalogs that can be queried to view live activity or lock activity.

Sometimes you'll want to simulate behavior from production that's difficult to reproduce. This could be to fix slow queries, or explore the effects of a lock.

Read on to learn how to create these types of experiments.

Generating Fake Data for Experiments

As you saw earlier, your server instance has many databases running on it.

Let's explore the other databases. You'll use the letter "l" after a backslash to "list" the databases. Because this is difficult to read, it's worth repeating this is the letter "l" and not the number "1".

From psql, run the \l meta-command to list databases.

You should see postgres listed, which is a built-in database. Run \c postgres to "connect" to the postgres database.

A database is a logical grouping of tables and other objects that exist on your PostgreSQL server instance.

Let's make another database that's dedicated to experimentation so that it's isolated from the Rideshare database.

You'll need to connect as a superuser, such as psql -U postgres, to create new databases.

---

11. https://www.postgresql.org/docs/current/explicit-locking.html
12. https://www.postgresql.org/docs/current/explicit-locking.html#LOCKING-DEADLOCKS

Once connected, type CREATE DATABASE experiments; to create the experiments database. Connect to it with \c experiments.

Create a table in experiments and populate it with fake data.

Try writing a CREATE TABLE DDL statement to create a table called tbl with a single column col with type smallint.

If you're a Rails developer, you normally use Active Record to create tables. It's OK to look up the SQL syntax for how to create tables. The goal is to get familiar with performing DDL changes using SQL so that you're able to when needed.

You'll want your tbl table to have rows. How might you insert ten rows with fake data? To do that, use the built-in GENERATE_SERIES() function. This function generates a series of values like integers or dates from a start value to an end value. Use this function to generate numbers from one to ten.

Generate a Series

 Get creative with the GENERATE_SERIES() function to generate a series of numbers or dates.

Here are the SQL statements to create the table and populate rows:

sql/create_table_generate_series.sql
```
-- create the table
CREATE TABLE tbl (col SMALLINT);

-- populate the table
INSERT INTO tbl(col) SELECT GENERATE_SERIES(1, 10);
```

You have now created an experiments database with a tbl table and populated ten rows.

What else can you practice using SQL?

Creating Indexes Using SQL

As a Rails developer, you may not have written many CREATE INDEX statements in SQL. You've used the Active Record create_index() method, which generates the SQL DDL to create an index.

Try creating an index using SQL. In query performance emergencies or for certain types of exploration, creating indexes from psql with SQL is useful.

This index should cover the col column on the tbl table and use the default B-Tree type. Don't worry about the purpose of the index; right now, you're just getting comfortable running SQL.

Toggle Timing

 Type \timing in psql to toggle timing.

This will show how long the CREATE INDEX statement takes. On large tables it can take a long time to create an index.

Adding indexes on live systems in production should be done using the CONCURRENTLY keyword, which means the table can continue to be queried while the index is being added. The trade-off with CONCURRENTLY is that it makes the operation take about twice as long. Feel free to skip it on your local instance for this example. It's not necessary.

Here is the SQL statement:

```
sql/create_index_basic.sql
CREATE INDEX test_index ON tbl (col);
```

Try dropping the index you just created using DROP INDEX. From psql, run DROP INDEX test_index;. Note that indexes should also be dropped using the CONCURRENTLY keyword on production systems.

When you've made a structural change that you'd like to undo, how might you accomplish that?

Rolling Back Schema Modifications

PostgreSQL has a feature called "transactional DDL."[13] Transactional DDL means that when structure changes are made, they either fully succeed or they're rolled back. This avoids a partially applied modification. Not all relational databases work this way, so this is a nice feature to have!

Speaking of transactions, what is a database transaction exactly? Rails developers may be less familiar with database transactions. Here are the basics.

By using an explicit transaction, you're able to make multiple changes as a single unit. Transactions can be explicitly created, but otherwise, they happen with every statement as implicit transactions opened by the statements you're

---

13. https://wiki.postgresql.org/wiki/Transactional_DDL_in_PostgreSQL:_A_Competitive_Analysis

sending. Transactions are also part of concurrency control, which you'll work with more later.

Try out transactional DDL a bit with an experiment. Make a DDL change and create an explicit transaction. You'll roll it back and confirm the change was not applied.

Open up psql and type BEGIN; to open a transaction.

Inside the transaction, create a DDL change. Create the index using the statement you used in the last section.

Since you're using an explicit transaction, you have "transaction control." With transaction control, you may decide to commit or roll back the transaction. After typing the CREATE INDEX statement and a semi-colon to end the line, on a new line type ROLLBACK; to roll it back.

sql/transactional_ddl_changes.sql
```
BEGIN;

CREATE INDEX test_index ON tbl (col);

ROLLBACK;
```

The ROLLBACK keyword rolls back a transaction. Before that point, from the perspective of your transaction, the index existed. After you rolled back the transaction, the index does not exist. Transactional DDL made these steps possible.

Now that you've seen transactional DDL, it may be tempting to experiment with structural modifications in your production database. You can create experimental changes, conduct experiments, and then roll them back. But is this a good idea?

Exploring and Experimenting Safely in Production

Most companies have a pre-production or staging environment that runs the application with a separate PostgreSQL database.

A staging environment is a great place to perform some kinds of experimentation. Take advantage of this if it's available to you! This is a much better place to perform structural modifications or load large amounts of data, because it doesn't add risk to the availability or operation of your production database.

To further reduce risk, create a read-only PostgreSQL user that you can use on your primary database. Grant the pg_read_all_data (14+) or the pg_monitor role to this user so that the role can access new tables. The post, "Creating a

Read-Only Postgres User,"[14] describes how to do this. Check out other "Pre-defined Roles"[15] in PostgreSQL. By having your team regularly use a read-only user, you may prevent accidental inserts, updates, or deletes. Rideshare includes a role, app_readonly, which is a read-only role you may try using.

New tables, constraints, data relationships, and indexes are common ways that databases evolve over time. Developers add and remove features or improve the data model. While schema evolution happens locally during the development cycle, it's not always practical to populate huge amounts of data in local databases to do performance testing.

Larger-scale performance testing is often required in order to reveal issues and areas for improvement.

Wouldn't it be nice to have a performance-testing database environment to use? How might you set that up?

In the next chapter, you'll set up a performance-testing database as a scrubbed clone of your production database. You'll build the performance database from scratch using the Rideshare database, but you'll make the data safe for your team to work with.

Read on to learn more.

---

14. https://www.crunchydata.com/blog/creating-a-read-only-postgres-user
15. https://www.postgresql.org/docs/current/predefined-roles.html

## CHAPTER 3

Building a Performance-Testing Database

In the previous chapter, you started working with PostgreSQL using psql. You learned about the Rideshare application, connected it to PostgreSQL, and are now ready to work with the application codebase and databases.

In this chapter, you'll learn tactics that you can use to create a scrubbed copy of your production database. By scrubbing the data, you'll remove sensitive column values and make the database safe to use for a wide audience where performance testing can be done.

The benefits of performance testing in a separate scrubbed database are that you can test large-scale changes to queries and indexes while the data remains production-like. Testing in a performance database gets you a close approximation of production without risking harm to it.

While there are other uses for a scrubbed database besides performance testing, the performance testing benefits are the most substantial. For that reason, we'll call this database the *performance database* going forward.

Note on Chapter Placement

The tactics in this chapter use advanced concepts like constraints, row copying, and database functions that readers have not yet seen. Why doesn't this chapter appear later in the book?

In later chapters, readers analyze performance and need a large database to work with. To provide a place for readers to test, this chapter suggests they can create a scrubbed copy of their production database on a separate instance to act as the database for performance testing.

Note on Chapter Placement

Alternatively, readers may want to complete Part II first to get more comfortable with these concepts, then return here in preparation for Part III.

A major emphasis of the chapter will be to help you learn *functions* and *procedures* in PostgreSQL, especially if you're new to them. If you've never worked with functions or procedures before, don't worry; no prior knowledge is expected.

There's a lot to learn here, so you might be wondering whether it's worth the effort. Certainly, you could use the alternative of generating entirely fake data.

Some cloud providers make it relatively straightforward to create a new instance from a backup. While that could work for performance testing, you'd get an exact copy of the data, which includes sensitive customer information. That means you'd need to limit access to this database, which decreases its utility. Building a scrubbed database unlocks greater access since sensitive information is removed. This means you can share it with the whole team.

Since Rideshare is fictional, and the book doesn't have a copy of your production database to start with, we'll need to pump up the Rideshare database a bit by generating data. To do that, you'll generate large amounts of fake data to get row counts that are more similar to a production database.

We'll make the data look realistic and treat the original data as if it were sensitive (even though it's fake and generated). That way, you can swap out this part of the process for one where you get a copy of your database data. You might get that copy from a backup.

What do we mean by sensitive data anyway? When columns have values that uniquely identify individuals, the data is considered sensitive. A good security practice is to limit access to sensitive data, even within your development team.

To make your production data safe to work with, you'll scrub (or "replace") any values that you've deemed to be sensitive with nonsensitive values that maintain the same characteristics.

A scrubbing process should be automated, and run quickly even for tables with millions of rows. While it increases the technical challenges around creating this, by automating it and having it run quickly, it's more likely to scale to your production database needs and be maintained over time by your team.

Another design goal is for the scrubbed data to maintain the statistical properties and distribution of the original data as much as possible. This way, your query performance analysis in your performance database will more closely match what you'd find in the production database without needing to test in production. With that said, to keep things as similar as possible, you'll also want to use similar system resources in both places, which means you might "double pay" to run a performance database that's sized the same as your production database. While this isn't necessary, if your budget only allows for a smaller instance, or you aren't able to preserve as many similar characteristics in scrubbed data, you'll start to lose some "fidelity" for the performance database as a reproduction.

Finally, a design goal for this scrubbing process is that it works with modern versions of PostgreSQL and doesn't rely on external dependencies.

To achieve those goals with a high level of flexibility, you'll need to build all of the pieces yourself.

This will be a lot of work, so let's get started!

Generating Bigger Data

The Rideshare users table is polymorphic, storing rows representing Driver and Rider class instances. Rideshare has data generator scripts that populate records with realistic-looking data from the Faker gem.[1]

In lieu of a large pre-made dump file to download, you'll start from the normal data generators in Rideshare, which create around 20,000 rows, and then pump that up by generating a lot more data.

To run data generators, run the following command in your terminal from the Rideshare directory:

```
sh/rails_data_generators_generate_all.sh
bin/rails data_generators:generate_all
```

This takes a few moments to run, creating around 20,000 records in the users table. While this is a nice amount of data to work with for many tasks, and you'll frequently be dropping your database, starting over, and running generators, for the performance database you'd like to have much more data.

To do that, you'll generate millions of records. When working with tens of millions of rows, you'll get a feel for how the row count affects things like query performance, index creation, and more.

---

1. https://github.com/faker-ruby/faker

To get you started, Rideshare has a bulk_load.sh script in the db directory. Run this script to populate ten million rows in your users table.

This script also raises the statement_timeout (which you'll learn about later) to ten minutes, which allows it to run longer than would normally be allowed. This script will take several minutes to run.

Check Available Space

 This script grows your users table by at least 4 GB. Make sure you've got enough space.

If the statement is canceled because it's taking longer than ten minutes to run, modify your local copy to increase the statement_timeout further. cd into the db directory in Rideshare, and run the following script:

```
sh/scripts_bulk_load.sh
cd db

time sh scripts/bulk_load.sh
```

You'll see output like this:

```
Creating 10_000_000 rideshare.users rows,\
  raising statement_timeout to 600000 (10 minutes)...

INSERT 0 10000000
Performing VACUUM (ANALYZE, VERBOSE) on rideshare.users
```

Once the script completes, connect to the Rideshare database: psql $DATABASE_URL. You'll work with psql for the most part in this chapter.

Check the size of the table by running the following query:

```
sql/pg_size_pretty_pg_total_relation_size.sql
SELECT PG_SIZE_PRETTY(
  PG_TOTAL_RELATION_SIZE('rideshare.users')
);
```

Let's explore sensitive fields in the users table. From psql, run \d users. Notice users has fields first_name and email. The values in these fields are unique to individuals, so they're considered sensitive. These are some of the fields you'll scrub!

> ## How Do I Identify Sensitive Data?
>
> To identify sensitive data, you'll look through all of the columns and find ones that describe personal information.
>
> Look for fields that have names, emails, phone numbers, national identifier numbers, document numbers, or that sort of thing.

If you wish to start over at any point, recreate the database (bin/rails db:reset) and rerun the data generator script (bin/rails data_generators:generate_all).

With data created, you're ready to jump into the scrubbing process. Imagine that your current local data with fake data represents your production data with sensitive values. For your production database, you start from a database dump or a backup. Here, you'll work directly with your Rideshare database.

As you saw earlier, one design goal for your scrubbing system is to keep the statistical properties and data distribution for any scrubbed columns intact. What does that mean?

Replacement Values That Are Statistically Similar

The distribution of the data in tables, columns, and indexes all affect query performance.

Query execution plans are determined dynamically on the fly. PostgreSQL uses the estimates and statistics it's collected to generate alternative query plans and compare them against one another. The query planner then chooses the lowest cost plan that produces the fastest data retrieval. This means the statistical properties of the data itself are part of the plan selection process. For the scrubber, we want to keep these intact so plan selection in the performance database is closer to what you'd see in your production database.

For example, you might make a query change or add an index in the performance database, verify it on scrubbed data with an execution plan, and then expect to see the same improvements as you promote your changes into the production environment.

Now that you know that collected statistics are important, let's learn about what's collected.

To do that, explore the pg_stats system view[2] to see some of the data it has. You'll see the most common values, rows with NULL values, and more pieces of information.

For the Rideshare database, let's look at the users table. We'll raise the amount of stats collected, then analyze the table, and finally, we'll inspect the pg_stats catalog.

To do those things, run the following statements from psql:

```
sql/table_statistics_users.sql
ALTER TABLE users
ALTER COLUMN first_name SET STATISTICS 5_000;

ANALYZE users;

SELECT
  attname,
  n_distinct,
  most_common_vals
FROM pg_stats
WHERE schemaname = 'rideshare'
AND tablename = 'users'
AND attname = 'first_name';

-- -[ RECORD 1 ]----+----------------------------------------------------
-- attname          | first_name
-- n_distinct       | -0.9931146
-- most_common_vals | {Alonso,Fred,Harris,Corey,
--                     Dominique,Jamal,Marion,Mary,Reed,Sam,Sandy,Stevie}

-- Set statistics target back to default of 1000
```

PostgreSQL uses a default amount of 100 for samples collected from tables, and the default_statistics_target parameter[3] can be changed. Here, we've changed the column level samples collected for the first_name field. This slows down the ANALYZE command considerably, so change it back to 100 when you're done with this.

With that change, you can now see some of the most common first names in the users table. The earlier, smaller, data generators task generates nicer fake names, while the bulk load task generates sequential names that aren't as realistic. However, with that increased statistics value, you should be seeing some realistic fake names that occur more than once in the data.

---

2. https://www.postgresql.org/docs/current/view-pg-stats.html
3. https://www.postgresql.org/docs/current/runtime-config-query.html

PostgreSQL tracks the frequency for each of the most common values. The frequency is the total number of occurrences divided by the total number of rows.

When you're working with the number of distinct values in a column, this is called the *cardinality* (see "What Does Cardinality Mean in a Database?"[4]). Speaking of fancy database terms, let's take a look at more terminology you'll see in this chapter:

Performance Database Terminology

- schema—In PostgreSQL, it's a namespace for tables and objects

- Scrubbing—Replacing sensitive text with nonsensitive values

- Functions—Database functions in SQL or the procedural language PL/pgSQL, for advanced operations

- Procedures—Similar to functions with more capabilities

- Cardinality—Unique values in a column

We know we want to replace sensitive columns. What should we use as data to fill in?

We want to choose replacement values that have the same length and use the same amount of space to keep the IO roughly equivalent.

One difference from a production system will be the level of bloat compared with your performance database, which will have low values to start. Bloat can affect IO, so we won't be able to create an exact replication. Bloat will be covered later and you'll learn how to simulate it.

Let's dive into a specific name within the users table. The name "Elroy" shows up a lot in the Faker gem generated data. Let's consider its characteristics.

The name is a string type that has five characters. "Elroy" is stored in a character varying column. A good replacement for Elroy would also be five characters long and stored in the same column type.

Another statistic for columns is the percentage of NULL and non-NULL values. PostgreSQL tracks this as the null_frac or null fraction.

---

4.   https://vertabelo.com/blog/cardinality-in-database/

NULL values in columns consume less space but are still maintained in indexes, at least in older versions of PostgreSQL. Newer versions added *index deduplication.*[5]

To recap, consider the column cardinality, frequency distribution, and the proportion of NULL values.

Open up the equivalent tables to "users" in your database, and start to take note of columns that have sensitive values. To do that, you might inspect a few rows, or it may be more obvious for columns like names, emails, phone numbers, tax identifiers, etc.

As you start to identify these columns with data you want to scrub, you might be wondering how to keep track of the columns. Let's explore one technique in the next section.

Tracking Columns with Sensitive Information

To maintain your list of columns with sensitive values, track that information within PostgreSQL.

PostgreSQL has database-level and table-level comments that we'll use for this purpose.

Database comments are dumped like other structural details when pg_dump runs. You'll use the column commenting capability to track sensitive columns.

Connect to the rideshare_development database from psql and run this SQL statement:

```
sql/create_comment_for_table_column.sql
COMMENT ON COLUMN users.email IS 'sensitive_data=true';
```

You'll see COMMENT as output, meaning the comment was added. The comment is on the users.email column and uses a key and value structure to annotate this column as having sensitive data.

To confirm the comment was added, run \d+ users. This expanded form of \d ("describe") includes additional information, like comments. If the output from \d+ users is difficult to read, try running \pset format wrapped to toggle wrapping and then run it again.

To the far right, you should have a Description column that shows sensitive_data=true.

For each sensitive field you've identified, create this type of comment.

---

5.   https://www.postgresql.org/docs/current/btree-implementation.html#BTREE-DEDUPLICATION

To keep all databases in sync, create database comments using Rails migrations. Database comments are added to the db/structure.sql file and committed like other DDL changes.

Now that you're identifying sensitive columns and tracking them in the database, you're ready to start the scrubbing process.

Comparing Direct Updates and Clone and Replace

For your scrubbing system, you'll compare two techniques that we'll call *direct updates* and *clone and replace.*

Direct updates are SQL UPDATE statements that overwrite values in place. Direct updates work well for smaller tables, for example, ones with less than one million rows. This strategy doesn't scale for very large tables because UPDATE statements slow down as row counts increase (you'll learn more about that later).

Direct updates are more straightforward to write and automate, but they do have a trade-off in that maintenance must run afterward. You haven't yet worked much with maintenance, so we'll just touch on the basics here. Due to the design of PostgreSQL, an UPDATE statement leaves a row version that represents what the content was "formerly," that's now considered "dead" and ready to be cleaned up. When no transactions reference it, an automatic process called Autovacuum will clean it up. To better control the timing of that, we'll immediately run a vacuum job that takes care of the dead row versions as part of the direct updates strategy.

That command is the VACUUM command. Besides that one, you'll also run the REINDEX command as part of your post-processing steps.

Because direct updates as a strategy is slow for large tables (for example, more than one million rows), you'll add a second strategy for those tables called clone and replace.

You might want to limit your use of clone and replace because it's more of a pain to set up, but it does run considerably faster. Clone and replace uses a trick where you replace the original table with a copy of it, or a "clone." You'll see how to do this in an upcoming section.

Clone and replace is faster because it doesn't create bloat, which was briefly touched on, so the post-scrubbing maintenance steps that were mentioned are not needed with this strategy.

Clone and replace uses some more tricks like deferring index maintenance and constraint checks. To achieve that, clone and replace temporarily removes constraints and defers index creation but adds them back later so that the resulting table appears as a clone of the original.

You've now seen a brief introduction and comparison of direct updates and clone and replace strategies. With that in place, you're ready to begin to put these into action.

Let's start from scratch with a basic scrubbing function, which we'll then expand out to be used in an automated process.

Starting an Email Scrubber Function

To scrub sensitive values, the crux of the implementation is based on a database function that you'll call on the fly to transform rows. Since you may not have written database functions before, let's start with a skeleton of the function and gradually build it up.

Let's use the users table and email column from Rideshare. This column has a varchar type and the email addresses have a variety of domains like gmail.com and others. Your goal is to preserve the email domain portion from the original values, because they don't uniquely identify individual people, but replace the first portion before the "@" symbol.

To do that, create a database function called SCRUB_EMAIL().

PostgreSQL functions can be written using SQL or a built-in procedural language called *PL/pgSQL*. The procedural language is available as an extension. Run \dx from psql to confirm that the plpgsql extension is listed. You'll see how to use these later, but for now, let's use a SQL function.

PostgreSQL calls SQL functions "query language (SQL) functions."[6] Query language functions have some similar properties to Ruby methods you're familiar with, like variable numbers of arguments or default arguments. Functions written with PL/pgSQL can use variables, conditional branching, and loops.

Let's get into it. The function "signature" accepts a single argument, which has a matching varchar type (types must match) and returns a varchar.

Run psql then type out or copy and paste the following:

---

6. https://www.postgresql.org/docs/current/xfunc-sql.html

sql/scrub_email_v1.sql

```sql
CREATE OR REPLACE FUNCTION SCRUB_EMAIL(email_address varchar(255))
RETURNS VARCHAR(255) AS $$
SELECT email_address;
$$ LANGUAGE SQL;
```

CREATE OR REPLACE FUNCTION creates a named function or overwrites one that was defined with the same name and arguments. The function accepts an email_address with the type varchar(255). The argument type is important and must match the input type exactly to be invoked.

Once you've pasted your function body into psql, you can call it using SELECT:

This function doesn't do anything yet. You're just calling it from SELECT on your input value to show how that works and as a way to verify that it's defined.

sql/select_scrub_email.sql

```sql
SELECT SCRUB_EMAIL(email)
FROM users
LIMIT 5;
```

Nice! What you've just done are the basics of the scrubbing process. You'll create a function, call it from SELECT, and use a transformed value (you haven't done that part yet) instead of the original value.

Functions you define are source code, just like your Ruby code in your Rails application. For that reason, you'll want to keep them in version control and use a code review process to manage changes over time.

Where do you keep your function source code? You could keep your functions in a directory called db/functions. That gives you a sensible place to keep them and manage them, but they won't automatically be versioned or added to your database.

Functions do not have a built-in versioning concept. Wouldn't it be nice to have versioned functions to make it easier to manage changes and for new versions to be automatically added to your database?

Fortunately, the fx Ruby gem ("Versioned Database Functions and Triggers for Rails"[7]) provides this functionality. Let's put it to use in Rideshare.

fx provides a Rails generator that generates a SQL file. This is where you'll place your function definition. fx also generates a migration file that adds the function definition into PostgreSQL.

---

7.   https://github.com/teoljungberg/fx

The fx gem was added to Rideshare so you can explore it there. Invoking the fx generator looks like this:

```
sh/rails_fx_gem_generate_function.sh
bin/rails generate fx:function scrub_email
```

Here's a migration from fx in Rideshare:

```ruby
ruby/migration_db_function.rb
class CreateFunctionScrubEmail < ActiveRecord::Migration[7.0]
  def change
    create_function :scrub_email
  end
end
```

You'll see that fx adds a .create_function() helper to Active Record that works the same as other helpers.

Functions are included in the application db/structure.sql file after running bin/rails db:migrate.

The first generation created a SQL file db/functions/scrub_email_v01.sql, with version "01". Check out the db/functions directory in Rideshare to see revisions to the function.

Now that you've seen the basics of managing functions with fx, you're ready to continue iterating on your scrubber function implementation.

Implementing the Scrub Email Function

PostgreSQL has a large amount of built-in functions for different purposes. These are roughly equivalent to the standard library in a programming language like Ruby.

Your custom function (or "user-defined" function) can build on top of these built-in PostgreSQL functions. Let's take a look at how to do that.

Use the PostgreSQL SPLIT_PART()[8] function to split a string into parts.

Pass an email address like SPLIT_PART(email_address, '@', 1) to return the first part before the @ symbol. The first part has a position of 1 (Not 0) so 1 is provided as the third argument.

Try out the SPLIT_PART() function from psql by calling it as follows:

---

8.   https://www.postgresqltutorial.com/postgresql-string-functions/postgresql-split_part/

```
sql/select_split_part_function.sql
SELECT SPLIT_PART('bob@example.com', '@', 1);
--  split_part
--  ------------
--    bob
```

Calling SPLIT_PART() returns bob, previously shown in the commented out portion. bob is the text you're replacing.

How long is bob? Use the built-in LENGTH() function. bob has a length of three. Bob is not long!

```
sql/select_length_function.sql
SELECT LENGTH('bob');
```

Alright. You'll now need some replacement text to use to overwrite "bob". What can you use as replacement text?

One option is to use the built-in PostgreSQL MD5() function. This function generates a hash value as a string, which serves as a random set of characters used to replace "bob".

Since the MD5() function generates 32-character long strings, but we only need three of them, we can slice out a portion. While you could use the original text as input to the function, MD5 hashed text is not considered cryptographically secure. The original text could be "guessed" by comparing hashed text to it.

Let's sprinkle in a bit of security here. For the performance database, we're OK to lose the original text values. Let's use the RANDOM() function as input to MD5() and then cast the output to ::TEXT. RANDOM() provides a semi-random input to MD5(), and we're purposefully not connecting it here to the original text.

Since we're using RANDOM(), we might want more consistent generated results on repeated runs of this process. How can we do that? Haki suggested using the SETSEED()[9] function to achieve that.

> **Haki:** For RANDOM(), calling the SETSEED() function makes the values deterministic.
>
> **Andrew:** Oh yeah? How does that work?
>
> **Haki:** With the same seed value for a given instance, 'RANDOM()' will generate the same random values in the same order, across sessions.

Let's add that for our scrubbing process. We'll use a value of 0.5 and call SELECT SETSEED(0.5); when we want to work with random values.

---

9.   https://www.techonthenet.com/postgresql/functions/setseed.php

From the long MD5() string, you'll take a slice out based on the length you need. Typically the unique email address portion will be less than 32 characters long, so we'll focus just on that in these examples.

One gotcha when generating MD5 text strings is there can be overlaps on the first few characters for short strings. Let's use a workaround to make sure that the strings you're working with are unique since we need unique email addresses per the constraints on the users table.

Use at least five characters of length for replacement text, even when the source text is shorter. To do that, use the built-in GREATEST() function to grab a slice that's either the length of the original text or five, whichever is greater.

Use the CONCAT() function to assemble each of the string parts together, crafting a full replacement email address.

The following version brings everything together. Overwrite the earlier function definition that didn't have a body by copying and pasting this function into psql.

```
sql/scrub_email_function_full.sql
-- replace email_address with random text that is the same
-- length as the unique portion of an email address
-- before the "@" symbol.
-- Make the minimum length 5 characters to avoid
-- MD5 text generation collisions
CREATE OR REPLACE FUNCTION SCRUB_EMAIL(
  email_address VARCHAR(255)
) RETURNS VARCHAR(255) AS $$
SELECT
CONCAT(
  SUBSTR(
    MD5(RANDOM()::TEXT),
    0,
    GREATEST(
      LENGTH(
        SPLIT_PART(email_address, '@', 1)
      ) + 1, 6
    )
  ),
  '@',
  SPLIT_PART(email_address, '@', 2)
);
$$ LANGUAGE SQL;
```

Let's call it again using SELECT:

```
sql/scrub_email_short.sql
SELECT SETSEED(0.5);

SELECT SCRUB_EMAIL('bob@gmail.com');
--      scrub_email
-- --------------------
--   2bffb@gmail.com
```

We're using the seed function mentioned earlier. You should see that "bob" was replaced now with a value like "2bffb". Great!

Let's try a longer email address to make sure the function works as expected:

```
sql/scrub_email_long.sql
SELECT SETSEED(0.5);

SELECT SCRUB_EMAIL('bob-and-jane@gmail.com');
--        scrub_email
-- ------------------------
--   2bffb502c463@gmail.com
```

You should see a longer value like "2bffb502c463" that has the same length as the source text.

With your scrubber function in place, you're now ready to scale this up to run across your entire set of rows using the replacement techniques introduced earlier. Read on to learn more.

Understanding Clone and Replace Trade-Offs

In this section, you'll dive into the clone and replace strategy introduced earlier. For clone and replace, the first step is to create a new destination (or "target") table that is a clone of the original (or "source") table. The destination table will be empty with no data rows to start. We'll assume the source table has around 20,000 rows. Reset if you've populated many more rows.

Run psql $DATABASE_URL to connect to the rideshare_development database. Run the following command to copy the users table structure to a new table called users_copy:

```
sql/table_copying_create_like.sql
CREATE TABLE users_copy (LIKE users INCLUDING ALL);
```

You now have a users_copy table that's a clone of the original users table structure with no data rows. Run \d users_copy from psql to describe it. Confirm there are no rows by running SELECT COUNT(*) FROM users_copy;.

The reason you didn't fill in any table rows is important. You'll find out why very soon.

Review the general form of the INSERT following statement, which takes query results from a SELECT statement.

By connecting these two statements, you'll copy rows from one table to the other. Since the destination table has all the database objects, including indexes, constraints, defaults, triggers, and more, the insert process is slower than it would be without all of those objects.

You don't need to run this statement now, and it doesn't include the function you've defined. You're just looking at the structure for now.

```
sql/table_copying_insert_into.sql
INSERT INTO users_copy(
  first_name,
  last_name,
  email,
  type,
  created_at,
  updated_at
)
(
  SELECT
    first_name,
    last_name,
    email,
    type,
    created_at,
    updated_at
  FROM users
);
```

As you saw earlier, you can call functions from a SELECT statement. Now that you've seen how to copy rows by inserting them into a new table following a select statement, you can bring these two things together.

The technique here is to call your scrubber function in the select clause so that you can transform values on the fly before they're inserted into the destination table. The "clone" step was the first part where you copied the table, and the "replace" portion is this on-the-fly text replacement that uses your scrubber function.

Run \df scrub* in psql to verify your scrubber function is listed.

You'll use the SCRUB_EMAIL() function for all rows in your users table. The function is modifying the value of the email column for all rows. You're ready to go. Go ahead and run this statement from psql for your table:

sql/scrubbing_on_the_fly.sql
```
INSERT INTO users_copy(
  id, first_name, last_name,
  email, type, created_at, updated_at
)
(
  SELECT
  id, first_name, last_name,
  SCRUB_EMAIL(email), -- scrubber function
  type, created_at, updated_at
  FROM users
);
```

If this ran correctly, you'll see something like INSERT 0 20200, meaning 20,200 rows were inserted into users_copy. You have now filled up the users_copy table with rows and their email address columns are scrubbed. Nice! Let's do some comparisons. Let's compare the same rows in each table by id:

sql/scrubbed_row_comparison.sql
```
SELECT
  u1.email AS original,
  u2.email AS scrubbed
FROM users u1
JOIN users_copy u2 USING (id)
WHERE id = (SELECT MIN(id) FROM users);
```

Although this technique may have been fast for 20,000 rows, as you scale it up to process tens of millions of rows, and for many tables in your database that you wish to scrub, you'll want to speed up all individual operations so the overall process runs faster.

How might you go about that?

Speeding Up Inserts for Clone and Replace

By using database functions inside PostgreSQL to perform scrubbing, you're removing latency that would otherwise be added to the process when the client application communicates with PostgreSQL.

To speed it up further, you'll use some common tricks to insert rows into the table faster.

A note upfront: these tricks speed up the insert rate but add complexity to the process. Try to avoid the complexity to start, then reach for these tricks if needed.

The tricks rely on removing database constraints and indexes on the destination table before the copying starts. They aren't permanently removed, but they're initially skipped and then added back afterward. To achieve this you will be doing a lot of manipulating of table objects directly, which can get complicated!

To get started, drop the users_copy table you created earlier since you're going to create it again. You'll be working in psql for this section. Earlier, you created the users_copy table using the INCLUDING ALL keywords, but this time, you'll do something different.

Create the table with the keywords INCLUDING ALL EXCLUDING INDEXES:

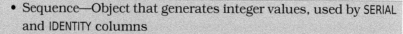
```
sql/table_create_like_including_all_excluding_indexes.sql
DROP TABLE IF EXISTS users_copy;

CREATE TABLE users_copy (LIKE users INCLUDING ALL EXCLUDING INDEXES);
```

Describe the new version of users_copy with \d users_copy. This version has many of the database objects from before, but neither the table indexes nor the primary key constraint on the id column were copied over.

Run the sql/scrubbing_on_the_fly.sql insert statement from earlier into this new version of the table. Run \timing in psql to toggle timing on, and compare the performance between the variations.

Besides indexes, you'll also defer creating foreign key and primary key constraints. Finally, you'll manipulate the *SEQUENCE* ownership and assignment to get the destination table back into place as a clone.

Let's do a quick refresher on sequences and primary key column values.

Primary Key Column Options

- Sequence—Object that generates integer values, used by SERIAL and IDENTITY columns

- serial or bigserial—PostgreSQL type that uses int or bigint types with a sequence

- identity—Newer primary key type, SQL standard, uses sequences, recommended over types SERIAL and BIGSERIAL

Active Record does not generate IDENTITY primary key column types by default as of Rails 7.1. However, the IDENTITY type is recommended over SERIAL and BIGSERIAL for a few reasons.

The IDENTITY type is a standards-based type that's used in other database systems. An IDENTITY column can't be overwritten as easily as Serial. Use the GENERATED ALWAYS option to make it impossible to overwrite a generated value. Another advantage for administrators is fewer privileges need to be granted for IDENTITY types when it's used for the primary key.[10]

Consider how you'll handle foreign key constraints. If you don't know what they are or are a little foggy on them, don't worry, they will be covered in more detail in an upcoming chapter. For now, you just need to know how to remove them and add them back as part of the scrubber system. Once you know the general technique, it's something you'll want to automate.

Since the users table does not have foreign key constraints, let's use a different table in Rideshare to show the general approach.

From psql, run the following SQL statement to list foreign key constraints in the rideshare schema. Take note of the constraints for the trips table. This query uses the pg_constraint[11] catalog:

```
sql/list_all_constraints.sql
-- list constraints in 'rideshare' schema
SELECT
  conrelid::regclass AS table_name,
  conname AS foreign_key,
  PG_GET_CONSTRAINTDEF(oid)
FROM pg_constraint
WHERE contype = 'f'
AND connamespace = 'rideshare'::regnamespace
ORDER BY conrelid::regclass::text, contype DESC;
```

Let's use a constraint on the trips table. Select the constraint fk_rails_e7560abc33, which is one that links the driver_id foreign key to the users table. The constraint name was generated by Active Record. While the name should be the same, refer to the latest copy of Rideshare if you run into issues.

Describe the trips table by running \d trips to verify the constraint definition:

```
Foreign-key constraints:
    "fk_rails_e7560abc33" FOREIGN KEY (driver_id) REFERENCES users(id)
```

---

10. https://stackoverflow.com/a/55300741/126688
11. https://www.postgresql.org/docs/current/catalog-pg-constraint.html

To restore the constraint after copying has been completed, if you'd made a copy of the trips table as trips_copy, you'd add the constraint to the trips_copy table. We haven't made this table here; we're just using trips as a source table for inspiration as an example of this technique.

Creating constraints manually can get very tedious. There could be dozens of constraints to create!

A better way is to list out the constraint definitions as creation DDL statements. This makes for straightforward copy-and-paste to recreate them.

To do that, run the following query from psql:

sql/constraint_definition_ddl.sql
```
SELECT
  FORMAT(
    'ALTER TABLE %I.%I ADD CONSTRAINT %I %s;',
    connamespace::regnamespace,
    conrelid::regclass,
    conname,
    PG_GET_CONSTRAINTDEF(oid)
  )
FROM
  pg_constraint
WHERE
  conname IN ('fk_rails_e7560abc33');
```

Before you can run this, you'll need to make a trips_copy table like you did for users_copy. Run the following statements to create a trips_copy table. Next, run the ALTER TABLE statement to add the foreign key constraint using the same name.

sql/create_table_like.sql
```
CREATE TABLE trips_copy (
  LIKE trips INCLUDING ALL EXCLUDING INDEXES
);

ALTER TABLE trips_copy
ADD CONSTRAINT fk_rails_e7560abc33 FOREIGN KEY (driver_id)
REFERENCES users(id);
```

You've now seen what a multistep process could look like, where you clone the table without constraints, copy all the rows, and then create an equivalent constraint on the destination table using the definition from the source table.

That covers the basics of migrating over the constraints. Next, you'll look at sequence objects.

Sequences are used with primary keys to generate increasing integer values. Note that trips and users are using the Serial type for primary keys and not

IDENTITY columns (see "Serial Type Versus IDENTITY Columns").[12] This is not following the best practice mentioned earlier but is intentionally left in here to show a mix of configurations.

The users table id column is the primary key and has a unique value enforced by the primary key constraint, handed out from a sequence. The sequence is named users_id_seq, which follows the naming convention for sequences created with Active Record.

Just like with foreign key constraints, you may list out all the sequences in the database. Run the following query to list all sequences[13] from psql:

```
sql/list_sequences_table_column_owner.sql
SELECT
  s.relname AS seq,
  n.nspname AS sch,
  t.relname AS tab,
  a.attname AS col
FROM
  pg_class s
JOIN pg_depend d ON d.objid = s.oid
AND d.classid = 'pg_class'::REGCLASS
AND d.refclassid = 'pg_class'::REGCLASS
JOIN pg_class t ON t.oid = d.refobjid
JOIN pg_namespace n ON n.oid = t.relnamespace
JOIN pg_attribute a ON a.attrelid = t.oid
AND a.attnum = d.refobjsubid
WHERE
  s.relkind = 'S'
  AND d.deptype = 'a';
```

You'll need to change the ownership of the sequence so that they're owned by the users_copy table. This is because eventually the users_copy table will take over for users.

Warning: you wouldn't want to modify the sequence ownership like this for a live system. However, since you're working locally, it's safe to do. In your database, you'd likely be working on a separate instance from production that would be disconnected from other client queries while you ran this transformation process.

The sequence must be in the same schema as the table, and the table owner must be the same. users_id_seq is in the rideshare schema. Check the owner of users and users_copy with the \dt meta-command.

---

12. https://wanago.io/2022/02/21/serial-type-identity-columns-postgresql-typeorm/

13. https://github.com/andyatkinson/pg_scripts/blob/main/list_all_sequences.sql

Run the following statement to set the OWNED BY for the sequence, linking it to rideshare.users_copy.id.

```
ALTER SEQUENCE users_id_seq OWNED BY users_copy.id;
```

To describe indexes for the users table from psql, run the \d users meta-command. The indexes are displayed at the bottom. Since you want to create them, it would be nice to display them in a way that makes creation easier, as you saw earlier, which means in a CREATE INDEX form.

Use the same trick from before, where you list the indexes as DDL creation statements.

To do that, run the following query:

```
sql/list_users_table_indexes.sql
SELECT PG_GET_INDEXDEF(indexrelid) || ';' AS index
FROM pg_index
WHERE indrelid = 'users'::REGCLASS;
```

Let's take a look at the UNIQUE index on the users.email column. To create that index again, you'd run the following statement to create on the users_copy table:

```
sql/create_unique_index_users_email.sql
-- Temporarily adding "2" to the index name,
-- so that it's unique (can remove the "2" later)
CREATE UNIQUE INDEX index_users_on_email2
ON users_copy USING btree (email);
```

You'll also need to make the name unique since index_users_on_email already exists for the users table. Add something unique on the end, like the number "2".

Repeat these general steps for each of the indexes.

To recap, you've seen how to bring over constraints, sequences, and indexes after you've copied the rows in. You've created them on the destination side tables.

With all of those objects recreated, the table is now equivalent in structure to the original. For your database, you may have even more objects on source tables that need to be brought over. What's shown here are some of the most critical objects, but it's not intended to be a comprehensive list.

With those objects copied over, the users_copy table can now "take over" from the users table. The last step in this process is to rename users_copy to users. Drop and rename operations are combined into one using a database transaction. This means they'll succeed or fail together and avoid a partial success or failure.

From psql, run the following SQL statements to DROP the source table and rename the destination table at once:

```
sql/finalize_table_copying_users.sql
BEGIN;
-- drop the original table and related objects
DROP TABLE users CASCADE;

-- rename the destination table to be the source table name
ALTER TABLE users_copy RENAME TO users;

COMMIT;
```

Note that CASCADE was used here, which drops all related objects for the table. Be careful using CASCADE in your system. You'll want to know exactly what's being dropped if you are to use it, so you should test on a separate database where that's acceptable and where you can easily recreate it from the source. Only use the CASCADE option when you understand all of the objects being dropped and wish to take advantage of the convenience of this option instead of more surgical drops.

Rideshare has more objects connected to the users table, like views and materialized views that are being discarded due to using CASCADE. For now, it's OK to remove them. Part of that decision is simply for the length of this exercise. In your real system, those views and materialized views are likely to be objects you'll want to bring forward for their functionality or performance benefits.

We know that we can always reset the Rideshare schema by running bin/rails db:reset if we want to start over. For your live system, you'll want to explore the connected objects further. Developing solutions to migrate views and materialized views will be left as an exercise for the reader.

Once the names are switched over and the transaction commits, the new table now appears the same as the old one to the Rails application. In other words, the new table works instantly with the driver and rider model classes since it has the same structure.

Phew! That was a lot. But you did it. This strategy is much more complex than the other one, so at this point, you can expect smoother sailing for the remainder of the chapter. Hopefully, each of these examples ran smoothly. If not, refer to code, issues, and pull requests for the latest version of Rideshare on GitHub, the appendix *Getting Help*, and the book forum.

You've now seen all the major steps of the clone and replace strategy. While this strategy works well for big tables, and each of the steps can be automated, moving all of the database objects around is a lot of work.

For smaller tables, directly updating rows is more straightforward and fast enough. You'll try that out next.

Using Direct Updates for Text Replacement

Direct updates are the alternative strategy that offer good-enough performance and much less complexity.

This strategy is "destructive" compared with clone and replace, because it mutates the table row data in place. Clone and replace has a "rollback" benefit because you've got the option before the table name swap, where both tables exist, and you can do checks to make sure everything is good before swapping. That's an important benefit that you'll lose with this strategy.

Let's try it out. Run the following UPDATE statement from psql to scrub email address columns for every row. You may want to reset all the way back to start from the "sensitive" fake generated values, or you may want to mutate the already-scrubbed values. We're mainly interested in how the process works here and not the exact output.

```
sql/direct_updates_users.sql
UPDATE users
SET email = SCRUB_EMAIL(email);
```

You should see something like UPDATE 20200, meaning all of the rows were updated in place.

If you were running this on a very large table with millions of rows, you wouldn't be able to update them all in a practical amount of time.

Instead, you'd update rows in batches. You might choose a batch size of 10,000 rows to update at a time and then iterate through all rows in the table.

The batched approach also controls the amount of server resources needed for this operation to run. Although the scrubbing is intended to be run on a separate instance without other client queries, the batching approach is a good approach in general because it can also be used on a live database with other queries. You'll explore working in batches in greater depth in an upcoming section. For now, you'll use single statements.

Notice how with direct updates, you don't need to worry about managing foreign key constraints, sequences, or indexes as you did earlier using the clone and replace strategy. This saves a ton of your time.

On the other hand, you learned earlier that large amounts of update operations cause bloat and that post-update maintenance is needed.

What does that look like?

Performing Database Maintenance

Because you've created a large number of updates, new row versions have replaced old ones, and those old ones are no longer needed. Remember row versions are immutable in PostgreSQL. The former version is now a "dead" row since no transaction will refer to it. The space it consumes contributes to bloat and that space could be re-used for storing other tuples from inserts and updates.

Autovacuum manages this for you, running with different processes in the background. Autovacuum uses a scheduler system and thresholds, running VACUUM operations once thresholds are met.

For manual operations like direct updates, you can intervene here and manually run VACUUM to ensure that it runs and does not wait around for thresholds to be met.

To do this, run the VACUUM command on each table you've updated. For a manual VACUUM operation using the analyze and verbose options, run the following statement from psql run:

```
sql/vacuum_analyze_users.sql
VACUUM (ANALYZE, VERBOSE) users;
```

ANALYZE updates table statistics that are collected for the table.

VERBOSE shows more information, listing the number of pages scanned, live rows, and dead rows.

Besides Vacuum, you'll also want to refresh your indexes. To do this, you'll perform *reindexing* operations using the REINDEX command. Reindexing replaces the original index with a freshly built one. The new index contains no entries that reference dead row versions.

In PostgreSQL version 12, REINDEX gained support for the CONCURRENTLY keyword, which makes this operation safe to run online while other queries access the table. This was a significant improvement, meaning that indexes could be refreshed safely without needing to disconnect the table from live queries.

For the Performance database, since you're scrubbing data offline, it's OK to skip CONCURRENTLY. Run REINDEX without CONCURRENTLY when there are no other users or transactions so that the command runs faster.

If you've rebuilt the Rideshare database, you should have an index named index_users_on_email. Try rebuilding it by running this statement from psql:

sql/reindex_users.sql
```
REINDEX INDEX index_users_on_email;
```

You've now seen how to use VACUUM, ANALYZE, and REINDEX following a big update for optimal query performance.

Earlier you learned that instead of a single update statement, updates for millions of rows should be performed in batches.

How does that work?

Performing Updates in Batches

Earlier you created a function using SQL, and learned that functions can also be written using the PL/pgSQL procedural language.

PostgreSQL offers another capability that extends functions further, called *procedures*, introduced in version 11. They're also written in PL/pgSQL.

Let's try it out. Create a procedure that calls the update function you developed earlier but moves it from a single update statement to using a batched approach.

Procedures can use loops and debugger output like you're used to having when working in Ruby. Procedures have transactional control, which means they can create their own database transactions.

To work on a batch of rows, use a range of values based on the id column of the users table. A variable sets the batch size, which is 1000 by default.

Read through the following SCRUB_BATCHES() implementation. After the code, the parts of the code will be explained.

sql/scrub_batched_direct_updates.sql
```
CREATE OR REPLACE PROCEDURE SCRUB_BATCHES()
LANGUAGE PLPGSQL
AS $$
DECLARE
  current_id INT := (SELECT MIN(id) FROM users);
  max_id INT := (SELECT MAX(id) FROM users);
  batch_size INT := 1000;
  rows_updated INT;
BEGIN
  WHILE current_id <= max_id LOOP
    -- the UPDATE by `id` range
    UPDATE users
    SET email = SCRUB_EMAIL(email)
```

```
    WHERE id >= current_id
    AND id < current_id + batch_size;

    GET DIAGNOSTICS rows_updated = ROW_COUNT;

    COMMIT;
    RAISE NOTICE 'current_id: % - Number of rows updated: %',
    current_id, rows_updated;

    current_id := current_id + batch_size + 1;
  END LOOP;
END;
$$;

-- Call the Procedure
CALL SCRUB_BATCHES();
```

Let's dig into the parts. First, a WHILE ... LOOP loop is used so the procedure runs indefinitely until meeting a condition to stop.

The GET DIAGNOSTICS rows_updated = ROW_COUNT; line captures the number of rows updated in one loop iteration for printing. The UPDATE statement updates all of the rows that are matched inside of the id column range. This will update up to 1000 rows for a batch if there are no gaps in the range.

Values are printed out in a similar way to puts in Ruby, using a RAISE NOTICE clause. The % symbol is used in a similar way to String interpolation in Ruby.

Try copying and pasting the CREATE PROCEDURE block into psql. This defines the procedure but doesn't call it. The last line, CALL SCRUB_BATCHES();, actually invokes (or "calls") the procedure.

Copy and paste the procedure into psql and run it. You'll see similar output to the following, which has lines per batch. On each line, the current_id is printed, and it gets updated in each loop operation starting from the MIN(id) value until the MAX(id) is reached.

```
NOTICE:  current_id: 1 - Number of rows updated: 1000
NOTICE:  current_id: 1002 - Number of rows updated: 1000
NOTICE:  current_id: 2003 - Number of rows updated: 1000
--…. And so on for each batch
```

Great! You've learned how to write a procedure using the PL/pgSQL procedural language and learned about some of the benefits of procedures over SQL query language functions.

You've seen how a batched UPDATE approach can be used for big tables to break up a big job into smaller pieces.

What's next?

What's Next for Your Performance Database

In this chapter, you saw how to build a data scrubbing system that could be used for your own production database to build a separate performance database that's safe to use.

By creating a safe-to-use copy of your production data and running on a server instance with a similar size, you'll have a place to do performance testing that closely approximates your production database while being safe to broadly share with your team. By automating the scrubbing process, you can run it repeatedly, iterating and improving over time, treating it as a foundational piece of your software development process.

For the strategies, you compared trade-offs between direct updates and clone and replace approaches, learning a lot about cloning structures and copying database objects along the way.

As you begin to automate your own system, you can reference an automation implementation in Rideshare. Check out the db/scrubbing/README.md file, which describes the scrubbing functions and a clone and replace implementation for a table that can be run repeatedly as a shell script.

Hopefully, you're now getting more comfortable using functions, procedures, and knowing what database objects are and how to manipulate them. With this foundation of tactics, you can solve unrelated and novel data migration challenges.

What's next?

In this chapter, we started to look at primary key and foreign key constraints but didn't have any broader investigation into what they're used for and how you might use them in your databases.

In the next chapter, you'll expand further into constraints and all the constraint types available in PostgreSQL, learning what they do, how and why to use them, and comparing and contrasting them to application-level data validation. You'll dive into how to improve the quality of your data by improving the correctness and consistency. Further, you'll learn to achieve improved data quality, even for huge tables and while lots of concurrent queries are running.

See you there!

## CHAPTER 4

Data Correctness and Consistency

In this chapter, you'll learn all about the *constraint* types supported by PostgreSQL. Beyond database constraints, we'll cover data integrity, consistency, and correctness more broadly by including application-level checks with Active Record. The overarching goal is to have high-quality data that matches what you expect and for your application to be free of data-related bugs.

PostgreSQL offers a variety of constraint types that you can use to both "describe" and "enforce" correctness and consistency. What's meant by describe? Besides enforcing a rule, constraints also document what's expected for values and rows. This information is accessible to all of your team members and all clients that use the database.

Since this chapter is aimed more at Rails developers, we'll assume you're less familiar with database constraints, particularly tricky nuances, and adding them for high-performance applications. We'll assume you're quite familiar with Active Record validations, but maybe less so with advanced concepts like custom validations (those will be covered later).

What are database constraints? Constraints are database objects that you add to your columns and tables to create rules for those. Rules can even span multiple tables (which you'll see later). These rules help improve the quality of your data by rejecting bad data at the source. If bad data never gets into your database, there will be a class of data bugs that you'll never see.

In most Ruby on Rails applications, you'll also validate data at the application layer using Active Record validations.

That brings up the question: do you really need both database constraints and Active Record validations? While they do overlap in purpose, there are some unique advantages to database constraints, and by the end of this chapter, you'll wonder how your application could go without them. That said, we'll work with both so that you can understand their benefits and drawbacks and make your own choices.

Let's start with an example use case. Constraints are used to describe and enforce *referential integrity* between related rows in two different tables.

What does that mean? Referential integrity basically means that PostgreSQL guarantees that data that's spread across multiple tables will stay intact when one side changes. If a data relationship exists expressed as a constraint, the relationship cannot be broken. PostgreSQL keeps the relationship intact and produces an error when there's an attempt to break it.

Referential integrity violations mean that one-half of the relationship is missing. How could that be the case if constraints enforce it? Integrity violations are usually due to the absence of a constraint, or due to a race condition from a client-level (application-level) data validation, where concurrent clients compete for the same sort of data change. An example of that would be duplicate data that's submitted from two clients at once without a database-side duplicate prevention mechanism.

When data bugs like that come up, they cause application errors, exceptions, and bad user experiences.

To make sure your data is referentially intact, you'll add foreign key constraints. Foreign key constraints are a constraint type that works with another type, primary key constraints, creating a linkage. Foreign keys refer to primary keys. When these two are used together, they describe a data relationship. When in place, PostgreSQL can now enforce the relationship when any DML operation like an insert, update, or delete (or SQL MERGE, which you'll see later) happens that may otherwise violate referential integrity.

Violations must be resolved before a constraint can be added. Does this mean you can't add constraints to an existing database that has invalid data? No. Although it's a bit trickier, you'll learn how to add constraints to any sort of high-performance database scenario in upcoming sections.

To avoid risk, developers may follow an antipattern of avoiding adding constraints entirely. You'll learn how to directly address those risks so that you can safely add constraints and take advantage of their benefits.

Let's take a look at some of the terminology you'll work with in this chapter:

Correctness Terminology

- Constraints—Database objects used to constrain values
- Correctness—Ensuring data is consistent with constraint definitions
- Referential integrity—Ensuring rows in two tables with a common value both exist
- enum—Database object that's an explicit list of values
- domain—Like an enum, but can be shared across tables

PostgreSQL provides the following constraint types,[1] which we'll explore:

- PRIMARY KEY
- NOT NULL
- UNIQUE (covered on page 69)
- REFERENCES (foreign key)
- CHECK (check)
- EXCLUDE (exclusion)

First up is the UNIQUE constraint. Let's take a look.

Multiple Column Uniqueness

One of the interesting challenges in data modeling is determining the definition for uniqueness in a set of table rows.

Uniqueness might mean no two rows can have the same value for a single column or even across multiple columns. The definition can also change over time. For example, an application that's limited to a single U.S. state might have unique city names for the system to start.

What happens when the system expands outside of a single state to all states? Well, now there's a data problem. Consider the city of "Portland." Portland...in which state exactly? Portland could refer to Portland, Maine or Portland, Oregon. At that point, you'd introduce a state concept and change the definition of uniqueness to be the combination of city name and state name.

---

1.   https://www.postgresql.org/docs/current/ddl-constraints.html

> ### Which Portland?
>
> Mention "Portland" to someone from the U.S. East Coast vs. someone from the West Coast, and see which one they think you're referring to.
>
> With consideration of your personal safety in mind, do *NOT* mention that one Portland has better beer than the other.

In Rideshare, there's a locations table with city and state columns. The table has a UNIQUE constraint on the address column.

You'll add a new unique constraint that defines uniqueness on both city and state.

Unique constraints can be added directly to a table. PostgreSQL then automatically adds an index to make enforcement of the constraint fast.

For a running system, adding the constraint using a unique index is more common because the index can be added CONCURRENTLY.

Without this mechanism, adding the unique constraint directly could cause a disruptive, long, lock period. With the CONCURRENTLY keyword, locking is minimized so other transactions accessing the table where the index is being added can carry on without disruption.

Let's dive into this example.

Review the following migration in Rideshare.

The unique: true option makes a UNIQUE index. The combination of disable_ddl_ transaction! and algorithm: :concurrently in Active Record migrations were used to create the index using CONCURRENTLY.

ruby/add_city_state_unique.rb
```ruby
class AddLocationsCityStateUnique < ActiveRecord::Migration[7.1]
  disable_ddl_transaction!

  def change
    add_index :locations, [:city, :state],
      unique: true,
      algorithm: :concurrently
  end
end
```

What about when there are duplicate city names, and we try to add the index? In that case, PostgreSQL won't allow the addition of a unique index that violates the constraint definition. You'll need to fix the duplicates that are in violation before the constraint may be added. How do we do that?

Fixing Constraint Violations

When adding constraints like NOT NULL or FOREIGN KEY, all existing rows in the table are checked. When the table has millions of rows, this might take a while. Querying batches of data to identify possible violations in Ruby code would also be slow.

How can you ensure there are no violations in advance?

To do that, you'll need to query for violations and fix them. You'd like that query to be efficient since your table may be large.

In the *SQL For Devs* post "Delete Duplicate Rows,"[2] two methods are shown to efficiently find duplicates and delete them. One technique is more complex but provides more flexibility.

The less complex technique finds and groups rows by their unique columns. Rows greater than the MIN(id) or less than the MAX(id) are deleted.

If you don't want to delete your duplicate rows, you could modify them (using an UPDATE) so that they don't violate the constraint you're trying to add. Keeping the rows around temporarily may be helpful, and they could always be deleted later.

The second approach from the post uses a more complex query. While the query is more complex, it provides flexibility with how to handle duplicate rows.

The technique uses a *Common Table Expression*[3] (CTE) for the main outer query, which we'll learn about in an upcoming chapter.

Result rows get a value from the ROW_NUMBER() *window function,*[4] which uses the PARTITION BY option. This "partitions" (or "segments") the results based on the columns that define uniqueness. You'll work with CTE queries and window function concepts in upcoming sections. For now, you can use these queries as is, and we'll work to understand their details more later on.

Each result row gets a row number. The rows can be ordered in different ways to get a different row number. The rows are deleted based on a row number condition, such as rows > 1. Once the duplicates are removed, you'll be able to add the constraint.

---

2.   https://sqlfordevs.com/delete-duplicate-rows
3.   https://www.postgresql.org/docs/current/queries-with.html
4.   https://www.postgresql.org/docs/current/tutorial-window.html

Here, we're just covering the general concept that duplicates need to be addressed and showing a couple of examples for efficient queries to do that. You've covered some basics for adding unique constraints to your system, including how to remove duplicates and how to use the CONCURRENTLY keyword to add them safely on a live system.

Next, you'll look at what FOREIGN KEY constraints are and how to use them.

Enforcing Relationships with Foreign Keys

For several major versions, Active Record did not support database-level foreign key constraints. Support for them was added to Rails version 4.2, which was released in 2014. By that time, a lot of developers who had been using Ruby on Rails may have missed the boat somewhat on the value and purpose of foreign key constraints and how to use them. Further, in that same era, the rise of *schemaless* databases happened, which further reduced knowledge and usage of constraints in data models.

The paper "Feral Concurrency Control: An Empirical Investigation of Modern Application Integrity"[5] explores how Active Record models use associations and validations to link models together. Using these mechanisms, data may be validated and checked for consistency.

Active Record callbacks[6] are triggered when objects are created, updated, or deleted. These events can be hooked into to perform validation of data, which can help prevent bad data from making it into your system.

Let's explore data validation and enforcing referential integrity in your database. First, you'll need to identify the foreign key columns. In Active Record, these are often columns you've set up that end in _id and hold a value that is the primary key value from a model or table that's being referred to.

Each table stores the same value in their respective columns, which then makes it possible to write SQL to create a combined row of data that has the columns from both tables. The foreign key constraint,[7] then, is a rule that you define that links these two columns together using some standard SQL. Active Record supports that by making helpers available that you can use in migrations to create your constraints.

---

5.   http://www.bailis.org/papers/feral-sigmod2015.pdf
6.   https://guides.rubyonrails.org/active_record_callbacks.html
7.   https://guides.rubyonrails.org/active_record_migrations.html#foreign-keys

The table being referred to can be thought of as a dependency for the referring side because, without that foreign side referred to, the referring side would be invalid.

If you're not using foreign key constraints, then you may not have any in your database at all. None are created by default. They are completely optional and left up to you as the programmer to use where appropriate. This means you'll need to know what they are, how they help, and how to safely add them (which implies they can be added in an unsafe way).

Let's review a foreign key example from Rideshare.

When a Driver accepts a TripRequest, a Trip is created. Trips depend on trip requests. Use a foreign key constraint to express and enforce this relationship.

Run the following SQL to add the constraint:

```
sql/foreign_key_constraint_trips.sql
ALTER TABLE ONLY trips
ADD CONSTRAINT fk_trips_trip_requests
FOREIGN KEY (trip_request_id)
REFERENCES trip_requests(id);
```

If this ran successfully, you'll see ALTER TABLE printed out, meaning the constraint was added. Be aware that this constraint already exists in Rideshare, so you've just added a duplicate. Say what?

Duplicate Constraints and Indexes

 Constraints and indexes can be duplicated definitions as long as they have unique names. Be careful to avoid duplicate constraints or indexes because they consume space and add latency. If you find a duplicate definition, remove one of them.

If you would like to remove the duplicate constraint you just added, run the following:

```
ALTER TABLE trips DROP CONSTRAINT fk_trips_trip_requests;
```

You've now seen how foreign keys define a relationship with primary keys and how to use foreign key constraints to enforce them.

Next, you'll work with check constraints, which is arguably the most versatile and underappreciated constraint type. Read on to learn more.

The Versatile Check Constraint

If constraints can be considered "cool," then the check constraint[8] has to be the coolest. This is a flexible type of constraint you'll use in multiple ways.

Any condition that you can express using SQL that evaluates to a Boolean result can be written for a check constraint. Create a Boolean condition rule that's checked any time data is inserted, updated, or deleted.

Like other types you've seen so far, check constraints are added to a table.

For Rails developers, you'll want to know that support for check constraints was added to Active Record in version 6.1,[9] and support for if_exists was added later.[10] This means helper methods can be used from migrations to create check constraints.

Check constraints are similar to Active Record model validations but offer stronger consistency guarantees, especially under high concurrency.

Check constraints can be used with Active Record validations. They can complement each other at different layers: the application layer and the data layer. Besides these two layers, your application may even have a third layer of front-end client-side data validation. All of these layers of data validation share a goal: to prevent bad data from entering your database.

Let's try creating a check constraint. You'll add one to the vehicle_reservations table in Rideshare. The following examples were inspired by "Postgres Constraints for Newbies"[11] from Crunchy Data.

Let's review an existing check constraint before adding a new one. Review the check constraints on the trips table.

Let's discuss what we'd expect to see for trips data. When a trip completes, the completed_at column captures the completion time. The completion time should always occur *after* the trip creation time to be "chronologically consistent." How can we make sure that our timestamps always match those expectations? Using a check constraint, of course.

To add them, you'll usually use an Active Record migration. Review the following migration to see how the existing check constraint was added.

---

8. https://blog.saeloun.com/2021/01/08/rails-6-check-constraints-database-migrations

9. https://blog.saeloun.com/2021/01/08/rails-6-check-constraints-database-migrations/

10. https://github.com/rails/rails/commit/25f97a66bdae6efe788b2d0ab7ab9cef6fc5a23a

11. https://www.crunchydata.com/blog/postgres-constraints-for-newbies

```
ruby/migration_trips_check_constraint.rb
class AddCheckConstraintTripsCompletedAt < ActiveRecord::Migration[7.0]
  def change
    add_check_constraint :trips,
      "completed_at > created_at", # Chronologic consistency
      name: "trips_completed_after_created"
  end
end
```

We can see the condition expressed in SQL, returning a Boolean result, and the constraint is given a name. That migration code generated this DDL:

```
sql/check_constraint_trips.sql
ALTER TABLE trips
ADD CONSTRAINT trips_completed_after_created
CHECK (completed_at > created_at);
```

Great. Now that you've reviewed an existing constraint on the trips model, try creating one yourself.

Take a look at the vehicle_reservations table. Vehicle reservation start and end times should also be chronologically consistent. Try adding one following the example you've seen for those two columns.

If there are rows that violate the constraint, PostgreSQL will display an error message:

```
sql/error_constraint_violation.sql
ERROR: check constraint "trips_completed_after_created"
of relation "trips" is violated by some row
```

If you've got rows that violate the definition, you'll need to clean those up before the constraint can be added. Otherwise, congrats, you've added a check constraint to the vehicle_reservations table. You may now start to think about other relationships the columns have to each other or how else you might validate their inputs. Later on, you'll see some command-line tools you can use that help make sure your database constraints are in sync with your Active Record model validations.

Let's try a more complex constraint. Imagine that vehicle reservations must be at least 30 minutes long. How would you do that? Remember that any condition that can be expressed in SQL can be used as the definition for a check constraint.

Before reading further, think about how you'd write a condition so that a second timestamp was equal to or greater than 30 minutes in the future.

When you're ready, keep reading to see one way.

OK, let's take a look. Both starts_at and ends_at already prevent NULL, so you can be sure they have values. You might want a condition in SQL like this:

```
ends_at >= (starts_at + INTERVAL '30 minutes')
```

For that condition to be true, ends_at must be at least 30 minutes greater than starts_at. Let's include that in a check constraint definition.

Run the following SQL statement in psql:

```
sql/check_constraint_reservation_length.sql
ALTER TABLE vehicle_reservations
ADD CONSTRAINT vehicle_reservation_minimum_length
CHECK (ends_at >= (starts_at + INTERVAL '30 minutes'));
```

If that runs correctly, you will see ALTER TABLE as output. Running \d vehicle_reservations in psql will show the check constraint.

Nice. What else can we do with check constraints? Earlier, you learned they can be used as a "transitional element." What does that mean?

Remember how we said check constraints can be cool? Check constraints and foreign key constraints can be added so that they are only enforcing their conditions for *new* row changes. By row changes, we mean DML changes like inserts, updates, or deletes to rows.

What about rows that existed before?

When check and foreign key constraints are created as NOT VALID, it's as if they're not there at all for existing rows. Why would we want that? The reason is that adding the constraint to the entire set of rows on large tables causes a long lock period that can block other transactions. With the constraint in effect initially only for new row changes, it can be added safely to any table. Granted, this means it's not fully applied since it is not in effect for all rows.

The NOT VALID in SQL can also be specified in Active Record. To do that, you'll use validate: false within your Active Record migrations. This is a bit confusing, but validate: false in Active Record generates NOT VALID in SQL.

Check constraints are cool because UNIQUE and NOT NULL constraints do not have support for NOT VALID (or validate: false)! Within the constraint community, it's a highly coveted option!

How can we safely add UNIQUE and NOT NULL constraints to tables, though, and make sure that all rows are eventually checked for compatibility with the constraint?

To do that, we can again use check constraints in a supportive, temporary role for UNIQUE and NOT NULL.

Even when the intended final constraint type is UNIQUE or NOT NULL, check constraints can stand in temporarily, to validate changes against new rows in preparation for adding the other constraint types on a permanent basis.

What does that process look like? Here's an overview of how a check constraint might be used temporarily:

- Add a check constraint and mark it NOT VALID option. Foreign key constraints also support the NOT VALID, so they are also cool. UNIQUE and NOT NULL need some help.

- With the NOT VALID check constraint in place, the constraint is enforced for new row changes.

- Separately, validate manually that all existing rows are compliant with the UNIQUE or NOT NULL, likely as batched operations. Then validate the check constraint, which means it's applied to all older rows but taking a less heavy lock.

- With all rows validated from the check constraint, you can now add the target UNIQUE or NOT NULL constraint more easily.

- With the target constraint in place, the check constraint is now redundant and can be removed.

While this process does involve several steps, and overall is optional, it adds more safety along the way, which can be critical for big and important tables with a lot of activity.

Besides a two-step process for validating new and existing rows, enforcement of constraints can also be deferred. This is a slightly different concept that's worth exploring.

Deferring a constraint refers to how a constraint is enforced but scoped to a transaction. Can we control enforcement for a constraint using a transaction? Read on to learn more.

Deferring Constraint Checks

As you've seen, constraints enforce a definition you've created. Enforcement happens as rows are inserted, updated, and deleted.

Some PostgreSQL constraints can *defer* when enforcement happens. UNIQUE, PRIMARY KEY, foreign key (REFERENCES), and exclusion (EXCLUDE) constraints support the deferrable capability. However, none of them are deferred by default, meaning they are "checked immediately."

If you wish to make the constraint deferrable, you'll need to create it that way from the beginning or replace it using the DEFERRABLE option in the definition.

The deferrable behavior can also be used on an as-needed basis or be configured as the default behavior. To use a deferrable constraint as needed, that's already configured to allow it, use SET CONSTRAINT[12] within a transaction.

When can we defer constraints, and how is that useful? In the Hashrocket post "Deferring Constraints in PostgreSQL,"[13] the author shows how unique list item positions can be shuffled around. By deferring constraint enforcement, duplicates are allowed temporarily, which can simplify the SQL statements.

To achieve that, updating the list item positions is done within a single transaction. The unique position value enforcement is deferred until the transaction commits. Since all positions are unique by commit time, the transition commits successfully. If the enforcement happened earlier when there were duplicates, PostgreSQL would have raised an error.

This behavior can be made the default, which makes sense for some use cases. To make it the default, define your constraint using DEFERRABLE INITIALLY DEFERRED. This makes the constraint enforcement always happen at the end of a transaction compared with being enforced immediately.

You've now seen how to defer constraint enforcement and looked at when that might be useful.

Next, you'll explore another constraint type. The exclusion (EXCLUDE) constraint is powerful and less commonly used. This constraint type can be used with multiple rows within the same table. How does that work?

Preventing Overlaps with an Exclusion Constraint

With the constraints you've seen so far, they work on single rows within a single table. *Exclusion constraints* are different. They work on multiple rows of the same table, creating rules that prevent two rows from having a certain overlap or some other condition.

Let's look at an example where we'd want to prevent overlaps. In Rideshare, vehicle reservations should not overlap. Since reservations are stored as rows,

---

12. https://www.postgresql.org/docs/current/sql-set-constraints.html
13. https://hashrocket.com/blog/posts/deferring-database-constraints

you can use an exclusion constraint to prevent newly created rows from overlapping with existing ones.

This is because two riders should not be able to reserve the same vehicle at the same time. Typically, this business logic is written into the application. Since this requirement is very important to how Rideshare works, you'd like to leverage the stronger consistency guarantees that an exclusion constraint offers.

Overlapping vehicle reservations would cause a bad user experience. Not only would the reservation be impossible to fulfill for both people simultaneously, it would be unclear which reservation to honor and which to cancel. The first one? The most recent one? One of the customers would be upset. Let's avoid that!

To create the exclusion constraint, you'll use a *GiST* index and set an *operator class* (more on these topics later). To create that index type, you'll enable the btree_gist extension for the Rideshare database. You haven't yet worked with GiST indexes; for now, it's enough to know they're the index type needed to enforce the exclusion constraint.

Run the following SQL in psql to add this constraint. Each of the pieces will be explained afterward.

```
sql/exclusion_constraint.sql
-- Remove existing constraint in Rideshare, we'll
-- add it back to practice (need double quotes)
ALTER TABLE vehicle_reservations
DROP CONSTRAINT IF EXISTS "non_overlapping_vehicle_registration";

-- Enable the extension
CREATE EXTENSION IF NOT EXISTS btree_gist;

-- Create the exclusion constraint,
-- using a GIST index
ALTER TABLE vehicle_reservations
ADD CONSTRAINT non_overlapping_vehicle_reservation
EXCLUDE USING GIST (
  vehicle_id WITH =,
  TSTZRANGE(starts_at, ends_at) WITH &&
)
WHERE (NOT canceled);

-- List exclusion constraints
SELECT conname FROM pg_constraint
WHERE contype = 'x';
```

Let's break down what's happening here.

A constraint named non_overlapping_vehicle_reservation is being added. The btree_gist extension was enabled because a GiST index is used for the constraint.

Identical vehicle_id values are selected using the WITH = clause and operator.

For the same vehicle_id, the starts_at and ends_at column values are compared using WITH &&.

The && operator is a special one that identifies overlaps comparing two timestamp values using the TSTZRANGE[14] range type. Overlaps here mean reservations *do* have overlapping time ranges, which is exactly what you want to detect so that it can be prevented.

The last part is a WHERE clause with WHERE (NOT canceled). This clause excludes canceled vehicle reservations. This makes sense because you don't want "canceled" reservations to block "active" reservations in the same time period.

And there you have it.

The exclusion constraint is complex with terse syntax. Once you've learned it, it's quite expressive and powerful. The constraint describes and enforces a nonoverlapping relationship between two rows in the same table. Besides enforcement, for those who can read the constraint definition, it also serves as documentation of what kinds of row data can be expected in the table.

In the next section, you'll switch gears away from constraints and explore Active Record application-level validations.

Active Record provides flexible and useful built-in validation types. Sometimes, these aren't enough for your custom requirements. Fortunately, Active Record allows you to write custom validators that can enhance built-in validations. How can you do that?

Creating Active Record Custom Validators

As an experienced Rails developer, you're probably familiar with Active Record validations.[15] Active Record provides a huge list of validations, and many of them can be combined together.

This system is extensible, meaning developers can create their own validations as *custom validators*. Custom validators[16] are created using object oriented design concepts we'll explore next.

---

14. https://www.postgresql.org/docs/current/rangetypes.html
15. https://guides.rubyonrails.org/active_record_validations.html
16. https://guides.rubyonrails.org/active_record_validations.html#performing-custom-validations

How are they set up? To create one, create a Ruby class that extends the ActiveModel::Validator class and implements a validate() instance method. The .validate() method accepts a record argument. When those two ingredients are in place, you've created a custom validator.

Individual attributes for a model can be validated by extending the ActiveModel::EachValidator class and implementing the .validate_each() method. This method has a signature of validate_each(record, attribute, value), allowing you to access the record, attribute, and the value.

The Rails Guides section "Performing Custom Validations"[17] is worth a read. We'll take inspiration from the email validator listed there. The email validator has been copied into the User model of Rideshare. Take a look at the following code:

```ruby
# ruby/email_validator.rb
class EmailValidator < ActiveModel::EachValidator

  EMAIL_REGEXP_FORMAT = /\A([^@\s]+)@((?:[-a-z0-9]+\.)+[a-z]{2,})\z/i

  def validate_each(record, attribute, value)
    unless value =~ EMAIL_REGEXP_FORMAT
      record.errors.add(
        attribute,
        (options[:message] || "is not an email")
      )
    end
  end
end
```

This custom validator is intended to validate the format of an email address column. To use the validator, specify email: true on the model attribute you want to validate using it. That short bit of configuration is all that's needed to wire up an attribute to this custom validator class.

Active Record supports multiple validations being listed out for an attribute. This means you can combine both built-in validations and custom validators that you've defined.

Now that you've seen the EmailValidator custom validator, it's time to try making your own.

Imagine you're developing a feature for Rideshare that validates driver's license numbers. You've got a driver's license from the state of Minnesota in the United States to validate. How would you do that?

---

17. https://guides.rubyonrails.org/active_record_validations.html#performing-custom-validations

Driver's licenses in the United States have different formats in each state. Some states share their formats.

According to "U.S. Driver's License Numbers,"[18] Minnesota driver's license numbers have one letter and 12 numbers. For example, P800000224322 starts with the letter "P" and then has 12 numbers.

A regular expression of [a-zA-Z]\\d{12} is even provided on the website to validate the format, nice! Use this regular expression as the core part of your custom validator implementation.

A skeleton is provided as follows. Try filling out the validate_each method using what you learned earlier. Once you're done or if you get stuck, then continue reading.

```ruby
class DriversLicenseValidator < ActiveModel::EachValidator
  def validate_each(record, attribute, value)
  end
end
```

A completed example for driver's license numbers for Minnesota has been added to app/validators in Rideshare and also copied here:

```ruby
ruby/drivers_license_number_validator.rb
class DriversLicenseValidator < ActiveModel::EachValidator

  DL_MN_REGEXP_FORMAT = /[a-zA-Z]\d{12}/i
  DEFAULT_MESSAGE = "is not a valid driver's license number"

  def validate_each(record, attribute, value)
    unless value =~ DL_MN_REGEXP_FORMAT
      record.errors.add(
        attribute,
        options[:message] || DEFAULT_MESSAGE
      )
    end
  end
end
```

Was your solution similar?

Let's go back to where you'd wire up the validator. As you saw, custom validators can be combined with built-in validations like presence and uniqueness. Let's give that a shot.

The driver model in Rideshare combines these validators as follows:

---

18. https://success.myshn.net/Data_Protection/Data_Identifiers/U.S._Driver%27s_License_Numbers

```ruby
ruby/driver_model.rb
class Driver < User
  validates :drivers_license_number,
    presence: true,
    uniqueness: true,
    drivers_license: true
end
```

Combining Validators

 Active Record validations and custom validators can be stacked up for an attribute, creating an expressive set of application-level validations.

You've now seen how to combine multiple Active Record validations. Pretty slick. These validations enforce that data is present, unique, and matches an expected format.

Although these rules are rigid, at other times you'll want more flexibility.

One example is case sensitivity. You probably have data in your system that could be supplied with a wide variety of casing, yet you want to avoid duplicate data that's only different by casing.

Email addresses are one example where you want to store only one unique value, but they can be supplied by users using any kind of mixed-up casing. To enforce uniqueness, you'd compare them using a case-insensitive approach.

For presentational purposes though, you may wish to store the emails exactly how the user has entered them. How can you rectify those two different requirements?

Significant Casing and Unique Constraints

In this section, you'll tackle the challenge introduced in the last section. You'll accept and store formatted strings with "significant" casing, exactly as the user has supplied the text. At the same time, when comparing values, you'll compare them without their original casing.

While there are multiple ways to accomplish this in PostgreSQL, we'll start by looking at a tactic that requires an extension.

Enable the citext[19] module (extension) for the Rideshare database. To do that, run the following statement from psql:

```
CREATE EXTENSION IF NOT EXISTS citext;
```

---

19. https://www.postgresql.org/docs/current/citext.html

Running \dx from psql should show the extension.

citext provides a case-insensitive character type you'll use as a column type.

To test out citext, create a new table in the Rideshare database using a separate temp schema. Use the temp schema for tables that aren't part of the application schema.

From psql, enter this statement to create the schema if it doesn't exist:

```
sql/create_table_temp_customers_citext.sql
CREATE SCHEMA IF NOT EXISTS temp;

CREATE TABLE IF NOT EXISTS
temp.customers (email CITEXT);
```

You should be able to create the new schema while connected as the owner user. After creating the temp schema, running \dn to describe schemas should display it.

Let's insert data into temp.customers. Run the following:

```
INSERT INTO temp.customers (email)
VALUES ('Customer1@example.com');
```

With that row inserted, try querying for it. Use a lowercase "c" in the WHERE clause, which doesn't match how the data was inserted since it used a capital C.

```
SELECT * FROM temp.customers
WHERE email = 'customer1@example.com';
```

Despite the query having a different case for "c" compared with how the data was inserted, your query successfully finds the row. How did that work? This was possible because the email was stored using the citext type, which ignores the casing at query time.

Another nice property for citext columns is that you can use unique constraints regardless of how the casing is for values.

Add a unique constraint to temp.customers for the email column. Try and insert a row that has the same email address value, but uses a different case. You'll see that the row cannot be inserted since it violates the unique constraint. Nice!

With the unique constraint in place, you can no longer accept email addresses that are the same but have different casing. This is probably the behavior that you want, but you'll need to make that determination for your system.

The benefit of using citext and a unique constraint with this combination is that you didn't need to normalize or transform email addresses in order to compare them to prevent duplicates.

Speaking of storing a normalized value, how might you go about doing that in PostgreSQL?

Storing Transformations in Generated Columns

PostgreSQL 12 added a feature called *generated columns* and it's supported by Active Record as "virtual" columns.[20] A virtual column is a second column that you create in your schema, but then PostgreSQL handles keeping it updated automatically on your behalf. It does that by transforming a value based on an expression that you've provided.

Let's see how it works.

Create a column for the temp schema customers table you've just made that adds a second column called email_downcased.

The email_downcased gets the result of calling the SQL LOWER() function on the email column value. Whenever the email column is modified, email_downcased is updated automatically. This is a "stored" generated column. Here's the snippet:

```ruby
ruby/migration_snippet_virtual_column.rb
create_table 'temp.customers' do |t|
  t.string :email
  t.virtual :email_downcased,
    type: :string,
    as: 'LOWER(email)',
    stored: true
end
```

Generate a new migration and paste the previous snippet into the change method. After doing that and running bin/rails db:migrate, the email_downcased column is added with the following definition for its column default:

```
GENERATED ALWAYS AS (LOWER(email::TEXT)) STORED
```

What does all of that mean? The GENERATED keyword indicates this is a generated column. The ALWAYS AS ... STORED portion means the transformed value is automatically stored. The SQL LOWER() function creates a lowercase version of email.

---

20. https://guides.rubyonrails.org/active_record_postgresql.html#generated-columns

How does this compare to citext you saw earlier, which is similar? Since stored generated columns are built-in, you won't need to add a separate extension.

On the downside, you'll be adding another column to your table.

That wraps up the basics for stored generated columns.

In the next section, we'll look at another useful capability in PostgreSQL called "enumerated types."

If you're a seasoned Rails developer, you may think of Active Record enums[21] (added in 4.1) in Active Record models when you see "enum".

Did you know that you can create enums in PostgreSQL?

Constraining Values with Database Enums

Enumerated types or "enums" are a way to express a limited set of possible values. In a database context, they are similar to constraints in that they "constrain" the possible values. Enums also act as documentation since they enumerate all possible values a column can have.

When adding an enumerated type object, it becomes part of your database structure, meaning it's dumped to the db/structure.sql file when migrations run.

In Active Record, an array of enum values can be used with an inclusion validation to ensure input data matches one of the types.

Let's look at an example. Although not an enumerated type specifically, the VehicleStatus class in the Rideshare codebase limits status values to DRAFT or PUBLISHED.

Rideshare uses an inclusion validation in the vehicle model to enforce this.

```
validates :status,
  inclusion: { in: VehicleStatus::VALID_STATUSES }
```

The status column also has a NOT NULL constraint which prevents nulls, a column default of VehicleStatus::DRAFT.

How can we implement something similar to the vehicle statuses as a PostgreSQL enumerated type?

Let's start by looking at the Rails Guides page "Active Record and PostgreSQL Enumerated Types."[22] Enumerated types have trade-offs worth knowing about upfront. Here are some details:

---

21. https://blog.saeloun.com/2022/01/05/how-to-use-enums-in-rails/
22. https://guides.rubyonrails.org/active_record_postgresql.html#enumerated-types

- Enums are a PostgreSQL type.

- When adding values to an existing enum, new values may be added before or after existing ones (to the front or back), but not in the middle.

- Enum values cannot be dropped.

These are significantly rigid requirements compared with code that's more flexible. If your enumerated type values rarely change, in exchange for this extra rigidity, you gain stronger consistency guarantees.

Imagine that you've decided to move forward with an enum in PostgreSQL. Let's look at how to do that.

The following migration does a few things:

- Creates the enum called vehicle_status using the create_enum helper in Active Record

- Adds the status column to vehicles

- Sets the column type to be enum and specifies the vehicle_status enum

- Prevents nulls for vehicles.status

Generate a new migration and work these pieces into the migration .change() method. When you've done that, run bin/rails db:migrate to apply it.

ruby/migration_snippet_vehicle_enum_usage.rb
```ruby
create_enum :vehicle_status, [
  VehicleStatus::DRAFT,
  VehicleStatus::PUBLISHED
]

add_column :vehicles, :status, :enum,
  enum_type: :vehicle_status,
  default: VehicleStatus::DRAFT,
  null: false
```

After migrating, you've created an enum database object and are now using it for a column. You'll see a new CREATE TYPE statement in db/structure.sql that looks like this:

sql/create_type_as_enum.sql
```sql
CREATE TYPE vehicle_status AS ENUM (
  'draft',
  'published'
);
```

If you'd like to explore this further within PostgreSQL, look at the pg_type catalog, which can show enums. Confirm the enum name and values match the migration.

sql/view_pg_types.sql
```
SELECT
  n.nspname AS enum_schema,
  t.typname AS enum_name,
  e.enumlabel AS enum_value
FROM pg_type t
JOIN pg_enum e ON t.oid = e.enumtypid
JOIN pg_catalog.pg_namespace n ON n.oid = t.typnamespace;

--  enum_schema |    enum_name    | enum_value
--  ------------+-----------------+-----------
--  rideshare   | vehicle_status  | published
--  rideshare   | vehicle_status  | draft
```

You may run into a compatibility problem between the database enumerated type and the Active Record model methods. Update the model code to include the enum information.

ruby/active_record_enum_usage.rb
```ruby
enum status: {
  draft: "draft",
  published: "published"
}, _prefix: true
```

The _prefix option adds a status_ prefix to the generated model methods. With that code in place, try calling status_draft?() on a VehicleReservation instance. You can instantiate model instances and call methods from bin/rails console.

To see all of the possible values for the enum, refer to the db/structure.sql file.

What else can you do with this enum now that you've created it? A benefit of enumerated types is that they can be used as column types on other tables. If another table has similar possible data values in the same order, there's an opportunity to re-use your enum.

The post, "PostgreSQL: ENUM is No Silver Bullet,"[23] lists examples of common enumerated types and trade-offs.

The post, "Enums vs. Check Constraints in Postgres,"[24] advocates for skipping enums entirely and using check constraints with an explicit list of values instead.

You'll have to determine what makes the most sense for your needs.

---

23. https://medium.com/swlh/postgresql-3-ways-to-replace-enum-305861e089bc
24. https://www.crunchydata.com/blog/enums-vs-check-constraints-in-postgres

Besides check constraints and enums for enumerating out values, there is one more option in PostgreSQL worth considering.

In the next section, you'll look at domains, which are another object type with some similarities to both enums and check constraints.

Read on to learn more.

Sharing Domains Between Tables

PostgreSQL *domains*[25] are another object type with similarities to enums and constraints. The post, "Enforcing a Set of Values,"[26] explores storing enums and domains.

The domain created in the post has the type text and uses a CHECK type constraint to verify the value. The domain is used as the column type.

From psql, try creating a domain by copying and pasting the following SQL:

```
sql/create_domain.sql
CREATE DOMAIN vehicle_statuses AS TEXT
CONSTRAINT valid_vehicle_statuses CHECK (
  VALUE IN ('draft', 'published')
);
```

If that ran correctly, you should see CREATE DOMAIN.

After running the statement, type \dD to "describe domains." Verify the domain you just created is listed. You've now created a freestanding vehicle_statuses domain that's not yet used by anything. How do we do that?

Let's use the vehicle_statuses domain for the status column in the Rideshare vehicles table.

Since we want to reconfigure the column, and we don't care about the data for this example, we'll first drop the column. Run the following statements from psql:

```
sql/vehicle_status_domain.sql
-- drop column so it can be added back
ALTER TABLE vehicles DROP COLUMN status;

-- add column with a Domain called "vehicle_statuses"
ALTER TABLE vehicles
ADD COLUMN status vehicle_statuses
NOT NULL
DEFAULT 'draft';
```

---

25. https://www.postgresql.org/docs/current/sql-createdomain.html
26. https://justatheory.com/2010/01/enforce-set-of-postgres-values/

After dropping the existing status column, it can be added back using the domain.

The vehicles.status column now uses a domain called vehicle_statuses. The column does not allow NULL values and has a default value.

Row modifications must pass the CHECK constraint definition that's part of the domain.

You might be noticing these are quite similar to enums and wonder what the difference is.

The main difference for domains compared with enums is that the NOT NULL constraint portion is part of the domain. Enums do not have a way to attach additional constraint types to them, but domains do.

Like enums, this domain can also be used by different tables that have the same needs.

Let's recap. You've now implemented a variety of mechanisms to help ensure that data is correct, consistent, and referentially intact. You've used check constraints, enums, and domains to do that.

These techniques are all intended to help prevent bad data from entering your system.

To help grow the knowledge around these capabilities for your team, you may want to add some tooling. In the next section, you'll explore some open source tools that can help.

Automating Consistency Checks in Development

Let's look at some command-line tools provided as Ruby gems that have been added to Rideshare.

Rideshare uses the active_record_doctor[27] gem to analyze the database and the application code.

To run it, go to your terminal and run bin/rake active_record_doctor from the Rideshare directory. This runs the built-in checks and makes recommendations.

One of the checks compares the column types between the primary key and foreign key columns to make sure they match. Some mismatches exist in Rideshare now, so try running the tool and finding them. Feel free to fix them in your local copy.

---

27. https://github.com/gregnavis/active_record_doctor

Validations defined in models are also compared against database constraints. For example, when a uniqueness validation exists but there's no UNIQUE constraint for the same column, the tool recommends adding a UNIQUE constraint. The tool also recommends adding missing foreign key constraints.

Another gem to try out is database_consistency.[28] Similar to Active Record Doctor, database_consistency analyzes Active Record models and database objects, making recommendations for greater data consistency.

For example, when a column LIMIT constraint exists without a corresponding Active Record length validation, the tool recommends adding it.

Active Record Doctor and database_consistency can be integrated into your development process. They could run automatically as part of your release process, or developers on the team could run them to help identify and apply data quality improvements.

We've come to the end of this chapter on data quality. You've built a solid foundation that you can use for your own applications.

It's now time to shift gears toward the structure of your database.

Over time, as you add to and modify your structure, you'll find that some types of structural changes are dangerous. Changes that are not dangerous on small, low-activity tables are fine, but they can suddenly cause problems for big tables with a lot of activity. Why is that? How can we avoid that?

How can we continue to safely evolve the database despite greater amounts of data and concurrency? Read on to find out.

---

28. https://github.com/djezzzl/database_consistency

Part III

Operate and Grow

## CHAPTER 5

Modifying Busy Databases Without Downtime

Over time, application codebases and database structures evolve. Your development team's velocity depends on being able to deliver new code and database changes quickly. Rails developers use Active Record migrations to evolve the database structure, creating DDL changes at a steady rate alongside application code changes.

When your application is new and query volume is low, modifying database structures has little to no risk. Since tables are locked for changes for a brief period, with low row counts and low numbers of concurrent users, this brief lock period is no big deal.

However, for applications that are successful and have grown in data volume and query volume, with increased numbers of concurrent sessions, making on-the-fly database structural changes adds more risk for downtime to concurrent user sessions contending for the same data.

One of the challenges you'll face in this phase is continuing to evolve your database structure at the same rate while avoiding risk and downtime.

How do you identify problematic database changes and avoid those pitfalls? You'll learn how to do that in this chapter.

Besides structural changes, you may also perform large-scale *data backfills* or *data migrations*. Backfills populate one or more empty columns, using queries and performing updates during a short period, where they run in high volume. Large backfill operations *also* carry risk to the running operations for concurrent sessions. For that reason, we'll include big backfills in the scope of riskier operations to design safeguards for.

With those goals in mind, let's look at some of the terminology you'll work with:

Busy Databases Terminology

- Strong Migrations—Library that adds safety to migrations

- Multiversion Concurrency Control (MVCC)—Mechanism for managing row changes and concurrent access

- ACID—Set of Guarantees that PostgreSQL makes including Atomicity, Consistency, Isolation, Durability

- Isolation levels—Configurable access level for transactions

- Denormalization—Duplicating some data for improved access speed

- Backfilling—Populating new empty columns for a new table design

- Table rewrites—Internal changes from schema modifications that cause a significant availability delay

You've learned some changes are dangerous at higher levels of scale. What are those and how do we find them?

Identifying Dangerous Migrations

As an experienced Rails developer and PostgreSQL user, you've likely had migrations that didn't run correctly. These might have resulted in failed deployments that blocked releases. You'd like to detect these earlier and avoid failed migrations.

One solution would be to take your database offline to perform changes. Structural changes would be perfectly safe this way!

Unfortunately, that strategy is usually impractical. Modern development teams don't take their databases down for structural changes. Modern teams continually ship code changes and schema changes every day. Fortunately, PostgreSQL can keep pace with these needs, but you'll need to learn some tricks and add processes around detecting riskier scenarios to achieve this.

Safe Migrations

Active Record migrations have no built-in concept of "safety" or "danger." All migrations are treated as being equally safe or unsafe.

Fortunately, third-party gems like Strong Migrations[1] can be added to introduce a concept of safety to your migrations process.

Strong Migrations identifies potentially unsafe migrations, by comparing the migration code to well known problematic patterns. Since it's hooked into the normal migrations process, it prevents unsafe migrations by default. To help developers out, Strong Migrations provides safer alternatives when an unsafe migration is detected.

Let's explore that further.

Learning from Unsafe Migrations

One of the goals in preventing unsafe migrations is to prevent blocking concurrent queries while a structure change is made, which causes application errors.

To learn more about how queries get blocked, you'll simulate the scenario. The unsafe migration you'll work with adds a "Volatile default" value.

To simulate the effect, you'll create a long-running modification and then run a query in that same time period. You'll use Rideshare and the temp schema that was set up earlier.

Launch psql, connecting to the Rideshare database. To reset the temp schema, use the CASCADE option, which drops any tables in that schema. Then create it again.

```
DROP SCHEMA IF EXISTS temp CASCADE;

CREATE SCHEMA temp;
```

Within the temp schema, create a slimmed down users table with an id and name column.

Populate the table with ten million rows. Use CREATE TABLE AS to create the table and populate it in a single statement.

Use GENERATE_SERIES() to get integer values from one to ten million for the id and to create a unique name.

Toggle timing on using \timing to see how long the operation takes.

This will take a bit of time to populate. Run the following statements:

---

1.   https://github.com/ankane/strong_migrations

```
sql/migration_dangerous_defaults_setup.sql
-- Enable timing
\timing

-- create users table (id, name)
-- populate it with 10,000,000 rows
CREATE TABLE temp.users AS
SELECT
  seq AS id,
  'Name-' || seq::TEXT AS name
FROM GENERATE_SERIES(1, 10000000) AS t(seq);
```

Verify the temp.users table structure by running \d temp.users. Confirm it has ten million rows.

Imagine you've made an application change and want to associate users to cities. You'll track a City for the User in a new city_id column. You want both new and existing users to have a city assigned.

In the application, you might prompt users to add their city after adding the column. But you'd like the column to have a default value to start.

Add a new city_id column and give it a default value.

You'll perform this two times to illustrate a difference between how a Volatile and Non-volatile Default works when being added. The first one is relatively safe since it uses a non-volatile, or "static" value. The second version is unsafe on a large table because of the Volatile Default.

Run the following statement to set the Non-volatile value of 1 for all rows.

```
sql/migration_safe_modification.sql
-- add column with a constant default value
-- This is safe to do and runs fairly quick
ALTER TABLE temp.users ADD COLUMN city_id INTEGER
  DEFAULT 1;
```

After adding the column, run \d temp.users and make sure city_id has the Default defined.

Drop the column you just added to prepare to add it a second time.

```
ALTER TABLE temp.users DROP COLUMN city_id;
```

For the next run, it will help to have two different sessions. The following examples have psql1 and psql2 in their name, referring to where you should run the statements.

In the unsafe version, you'll run the ALTER TABLE statement from the psql1 session.

Run that now.

sql/migration_dangerous_modification_psql1.sql
```
-- !!! Dangerous Version !!!
-- Adds a "non-constant" or "volatile" DEFAULT
-- This takes a LOT longer
-- Table is locked in `ACCESS EXCLUSIVE` mode for duration
ALTER TABLE temp.users ADD COLUMN city_id INTEGER
  DEFAULT 1 + FLOOR(RANDOM() * 25);
```

While that's running, from the psql2 session, run the following SQL query, which is normally very quick:

sql/migration_dangerous_modification_psql2.sql
```
SELECT * FROM temp.users LIMIT 1;
```

The DDL in psql1 can take ten seconds or more to run. In that time, the query in psql2 will appear "hung" until psql1 finishes. Once psql1 finishes, psql2 instantly finishes.

psql2 appeared hung because psql1 had locked the table with exclusive access while the Default value was added to all rows. Since there are ten million rows, performing this change took a long time, and the table was locked, even blocking SELECT queries until it finished.

Imagine instead of the single query from psql2, there are hundreds of queries running during that lock period, all getting blocked. This could quickly cause thousands of errors in your application, something you'd like to avoid!

What steps can be put in place to help detect these issues?

Learning to Use CONCURRENTLY by Default

One of the ways you'll make some operations safe to run, is by using the CONCURRENTLY keyword.

PostgreSQL supports the CONCURRENTLY option for a number of operations. Learn to use the CONCURRENTLY keyword whenever it's available as the default way that you work.

CONCURRENTLY is *not* added by default, so it's up to you to know where it can be used, and use it. When a table has no other concurrent activity, using CONCURRENTLY won't provide a benefit.

Let's start with some of the places where you'll use it. You haven't yet learned about rebuilding indexes or managing partitions. For now, you don't need an understanding of what those are, only that they support the CONCURRENTLY keyword.

The following list of operations support it:

- Adding an index
- Dropping an index
- Rebuilding an index (reindexing)
- Adding a partition
- Detaching a partition

A trade-off with the CONCURRENTLY option is that the operation takes twice as long. For offline modifications or when there's low or no concurrent activity, using CONCURRENTLY is not needed. In those cases, you want to prioritize the speed of the operation.

Using CONCURRENTLY is part of your set of tricks for safe migrations. What other safety mechanisms can you add?

Adopting a Migration Safety Check Process

Each Active Record migration file is a new source code file. At organizations that use pull requests or merge requests to introduce changes, each change is up for review, and often a review is required before merge.

Experienced developers might identify dangerous database changes from mistakes they'd made in the past. Raising these concerns in a code review helps prevent them from getting released.

While code reviews are valuable (and often required), team members must have the necessary skills to identify unsafe migrations and be available for a review. This process is more difficult to scale as the volume of these changes increases.

Tooling can help augment a human review process, identifying unsafe migrations like an experienced developer. Ideally, the tool could even be integrated into the local development process so that feedback is received early and often.

Fortunately, this tool exists, and it's called Strong Migrations!

Exploring Strong Migrations Features

Strong Migrations strengthens the uptime and resiliency of Rails apps and grows engineering team skills by detecting unsafe migrations and providing safer alternatives.

Most unsafe operations are detected and prevented by default. Besides stability benefits, safe variations provide education on known problematic patterns and solutions. The Strong Migrations GitHub README includes a wealth of information.

These are some of the operations that are detected:

1. When adding constraints (CHECK, FOREIGN KEY, and NOT NULL) to an existing column, Strong Migrations checks whether they're validated immediately or not.

2. Strong Migrations checks for table modifications *and* data backfills that would extend the duration of an exclusive lock.

3. When removing or renaming a column or table, Strong Migrations checks whether this will create a problem with the *schema cache* (see Avoiding Schema Cache Errors, on page 109)

4. Strong Migrations prevents changing the type of a column to an incompatible type.

5. When adding or dropping an index without the CONCURRENTLY keyword, Strong Migrations prompts the developer to use CONCURRENTLY.

How does it work?

Strong Migrations hooks into the Rails migration process when developers run bin/rails db:migrate.

When a potentially unsafe migration is detected, an exception is raised that prevents the migration from being applied.

This forces the developer to either abandon it, rewrite it using a safer alternative, or override the safety check with the .safety_assured() Ruby block. Review the db/migrate directory of Rideshare for examples.

Next, you'll look at a specific example from Rideshare.

Trips can have a rating of integer values between one and five. As an Active Record Validation, Rideshare uses a "numericality" validator configured in the *Trip* model to enforce this Integer range. The rating value can also be nil since trips aren't rated until after they're completed.

Review the rating field validation in app/models/trip.rb.

The rating validation can also be implemented in PostgreSQL using a check constraint (type CHECK).[2] This check constraint was added to Rideshare. Review the following migration file:

---

2. https://www.postgresql.org/docs/current/ddl-constraints.html#DDL-CONSTRAINTS-CHECK-CONSTRAINTS

```ruby
# ruby/migration_trip_rating_check_constraint.rb
class AddTripRatingCheckConstraint < ActiveRecord::Migration[7.0]
  def change
    add_check_constraint :trips,
      "rating >= 1 AND rating <= 5",
      name: "rating_check"
  end
end
```

The migration used the .add_check_constraint() method added in Rails 7. This migration was flagged by Strong Migrations as unsafe. Initially, it did not use the validate: false option, which means it would have been applied immediately to all rows of the table.

The technical solution to avoid applying the constraint immediately for all rows requires two steps. In the first step, you create a migration that adds validate: false to what you did earlier. Then you deploy that first.

What does that do? When that deploys and lands on PostgreSQL, it creates the constraint using the NOT VALID clause. This is kind of a misnomer because the constraint is valid. What this constraint state means is that it is only in effect for *new* inserts, updates, and deletes, but not for the rows created before that constraint was in place. That leaves a gap, but you'll close that gap in the second phase.

For the second phase, you'll generate an entirely new migration, which has the purpose of "validating" the constraint. Note that you will need to validate for the "validation" to be successful, or it will fail.

The combination of these two migrations are combined into a single code example and form the "tactic" to add constraints to big and busy tables to work around what would be a long and disruptive lock:

```ruby
# sh/migration_check_constraint_dangerous.rb
# Example message from Strong Migrations:
#
# === Dangerous operation detected #strong_migrations ===
#
# Adding a check constraint key blocks
# reads and writes while every row is checked.
# Instead, add the check constraint without
# validating existing rows, then validate them
# in a separate migration.

# Migration #1: Add Check Constraint using "validate: false"
# Add a migration with "validate: false"
class AddTripRatingCheckConstraint < ActiveRecord::Migration[7.0]
  def change
    add_check_constraint :trips,
```

```
    "rating >= 1 AND rating <= 5",
    name: "rating_check",
    validate: false
  end
end

# Migration #2 (generate new file): Validate Check Constraint
# using `.validate_check_constraint()` method
class ValidateAddTripRatingCheckConstraint < ActiveRecord::Migration[7.0]
  def change
    validate_check_constraint :trips,
      name: "rating_check"
  end
end
```

Let's dig into this more so that it's clear. Adding a check constraint to a table requires an Exclusive Access lock while being added. With validate: false option, the lock period is extremely brief, causing little or no interruption to concurrent access.

To enforce consistency for *all* rows, you're following up the original migration by *validating* the constraint. This used the .validate_check_constraint() method in Active Record.

Before the constraint was validated, running \dt trips from psql shows the constraint with the NOT VALID keywords:

```
Check constraints:
    "rating_check" CHECK (rating >= 1 AND rating <= 5) NOT VALID
```

Validating the constraint removes the NOT VALID keywords. You can check this yourself by reviewing the constraint definition before and after.

If there are constraint violations on old rows, you'll learn about them at validation time because the operation will fail. You'll need to fix the data before the constraint can be validated. To do that, you'll need to see what makes sense before updating the data, deleting it, or something else. Technically speaking, validating the constraint is *not required*. However, without validating the constraint, it's *not* in effect for data created before it was added, and it's difficult for other programmers on your team to see when it was added.

With a validated constraint, you know all rows are consistent with the check constraint definition. This makes the whole team happy.

Using the previous tactics, you're now able to add the check constraint even to large and busy tables without causing downtime.

Now that you've started to work with locks, blocked queries, and concurrency, let's refresh your knowledge on these topic areas in the next section.

Locking, Blocking, and Concurrency Refresher

As you learned earlier, one of the operational challenges with PostgreSQL is minimizing disruptive table locks when modifying the table structure. This section will go into more depth on that.

All SQL statements, including SELECT statements (DQL), DML, and DDL, run inside a transaction.

Transactions are normally automatic and implicit, although as the developer you may use explicit transaction blocks with the keywords BEGIN and then COMMIT or ROLLBACK. You may also lock resources explicitly.

To further confuse the matter, the Active Record disable_ddl_transaction! is problematic. See "PR #21044,"[3] which explains how disabling the wrapping transaction is not limited to DDL but could be for a DML operation. Other databases don't support transactional DDL. Even with this option set, a Rails client application can't change the PostgreSQL transactional DDL feature, meaning DDL still runs inside an implicit transaction.

What about lock types? PostgreSQL reports which lock types conflict with each other in the "Conflicting Lock Modes" table on the "Explicit Locking"[4] documentation page. Familiarize yourself with different DDL and DML statement types and which locks they take. The PostgreSQL Lock Conflicts[5] tool is an excellent resource that maps operations to lock types.

If you have lock contention issues, how can you gain more insight into what's happening?

Another catalog to use is the pg_locks view. Review the "Lock Monitoring"[6] PostgreSQL wiki for examples of using it.

Lock contention is not something you'll usually see and fix in real time, so it can be difficult to have a mental model of it. One way to build that up is to simulate a lock scenario. You'll do that next!

In this exercise, you'll create two transactions that contend with one another.

Open two psql sessions named psql1 and psql2 as you did earlier.

---

3. https://github.com/rails/rails/issues/21044
4. https://www.postgresql.org/docs/current/explicit-locking.html
5. https://postgres-locks.husseinnasser.com
6. https://wiki.postgresql.org/wiki/Lock_Monitoring

sql/locks_and_blocks_part_1_psql1.sql

```
-- From "psql1" connected to Rideshare:

-- psql $DATABASE_URL

-- Start a Transaction
BEGIN;

-- create explicit EXCLUSIVE LOCK of trips table
LOCK trips IN ACCESS EXCLUSIVE MODE;
```

sql/locks_and_blocks_part_2_psql2.sql

```
-- From "psql2"
-- Inspect pg_locks view
-- Find the "AccessExclusiveLock" for "trips"
SELECT
  mode,
  pg_class.relname,
  locktype,
  relation
FROM pg_locks
JOIN pg_class
ON pg_locks.relation = pg_class.oid
AND pg_locks.mode = 'AccessExclusiveLock';

-- -[ RECORD 1 ]-----------------
-- mode     | AccessExclusiveLock
-- relname  | trips
-- locktype | relation
-- relation | 461492

-- "psql1", inspect the current lock_timeout;
-- A lock_timeout of 0 means it is disabled, so
-- a statement waiting on a lock will run forever
SHOW lock_timeout;

-- "psql2"
-- Create the DDL statement from earlier.
-- DDL statement acquires an exclusive lock
-- But it will get blocked!
ALTER TABLE trips ADD COLUMN city_id INTEGER DEFAULT 1;

-- Since this hanging go back to "psql1"
```

sql/locks_and_blocks_part_3_psql1.sql

```
-- Query pg_stat_activity from "psql1"
-- Look for waiting transactions
-- Confirm the ALTER TABLE is listed and blocked
SELECT
  wait_event_type,
  wait_event, query
FROM pg_stat_activity
WHERE wait_event = 'relation'
AND query LIKE '%ALTER TABLE%';
```

```
-- -[ RECORD 1 ]---+-------------------------------------------------------
-- wait_event_type | Lock
-- wait_event      | relation
-- query           | ALTER TABLE trips ADD COLUMN city_id INTEGER DEFAULT 1;

-- NOTE: UNBLOCK
-- To unblock, COMMIT or ROLLBACK the original transaction from "psql1"
ROLLBACK;
```

The ALTER TABLE statement gets blocked trying to modify the trips table because the trips table is locked with exclusive access. The statement is waiting to acquire the same lock type.

How might you prevent the statement from waiting forever?

Prevent Excessive Queueing with a Lock Timeout

When a statement is waiting, it's in a queue for the lock type, so it can be said to be *queueing*. One protection to add is a lock_timeout.[7] The purpose of the lock_timeout is to set the maximum allowed time a transaction can wait before it's canceled.

The lock_timeout parameter can be set database-wide, within a session, or for a single statement.

In the example from the last section, the lock_timeout was not set.

Try running the experiment again, but this time set a lock_timeout. You'll need two psql sessions, psql1 and psql2, as you did earlier.

Use the following statements. The main difference from earlier is that you're using SET LOCAL lock_timeout = '5s'; to set a lock_timeout of five seconds within a transaction.

```
sql/set_lock_timeout_psql1.sql
-- create psql1
-- start a transaction
BEGIN;
LOCK trips IN ACCESS EXCLUSIVE MODE;
```

```
sql/set_lock_timeout_psql2.sql
-- create psql2
-- set a transaction level lock_timeout
BEGIN;
SET LOCAL lock_timeout = '5s';
```

---

7. https://postgresqlco.nf/doc/en/param/lock_timeout/

```
-- Run the modification
-- It should hang since the table is locked for exclusive access
-- But it should get canceled after 5s
ALTER TABLE trips ADD COLUMN city_id INTEGER;

-- In psql2 notice the statement is canceled
-- ERROR:  canceling statement due to lock timeout

-- run rollback in both psql1 and psql2
ROLLBACK;
```

With the timeout in place, the statement will be canceled after waiting the maximum amount of time. This adds a safeguard that prevents your transactions from waiting forever.

What other kinds of safeguards can be added?

Exploring Lock Type Queues

Statements requesting access for a lock type are put into a queue where they wait in order.

If transaction B is waiting to acquire the lock type that transaction A holds, B must wait for A.

As described in "PostgreSQL and the Lock Queue,"[8] the pids for the backend processes are logged, including the statement holding a lock type and the statements waiting to acquire it.

Some helpful lock parameters to set are log_lock_waits to on and setting a value for deadlock_timeout to gain visibility into locks or blocked queries. When these timeouts cause cancellations, the events and queries will be logged to postgresql.log. See the post, "Cost of log_lock_waits and deadlock_timeout,"[9] for more.

Take a look at the following example. This example shows the pid holding a lock and all pids waiting to acquire the lock type.

```
DETAIL: Processes holding the lock: 29386. Wait queue: 31025, 30551, ...
```

The pids 31025 and 30551 are blocked waiting on pid 29386. Once the query associated to the backend pid 29386 completes, the pids that are waiting will be processed in the order of how they appear.

Besides the pg_stat_activity catalog you saw earlier, use a log analyzer for your postgresql.log log file to find lock issues.

---

8. https://joinhandshake.com/blog/our-team/postgresql-and-lock-queue/
9. https://dba.stackexchange.com/a/249904

pgBadger[10] organizes lock-related query information from your postgresql.log. The lock information is put into categories like "Most frequent waiting queries" and "Queries that waited the most," which can help your investigations. Install it by running brew install pgbadger. Using it is straightforward; just run it and supply it with the path to your postgresql.log file. Next, you will look at the statement_timeout.

Setting a statement_timeout

The statement_timeout[11] can be set from the client application to set a maximum allowed time for statements. When the time is reached, the statements are canceled. A statement_timeout is set in Rideshare in the config/database.yml.

When queries are canceled for taking too long, they'll need to be fixed so they run in less time. This is especially crucial for user-facing queries, although even queries for background jobs should be sped up when they're excessively long.

Setting too low of a value for statement_timeout cancels queries unnecessarily. Not setting it at all means queries are allowed to run forever, consuming limited resources like database connections. A happy middle ground is to set a reasonable statement_timeout value that balances these two extremes.

For most Ruby on Rails web applications, user-facing actions should return their responses in less than 250ms. However, the maximum allowable time may depend on the type of application being run and how much effort the team can put into query optimization.

For e-commerce applications, teams may want an upper bound of 50ms to avoid lost sales.

For B2B Enterprise SaaS applications, teams may tolerate much slower response times, into the single-digit seconds.

Why bother with optimizing queries? Reducing the execution time of queries improves the scalability of the server through increased concurrency, reduction of lock contention, and minimization of needed server resources.

With the increased efficiency, we may avoid needing to spend more money on scaling up instances, adding server resources, or adding auxiliary caching or specialized mechanisms.

---

10. https://github.com/darold/pgbadger
11. https://www.postgresql.org/docs/current/runtime-config-client.html

If your application does not have a statement timeout set at all, try starting with a high value, like five or ten minutes. As you eliminate slow queries, and as time passes without cancellations, continue to lower the timeout value. Repeat this pattern.

You may want to make some exceptions. One might be to allocate a small portion of the total database connections to a configuration that's intended to allow more time for slow queries.

To do that, you'd create a separate configuration in config/database.yml that has a limited number of database connections (the pool size) and a higher statement timeout value allowing for longer running statements. This configuration would be used exclusively for queries from background job workers. When selecting a pool size for Active Record, check out the post "Why the Advice to Have a Connection Pool the Same Size as Your Puma Threads Is (Probably) Wrong for You."[12] This post shows how additional database connections are used when new threads are created. Specific links to topics here are .load_async() (see Backgrounding Queries Using load_async, on page 126) and GoodJob (see Background Jobs Without Sidekiq, on page 389).

To see a sample of how you might accommodate slow clients, check out the slow clients configuration example in the Rideshare db/README.md. The example shows a configuration block, Active Record class, and usage of the class. Within the usage, a query that would normally be canceled runs successfully, thanks to the higher statement timeout.

This concludes the coverage on timeouts. In the next section, you'll shift gears and look at how Active Record caches your schema and some possible pitfalls.

Avoiding Schema Cache Errors

When Active Record starts up, for each model that's backed by a database table, the table fields are scanned and cached in the schema cache[13] for as long as the application is running.

Dropping a database column without considering Active Record and active instances of the application means that a schema change may cause an application error. This is due to the application trying to write or read to a cached column that's been removed.

---

12. https://tekin.co.uk/2023/07/active-record-connection-timeout-errors-with-puma
13. https://api.rubyonrails.org/classes/ActiveRecord/ConnectionAdapters/SchemaCache.html

To drop a column safely, use the Active Record ignored_columns()[14] mechanism. Add the field you're planning to drop to this list, and deploy and restart the application instances.

A field added to ignored_columns(), after the application has restarted, can safely be dropped from the database without issues from a stale schema cache.

Next, you'll jump into *backfilling* and how to perform it for large-scale operations safely.

Backfilling Large Tables Without Downtime

Over time, your database structure will evolve to meet the needs of the application. This could be from new features or more efficient designs. You may introduce a new empty column that needs to be populated for rows that existed before it was added. The column would be NULL to start.

The process of filling in data for existing rows is called "backfilling." As your table row counts increase, backfills take longer and can become very complicated and risky. One approach is to try and avoid them and provide application-level data in lieu of data from the database.

This can be a worthwhile trade-off to spare the development for some cases. In those cases, the backfill could be called *optional* when the application can *fall back* to a different or default value. What about when backfills aren't optional, but *required*?

In those cases, you'll need some tactics to backfill large numbers of rows without interrupting other work being done in the database. While you could create backfills using Ruby code with Rake tasks, in this section, you'll focus exclusively on backfill techniques with SQL code you'll run from psql.

One of your goals with backfill queries should be to avoid harming other concurrent client activity. To achieve that, your backfill operations need to run efficiently and consume few resources. Ideally, your server instance is over-provisioned, which means there's a lot of spare capacity for CPU, memory, and storage access operations. If your instances don't normally run as over-provisioned, if possible, consider adding more resources temporarily while backfill operations run, then removing them once they're complete.

Take advantage of low activity periods to perform your backfill operations. Since we'll focus on SQL backfills, let's consider some basic process steps.

---

14. https://www.bigbinary.com/blog/rails-5-adds-active-record-ignored-columns

As you develop them, list out the SQL commands that are part of the process. Share the steps with your team to gather feedback and share knowledge about this significant planned operation. Validate the steps using a pre-production database like the Performance Database you set up earlier. If you're using a cloud provider, try using a separate detached instance created from a snapshot as a test run of any steps. Detached instances are useful, but since they don't have live traffic, this test method does not fully simulate what you'll see in your production database.

Here are some backfilling concepts you'll work with:

- You'll learn how *double writing* (or *dual writes*) works

- You'll learn how to use an intermediate table to assist in the backfill

- How to use batched operations to limit resource consumption

- Adding a throttling mechanism to slow things down, providing time to PostgreSQL for index maintenance and replication

- Creating specialized indexes supporting the backfill queries

- Using UNLOGGED tables and disabling Autovacuum to speed up and smooth out operations

Let's dive in.

Backfilling and Double Writing

Modern engineering organizations are able to perform data migrations online for most cases, avoiding the need for downtime. Downtime halts business operations, application availability, and should be avoided when possible.

Zero or minimal downtime approaches are technically challenging and risky compared with offline backfills. Online backfills require careful planning, lots of testing in local development, and coordinated timing.

After introducing a new database column, you may want to plan out multiple release phases, cutting over write operations, then reads, and progressing from lower-impact to higher-impact environments.

Double writing can help as a transitional technique to minimize the time needed in a cutover. Two locations receive writes actively. Reads are switched from the original location to a target location. While writes continue to happen, rollbacks are possible if there are issues in the new location.

How can you separate reads and writes?

Separating Reads and Writes for Backfills

Backfills are straightforward when they can SELECT from one table and UPDATE another table.

When the table being queried is under heavy load, it may be too slow to query it in high volume for backfill purposes. Determine if you can modify the source table by adding special-purpose backfill indexes so backfill queries run faster.

If the queries to read and write aren't fast enough, you may want a specially built table as a transitional element.

Specialized Tables for Backfills

When optimizing the read side and write side queries is not enough, you may need an intermediate table to assist in the backfill process.

The data in this table is duplicated from a source. As a special table, there are no other connections to this table or contention for accessing data. This separate table can also be updated to track progress.

A trade-off with special indexes or tables is more (temporary) space consumption.

When designing a table for backfills, make it as narrow (as few columns) as possible.

To make writes faster, set the table to UNLOGGED, which disables crash protection.

From psql, run SET UNLOGGED for the table. An unlogged table doesn't use the Write Ahead Log (WAL), thus, it doesn't receive the crash protection benefit. If Postgre-SQL restarts unexpectedly when the recovery process begins, any unlogged tables are truncated.[15] That's a severe concern, but since this table contains data that's been copied from elsewhere, the truncation possibility with unlogged tables is an acceptable trade-off for the benefits of faster write operations.

Unlogged to Logged

When working with unlogged tables, if you plan to make them logged later, keep in mind that transition will create a lot of Write Ahead Log (WAL) changes suddenly, which can cause a lot of resource load.

The intermediate table here will remain unlogged and can be dropped when it's no longer needed, avoiding this issue.

---

15. https://pganalyze.com/blog/5mins-postgres-unlogged-tables

Autovacuum can also be disabled, which keeps it from consuming resources. Let's do that now. For the table trip_requests_intermediate, run the following statement from psql to disable Autovacuum for the table:

sql/alter_table_disable_auto_vacuum.sql
```
ALTER TABLE trip_requests_intermediate
SET (autovacuum_enabled = false);
```

Keep reading to put these techniques into practice.

Practicing Backfilling Techniques

Let's practice some of the backfill techniques you've seen.

Using the earlier example that added a city_id column to the users table, imagine that you were creating a purpose-built intermediate table to act as the data source.

This table has these characteristics:

- A minimal set of columns
- Purpose-made index for a single query
- No constraints
- Unlogged
- Autovacuum disabled
- No other indexes if updating or deleting rows

Run these statements in psql:

sql/create_backfill_intermediate_table.sql
```
CREATE SCHEMA IF NOT EXISTS temp;

CREATE UNLOGGED TABLE temp.users_intermediate (
  user_id BIGINT, city_id INTEGER
);

ALTER TABLE temp.users_intermediate
SET (autovacuum_enabled = false);
```

Generate some rows:

sql/backfill_intermediate_generate_rows.sql
```
INSERT INTO temp.users_intermediate (user_id, city_id)
SELECT GENERATE_SERIES(1, 10, 1), GENERATE_SERIES(1, 10, 1);
```

For your backfill, you'll UPDATE the users.city_id column using matching rows from the temp.users table. If the users.city_id column does not exist, you can add it by running this statement:

sql/backfill_alter_table_add_column.sql
```
ALTER TABLE users ADD COLUMN IF NOT EXISTS city_id INTEGER;
```

Let's imagine temp.users_intermediate has millions of rows. You want accessing rows to be as fast as possible.

To achieve that, add a *multicolumn index* covering both columns:

sql/backfill_add_index.sql
```
CREATE INDEX temp_users_user_id_city_id
ON temp.users_intermediate (user_id, city_id);
```

You'll learn more about multicolumn indexes in an upcoming chapter.

From psql, run the following query and add EXPLAIN in front of it. You haven't started working with EXPLAIN and the query planner yet, but they'll be covered more in an upcoming chapter.

The query execution plan should show an index scan was used and list the index name you created.

sql/backfill_update.sql
```
UPDATE users
SET
  city_id = temp.users_intermediate.city_id
FROM temp.users_intermediate
WHERE users.id = temp.users_intermediate.user_id
AND users.id > 0
AND users.id < 10000;
```

Try setting SET enable_seqscan = OFF; if you got a sequential scan, or try adding more sample rows to the table.

For your batch size, use a range that is sized appropriately for your database server. Iterate through the users table using the primary key id column. There will be up to 10,000 updates at once for this batch size, given no gaps.

Use the PL/pgSQL procedure you saw in an earlier chapter to turn this single statement into a batched, looping version that can process all rows.

Besides batched updates, consider adding pauses in between batches, to throttle down the speed and add time for index maintenance and replication. Monitor server resources while your statements are running, and stop them if needed.

Once the destination table is updated, you can safely remove the temp.users transitional table.

Wrapping Up

In this chapter, you learned how to make structural database changes safely, even on large and busy databases. You learned about lock types, queues, and saw how queries can become blocked. You simulated lock behavior, blocked queries, and added safeguards by setting a lock_timeout and statement_timeout.

You learned about backfill techniques and how to optimize them for large-scale operations.

You worked a lot in PostgreSQL. In the next chapter, you'll shift gears and work more with Active Record and Ruby code. You'll learn how to optimize queries from application code. Read on to get started.

## CHAPTER 6

Optimizing Active Record

In this chapter, you'll analyze the Active Record code that you write and the SQL queries that are generated, focusing on their performance and scalability.

You'll see a variety of ways to improve the performance of your application by eliminating unnecessary queries using caches and by incorporating advanced query design.

Active Record is the *Domain Specific Language* (DSL) that Rails developers use to create SQL queries from Ruby code.

If you've written SQL before and are newer to Rails, you may wonder whether writing your queries as Active Record code instead of directly as SQL is worth it. You may prefer to write SQL directly. What are some of the reasons for preferring Active Record?

Preferring Active Record over SQL

As you saw earlier, Ruby on Rails uses Convention over Configuration in its design. Active Record is the conventional way to write queries after you've configured your data model layer with model classes, relationships, validations, and callbacks. Embracing the conventional way to write queries helps ease maintenance by keeping the application codebase more conventional, making it easier for new team members to guess where to look for code and to quickly understand how it works.

While SQL is great, and is more of a focus in upcoming chapters, in this chapter, we'll leverage everything we can from Active Record to create high-performance code.

Many times, fragments of a query exist in other queries. In Active Record, fragments of SQL queries, for example, WHERE clauses that perform filtering, can be grouped into *named scopes*. Named scopes provide a convention to re-use query fragments that can be shared across models.

One example where filters are re-used is for the "soft deletes" pattern. In lieu of featuring a specific gem here, check out the category of gems dedicated to Active Record soft deletes[1] over at the Ruby Toolbox.

With soft deletes, the table gets a deleted_at timestamp column. When records are soft deleted, the timestamp is set, and the record is hidden from the application using a shared SQL fragment that the application uses to hide those rows. By implementing this as a default scope added to all application models, there's a conventional re-use of this SQL fragment at the data layer.

Finding Your postgresql.log

If you get tired of looking up where your postgresql.log is, make a script to do it for you!

- Download tail_log.sh from https://github.com/andyatkinson/pg_scripts
- chmod +x tail_log.sh
- Copy tail_log.sh to /usr/local/bin in your PATH (echo $PATH)
- Now you can run sh tail_log.sh from anywhere, which immediately starts live tailing (tail -f) your PostgreSQL log!

As you explore SQL queries in your postgresql.log (see previous note) or in your Application Performance Monitoring (APM) tool, you'll need a way to connect generated SQL queries back to Active Record application code.

How can you do that?

Query Logs to Connect SQL to App Code

The Marginalia[2] gem was a popular option to add source location information to queries prior to Rails 7.

Marginalia adds statement-level comments to SQL queries, with segmented parts that describe the application code that generated them.

The Marginalia comment segments include the application name, controller name, and controller action name and can be extended with your own segments. Here is an example comment:

```
/*application:Rideshare,controller:trips,action:index*/
```

---

1. https://www.ruby-toolbox.com/categories/Active_Record_Soft_Delete
2. https://github.com/basecamp/marginalia

This comment shows the query was generated from the Rideshare application in the trips controller and index action. With this comment, you're able to navigate directly to the specific line number in the TripsController#index action where the query was generated. From there the query may be edited or replaced.

In Rails 7, the functionality of Marginalia was added to Rails and called *query logs* (or query log tags).

Rideshare enables query log tags by setting config.active_record.query_log_tags_enabled to true in config/application.rb. Note that prepared statements are incompatible with query log tags (See the Warning in config.active_record.query_log_tags_enabled[3]).

You haven't yet worked with prepared statements, but you will do that in upcoming chapters. For now, to disable prepared statements, set prepared_statements = false in config/database.yml.

With prepared statements disabled and query log tags enabled, Rideshare has statement-level comments directly from Rails, similar to the ones provided by the Marginalia gem, without requiring the gem.

Besides seeing these comments in the PostgreSQL log and Rails server log, you'll see them in the Rails console output. For example, notice /*application: Rideshare*/ from bin/rails console this output:

```
irb(main):020:0> Trip.first
  Trip Load (0.5ms)  /*application:Rideshare*/ SELECT "trips".*
  FROM "trips" ORDER BY "trips"."id" ASC LIMIT $1  [["LIMIT", 1]]
```

Query log tags improve your observability by helping you connect SQL to Active Record code. How can you use this observability information to help your platform?

One way is to find and fix common Active Record query problems. What are some examples of those?

Common Active Record Problems

Before diving into common Active Record query pattern problems, we'll want to build more context. Let's look at the following terminology that you'll work with in upcoming sections:

---

3.   https://guides.rubyonrails.org/configuring.html#config-active-record-query-log-tags-enabled

Active Record Optimization Terminology

- Lazy loading—Loading data "late", on-demand
- Eager loading—Loading data "early" or "upfront"
- Strict loading—Preventing lazy loading, requiring eager loading
- Counter cache—Incrementing a counter at INSERT time, storing the computed value for fast access

Let's take a brief detour and refresh our knowledge on data *normalization*. Good data normalization practices dictate the removal of duplication of fields between tables. In a fully normalized database, each table has a unique set of fields. To display screens of data in an application, data is joined together from two or more tables, given that most screens of information presented to users wouldn't be limited to the data in a single table. This is where you come in, as you'll be writing a lot of queries that join rows together.

To join rows together, you'll use foreign key and primary key columns, which form a relationship, and each stores a shared value. As you know, the primary key from one side is copied into the foreign key column on the other side of the relationship so that those rows can be combined (joined).

Once models are configured with Active Record, it becomes quite expressive and straightforward to pull data from many tables. Admittedly, since Active Record works so well as Ruby code, you're able to write complex queries and think less and less about the relational model or generated SQL.

The flip side of that is that it's possible, when lacking awareness of the generated queries, to create loops and other SQL queries that are inefficient or even unnecessary. The impact of that could be extra latency from your queries.

The remedy, of course, is to better understand the SQL that's generated and how it performs.

With that background context in place, let's jump into some specific query patterns that are problematic.

Active Record uses *lazy loading* to defer query generation. This makes for a nice developer experience since scopes can be built up from method calls on the same base object class. The inverse of lazy loading is to load data upfront, which Active Record calls *eager loading*.

Let's start from the solution side. Eager loading is commonly a quick fix or solution for inefficient queries that use lazy loading. The most notorious query pattern there is the *N+1* pattern. The N+1 pattern involves queries for two tables: an outer query and an inner query. The outer query runs once, but the inner query runs N times (repeatedly), querying the same table. Those repeated queries can be consolidated into a single query for the table, which will generally perform better.

Let's explore this with an example. Open bin/rails console from your terminal.

Make sure SQL queries are logged in your console by running this code:

```ruby
# ruby/n_plus_one_example.rb
# Show SQL if not already enabled in bin/rails console
ActiveRecord::Base.logger = Logger.new(STDOUT)

Vehicle.all.each do |vehicle|
  vehicle.vehicle_reservations.count
end; nil
```

Notice how the count of vehicle_reservations is queried for every vehicle.

The SQL queries will look as follows, with repeated queries to the reservations table, only varying the vehicle_id field:

```ruby
# ruby/n_plus_one_queries.rb
Vehicle Load (2.1ms)  \
  SELECT "vehicles".* FROM "vehicles" /*application:Rideshare*/
SELECT COUNT(*) ... WHERE "vehicle_reservations"."vehicle_id" = 1
SELECT COUNT(*) ... WHERE "vehicle_reservations"."vehicle_id" = 2
SELECT COUNT(*) ... WHERE "vehicle_reservations"."vehicle_id" = 3
SELECT COUNT(*) ... WHERE "vehicle_reservations"."vehicle_id" = 4
```

N+1 queries can happen in most Active Record code, including models, views, or serializers. Monitor your local server development log for N+1 queries and keep an eye out for them in code reviews.

Besides manual identification, are there other ways to find them?

Tooling to Find Problematic Query Patterns

While manual checks are useful, the Rails ecosystem has many gems and tools to detect N+1 queries. These tools could be integrated into your development flow to add some automation.

The Ruby gem Prosopite[4] is an N+1 detection gem that's been added to Rideshare, along with pg_query,[5] which it depends on.

Let's see if Prosopite picks up this deliberate N+1. Run the code again in Rideshare from bin/rails console inside of a Prosopite block, as this shows. Set Prosopite.rails_logger = true.

---

4. https://github.com/charkost/prosopite
5. https://github.com/pganalyze/pg_query

```ruby
ruby/n_plus_one_detection.rb
Prosopite.rails_logger = true

Prosopite.scan do
  Vehicle.all.each do |vehicle|
    vehicle.vehicle_reservations.count
  end
end
```

Hopefully, you saw that Prosopite displayed a message, N+1 queries detected, in the Rails console. Great! Prosopite can even be configured to detect N+1 patterns in test code, causing a test failure. By setting this up in your test suite, you will more quickly identify N+1 code to fix due to failing tests in the CI environment.

Now that you can detect N+1 queries manually or automatically, how do you fix them?

Use Eager Loading to Reduce Queries

To fix N+1 queries, use eager loading tactics that load required data with fewer queries. Test to make sure you get the same query results.

Active Record *Associations* (see "Types of Associations"[6]) like has_one(), has_many(), or belongs_to() generate different SQL queries, joining rows of data from tables together between the six types (see Join Types[7]).

For SQL joins, use the Active Record .left_joins() and .includes() helper methods to create LEFT OUTER JOIN and INNER JOIN join types, respectively.

For join types not supported by Active Record, specify the SQL fragment for the join type within the .joins() method as text.

Besides eager loading, there's another method we'll look at. Data can be "preloaded" using the .preload()[8] method. The preload method is one of the eager loading method types. Let's try it out.

In bin/rails console, run the same code again but add .preload() after the Vehicle class name, as shown:

```ruby
ruby/active_record_preload.rb
Vehicle.preload(:vehicle_reservations).all.each do |vehicle|
  vehicle.vehicle_reservations.size
end; nil
```

---

6. https://guides.rubyonrails.org/association_basics.html#the-types-of-associations
7. https://guides.rubyonrails.org/active_record_querying.html#joining-tables
8. https://api.rubyonrails.org/classes/ActiveRecord/QueryMethods.html#method-i-preload

What did you see? Hopefully, using .preload() here avoids the N+1 query pattern. There was one more change in this snippet. The .count() method from earlier was replaced here with the .size() method.

Since the vehicle reservations association was already loaded, the .size() method avoids sending another SQL query (a COUNT() query),[9] which helps reduce latency.

Preloading isn't the only method to eager load associated data. What other methods are there?

Eager Loading with .includes()

Besides .preload(), .includes() is another method for eager loading. This method produces an equivalent SQL query to .preload().

Try running the following example using .includes() and compare the generated query to the one from earlier:

```ruby
ruby/active_record_includes.rb
Vehicle.includes(:vehicle_reservations).each do |vehicle|
  vehicle.vehicle_reservations.size
end; nil
```

With .preload(), the WHERE clause conditions for the second table being joined cannot be modified. The SQL query used an IN clause for the top-level query with a list of primary key values from the second table.

If .includes() generates the same SQL query, then why does this method exist?

Another trick that .includes() has is that it can pick between two strategies. .includes() will work equivalently to .preload(), or it will generate a LEFT OUTER JOIN to join the tables together. How does it decide?

Active Record chooses a LEFT OUTER JOIN when there are conditions on the associated table. Let's look at an example with query conditions. Conversely, the IN clause strategy is used when there are *not* conditions on the associated table.

Modify the example from earlier that fetches vehicle reservations. This time, fetch only the active reservations (the ones that aren't canceled), which we're doing here to create conditions on the associated table.

Run this code from bin/rails console and look at the generated SQL:

---

9. https://www.speedshop.co/2019/01/10/three-activerecord-mistakes.html

```ruby/eager_load_includes_left_outer_join.rb
Vehicle.includes(:vehicle_reservations).
  where(vehicle_reservations: { canceled: false }).
  size
```

Notice it generated a LEFT OUTER JOIN to load the vehicle_reservations data. This was so that the vehicle reservations could be filtered only to canceled reservations.

If we load vehicle reservations via .includes() without any filters for that table, we see two generated SQL queries. A limit of 2 is applied to the vehicles. For each of their vehicle_id foreign key columns, there's a single SQL query that loads vehicle reservations using an IN clause, which is a list of those two values. Note that an IN clause with a big list of values will perform poorly at a certain point.

```
Vehicle.includes(:vehicle_reservations).limit(2)
```

You've now seen a couple of ways to use eager loading, both the .preload() method and .includes() method, to help you avoid the N+1 query pattern with unnecessary queries that add latency.

Imagine you wanted to prevent N+1 queries entirely. How could you do that?

Prefer Strict Loading over Lazy Loading

Active Record introduced a feature called *strict loading* in Rails 6.1[10] that disables the ability to perform lazy loading.

Strict loading can be specified globally, at specific source code caller locations, or even on associations.

Let's try putting strict loading into practice using Rideshare.

Run the following code in bin/rails console:

```ruby/vehicle_reservations_strict_loading.rb
vehicles = Vehicle.strict_loading.all

vehicles.each do |vehicle|
  vehicle.vehicle_reservations.first.starts_at
end

# `Vehicle` is marked for strict_loading. The VehicleReservation association
# named `:vehicle_reservations` cannot be lazily loaded.
# (ActiveRecord::StrictLoadingViolationError)
```

This code enables strict loading for a specific query for vehicles. Trying to combine vehicle reservation data with vehicle data that's already been loaded

---

10. https://github.com/rails/rails/pull/37400

raises an ActiveRecord::StrictLoadingViolationError exception. With this exception being raised, this effectively prevents lazy loading. That's great, but we still need to load the associated data. How do we do that?

As you did earlier, you'll use eager loading to load associated data upfront, which works within the constraints of strict loading. Modify the previous query using eager loading based on what you saw earlier. Confirm that the strict loading exception is no longer raised. Cool!

You've now worked detection of N+1 query patterns into your system, and learned how to use eager loading to fix them. Besides that, you learned how to disable lazy loading entirely using strict loading, which means you can selectively avoid N+1 queries by loading required data upfront.

What other kinds of Active Record query-level optimizations can you make?

Optimizing Active Record Queries

You may be wondering whether it's worth eliminating individual queries. What are the benefits of doing that? One benefit of eliminating an unneeded query is that it reduces the number of concurrent database connections needed.

You haven't yet worked with database connections, but you'll explore them in an upcoming section. For now, it's enough to know they're a limited resource that you want to use only when necessary.

Besides connections, eliminating unnecessary queries reduces IO because those storage accesses don't happen when the query is removed.

Let's explore reducing IO a bit. As you work on query optimization, you'll find a common theme of reducing how much data you pull, whether it's from tables, indexes, or elsewhere. This is because the data access adds latency, and depending on how PostgreSQL is deployed for you, it may add cost or have an associated quota that you do not wish to exceed.

How can we reduce IO? One way to reduce the IO is to restrict the fields in the SELECT portion of your queries. Use the Active Record .select() method to do that.

Active Record 7.1 added the ability to select fields from the local table and associated tables using a nice Ruby hash style.[11]

---

11. https://blog.kiprosh.com/rails-7-1-allows-activerecord-querymethods-select-and-reselect-to-receive-hash-values/

When field data is already loaded into memory, .select() reads from the loaded collection and avoids a SQL query. (see "Rails Pluck vs. Select and Map/Collect"[12]). As you'll see in an upcoming chapter, accessing fewer fields opens up the possibility of more efficient index scans and index-only scans, which can greatly reduce the IO for a query.

Besides .select(), you may have also used .pluck() which returns an Array object. This prevents chaining but still selects fewer fields. Try running this code from bin/rails console:

```ruby/active_record_pluck.rb
Vehicle.includes(:vehicle_reservations).
  pluck('vehicles.name',
        'vehicle_reservations.starts_at',
        'vehicle_reservations.canceled')
```

We've now seen how to use .select() and .pluck() to reduce IO and possibly achieve a more performant index scan (we'll look at indexes in an upcoming chapter).

Next up, let's look at how we can use the newer .load_async() capability added to Active Record version 7.

Backgrounding Queries Using load_async

Rails 7 supports *Asynchronous Query Loading*[13] with the .load_async() method. When running queries asynchronously, they use a new thread of execution, which grabs its own database connection. While this runs the query in the background, keep an eye on how many database connections are being used.

The post, "Running Queries in Parallel with Rails 7 and load_async,"[14] shows a nice example of where this can help. The post shows a number of queries in a Rails controller without .load_async(), showing multiple database fetches. Each fetch executes serially, meaning one by one.

Looking at the same example, but using .load_async(), the second query right after the first query is not blocked on starting. Since each of the fetches uses .load_async(), the reduction in blocking due to serial execution produces an overall 35 percent reduction in loading the data.

Take note, though, that individual slow queries will still ultimately dictate overall endpoint performance. The post, "Parallelizing Queries with Rails 7's

---

12. https://www.rubyinrails.com/2014/06/05/rails-pluck-vs-select-map-collect/

13. https://rubyonrails.org/2021/12/15/Rails-7-fulfilling-a-vision

14. https://www.mikecoutermarsh.com/running-queries-in-parallel-rails-7-load-async/

load_async,"[15] shows in one example where, despite using .load_async(), an individually slow query took more total time compared with two others running asynchronously that had already finished.

Let's continue the discussion on removing queries to reduce latency and IO.

In the next section, you'll see how to do that using the RETURNING keyword.

Save a SELECT by Using RETURNING

PostgreSQL supports the RETURNING keyword, which allows you to specify the fields in your query result following an INSERT that you wish to get back.

This is very handy for fields that are populated by the database since you'd need to send another query afterward to fetch them without it.

For example, a sequence that populates a primary key is one type of database-produced value.

Let's try this out. Let's re-use the temp.users schema and table set up earlier (see Learning from Unsafe Migrations, on page 97). The table does not currently have a sequence, so let's add one.

Create a sequence and configure temp.users to use it by running the following from psql:

```
sql/returning_keyword_sequence.sql
CREATE SEQUENCE temp_users_id_seq INCREMENT 1 START 1;

ALTER TABLE temp.users ALTER COLUMN id
SET DEFAULT nextval('temp_users_id_seq');
```

Now temp.users.id will be populated with values from the sequence.

Try inserting a row using SQL, adding the RETURNING keyword, specifying the id and name column:

```
INSERT into temp.users (name) VALUES ('bob') RETURNING id, name;
```

You should get the id and name values back in the result, even with id being generated by the sequence at insert time.

Now, let's try this from Active Record. Active Record also supports the RETURNING keyword for inserts. At publication time, RETURNING is not supported by Active Record for other DML operations (see PR #48241[16]).

---

15. https://blog.skylight.io/rails-7-load_async/
16. https://github.com/rails/rails/pull/48241

Experiment in bin/rails console. Insert a single Driver using .insert_all() and specify the id column in your returning clause:

```ruby
ruby/insert_all_with_returning.rb
driver = Driver.insert_all([
  {
    first_name: 'Andrew',
    last_name: 'Atkinson',
    email: "andrew.atkinson@example.com",
    password_digest: SecureRandom.hex
  }],
  returning: [:id]
).first

driver["id"]
```

After running that code, the driver variable should have an id property that's populated with the id sequence value from PostgreSQL, which you have received without needing to query a second time for it.

You've now used RETURNING to eliminate a query.

Imagine that you've focused your efforts on eliminating as many queries as possible. After you've done that, what's next? Let's assume we can't eliminate the queries, so we'll want to make them more efficient.

Restricting Queries Using a LIMIT

A common way to improve poor query performance is to add more restrictions to the query. These restrictions could be filters that reduce the data being accessed.

Restrictions should be added to WHERE clauses, JOIN clauses, or using a LIMIT clause whenever possible. This helps lessen the storage access and the result size, making the query more efficient. To do that from Active Record, use the .limit() method.

A common issue is a query with no limit where the intention was more flexibility for the client. While providing the client flexibility, as the engineer building and scaling the product, you'll also need to be mindful of initial performance and performance as data volumes and query volumes increase.

For tables with small row counts, no-limit queries could perform OK. They slow down as row counts increase, producing huge results that may be more data than is needed by the client. The nontechnical part of this evaluation is to determine what's needed by the client and provide the minimal result set to achieve that.

Related Active Record concepts for working with large amounts of data are batch operation methods like .find_each(), .find_in_batches(), and .in_batches() (see "Rails—find_each vs. find_in_batches vs. in_batches"[17]). These will be covered in an upcoming chapter.

As queries become more complicated, you may need to bring in more advanced query design techniques to reduce the total number of queries. What are those?

Advanced Query Support in Active Record

Subquery expressions[18] or "subqueries" combine multiple queries into a single statement. An outer query uses an inner query as a way to filter rows. Filtering is usually conducted with a WHERE clause or IN clause. Generating subqueries has been possible with Active Record dating back to version 3.

To get familiar with subqueries in Active Record, adapt an example from the "PostgreSQL Tutorial on Subqueries"[19] to Rideshare. Create an analytical query to show how multiple queries can be combined in a single statement. First, write the query using SQL and then convert it to Active Record. The query has these goals:

- Find the average number of trips provided by drivers.
- Find drivers who have completed more trips than the average.
- From that filtered list, order the drivers by their trip count.

Since we're combining aggregations and filtering and ordering, using a sub-query here is helpful. To get the average, use the AVG() PostgreSQL aggregate function. Run the following from psql:

```
sql/select_avg_trips_count.sql
SELECT ROUND(AVG(trips_count))
FROM users
WHERE type = 'Driver';
```

After rounding the average, we're seeing a value of 3. Use that value as input to a WHERE clause to filter to drivers that have a trip count greater than the average. These could be thought of as the most active Rideshare drivers.

---

17. https://medium.com/lynns-dev-blog/rails-find-each-v-s-find-in-batches-v-s-in-batches-d5ca9bfe37d

18. https://www.postgresql.org/docs/current/functions-subquery.html

19. https://www.postgresqltutorial.com/postgresql-tutorial/postgresql-subquery/

```sql/trips_count_subquery.sql
SELECT
  users.id AS driver_id,
  trips_count
FROM users
WHERE type = 'Driver'
AND trips_count > (
  -- the earlier ROUND(AVG(trips)) query
  SELECT ROUND(AVG(trips_count))
  FROM users
  WHERE type = 'Driver'
)
ORDER BY trips_count
DESC LIMIT 5;
```

Run that query and you should see results like this:

```
 driver_id | trips_count
-----------+-------------
     20064 |          19
     20097 |          17
     20024 |          16
     20007 |          16
     20036 |          16
```

Great! You've now got a sorted list of drivers that have provided more trips than the average. To do that, you created a subquery using SQL.

How can you adapt this Subquery to Active Record?

Use the post "Advanced Active Record: Using Subqueries in Rails"[20] from PgAnalyze as a guide. Run the following code in bin/rails console and confirm the generated SQL query is equivalent to the previous one:

```ruby/active_record_subquery.rb
Driver.where('trips_count > (:avg)',
             avg: Driver.select('ROUND(AVG(trips_count))')).
  order(trips_count: :desc).
  limit(5)
```

Nice. We've confirmed the results have the same set of drivers and in the same order.

In the previous code, :avg is a placeholder. The value for :avg is supplied from an Active Record fragment. The advantage of creating a subquery using Active Record is that your result will be Active Record instances to work with. You can then continue to chain and compose query parts with that result or present it to the client. Pretty cool.

---

20. https://pganalyze.com/blog/active-record-subqueries-rails

Subquery expressions in SQL are useful, but they can become complicated to maintain. To help, let's use a common table expression, a technique we saw earlier.

Read on to learn more.

Using Common Table Expressions (CTE)

Common Table Expressions (CTE) are a technique in PostgreSQL to combine two or more standalone queries into a single statement. Each statement gets a name, helping you better organize your multiquery statements.

Support for PostgreSQL CTE queries was added in Active Record 7.1. Active Record added a .with() method (see "Rails 7.1 Construct Common Table Expressions"[21]) which generates a CTE. Prior to Rails 7.1, a CTE could be integrated in Active Record using the activerecord-cte[22] gem.

A CTE can be used recursively by combining a nonrecursive portion and a recursive portion, then using a UNION to combine the parts. A Recursive CTE will not be covered here, but PostgreSQL Tutorial has a nice example in the post "Learn PostgreSQL Recursive Query By Example."[23] The example shows how to find direct reports for a manager for various levels of depth.

In this section, create a CTE to answer questions about Rideshare drivers. As you did in the last section, you'll write the CTE first using SQL and then translate it into Active Record.

To start, let's find drivers created in the last 30 days. Run the following query from psql:

```
sql/trips_new_drivers.sql
-- Drivers created in the last 30 days
SELECT *
FROM users
WHERE type = 'Driver'
AND created_at >= (
  NOW() - INTERVAL '30 days'
);
```

Imagine a Rideshare feature that shows ratings for new drivers. To fetch the data, use the rating column on the trips table.

---

21. https://blog.kiprosh.com/rails-7-1-construct-cte-using-with-query-method

22. https://github.com/vlado/activerecord-cte

23. https://www.postgresqltutorial.com/postgresql-tutorial/postgresql-recursive-query/

The CTE will have named query parts so the query stays organized and maintainable. To populate a lot of rated trips, run bin/rails data_generators:trips_and_requests from your terminal. Once you've got a lot of rated trips loaded, run this SQL query from psql:

```sql
sql/trips_top_drivers_cte.sql
WITH new_drivers AS (
  SELECT *
  FROM users
  WHERE type = 'Driver'
  AND created_at >= (NOW() - INTERVAL '30 days')
),
rated_trips AS (
  SELECT id, driver_id
  FROM trips
  WHERE rating IS NOT NULL
)
-- Display Driver names and
-- the Average rating for their trips
SELECT
  trips.driver_id,
  CONCAT(users.first_name, ' ', users.last_name) AS driver_name,
  ROUND(AVG(trips.rating), 2) AS avg_rating
FROM trips
JOIN users ON trips.driver_id = users.id
JOIN new_drivers ON trips.driver_id = new_drivers.id
JOIN rated_trips ON trips.id = rated_trips.id
WHERE users.type = 'Driver'
GROUP by 1, 2
ORDER BY 3 DESC
LIMIT 10;
```

Let's break down what's happening in the CTE. The CTE has named parts new_drivers and rated_trips that could be standalone queries but are being brought together to combine Driver and Trip data. With the data sources combined, the drivers are presented with their names and ratings in descending order, showing the top-rated drivers first.

Let's try working with equivalent Active Record code for this CTE. Run the following from bin/rails console:

```ruby
ruby/active_record_cte_with.rb
# use the ".." endless range
Trip.with(recently_rated:
        Trip.where.not(rating: nil).
        where(created_at: 30.days.ago..)
).
from("recently_rated").
count
```

This Active Record code also combines multiple queries into one. The .with() method is used as an outer query. The name recently_rated is given as a name to the inner query. Review the generated SQL and compare it to CTE written previously. You should find that it's equivalent. Notice how the Active Record code is more compact. Nice!

You've now seen how to create subqueries and CTE queries using both SQL and Active Record.

When queries become complex and are commonly used, it can be nice to encapsulate their details. Fortunately, such a capability exists in PostgreSQL, called a database view. Read on to learn how to create and manage them using Ruby on Rails.

Introducing Database Views for Rideshare

In this section, you'll work with *database views* in PostgreSQL and manage them from Rails.

A database view *encapsulates*[24] a query, gives it a name, and is stored as an object within PostgreSQL. The query text itself is stored, not the query results. Each invocation runs as a "live" query.

Database views are not supported natively by Active Record, however, they can be integrated into Rails using a Ruby gem.

Since views have a query definition that may change over time, you'll evolve your database views in Rideshare the same way that you evolve other database objects like tables. PostgreSQL views do not have a versioning concept, so versioning will be added.

Database views, while not offering performance advantages themselves, are closely related to another type called *materialized views*, which do offer performance advantages. We'll explore all of this here in this section.

Some of the terminology used is listed here:

Administration Terminology

- Database view—Encapsulates a SQL query
- Materialized view—A view type that pre-calculates and stores results

---

24. https://en.wikipedia.org/wiki/Encapsulation_(computer_programming)

Imagine that you frequently queried new drivers in Rideshare and wanted to have a shared definition for what constituted a new driver. Once way to do that might be to express it in SQL and give it a name. You could use a real creative name, like "new_drivers", with a query like this:

sql/create_view_new_drivers.sql
```
DROP VIEW IF EXISTS new_drivers;

CREATE VIEW new_drivers AS
  SELECT * FROM users
  WHERE type = 'Driver'
  AND created_at >= (NOW() - INTERVAL '30 days');
```

You've just created your first view in Rideshare! new_drivers is a view that you can now reference in other queries.

Additional queries can be based on this view, although you'll want to be wary of the performance impact. Writing a query like SELECT * FROM new_drivers; runs as a live query and abstracts away the implementation details for the definition of a new driver. The details are said to be "encapsulated."

What is a materialized view? A materialized view is a special type of view that saves the results.

With materialized views, since query results are pre-calculated and saved, they are very fast to access. The trade-off is that pre-calculated results become stale over time, and refreshing the view may be performance intensive. View refreshes need to occur on a regular cadence to provide close to real-time results for tables that are heavily modified.

For materialized views to be viable, your use case should tolerate some staleness in the result data. Ideally the source data changes infrequently. With that said, materialized views can be a great solution offering huge performance increases.

To refresh the query results for a materialized view, use the REFRESH keyword. Fortunately, refreshes can be performed CONCURRENTLY, which means queries accessing the materialized view results computed earlier can continue to do so while they're being refreshed.

Let's see how to create both types of views in the next section. For the materialized view, you'll also configure automatic refreshes.

Creating the Search Result Model with Scenic

In this section, you'll work with the Ruby gem *Scenic*[25] to create database views.

Scenic works like Active Record. Similar to how create_table generates a SQL CREATE TABLE DDL statement, Scenic adds a create_view helper to generate DDL for creating database views.

The Scenic generator creates two files. The first is a plain text .sql file where you place the SQL query definition of your view. The second file is an Active Record migration that has the .add_view() method which adds the view based on the .sql file SQL definition.

Scenic was added to Rideshare, along with a view to search for drivers. Open psql and run \dv to *describe* the views. You should see a view named search_results.

Using Scenic, this view has been wired up to a model in Rideshare called *SearchResult*. This is a view-backed model, copied here:

```ruby
ruby/search_result.rb
class SearchResult < ApplicationRecord
  belongs_to :searchable, polymorphic: true

  # this isn't strictly necessary, but it will prevent
  # rails from calling save, which would fail anyway.
  def readonly?
    true
  end
end
```

The SearchResult model acts as an Active Record interface to the view. Let's try it out. Run bin/rails console and type SearchResult.first. This executes the query for the view and maps query results to Active Record objects. The SQL query text is logged to the bin/rails console output.

With Scenic, you can even evolve the query as you do with migrations. To do that, you'll use versions for your views. Refer to the documentation to explore how to revise the current search_results_v01.sql "Version 01" of the view.

Now that views have been introduced, and you've worked with them using Scenic, let's continue with materialized views, and how to refresh and manage them.

---

25. https://github.com/scenic-views/scenic

Improving Performance with Materialized Views

Materialized views are fast to access because they've already been computed with their results stored. When you query a materialized view, you're accessing pre-computed query results.

The access performance can even be improved further by adding indexes to materialized views. Just like tables, materialized views support indexes.

That sounds great; is there a catch? A limitation with materialized views is that even when they query many data rows, if even one row changes, the entire view needs to be recalculated.

Materialized views do not offer a partial refresh mechanism for only the changed bits.

Open source and commercial offerings attempt to solve this problem by offering solutions that partially update materialized views. The pg_ivm extension (which stands for "incremental view maintenance")[26] provides the ability to incrementally refresh materialized views. In this section, we'll focus only on what's available within PostgreSQL.

Let's look at a materialized view integrated into Rideshare. In the last section, you looked at the SearchResult model backed by the nonmaterialized search_results view.

Take a look at the FastSearchResult model in Rideshare. Both views were added to db/structure.sql. Search in the file for CREATE MATERIALIZED VIEW to view the definition. The db/structure.sql file shows only the definition of the view, just like regular views, with no query results in the dump file.

To view information about materialized views, use the pg_matviews[27] system catalog by running a query as follows:

```
SELECT * FROM pg_matviews;
```

Let's review the results from that system catalog. The ispopulated (bool) field shows whether the materialized view was populated. hasindexes shows whether any indexes were added. The \d+ fast_search_results meta-command is another way to view the definition.

To refresh the query results, use the REFRESH keyword.

---

26. https://github.com/sraoss/pg_ivm
27. https://www.postgresql.org/docs/current/view-pg-matviews.html

To refresh a view from Ruby, use the .refresh() method on the FastSearchResult model. Try calling it from bin/rails console as follows:

ruby/fast_search_result_refresh.rb
```
 FastSearchResult.refresh
   (20.7ms)  REFRESH MATERIALIZED VIEW "fast_search_results";
=> #<PG::Result:0x0000000115bc40d8 status=PGRES_COMMAND_OK \
    ntuples=0 nfields=0 cmd_tuples=0>
```

Compare the query response times between SearchResult.first and FastSearchResult.first. As your data size increases, the materialized view-based search should be much faster over time. If you want to experiment, try running the bulk_load.sh script mentioned earlier (see Generating Bigger Data, on page 41) to populate 10 million user rows, then compare the performance.

In Rideshare, the materialized view is refreshed periodically from a cron job. Since Ruby on Rails does not offer cron job scheduling within the framework, the gem whenever[28] was used to provide this.

Review config/schedule.rb, which lists the jobs and when they run. The following code uses the Rails runner[29] (CLI program) to call the same code you called earlier.

ruby/whenever_cron_job.rb
```
every 15.minutes do
  runner "FastSearchResult.refresh"
end
```

To refresh materialized views concurrently, add the CONCURRENTLY keyword, running the following from psql:

sql/refresh_materialized_view_concurrently.sql
```
REFRESH MATERIALIZED VIEW CONCURRENTLY "fast_search_results";
```

Materialized views must have a unique index to be refreshed concurrently. A unique index was added to enable concurrent refreshes:

sql/create_unique_index_materialized_view.sql
```
CREATE UNIQUE INDEX CONCURRENTLY
"index_fast_search_results_on_driver_id"
ON "fast_search_results" ("driver_id");
```

You can now refresh the materialized view concurrently, from psql as before, or from the Rails console. Try passing the concurrently: true option to the .refresh() method for the bin/rails console version as follows:

---

28. https://github.com/javan/whenever
29. https://guides.rubyonrails.org/command_line.html#bin-rails-runner

ruby/fast_search_result_refresh_concurrently.rb
```
FastSearchResult.refresh(concurrently: true)
```

Great. You've now seen how to leverage database views to encapsulate and name queries and how to create materialized views that are indexed and can be refreshed concurrently to improve access performance.

Besides making queries more efficient, Ruby on Rails offers a number of cache types that are used to help avoid database queries. Let's see what types are available and how to use them.

Reducing Queries with Active Record Caches

Active Record has a variety of caches that can be used to improve the performance of your Rails application.

The *query cache*[30] is a cache of SQL query results that lives for the duration of a Rails controller action. Since you're likely running Rideshare in development mode where the query cache is not enabled, Rails Guides shows how to enable it.[31]

Toggle Caching in Dev

 Run bin/rails dev:cache to toggle caching in development mode.

Take the query TripRequest.where(rider_id: 1).first, which loads the rider's first trip request.

After running it at the beginning of an action, the query and result are placed into the query cache while the action is processed. The second time the same query is run inside the same controller action, the query matches against the cached version and the result is returned from cache.

The Active Record query cache helps you avoid unnecessary queries. In development, you'll see CACHE printed in your Rails server logs whenever the query cache was accessed. Execution times will show as (0.0ms). CACHE statements in the Rails log can also be disabled (see "Disable Rails CACHE Logging"[32]).

---

30. https://guides.rubyonrails.org/caching_with_rails.html#sql-caching
31. https://guides.rubyonrails.org/caching_with_rails.html#basic-caching
32. https://heliom.ca/blog/posts/disable-rails-cache-logging

A trade-off with the query cache is that more memory is used to hold the query and the result. Memory is used to instantiate Active Record objects and their relationships for the query cache (see "Cached Queries Guidelines"[33]). As with all caches, there's also the possibility of stale data.

While being a very useful cache, an overreliance on it for good performance might indicate that you're underinvesting in optimizing your query performance.

In the next section, you'll continue the caching theme, looking at *prepared statements*[34] in PostgreSQL, then seeing how they work in Active Record.

Prepared Statements with Active Record

Prepared statements[35] are object types in PostgreSQL that separate parameter values from queries. The parameterless variation gets a name and gets stored for future variations where it can be re-used.

In future re-uses, the specific parameters are substituted into the prepared statement parameterless version. This substitution cuts down on some query statement parsing that otherwise happens and adds latency.

View prepared statements in your database using the pg_prepared_statements catalog view. To do that, run SELECT * FROM pg_prepared_statements; from psql. If the results are empty, you don't have any prepared statements.

Prepared statements are enabled by default in Active Record, storing up to 1000 statements per connection. Prepared statements are incompatible with some aspects of Active Record, including query log tags. Since it's enabled in Rideshare, to try out prepared statements, change config.active_record.query_log_tags_enabled = false in config/application.rb before starting up Rails console.

Let's assume you've made the previous change and want to use prepared statements. From bin/rails console, run some Active Record queries:

User.**first**

Trip.**first**

When those run, prepared statements are now populated. Explore them by running this code:

---

33. https://docs.gitlab.com/ee/development/cached_queries.html

34. https://www.postgresql.org/docs/current/sql-prepare.html

35. https://guides.rubyonrails.org/configuring.html

```ruby
ActiveRecord::Base.connection.execute(
  'SELECT * FROM pg_prepared_statements'
).values
```
ruby/active_record_prepared_statements.rb

Ruby on Rails keeps expanding support for prepared statements. Prior to Rails 7, SELECT * was cached when explicit fields weren't listed. In Rails 7, a setting, enumerate_columns_in_select_statements, was added[36] that enumerates the list of columns. Why enable this? Enabling this option helps increase the re-use of prepared statements, which can improve your overall performance.

You've now seen how to use the query cache and prepared statements. Let's continue with caches, looking at the counter cache.

Replacing Slow Counts with Counter Caches

The Active Record *counter cache* improves slow COUNT() queries by replacing them with a pre-computed count. They work by keeping a running tally of the count, stored in an integer column that's fast to access. As you will see elsewhere, the trade-off here is space consumption for improved access performance.

In Rideshare, imagine that you'd like to count the number of trips a Driver has performed. This query could be run in high volume, so you'd like to make it efficient. The code might look like this:

```
Driver.first.trips.count
```

This code uses the .count() Active Record method, which always generates a SQL COUNT() query. Before adding a counter cache column, one improvement would be to replace .count() with .size(). The .size() method uses the size of a pre-loaded collection in memory when it's available and then falls back to a COUNT() query when it's not.

Another reason to prefer .size() over .count() is that it will automatically use a counter cache column when it's available.

Counter cache columns have trade-offs to be aware of. First, they require adding a new column. The tallying mechanism adds a tiny bit of latency at write time, which is usually fine.

Since the counter cache's value is populated from a separate process, it opens up the possibility of a count inconsistency. Another trade-off on the Postgre-SQL side is that high-volume UPDATE statements can cause excessive bloat for

---

36. https://www.bigbinary.com/blog/rails-7-adds-setting-for-enumerating-columns-in-select-statements

the table, which requires more vacuuming. Finally, there can also be lock contention as rows are updated if there are concurrent updates that get blocked.

Despite these downsides, counter caches are a great built-in mechanism in Active Record that can dramatically improve the performance of your slow SQL COUNT() queries. You'll see how to handle the trade-offs listed here in upcoming chapters. Besides that, check out the post "Caching Counters with ActiveRecord's Counter Caches"[37] for more information.

Let's explore a counter cache column in Rideshare. A counter cache was added to the users table (remember it's polymorphic) to track the number of trips performed by the Driver.

Besides the new table column, the counter_cache: true configuration was added to the :driver association on the Trip model, which is used at *write time* to automatically keep the column value updated. That configuration looks like this:

```ruby/active_record_counter_cache.rb
class Trip < ApplicationRecord
  belongs_to :driver, counter_cache: true
end
```

When adding a counter cache to an existing table, the value won't be populated initially. You'll need to catch it up. Populate it before you access it, or you'll have an inaccurate count.

Explore the following methods in bin/rails console to reset the counter cache:

```ruby/reset_counters.rb
driver = Trip.first.driver

driver.trips.count

Driver.reset_counters(driver.id, :trips)

driver.trips.size
```

Once you've manually reset your counter cache, you're ready to use it. Anywhere you were previously counting trips for a driver, you can now use the precomputed count value. Rails automatically handles keeping the column value updated for you.

You've now seen a variety of ways to use Caches to eliminate queries and improve overall system performance.

---

37. https://blog.appsignal.com/2018/06/19/activerecords-counter-cache.html

Another type of performance improvement can be moving calculations from being performed in Ruby to being performed in PostgreSQL. How does that work?

Performing Aggregations in the Database

PostgreSQL has built-in SQL *aggregate functions*, which may improve performance for calculations. You'll have to test with your queries to be sure. Here you'll see your options.

Aggregate operations are designed to work on sets of data. Performance could improve due to less round-trip time when performed in the database, as compared to a solution that's split between the client application and the database.

Check out the available aggregate functions in the following table and their counterparts in Active Record:

Active Record	SQL
.count()	COUNT()
.average()	AVG()
.minimum()	MIN()
.maximum()	MAX()
.sum()	SUM()

Table 1—Aggregations Comparison

Explore the Active Record ActiveRecord::Calculations[38] module. For PostgreSQL, refer to documentation on "Aggregate Functions."[39]

PostgreSQL has more aggregate functions beyond those supported by Active Record. PostgreSQL even allows users to *create their own*, which are called user-defined aggregates.[40]

To close out the coverage on Active Record, in the next section, you'll explore how to reduce memory consumption, by creating fewer objects.

Object Allocations in Active Record

Active Record may be used as a thinner layer, working with SQL as input text, instantiating lighter weight objects that use "primitive" Ruby types.

---

38. https://api.rubyonrails.org/classes/ActiveRecord/Calculations.html
39. https://www.postgresql.org/docs/current/functions-aggregate.html
40. https://www.postgresql.org/docs/current/xaggr.html

Active Record has a number of methods that support direct SQL. The first one you'll look at is .find_by_sql().

Results from .find_by_sql() are mapped to instances of the caller class, but stored in a Ruby array. Active Record normally puts results into an ActiveRecord::Relation object, which allows lazy or deferred execution with support for chained methods. You'll lose that with .find_by_sql().

Try running this from bin/rails console:

```
ruby/find_by_sql.rb
TripRequest.find_by_sql("SELECT * FROM trip_requests LIMIT 1")
```

This loads records from the trip_requests table and creates TripRequest instances.

Another option when working with SQL in Active Record is to use the .execute() method. This method maps results to *primitive types* like String or Integer.

Try this out by running this code from bin/rails console:

```
ruby/active_record_execute.rb
ActiveRecord::Base.connection.execute("SELECT * FROM trips LIMIT 1")
```

For .execute() you're not working with a specific Active Record class, so results are mapped to PG::Result instances. This class is at a lower level than Active Record models. The fields ntuples=1 and nfields=7 show how one row (or *tuple*) was returned that has seven fields of data.

If primitive types are OK for your uses, .select_all() and .select_one() can be used with ActiveRecord::Base and a string of query text.

.select_one() works like .select_all() but returns only the first item.

Consider using primitive types to reduce memory consumption for critical performance areas where it's worth losing Active Record abstractions and conveniences. What kinds of memory savings are possible?

Let's use the Ruby benchmarking techniques demonstrated in "Optimizing Active Record Queries"[41] to compare these methods.

The following results were collected running the bin/rails benchmarks:active_record benchmark code in Rideshare, using Benchmark.memory. You may also run this code on your system. After running this several times, the Active Record Trip.first consistently used three times more memory compared with similar versions written using SQL that also selected a single row.

---

41. https://dev.to/kattyacuevas/optimizing-active-record-queries-4i84

Here are the results:

```
sh/benchmarks_memory_active_record.sh
Comparison:
.select_all() single User:     548754 allocated
            User.first:     1683706 allocated - 3.07x more
```

This was a huge chapter, so let's wrap it up!

Wrapping Up

You've now used several ways to optimize your Active Record code. You started from improved observability connecting SQL queries to Active Record application code, and then worked to optimize and eliminate queries.

By eliminating queries or making them more efficient, you're conserving limited database server resources.

You identified the N+1 query patterns manually and automatically and saw how to fix them using eager loading or avoid them with strict loading.

You created subqueries, Common Table Expressions, and database views. You worked with materialized views, refreshing them concurrently.

You learned about caches provided by Rails, including the query cache and counter cache.

With Active Record well covered, it's time to broaden your query performance focus to SQL queries.

In the next chapter, you'll explore SQL query performance, observability, and optimizations. See you there!

## CHAPTER 7

Improving Query Performance

In this chapter, we'll focus on SQL queries and factors that influence their performance.

You'll learn about query execution plans and how to read them, identifying the most costly parts. With an understanding of the costs, you'll learn tactics to lessen them, speeding up queries and reducing use of system resources.

Query optimization is a complex subject with entire books dedicated to it. In this chapter, you'll get set up with the basics.

Review the following terminology you'll see in upcoming sections:

Query Performance Terminology

- Selectivity—How narrow or wide a selection is
- Cardinality—How many unique values there are
- Sequential scan—Reading all rows for a table, also called *table scan*
- Index scan—Fetching values from an index
- Index-only scan—Fetching values *only* from the index, without needing to access table data

Although you'll primarily deal with SQL and PostgreSQL in this chapter, let's start out by discussing slow query visibility in Active Record.

How can you find slow queries?

Active Support Instrumentation for Queries

Without adding extra Ruby gems or PostgreSQL extensions, you can capture slow queries to the Rails log. *Active Support Notifications*[1] are a mechanism

---

1. https://guides.rubyonrails.org/active_support_instrumentation.html

that emit events with event data. The relevant events here are sql.active_record events.

How does that work? Take a look at the following slow query *Subscriber* class, which was added to Rideshare.

The Subscriber listens for sql.active_record events, calculating a query duration from the start and finish values. When the query takes more than one second, the query text is logged.

```ruby/slow_query_subscriber.rb
# Inspiration: https://twitter.com/kukicola/status/1578842934849724416
class SlowQuerySubscriber < ActiveSupport::Subscriber
  SECONDS_THRESHOLD = 1.0

  ActiveSupport::Notifications.subscribe('sql.active_record')
    do |name, start, finish, _, data|
    duration = finish - start

    if duration > SECONDS_THRESHOLD
      Rails.logger.debug "[#{name}] #{duration} #{data[:sql]}"
    end
  end
end
```

Open bin/rails console to test this out. Run SELECT PG_SLEEP(1); within ActiveRecord::Base .connection.execute() to create a query that will take one second. You'll see the Subscriber is triggered, and the query is logged with sql.active_record prepended:

```ruby/active_record_slow_query_subscriber.rb
ActiveRecord::Base.connection.execute("SELECT PG_SLEEP(1)")
[sql.active_record] 1.008904 SELECT PG_SLEEP(1) /*application='Rideshare'*/
   (1009.2ms)  SELECT PG_SLEEP(1) /*application='Rideshare'*/
```

While this technique can be used for the Rails log, how might you capture slow queries in PostgreSQL?

Capture Query Statistics in Your Database

The queries in your database consume resources. You'll want to optimize them to be less costly, focusing your optimization efforts on the biggest beneficiaries.

To find costly queries and make data-driven decisions, you'll need a global view of all queries and their statistics. To do that, use the pg_stat_statements[2] module you configured earlier (see Modifying Your PostgreSQL Config File, on page 28), which we'll abbreviate PGSS.

---

2. https://www.postgresql.org/docs/current/pgstatstatements.html

PGSS performs a normalization process for each query, removing specific parameters and replacing their values with placeholder characters (question marks).

The normalized query gets a *query identifier* (queryid), which represents a query group. Similar normalized queries placed into the same group are grouped together. Statistics are collected at the group level. PGSS presents the statistics in a catalog view that you can enable access to for your database.

More than 40 fields of information are collected as statistics[3] for PGSS. Some of the information includes the number of calls for queries within that group and their execution time min, max, mean, and standard deviation. These statistics are cumulative, growing until less-used query groups are evicted or statistics are reset. Rows and blocks that are accessed are included in the stats, which can be used to help identify excessive IO.

Since you added PGSS to shared_preload_libraries in postgresql.conf and restarted PostgreSQL, we'll assume it's ready to be used.

To make the system view available, connect to the rideshare_development database as the postgres superuser:

```
psql -U postgres -d rideshare_development
```

From there, run the following statement to create the extension within the rideshare schema:

```
CREATE EXTENSION IF NOT EXISTS pg_stat_statements
WITH SCHEMA rideshare;
```

Editing Config File

ALTER SYSTEM can modify shared_preload_libraries as an alternative to editing postgresql.conf. This method generates a value in postgresql.auto.conf that overrides the value in postgresql.conf.

To avoid confusion about where the active value originates, skip ALTER SYSTEM and edit postgresql.conf directly.

You've now enabled PGSS and are ready to use it.

Using Query Statistics

Since Rideshare isn't a running system, you'll need to simulate application activity so that query statistics can be calculated from it.

---

3.   https://www.postgresql.org/docs/current/pgstatstatements.html

Start the Rideshare server by running bin/rails server in your terminal.

In another terminal window, run the Rake task:

sh/simulate_app_activity.sh
```
bin/rails simulate:app_activity
```

As queries are received in PostgreSQL, PGSS places them into groups, gives the group an identifier, and captures group-level statistics. PGSS tracks 5000 normalized queries (or query groups) by default, which can be increased by setting pg_stat_statements.max.

The least-executed queries are discarded when the max is reached. To reset the statistics, run SELECT rideshare.PG_STAT_STATEMENTS_RESET(); from psql.

Great. If you reset the statistics, run the simulation again. Once you've done that, you should now have some stats to work with. Let's use the stats to find some of the ten slowest queries by mean execution time:

sql/ten_worst_queries.sql
```sql
SELECT
  mean_exec_time,
  calls,
  query,
  queryid
FROM pg_stat_statements
ORDER BY mean_exec_time DESC
LIMIT 10;
```

Great, you're able to view the PGSS information in psql and see some of the worst-performing queries.

Use pspg pager

pspg pager can be added to make the wide query results like the ones from PGSS more legible. With pspg configured as the pager, you're able to navigate horizontally within psql.

Refer to the Development Guides[4] repository or db/README.md in Rideshare for instructions and usage.

Rideshare queries should be displayed in descending order. An example result is shown as follows:

---

4.   https://github.com/andyatkinson/development_guides

```
sql/pg_stat_statements_result.sql
-[ RECORD 8 ]--+-------------------------------------------------------
mean_exec_time | 2878.5335836666663
calls          | 3
query          | SELECT COUNT(*) FROM "users" \
                   WHERE "users"."type" = $1 /*application:Rideshare*/
queryid        | 5435614976858805274
```

In this example, we can see the mean_exec_time, the number of calls, the query text, and the queryid.

While viewing statistics from psql works, you'd like to make this information more accessible to your team.

How can you do that?

Introducing PgHero as a Performance Dashboard

PgHero[5] is an open source PostgreSQL *performance dashboard*. PgHero ships as an open source Rails Engine and has been added to Rideshare as a Ruby gem. It's also available as a Docker container.[6]

When PGSS is enabled, PgHero captures and stores results in its own tables from the system view.

PgHero presents the following data on the Queries screen:

- Total number of calls
- Average duration
- The percentage the query represents among the total number of query executions

Since PgHero was added to Rideshare, run bin/rails server from your terminal and then visit /pghero in your browser to open up the dashboard. Once that's loaded, let's explore the various screens.

Navigate to the Queries tab. The following shows an example of what's presented there:

Total Time	Average Time	Calls	
1 min 41%	752 ms	58	postgres
SELECT "users".* FROM "users" WHERE "users"."type" = $1			

Table 2—PgHero Query Statistics

---

5.   https://github.com/ankane/pghero
6.   https://hub.docker.com/r/ankane/pghero

While the Queries screen may be one of the most useful, PgHero has a number of other screens. Let's take a brief tour through some of the others. First, we'll look at the Explain screen. PgHero has a built-in EXPLAIN (ANALYZE) interface on that screen that can be used to manually collect a query execution plan. Queries are safe to execute there because they're placed in a transaction that's rolled back. To do that, SET LOCAL is used with a statement_timeout set within the transaction.

Here's an example:

```
sql/set_local_statement_timeout.sql
SET LOCAL statement_timeout = 1000;
```

From there, you can paste in queries and generate explain plans. You may also copy and paste the explain plans into a linked visualization tool.

Let's move on to the PgHero Space screen. This screen shows the largest tables and indexes. If there are unused indexes, they're mentioned at the top, and they're labeled on their respective lines.

The Maintenance screen shows when tables were last vacuumed and analyzed. You'll go into greater depth on maintenance operations in an upcoming chapter.

Since PgHero is open source, you may fork it and extend it with your own features. (See andyatkinson/pghero[7] for an example)

You've now seen the basics of using PgHero as a performance dashboard.

Once you've identified individual queries to optimize, you'll want to understand which parts are the most costly. To do that, you'll use the EXPLAIN tool.

EXPLAIN Basics

SQL is a declarative language. When you write SQL, you declare the results you want, and PostgreSQL determines how to get them.

PostgreSQL allows you to see the *query execution plan* for a given query. Interpreting query execution plans is critical to understanding the performance of your queries.

Let's get into the basics. Open up psql and add EXPLAIN to the front of a basic query:

---

7.   https://github.com/andyatkinson/pghero

```
sql/explain_basics.sql
EXPLAIN SELECT 1;

                QUERY PLAN
-----------------------------------------
 Result  (cost=0.00..0.01 rows=1 width=4)
(1 row)
```

Even with this basic query, the plan shows useful information. From the plan, we can see one row was retrieved with a width of 4, which matches the width of the smallint type.

To display more information, EXPLAIN accepts arguments including ANALYZE, BUFFERS, FORMAT, and others. More on that soon.

Plans are broken into nodes, and each node has a cost. When plans are compared, the total costs are compared between alternatives, and the lowest cost plan is selected. Since the planning and comparison happen at runtime, this process does add latency to query execution. Fortunately the planning time is usually quite short, and it can always be inspected when using the right option.

To see the planning time, add the ANALYZE argument to EXPLAIN. Run EXPLAIN (ANALYZE) SELECT 1; from psql. With this version, the query actually runs instead of showing only the estimated plan.

The plan now shows estimated and actual costs. Both the *Planning Time* and *Execution Time* are visible.

To achieve a short planning time, PostgreSQL uses statistics, available indexes, and estimates to quickly make determinations. As you saw earlier, the default_statistics_target is to collect 100 samples for a table. Manual statistics collection can be triggered as well. Let's give that a shot.

To collect statistics, use the ANALYZE command. From psql run ANALYZE VERBOSE trips;.

The ANALYZE keyword shows up in two places. ANALYZE can be an argument to VACUUM as in when it's called by Autovacuum.

ANALYZE is also an optional argument to EXPLAIN, which is the version you're using here.

With all of that in mind, it's time to start diving into query plan specifics.

Reading Query Execution Plans

Query execution plans are packed with information. Besides the tables, indexes, and columns, there are many pieces of data. Some of the information is presented here:

- Costs (which can be disabled by setting COSTS OFF)

- Timing

- Scan Types like *sequential scan, index scan,* or *index-only scan*

- Filtering. How many rows were filtered, and which columns were filtered on?

- Indexes. Which indexes are listed? Were any not used that you expected to see?

- Loops. When the loops value is greater than 1, this means the plan node was repeated.

- Ordering. Are results ordered? An index should be used to support ordering operations.

- Buffers. How many buffers were accessed?

For an index scan, compare the list of fields and their order in the query to any supporting index definitions. You want the fields in the query and index definition to match when possible.

Can the fields in the SELECT be reduced? When selected fields are fully covered by an index definition, an *index-only scan* may be selected, which is the fastest type.

Add the BUFFERS argument to EXPLAIN to get insight into the amount of data being fetched (the IO). The amount of data being fetched adds latency to retrieval speed. Selecting less data will likely result in faster queries.

Look for TIMESTAMP and TIMESTAMPTZ columns in the query and find out if those are indexed. B-Tree index entries for timestamp fields are stored chronologically, which means the index can be used for ORDER BY operations. You'll explore that more in the next chapter.

As you begin reading PostgreSQL query execution plans, you'll learn a lot of new terminology. Free and commercial analysis tools are available to help you process all of this information.

A query plan visualizer is built-in to the PgAdmin[8] GUI client, and there are various web clients available. The https://explain.depesz.com[9] tool is a free plan analysis tool.

PgMustard is another company that offers a plan analysis tool. While the tool is a commercial paid tool, the business offers a wealth of community contributions in the form of guides and blog posts. One example is the free EXPLAIN Glossary,[10] which is filled with terms and definitions related to query planning.

Now that you've got a query to work with, and are familiar with the basics of collecting an execution plan, you're ready to dive into exploring fixes.

What sort of fix should we look for? One of the most common causes of slow query execution is inefficient filtering due to missing indexes.

How can you find whether your system is missing indexes?

Finding Missing Indexes

Missing indexes are a class of performance problem where sequential table scans are used because supporting indexes don't exist.

For tables with row counts in the millions, particularly when data is scattered on various pages and the table has a high amount of bloat, scanning the whole table to then filter down to a few rows is very inefficient.

To identify opportunities to add indexes, try running a query like find_missing_indexes.sql[11] on your database. This query shows counts of sequential scans and index scans for a given table.

When a table has a lot more sequential scans than index scans, the table might be missing indexes. From there, you'll want to then drill into the queries for data in that table by using PGSS.

PgHero helps you shortcut this with a *suggested indexes* feature. This feature uses row estimates and analyzes the existing table indexes in order to make suggestions.

The rails_best_practices[12] gem is another tool that can be used to help find missing indexes. This gem was added to Rideshare. Try running it by typing

---

8.   https://www.pgadmin.org
9.   https://explain.depesz.com
10.   https://www.pgmustard.com/docs/explain
11.   https://github.com/andyatkinson/pg_scripts/blob/main/find_missing_indexes.sql
12.   https://github.com/flyerhzm/rails_best_practices

bin/rails_best_practices . (the period on the end is for the current directory) in your terminal.

VehicleReservation has a foreign key column referencing a TripRequest. Earlier, the Rails Best Practices tool suggested adding an index to that column to help with constraint enforcement.

Let's look at one more tool. PgAnalyze has a free tool called PgAnalyze Index Advisor[13] that can also suggest indexes.

Index creation can even be automated. The hypopg[14] extension can test out speculative indexes to try and improve performance. Combined with the dexter[15] tool, indexes can be created automatically. Instructions for these tools are out of the scope of this chapter.

Although you may wish to eagerly or speculatively add indexes to your tables, consider waiting until you know they're needed. Remember that indexes have downsides, like adding latency for writes and consuming space. They should be added when you know those downsides are worth it for their benefits.

You'll also want to periodically find unused indexes and then remove them. You'll learn more about that type of database maintenance in an upcoming chapter.

Besides identifying missing indexes, you'll also want to find your slow queries. Let's look at that next. Where should we start?

Logging Slow Queries

Earlier you saw how to log slow queries to the Rails log. In this section, let's look at logging them in the postgresql.log.

Open up your postgresql.conf file. Set the following log_min_duration_statement value and save your changes. Reload the config file values by running pg_ctl reload. This assumes you've set the PGDATA environment variable (see Set PGDATA for pg_ctl, on page 406).

Start with a value of one second, with an entry like this:

```
sh/set_log_min_duration_statement.sh
log_min_duration_statement = 1000
```

---

13. https://pganalyze.com/index-advisor
14. https://github.com/HypoPG/hypopg
15. https://github.com/ankane/dexter

After reloading, tail the PostgreSQL log file to see the output. From psql, run SELECT pg_sleep(1); to create a query that's one second long and verify it's logged. Refer to the pg_scripts repo[16] administration directory for a tail_log.sh script that finds and live tails your PostgreSQL log file.

Running that script looks like this:

```
sh tail_log.sh
```

The log file output should look like this once you've configured log_min_duration_statement, and when you've run a query that exceeds that time:

```
sh/postgresql_log_min_duration_statement.sh
pid=90062 query_id=440101247839410938: LOG:  |
duration: 1000.963 ms  plan:
        Query Text: select pg_sleep(1);
        Result  (cost=0.00..0.01 rows=1 width=4)
pid=90062 query_id=440101247839410938: LOG:  |
duration: 1001.715 ms  statement: select pg_sleep(1);
```

Log Formatting

Refer to the sample file postgresql.sample.log in the Rideshare postgresql directory to configure your log file. Additional data points can be added to the output by customizing the log_line_prefix parameter.

For your production instance, start with a much higher value like 60 seconds, and fix any queries that exceed that. Once you've done that, you can lower the value to 30 seconds, which may result in more query cancellations. Fix those, and then lower it again.

Using the PostgreSQL log file, we're able to get the full logged query text instead of the normalized version with placeholder characters. With the full query text, we're able to manually run EXPLAIN (ANALYZE) and capture a query plan.

Wouldn't it be nice to get those plans automatically? How can we do that?

Automatically Gathering Execution Plans

To get plans automatically, we can use the PostgreSQL auto_explain module.

In the same way, you configured a minimum statement duration, which logged query text when queries exceeded that duration, auto_explain can log plans when a statement exceeds a certain duration.

---

16. https://github.com/andyatkinson/pg_scripts

auto_explain does add some overhead. Review the section that describes how "repeatedly reading the system clock can slow down queries" in the documentation.[17]

Once you've determined the overhead is acceptable, start with a high value for your system, like one second, as the value for auto_explain.log_min_duration. This means that queries that take more than one second will have their execution plans logged to the postgresql.log.

When working locally with Rideshare, queries may be very fast, executing faster than the timeout value you've set. When that happens, you won't get query plans logged by auto_explain.

One trick to avoid this in local development is to temporarily set auto_explain.log_min_duration to 0, so that all queries are logged. Try this by making this change and then reloading your PostgreSQL configuration.

Once you have done that, if you're live tailing postgresql.log using tail -f, you will immediately see multiline query execution plans in the log file. If you've configured your log_line_prefix per the example in Rideshare, you'll see the queryid in your logs. Note that this requires PostgreSQL version 16 or newer and setting compute_query_id to on. The post, "Using Query ID in Postgres 14,"[18] describes what the *query ID* is and why it's useful.

For Rideshare, we'll be using the query ID. It's quite an important linkage between various observability tools. What does that mean?

With the queryid, you can now have a common identifier to use whether you're working in PGSS, query text that's logged in the PostgreSQL log, or from manually or automatically collected query plans. This is a common identifier that produces the same value in all of those places!

How can you use the query ID to link up the data between these tools?

1. Get the queryid for a normalized query from PGSS.
2. Enable query plan logging using auto_explain.
3. Find matching queryid values in postgresql.log from automatically logged plans for queries that exceeded the configured timeout.

Great! Experiment with queries and try to find them using their query ID in all three places.

---

17. https://www.postgresql.org/docs/current/auto-explain.html
18. https://blog.rustprooflabs.com/2021/10/postgres-14-query-id

As you troubleshoot slow queries, you'll want to rule out maintenance operations as being causes of poor performance.

How do you do that?

Perform Maintenance First

Before diving too far into query performance, make sure the tables and indexes for the query are in good shape.

To do that, check off the following items:

1. For each table, run a manual VACUUM (ANALYZE) operation on the table. This makes sure VACUUM updates the *visibility map*[19] and ANALYZE updates statistics.

2. For indexes used by the query, check their estimated bloat percentage. Compare the estimated and actual figures. Consider a REINDEX CONCURRENTLY for indexes to rebuild them (more on this later).

3. If Autovacuum seems to be falling behind (more on this later), add more resources to Autovacuum globally or per table. You may also schedule supplemental maintenance operations.

You'll work with each of these maintenance operations in an upcoming chapter, so here you're just getting a quick peek into that. The general takeaway is to make sure maintenance is in a good spot before spending time on performance optimization.

When you've made sure maintenance is taken care of, you're ready to dive into query optimization.

First up, let's look at index scans. What are they?

What Are Index Scans?

When a column is listed in a WHERE clause, PostgreSQL needs to load a large set of data, and then filter down based on the conditions in the clause.

That could be done from table data or from index entries. The problem with table data is that it's scattered across a lot of pages, fragmented, and bloated. On the other hand, an index is pre-sorted and designed for fast retrieval for operations like filtering. You'll want your queries to use *index scans* as much as possible.

---

19. https://www.postgresql.org/docs/current/storage-vm.html

A good rule of thumb is to make sure that any WHERE clause conditions have a supporting index definition for those same columns, in the same order. The index could be a multicolumn or covering index (more on those later) or a single column index, but the leading column should be the most significant column that is highly selective, representing one row or a small proportion of values relative to the total. This will make the index quite "profitable" with a highly efficient lookup.

PostgreSQL won't always choose your index though. That can be surprising. Why is that? PostgreSQL considers the *selectivity* of the query and the *cardinality* for column values (their unique values), and then compares the costs between scanning a table or accessing an index and the table. Accessing indexes is often faster because entries are stored in sorted order. Sequential scans could be chosen when all the data resides in a single page. Since PostgreSQL loads whole pages at a time, it may be faster to load the page with a sequential scan over an index.

When an index is selected, what does that look like in the planner? The planner shows an index scan and prints the name of the index. You may want to give your indexes funky names so they're more easily identified in plans.

Another reason that scanning an index is faster is because entries are usually only row pointers, compared with table access that has many columns of data.

An even more efficient scan type than an index scan is an *index-only scan*.

With index-only scans, PostgreSQL fetches *all* of the data needed from the index, without needing to access table pages.

Index-only scans are supported for B-Tree indexes but fewer index types overall. As you saw earlier, try and limit the fields being selected in queries to increase the chances of index-only scans. You'll dive deeply into indexes as the sole topic of the next chapter.

Let's get back to analyzing and optimizing specific SQL queries.

For the next type of query to explore, let's look at COUNT() queries and how to make them fast.

Tricks for Fast COUNT() Queries

Bare COUNT(*) queries are known to be slow, although optimizations have been made in newer versions of PostgreSQL. To learn more, check out the post, "Faster PostgreSQL Counting."[20]

---

20. https://www.citusdata.com/blog/2016/10/12/count-performance/

In the last chapter, you learned how they can also be avoided using application-level caches with tactics like a counter cache column and the .size() method in Active Record that reads from that column.

While caches are nice, what if you'd like to directly improve the performance for SQL COUNT() queries? How could you do that?

Count queries can exist as two types: an unfiltered count of all rows for a table or a filtered count, for a portion of the rows in a table. The filtered type can be very slow but can be made fast using some tricks.

Let's look at the total row counts first. One way to speed them up uses a trick, which is to avoid running a count query entirely. Instead of the count query, PostgreSQL collects row count estimates, and the estimate can be queried from the catalog view.

While they can be slightly off (<= 5 percent), they are extremely fast and inexpensive to query. Try using them if you can.

Let's look at an example. Run the following statements for Rideshare from psql:

sql/estimated_count_reltuples.sql
```
-- Ensure stats are updated
ANALYZE users;

-- Use reltuples for estimate
SELECT reltuples::NUMERIC FROM pg_class WHERE relname='users';
```

You ran ANALYZE on the users table to update stats. Next, the query fetched the estimated row count for the users table as reltuples (short for *relation tuples*) from the pg_class catalog view.

Estimated counts can even be used within Active Record, although not natively.

To use them, the fast_count[21] gem was added to Rideshare for this purpose. The gem has a migration that adds a database function. Since you ran migrations in Rideshare, this function was added to PostgreSQL and is available to try out.

Let's do that. Run bin/rails console, and from there, run User.fast_count to see it in action. Compare the speed with User.count for the normal set of around 20K rows. At that size, .fast_count() may be slower.

ruby/fast_count_gem.rb
```
User.fast_count
```

---

21. https://github.com/fatkodima/fast_count

Let's try loading the ten million user records using the bulk script. With ten million users, the regular .count() query takes about 3.5 seconds initially, then around 400ms on repeated runs. On repeated runs of the .fast_count() method, the results are shockingly faster. The following example returns the same count figure but in less than 4 ms.

```
irb(main):020> User.fast_count
   (3.7ms)  SELECT fast_count('users', 100000)
=> 10020210
```

Did you know the query execution plan text you saw earlier can be treated as a data source?

Using the query execution plan text is a trick fast_count uses for fast estimated and filtered counts. Try running bin/rails console in the Rideshare directory and comparing these two Active Record counts.

```
ruby/fast_count_estimated_count.rb
User.where("last_name ILIKE 'lname123%'").count

User.where("last_name ILIKE 'lname123%'").estimated_count
```

The .estimated_count() method is provided by the fast_count gem and is under active development at publication time. Make sure to compare the estimated results to the actual query results. If they're not equivalent, then the estimated count can't be used. You can also try raising the statistics value for the last_name column that's being queried.

```
ALTER TABLE users ALTER COLUMN last_name SET STATISTICS 5000;
ANALYZE users;
```

Verify Estimated Counts

 The .estimated_count() method is under active development at publication time and may produce incorrect results. Make sure to verify that it has an accurate result. Check the latest version of the fast_count Ruby gem source code.

If you need to count distinct values, the PostgreSQL wiki documents some tricks to perform this quickly (see "Selecting Distinct Values"[22]). Fast distinct counts are being worked on in the fast_count gem at publication time.

Another advanced technique for quick, estimated distinct values in a set is to leverage the HyperLogLog data structure. You can use that in PostgreSQL

---

22. https://wiki.postgresql.org/wiki/Loose_indexscan

with postgresql-hll.[23] The HLL data structure estimates the number of distinct values in a large set. HyperLogLog is described as a *cardinality estimator*.

After installing and enabling the PostgreSQL extension, it may be used from Rails by adding the active-hll[24] Ruby gem. At publication time, instructions for configuring this with Rideshare are not provided but may be added in future Rideshare updates on GitHub.

When reporting multiple COUNT() values, a CASE statement can be used. A common pattern is to use a CASE statement for positive and negative conditions, producing an integer, and then summing the integers up.

While the SUM approach with a CASE statement works, FILTER is a less-complex alternative command that you may not know about.

The benefit of FILTER is that multiple filtered counts are possible from a single table scan. The post, "The FILTER Clause in Postgres 9.4,"[25] shows how to use FILTER for *scoped aggregate functions*.

When analyzing the data distribution for a column, FILTER is very handy because you can use it to get an overall count and then filter counts with different conditions. This could help you determine the most selective leading column for a multicolumn index, for example.

Try out the FILTER keyword by running this statement from psql:

```
sql/count_with_filter.sql
SELECT
  COUNT(*) AS total,
  COUNT(*) FILTER (WHERE type = 'Rider') AS riders,
  COUNT(*) FILTER (WHERE type = 'Driver') AS drivers
FROM users;
```

The query displays the overall total, followed by individual counts for riders and drivers from a single scan of the table.

You've now seen some various ways to improve the performance of COUNT() queries for your Rails app.

In the next section, you'll learn the basics of query hinting.

---

23. https://github.com/citusdata/postgresql-hll

24. https://github.com/ankane/active_hll

25. https://medium.com/little-programming-joys/the-filter-clause-in-postgres-9-4-3dd327d3c852

Query Plan Hints

As we saw earlier, SQL uses a declarative model. This model has an intentional separation between the queries that clients provide and the execution plan that PostgreSQL chooses.

While programmers can "influence" execution plans to an extent via their query or schema designs and indexes, they cannot directly "control" plans that PostgreSQL chooses.

Right? Well, that's true, but there's another concept that's sort of a middle ground that can be used to control portions of a plan. The concept is called *hinting* or "query plan hinting." With query plan hints, we can control part of the query plan using hints that are passed to queries as text comments.

Query plan hinting is not available in core PostgreSQL but can be added using the widely supported pg_hint_plan[26] extension. Further, Active Record supports query plan hints using pg_hint_plan. They tend to be underused in Rails, so let's take a look.

> **Robert:** *You know, pg_hint_plan is pretty useful for performance work in PostgreSQL.*
>
> **Andrew:** *Hm, maybe they should be included in this chapter.*
>
> **Franck:** *Does Ruby on Rails support plan hints with PostgreSQL?*
>
> **Andrew:** *Hints are supported. Active Record has a special method, "optimizer_hints," that passes them through.*

Active Record Supports Hints

 Queries can be generated with Active Record that include plan hints. For PostgreSQL, Active Record uses pg_hint_plan for hints.

The Active Record .optimizer_hints() method[27] was added in Rails 6, supporting query plan hints. This method accepts a comma-separated list of hint identifiers. Some of the hints accept optional arguments.

Hints are provided as a special "hint comment" that has a plus sign in front, and the comment is added in front of the query text. In other chapters, you're working with Marginalia and query logs, which also add comments to queries. Fortunately, hint comments are added in front of the query text, and those other comments are added after, so they don't conflict.

---

26. https://github.com/ossc-db/pg_hint_plan
27. https://api.rubyonrails.org/classes/ActiveRecord/QueryMethods.html#method-i-optimizer_hints

Successfully identifying and using hints is complex. Knowing where to use them involves knowing how the query planner works, how your schema and indexes are designed, and knowing your queries and data well. Some have asked whether hints should be used at all. What's the thinking behind that?

Well, hints partially break the declarative paradigm. Also, hints can become stale over time, where a stale hint could lead to a *worse* plan.

With those caveats in mind, hints can also be very useful. Since they're supported in Active Record, it's worth knowing about on the chance you'll need them. Let's look at an example in Rideshare that covers the basics. Refer to the appendix *Getting Help* for pg_hint_plan compilation instructions for macOS.

Once the extension is installed and available for Rideshare, you're ready to create a hint.

This example weaves in a new feature in Rails 7.1, which is that EXPLAIN in Active Record now supports the ANALYZE argument. To see that in action, run the following code in bin/rails console:

```
User.where("id <= 10").explain(:analyze)
```

The previous query execution plan uses an index scan using the primary key index for id. How can we work a hint in? Let's cook up a contrived example.

Imagine that you're a glutton for punishment, and you like your queries to run *much slower* instead of running faster. Weird!

To do that, you'd like to swap your speedy index scan for a slower sequential scan.

That's something we can do using the special hint identifier, "SeqScan," and passing in the users table name as an argument.

To do that, run the following code from bin/rails console. To start, this just prints the generated SQL:

```
User.optimizer_hints("SeqScan(users)").
where("id <= 10").to_sql
```

You should see the special "plus" comment in the generated SQL. The plus sign is inside of two forward slashes with asterisks inside of each. You should see users as the argument to SeqScan:

```
/*+ SeqScan(users) */
```

In case pg_hint_plan is toggled off, make sure it's set to on:

```
ActiveRecord::Base.connection.execute("SET pg_hint_plan.enable_hint = ON")
```

With that all in place, let's run it. As you did before, use EXPLAIN (ANALYZE) via Active Record from bin/rails console by running the following:

```
User.optimizer_hints("SeqScan(users)").
where("id <= 10").explain(:analyze)
```

This will run very slowly, especially if you ran the bulk load earlier and have 10 million users. You should see that the plan now selects a sequential scan (or a parallel sequential scan) thanks to the hint comment.

Toggle pg_hint_plan to off and re-run the same query, verifying that it's gone back to using an index scan. Or, run the prior code but remove the .optimizer_hints() method from the code, and verify that it goes back to using an index scan.

If pg_hint_plan is not installed or enabled, or if the hint is incorrect or the table doesn't exist, the hint is ignored and the query runs normally.

With that, you've seen the basics of integrating pg_hint_plan with Active Record. pg_hint_plan can be used for learning by forcing the use of some indexes and seeing what the performance is like, even if you don't commit hints that you used for learning purposes.

Next, you'll look at some tools to help you manage database performance and improve your designs.

Using Code and SQL Analysis Tools

To improve the performance of your system and your schema designs, consider adding command-line tools into your development flow. The rails-pg-extras[28] gem has many helpful capabilities worth a look. Let's try it out with Rideshare.

In your terminal, call the Rails runner with the following option to make sure the rideshare schema is accessed:

```
bin/rails runner 'RailsPgExtras.table_cache_hit(args: { schema: "rideshare" })'
```

We can also set the rideshare as the default schema for RailsPgExtras:

```
PG_EXTRAS_SCHEMA=rideshare
```

Look at the index hit rate and table hit rate ratios. A low index hit ratio could mean there are too few indexes. PostgreSQL keeps a cache of indexes in memory, and a low hit ratio means there are many cache misses.

In an earlier chapter, you learned about the log analysis tool, pgBadger. An additional use for PgBadger is historical query analysis.

---

28. https://github.com/pawurb/rails-pg-extras

Queries are presented in percentile groups like p90, p95, or p99. If you're just getting started, focus on the smaller percentiles first, like the 90th percentile. Remember that improvements there benefit 90 percent of requests. Once those are solved, you'll be ready to pursue bigger percentiles, which likely involve more challenging issues that benefit fewer requests.

Wrapping Up

In this chapter, you improved your visibility into SQL query performance using a variety of tools and techniques. You set up automatic slow query logging and learned how to analyze slow queries to find which parts performed poorly.

You found slow queries using a data-driven approach with PGSS. You learned how to manually and automatically collect query text samples and query execution plans in your PostgreSQL log. You identified common performance problems like missing indexes and developed fixes.

You started to scratch the surface of query execution plans and how important indexes are for high performance.

In the next chapter, you'll go into greater depth, focusing solely on the wide variety of indexes available in PostgreSQL.

You'll explore general purpose and specialized indexes. You'll deepen your knowledge of interpreting query execution plans, expanding on what you learned in this chapter.

## CHAPTER 8

Optimized Indexes for Fast Retrieval

Let's talk about indexes! Indexes are amazing data structures that you'll use to make your queries faster. You've seen how to use indexes for filter operations. With well-placed indexes, you'll reduce the IO needed to efficiently filter down a large set to the exact rows needed. You'll do that by making sure that your query conditions match the columns defined in the index.

Indexes aren't limited to filtering, though. In this chapter, you'll work with indexes in greater detail, exploring use cases and even options within indexes you may not have worked with before. Equipped with that knowledge and the hands-on experience you'll get here working in Rideshare, you'll be able to take that knowledge to your database work to identify good indexes, design them, and verify they're doing their job for your queries.

You'll create single-column, multicolumn, and partial indexes. You'll create indexes on expressions and different types of covering indexes. When you see the terms "composite" or "compound" indexes elsewhere, these are referring to *multicolumn* indexes in PostgreSQL.

Creating Indexes from psql

 You'll primarily create indexes from psql, although in a Ruby on Rails application, you'll generally create them using the Active Record helper methods.

Since you're learning to use psql more regularly, index creation examples are shown mostly as SQL. In a Ruby on Rails application, they'll generally be added by team members as new migrations files. The benefit of migrations is to keep all databases in sync.

Remember that DDL changes like CREATE INDEX on tables with high row counts and high transaction volume (transactions per second (TPS) or queries per second) should be created using the CONCURRENTLY option. This applies to both creating an index and dropping an index. If your index creation gets canceled, you'll need to raise your statement_timeout and try again. You'll see examples here to raise the timeout within a transaction.

The most common index type is the B-Tree[1] type, which is also the default type. You'll create different index types and supply them with different options. Index definition options include the operator class and storage parameters,[2] set using the WITH keyword.

Additional types you'll work with are GIN, GiST, BRIN, and HASH types. You'll know which types to use to best support your queries and what the trade-offs are for that type.

Let's look at terminology you'll see in this chapter:

Indexes Terminology

- Index definition—The columns the index covers

- Multicolumn indexes—Index that includes multiple columns in the definition

- Partial indexes—An expression that reduces the set of rows covered for a table, in the index definition

- Covering indexes—An index that covers all columns needed for a query

- Operator classes—Operators to be used by the indexes, specific to a column type

Since you're comparing the performance of queries with different index types, you'll need a lot of data to work with.

How might you generate large amounts of data?

Generating Data for Experiments

One of the best ways to learn about PostgreSQL is to conduct experiments on databases with large tables. For specific queries, you can then iterate on different index types, varying their definitions to cover different columns, orderings, and index options. Using the query planner, you can verify that the candidate indexes have the intended benefit or discard them.

---

1. https://www.postgresql.org/docs/current/btree-implementation.html
2. https://www.postgresql.org/docs/current/sql-createindex.html

Let's explore that process. Create a temp schema locally if one doesn't exist already from earlier work. Add a users table to the temp schema. Insert a large amount of rows into temp.users; ten million should do it! Run the following statements from psql to do that:

sql/insert_users_generate_series.sql

```
CREATE SCHEMA IF NOT EXISTS temp;

DROP TABLE IF EXISTS temp.users;

BEGIN;

SET LOCAL statement_timeout = '120s';

-- Requires PostgreSQL 16+ for underscores
CREATE TABLE IF NOT EXISTS temp.users
WITH (autovacuum_enabled = FALSE) AS
SELECT
  seq AS id,
  'fname' || seq AS first_name,
  'lname' || seq AS last_name,
  'user_' || seq || '@' || (
    CASE (RANDOM() * 2)::INT
      WHEN 0 THEN 'gmail'
      WHEN 1 THEN 'hotmail'
      WHEN 2 THEN 'yahoo'
    END
  ) || '.com' AS email,
  CASE (seq % 2)
    WHEN 0 THEN 'Driver'
    ELSE 'Rider'
  END AS type,
  NOW() AS created_at,
  NOW() AS updated_at
FROM GENERATE_SERIES(1, 10_000_000) seq;

COMMIT;

-- Update VM and stats
VACUUM (ANALYZE) temp.users;
```

Bulk Load Script

 A newer version of this script may be available in Rideshare at db/scripts/bulk_load.sh.

What is this script doing? This script fills the temp.users table with rows created on the fly from a SELECT statement. The temp.users table is similar to the Rideshare users table but has fewer columns.

When filtering rows for tables with low row counts, PostgreSQL may decide to scan the whole table instead of using an index. This can be surprising!

Index scans outperform sequential scans when filtering for a very small number of rows in a very large table. Since row data is stored in pages on disk behind the scenes, if the data is stored densely in a single page or a limited number of pages, PostgreSQL may also determine that it's less costly to read in the whole tables vs. use indexes.

When does it flip from sequential scans to index scans? For a given query that specifies a lot of fields of data, indexes often do not cover all the fields needed based on the SELECT clause.

Even when the planner chooses an index scan for filtering, a second *heap scan*[3] (the table data) is needed to retrieve the additional field data. This involves two scans. PostgreSQL keeps estimates for how costly these scans will be.

PostgreSQL may determine these two scans, an index scan and a heap scan, are more costly than a single heap scan (or sequential scan). To determine that, the query planner calculates the costs of the two scans as a plan and compares that to the cost of an alternative plan with the single scan. The single sequential scan can be less costly. In newer versions of PostgreSQL, sequential scans can be parallelized using multiple workers taking on different chunks of the total job in parallel.

What are some of the other influencing factors? PostgreSQL looks at parts of the query like how many total rows are being requested, what kinds of filters are present.

These factors are part of how selective the query is. Using the table's indexes, there may be a good match for the query conditions and the index content.

Other factors include the data distribution (whether it's skewed or uniformly distributed), the total table row count, and the costs associated with operation types like sequential access or random access. The planner uses the costs to make a runtime decision, identifying the lowest cost plan. Take note of the "Planning Time" when using EXPLAIN (ANALYZE) for a query.

With those explanations in place, you're ready to conduct some experiments on the temp.users table with ten million rows. If you conducted these same tests on a table with fewer rows, you'd likely see sequential scans when accessing the table.

---

3. https://www.postgresql.org/docs/current/glossary.html

Run this query from psql, prepending EXPLAIN (ANALYZE, BUFFERS):

```
sql/select_temp_users.sql
SELECT * FROM temp.users
WHERE last_name IN ('lname10000', 'lname100000', 'lname1000000');
```

With these options prepended to the query, you're presented with a query plan. Let's break down the details from the plan.

In PostgreSQL 16, this uses a parallel sequential scan. This makes sense because there aren't any other options at this point, as there are no indexes on the temp.users table. The execution time was over 500ms, and more than 100,000 buffers were read:

```
sql/explain_plan_buffers.sql
Buffers: shared hit=2176 read=125504
```

Shared hits mean the data was accessed from shared buffers (memory) without needing disk access. The read figure on the "Buffers" row means those blocks *were not* in shared buffers. Those were storage accesses or reads from your disk, which are slower. You might see a figure like read=130720.

Take a moment to think about what's happening here. PostgreSQL loads entire pages, not just rows within pages. To filter to the three requested last_name rows, the *entire set of pages* holding all data for the table is accessed.

After all of that data is loaded, the query asks for all fields of data, but from only three rows of ten million. Whoa. That's pretty dang inefficient! As you begin to explore the buffers information and think about how many bytes of data are moving around for operations like this, you'll develop a sense of heaviness (possibly an eye twitch) when seeing these kinds of inefficiencies. The upshot is these are the exact places where indexes can offer tremendous efficiency gains.

Let's consider the timing. While 500ms might feel pretty fast on your laptop while nothing else is running, in a busy web application with OLTP transactions, 500ms is *not good*. This is a long time for one query to run while it's reading a lot of data from storage and using server instance resources to conduct the filtering and processing needed.

What you might be thinking at this point is, how can we make this much more efficient? We know that we're loading only three rows, but starting from ten million. Can we start from a much smaller set than ten million? We can do that using an index. Especially for field data with high cardinality, B-Tree indexes stored using a tree structure, with leaf nodes, are much faster to navigate to and identify the requested three rows.

Which fields should be indexed? Since we're filtering on the last_name, the last_name should be covered in a B-Tree index either as a single column index or be the leading column for a multicolumn index. In either of those cases, the index can be used to support a much more efficient retrieval of the desired rows.

Let's do it! Create an index for temp.users covering the last_name column.

This is a big table, so creating the index will take a while. Toggle \timing on from psql to see how long it takes. Since you're adding the index to a nonlive system, let's skip the CONCURRENTLY option here so that the index is added as quickly as possible. Remember, though, that in live systems for big tables, you should consider using CONCURRENTLY as the default way of adding indexes.

Run the following from psql:

```
sql/create_index_users_last_name.sql
-- \timing
-- Timing is on.

CREATE INDEX users_last_name_idx ON temp.users (last_name);
```

Creating the index took around 12 seconds. In a live system with concurrent queries, you'd want to use the CONCURRENTLY option so that during those 12 seconds, other queries accessing the table are not blocked.

Run the query from earlier requesting the rows that match the three last names using EXPLAIN (ANALYZE, BUFFERS).

You should see some, frankly, staggering results. The query now runs tremendously faster, with both planning and execution time completing in a few milliseconds. Compare that time to 500ms.

What else do we see in the query plan? We see that the users_last_name_idx index was used with an index scan. Let's look at Buffer information. You may see one buffer or a small number accessed on the first time you run the query. Since we loaded all of these data rows sequentially, if they're small, they may all fit on a single page.

Running this query a second time shows all buffers were in the shared buffers cache, and none were read outside it. You might see shared hit=12 and no read buffers. If that's the case, you're now seeing query execution time in fractions of a single millisecond. Compare that with where we started, at 500ms, to now finding three values within ten million in two-tenths of a millisecond, or 200μs (200 microseconds).

Indexes are amazing! With this well-placed index, you've made the execution of this query extremely efficient by minimizing the latency, as the query results are served solely from the index, and the content fits within the buffer cache.

Serving results from the buffer cache and only scanning indexes allows PostgreSQL to retrieve the needed data with few resources (low cost).

Imagine that you added this index (using CONCURRENTLY) to your production system and now wish to keep all databases in sync.

To do that, create a migration that adds the index and use the if_not_exists: true option to add it conditionally. That could look like the following example:

```ruby
ruby/add_index_users_last_name.rb
class AddIndexUsersLastName < ActiveRecord::Migration[7.0]
  disable_ddl_transaction!

  def change
    add_index 'temp.users', :last_name,
      algorithm: :concurrently,
      if_not_exists: true
  end
end
```

Let's recap. You've added a single-column index to make the filtering operation very efficient, retrieving row data for three matching rows from ten million.

Although you're filtering on a single column, queries commonly work with multiple columns from one or more tables. How can you get these efficiency gains when filtering on multiple columns?

Single Column and Multiple Column Indexes

Multicolumn indexes[4] are indexes in PostgreSQL that include multiple columns in their definition. The definition in the last section for the index you made included a single last_name column.

You want to explore this section by first understanding the single and multi-column indexes you have in your database. To do that, check out the "Index Maintenance"[5] page from the PostgreSQL wiki, which has a nice index summary query that you can use.

Try it out with Rideshare. Run the query from psql for the Rideshare database by changing the schema from public to rideshare. The query shows a table-by-table

---

4. https://www.postgresql.org/docs/current/indexes-multicolumn.html
5. https://wiki.postgresql.org/wiki/Index_Maintenance

breakdown of the indexes for each, including their size, rows covered, and whether they're unique, single, or the multicolumn type.

Multicolumn indexes are specialized indexes because they support a single query or a limited set of queries. For their performance benefit, they consume more space and, like all indexes, add some write latency. Most indexes in Rideshare are single-column indexes, chosen to follow the guidance from the PostgreSQL "Multicolumn Indexes" documentation:[6]

> In most situations, an index on a single column is sufficient and saves space and time.

A database with a large number of multicolumn indexes might be "excessively indexed" or have redundant indexes. We'll look at both of these scenarios. In the first one, it may be worth comparing the performance for a set of queries using single-column indexes that replace multicolumn indexes. If they offer similar retrieval performance, you will benefit from less write latency and space consumption. You'll need a separate database instance with the same data and resources to test out indexing alternatives. That's outside the scope of this chapter, but you may be able to use the performance database approaches to help.

Let's consider multicolumn index benefits. Multicolumn indexes can provide some of the best performance when all columns needed are available in the index. Since indexes can be so beneficial, it makes their design challenging. The optimal index design depends on many factors, including the queries, the distribution of the data, how selective the queries are, the selectivity of the indexes, the cardinality of columns, and other factors.

Let's keep focusing on the fundamentals. From the same PostgreSQL wiki page, copy the *index size/usage statistics* query and run it for Rideshare. Every time an index is used in a query plan, PostgreSQL keeps track of that. Cool! Information like number_of_scans can be used in various ways. In a sense, they show how valuable an index is. An index only adds value when it's supporting one or more important queries.

Indexes have different levels of value depending on the queries you're trying to design for, which in turn also have different values for your application or platform. Some queries are critical; they must be fast and efficient, while others run very rarely, in a low-value or low-usage area of the product. They may even run unnecessarily. Those are some of the nontechnical factors that are also worth learning about to help inform your technical designs.

---

6.   https://www.postgresql.org/docs/current/indexes-multicolumn.html

Since we're testing in Rideshare, we'll again need something to simulate live traffic we'd have in a real-world application.

Generate queries for Rideshare by running the activity simulator script you saw earlier.

Start the Rails server by running bin/rails server in the Rideshare directory from your terminal.

In another terminal, run bin/rails simulate:app_activity.

Once this completes, you'll have index scan information to look at. Using the queries from earlier from the PostgreSQL wiki, review the number_of_scans for each index. The tuples_read and tuples_fetched columns show the number of tuples retrieved from an index.

The indexes in Rideshare for the primary key columns of the users, trips, and trip_requests table stand out as having a lot of index scans. From those index scans, a lot of tuples are returned. Indexes with no scans and no tuples fetched may be unused or infrequently used (or just not accessed as part of this simulation script). Use this data, or the absence of data in these fields, to help determine whether your indexes are beneficial or not.

For multicolumn indexes, another challenge is figuring out which order the columns should appear in. After all, the order does matter—a lot!

How does that work?

Understanding Index Column Ordering

The order of columns in the definition of a multicolumn index is significant. A good rule of thumb is that the leading column (the first column) should cut the list down as much as possible. In other words, for this leading column, it should be the most selective column from the columns you want to add.

Let's look at an example. Consider a multicolumn index covering columns "a" and "b", ordered (a, b) (a then b) from left to right. "a" is the leading column.

While queries that use column "b" can use this index, it won't be optimal. From the documentation:[7]

> The condition on the first column is the most important one for determining how much of the index needs to be scanned.

---

7.   https://www.postgresql.org/docs/current/indexes-multicolumn.html

The documentation describes how queries for columns that are nonleading columns in the multicolumn index may even skip a multicolumn index and choose a sequential scan when it offers a lower cost. If you're facing a scenario where you expected a multicolumn index to support a query, double check the columns defined and their order.

What if your application needs to efficiently filter on column "b"? PostgreSQL recommends creating separate single column indexes for "a" and "b".

The documentation "Combining Multiple Indexes"[8] shows how multiple indexes can even be used in a plan. There can also be multiple scans of the *same* index, used to combine index data when the query has AND and OR conditions.

Having single-column indexes on "a" and "b" allows PostgreSQL to combine the results of individual index scans for some operations.

> To combine multiple indexes, the system scans each needed index and prepares a bitmap in memory.

> The bitmaps are then ANDed and ORed together as needed by the query.

Great. Should we add single-column indexes then for every single column? Nope. Since indexes add latency to all DML operations (inserts, updates, deletes, and merges), we don't want redundant and unneeded indexes, as they don't provide benefits and slow things down.

Having all three indexes mentioned so far, a single column covering "a", a single column covering "b", and a multicolumn covering "a" and "b" means there are redundancies.

On the other hand, a multicolumn index that covers two columns, the first for filtering and the second for ordering, may provide the best query performance. This investigation and balancing act is where you, the professional programmer, come in as you evaluate these on a case-by-case basis.

While avoiding redundant indexes is a good guideline, you'll need to leverage your knowledge of the data distribution and conduct experiments using the planner to determine which index definition is best.

With that sort of general advice in place, let's shift gears and focus on more narrow index designs for specific scenarios.

First up, let's consider Boolean columns. Tables commonly have Boolean columns. What types of indexes work best for Booleans?

---

8.   https://www.postgresql.org/docs/current/indexes-bitmap-scans.html

Indexing Boolean Columns

While Boolean value columns are common, indexing them efficiently has some pitfalls to be aware of. Consider which values are allowed. When nulls are allowed, a Boolean column has three possible values: true, false, and NULL. Without nulls, there are only two possible values. These are *low cardinality* columns with a limited set of possible values. Right off the bat, this might indicate that indexes won't be very beneficial.

Let's keep going on this example. Imagine a "soft deletes" implementation that uses Boolean columns, with an is_deleted column that's false by default. Nulls are not allowed. As a reminder, soft-deleted rows aren't physically removed, but their timestamp is set, and then that value means they're hidden from the application.

Let's assume the majority of the rows are active, meaning their is_deleted column is false.

Is it a good idea to index is_deleted? It depends on the queries. For active deleted rows, since they represent the biggest proportion—the majority of rows—PostgreSQL would likely load the whole table with a sequential scan and then filter out the smaller proportion of soft-deleted rows.

When querying only for deleted rows, since PostgreSQL has indexed those rows, the query and index is more selective, and the index would likely be chosen. However, you'd need to test to be sure. The index is not efficient since the majority of rows are active. Indexes work best for retrieving data based on highly selective conditions or high cardinality data. They're also more efficient from a storage perspective when they contain only data that's queried.

Do we have options to make a more efficient index for Boolean data?

Filtering Rows with Partial Indexes

Partial indexes are B-Tree indexes that have an expression baked into their definition. The expression can serve the purpose of restricting the rows that are included in the index.

We'll apply that to soft deletes in a moment. Restricting the rows in an index provides multiple benefits but also trade-offs. Let's consider the benefits. The index consumes less space. The index contributes less to write latency since entries are only maintained in the index when the expression matches a particular DML operation.

A partial index is a *specialized* type of index that's optimized for specific queries by both providing efficient retrieval and efficient storage.

Let's go back to the soft deletes example. Let's mix it up a bit, though, and use a deleted_at column that also allows nulls. The earlier example did not allow nulls. Since we're allowing nulls, that means there are three possible values.

Let's imagine that deleted_at is null by default. Users can deactivate their accounts, which sets the deleted_at column to the current time. Those rows are then hidden from the app.

Imagine the Marketing department wants to investigate churn patterns. The deleted_at column starts getting used in queries that are designed to find deleted users. Imagine there's even a feature related to this, where recently deleted users are offered incentives to return to the platform. Besides ad hoc analysis queries, application queries are now running against this table in regular volume.

Let's set this up in Rideshare. Since Rideshare does not have soft deletes, you'll add the column and then add a partial index that restricts the rows picked. After that, you'll delete about ten users and analyze the table. Run through the following statements from psql:

sql/index_users_deleted_email_partial.sql
```sql
ALTER TABLE users ADD COLUMN deleted_at timestamptz;

-- Index supporting queries for "soft deleted" users
CREATE INDEX IF NOT EXISTS index_users_deleted_email_partial
ON users
USING BTREE (email)
WHERE deleted_at IS NOT NULL;

-- "soft delete" some users
UPDATE users
SET deleted_at = NOW()
WHERE id <= 10;

-- Update stats following deletes
ANALYZE (VERBOSE) users;
```

You've now got the column and index in place and have analyzed the table. Now run this query:

sql/users_soft_deletes.sql
```sql
SELECT email
FROM users
WHERE deleted_at IS NOT NULL;
```

The query should return the ten users you've just soft-deleted. Let's look at the plan and buffer information. Run the query again, prepending EXPLAIN (ANALYZE, BUFFERS).

Verify the plan used the index index_users_deleted_email_partial. You should see a very fast result, in fractions of a millisecond, for these ten rows. A number of factors are contributing to this being a very efficient lookup. Only the email address is included in the index. Only rows from the users table that match the condition deleted_at IS NOT NULL. We know that's only ten rows of the total. By querying for that very selective condition, the index is used not only because it matches the query conditions, but it even provides the email value directly, resulting in an "index-only scan." Nice![9]

Partial indexes aren't your only option. An alternative here could be a multi-column index with a leading deleted_at column.

Add an index covering deleted_at to filter down to the soft-deleted rows. Include the email column as the second column so the email can be fetched from the index.

Run this in psql:

sql/users_multicolumn_soft_deletes.sql
```
CREATE INDEX IF NOT EXISTS index_users_deleted_email_multi
ON users USING BTREE(deleted_at, email);
```

Describe the users table by running \d users, then verify that both indexes, index_users_deleted_email_partial and index_users_deleted_email_multi, are listed at the bottom.

Drop the partial index created earlier so that the multicolumn index is picked. Run this from psql:

sql/drop_index_if_exists.sql
```
DROP INDEX IF EXISTS index_users_deleted_email_partial;
```

Run the query again, still using EXPLAIN (ANALYZE, BUFFERS) to view the plan, and confirm the multicolumn index (index_users_deleted_email_multi) was used. The scan type should still be an index-only scan.

For those two alternatives that both result in an efficient index-only scan, let's review their trade-offs.

---

9. https://www.youtube.com/watch?v=2njVcg-O9Bg

Each index consumes different amounts of space and has different write latency impacts. Let's look at their sizes. Check out the size of the multicolumn index. Run this SELECT to see the size:

```
sql/users_multicolumn_index_size.sql
SELECT
PG_SIZE_PRETTY(
  PG_TOTAL_RELATION_SIZE('users_deleted_email_multi')
);
--  pg_size_pretty
-- ----------------
-- 1360 kB
```

Now check the size of the partial index:

```
sql/users_partial_index_size.sql
SELECT
PG_SIZE_PRETTY(
  PG_TOTAL_RELATION_SIZE('index_users_deleted_email_partial')
);
--  pg_size_pretty
-- ----------------
--   16 kB
```

We'll assume you've generated the 20K rows for users. With that number of rows, we can see that the partial index is *much* smaller, at just 16 KB compared with 1360 KB for the multicolumn index.

As you make index design choices, consider their space consumption and write effects. The multicolumn index includes two columns (email and deleted_at) vs. one in the index definition, which means index maintenance is required for all DML operations on this table that touch either row. The multicolumn index adds some additional write latency compared with the partial index.

Partial Indexes for Nullable Foreign Keys

 In the post The Unexpected Find That Freed 20 GB of Unused Index Space,[10] the author shows how partial indexes can be a good fit for nullable foreign key columns. The index supports enforcement of the constraint. The size is more efficient because NULL values are excluded.

You've now seen some of the benefits of partial indexes for space consumption and for reducing latency. You compared both for their usefulness in efficient retrieval.

---

10. https://hakibenita.com/postgresql-unused-index-size

Besides expressions written for partial indexes, what other kinds of expressions can you use with indexes?

Transform Values with an Expression Index

Expression indexes are indexes that have an expression in their definition, transforming a value before it's stored. PostgreSQL calls this an *index on an expression*.[11] These are also referred to as *functional* indexes when the expression uses a function like LOWER(), or colloquially as a synonym for "expression indexes."

Match Queries to Expressions Exactly

 Always confirm that indexes are *actually used* when you expect them to be. Inspect the query plan on the server where the query runs and review index usage stats. For expression indexes, this is very important since the query conditions must match the expression *exactly* for the index to be used.

Imagine that you want to search users by email address in a case-insensitive way. One solution would be to transform the email addresses using the LOWER() function before storing it within an index. Let's try that out.

Use the temp.users table you set up earlier, referring to code/sql/insert_users_generate_series.sql. The temp.users table should still have around ten million rows in it. If it doesn't, run the bulk load script again to bring it up to a size where differences in query performance are more obvious.

With the ten million rows populated, let's add more rows in with a mix of upper and lowercase. Review the following statement, which does that, but don't run it yet. We're adding an index first.

sql/insert_into_temp_users.sql
```
INSERT INTO temp.users (
  first_name, last_name, email, type, created_at, updated_at
)
VALUES
  ('Jane', 'Example1', 'Jane@example.com', 'Driver', NOW(), NOW()),
  ('jane', 'example2', 'jane@example.com', 'Driver', NOW(), NOW());
```

This statement deliberately creates email address duplicates. The table doesn't have a unique constraint on email addresses or any concept of case sensitivity, so this will be allowed.

---

11. https://www.postgresql.org/docs/current/indexes-expressional.html

You'd like to avoid these kinds of duplicates though. How can you do that? Let's use an expression index to accomplish that.

First, normalize the email addresses by applying the lowercase function to the input value. Besides that transformation, make the index a unique index, which enforces a unique constraint for email addresses on the table.

The following statement does all of that. The statement uses the LOWER() function to normalize the email addresses. On ten million rows, this will take a while to add. Enable \timing to find out how long it takes if desired.

```
sql/create_unique_index_users_email_lower.sql
CREATE UNIQUE INDEX index_temp_users_lower_email_unique
ON temp.users (LOWER(email));
```

With the unique constraint in place, try running the insert statement from earlier that you hadn't yet run.

You'll see that the statement fails. As expected, the unique constraint detects the duplicate email addresses that violate the constraint within the same insert statement (the two rows) and prevents the operation. Even though the email addresses used a mix of upper and lower case, and there's no concept of case sensitivity at the column level, the index definition itself uses both the expression and the constraint to validate the input data. Great!

With B-Tree expression indexes covered, let's move on and try out another type.

In the next section, you'll explore the GIN type, which is not one you've worked with yet.

Using GIN Indexes with JSON

Generalized Inverted Index types or GIN indexes[12] are a bit different from B-Tree indexes. Usually, B-Tree index entries point to single items. Exceptions to this are when columns hold nonunique values like names and duplicates are allowed. In those cases, a single B-Tree entry points to multiple rows.

However, even in that scenario, the row is present multiple times but is a single value (the name). What about data where the columns always contain multiple values or even data structures?

For example, jsonb columns with JSON formatted text could contain lots of "keys" within a structure of data. Despite that structure of data that's not one

---

12. https://www.postgresql.org/docs/current/gin-intro.html

single value, you still may have the need to efficiently query for data within that structure. Fortunately, thanks to the breadth and depth of indexes in PostgreSQL, you've got options to do that.

Let's look at an example in Rideshare. Imagine that you would like to collect "metrics" for rides that drivers provide. You aren't sure what the metrics will be in advance or what types of data they'll store. You'd like to have some flexibility so other people in the business can add new metrics. Imagine a specific type of metric for Ridesharing or car servers. A common one may be knowing how many suitcases (or "bags") a driver picks up for a particular ride.

The "bags" metric may inform future decisions as part of driver dispatching, knowing their size of vehicle and the quantity of bags picked up at different times or locations.

Let's consider another one. Imagine you want to track whether drivers played music or offered bottles of water. These metrics could be correlated with trip ratings to produce recommendations for drivers based on rider feedback that could help improve their ratings.

To store these metrics, you're considering whether they'll be strings, Booleans, or numbers.

Since the types are unclear, and the list of metrics may expand, you decide to store them as JSON data. You expect to add more attributes to the list over time. Will you be able to efficiently query into the list of metrics when row counts grow large?

To store JSON compatible strings, you can choose between json or jsonb. Choose the jsonb type because it supports indexes.

The metrics you're starting with are:

- bags_in_trunk (a number)
- music_on (true or false)
- water_offered (true or false)

In the following snippet, \gset is used to create a *dollar quoted literal* (see "Defining Multi-Line Strings in psql"[13]) to display an example metrics entry as JSON, formatted vertically. Run this command just to learn how to use this block, as you'll be using it later on.

---

13. https://stackoverflow.com/a/31457183

```
sql/select_json_string.sql
SELECT
$$'{
  "ride_details": {
    "bags_in_trunk": 1,
    "music_on": true,
    "water_offered": true
  }
}'$$ AS json_string \gset
```

The dollar quoted literal here in SQL is similar to a *Heredoc* or multiline string in Ruby. It is being used here only for legibility.

Let's use the data. To present the data assigned to json_string, use the JSONB_PRETTY() function. This also ensures the JSON is valid.

Run this statement in psql:

```
sql/select_json_string_jsonb_pretty.sql
SELECT JSONB_PRETTY(:json_string);
          jsonb_pretty
-------------------------------
 {                            +
     "ride_details": {        +
         "music_on": true,    +
         "bags_in_trunk": 1,  +
         "water_offered": true+
     }                        +
 }
(1 row)
```

We now have a multiline JSON string that we know is formatted correctly. This helps avoid headaches later on. With that in mind, create three JSON variables, one that represents an example of each metric. You'll invent these little blocks and then use them as input data to store.

To store the data, let's put them in a new column on the trips table called...wait for it...data.

Let's allow null values for the column and use the jsonb type.

Run each of the steps in the following SQL snippet individually, to add the column, and then put data into it.

Note that the statement assumes there are existing trips records with primary key id values 1, 2, and 3. The dollar quoted literal technique you saw before is used here to format the JSON data.

Run these statements from psql:

```
sql/jsonb_trip_details_multi_insert.sql
-- NOTE: Run these *individually* in psql
-- These set variables: json_string1, json_string2, and json_string3
SELECT $$'{"ride_details":
{"bags_in_trunk": 1, "music_on": true,"water_offered": false}
}'::jsonb$$
AS json_string1 \gset

SELECT $$'{"ride_details":
{"bags_in_trunk": 2, "music_on": true,"water_offered": true}
}'::jsonb$$
AS json_string2 \gset

SELECT $$'{"ride_details":
{"bags_in_trunk": 3, "music_on": false,"water_offered": true}
}'::jsonb$$
AS json_string3 \gset

-- Make sure three rows appear
\x -- vertical presentation
SELECT :json_string1, :json_string2, :json_string3;

-- Add the `data` column to the trips table
ALTER TABLE trips ADD COLUMN data jsonb;

-- Insert the 3 json strings above
-- into the `rideshare.trips` table
-- for ids 1, 2, 3
--
-- Assumes these exist:
-- SELECT id FROM trips WHERE id IN (1,2,3);
--
-- use UPDATE ... FROM for a multi-row UPDATE
-- https://stackoverflow.com/a/18799497
UPDATE trips AS t
SET data = c.json_string
from (VALUES
  (:json_string1, 1),
  (:json_string2, 2),
  (:json_string3, 3)
) AS c(json_string, trip_id)
WHERE c.trip_id = t.id;
```

Great. After running the last line you saw UPDATE 3, meaning three updates succeeded. Query the trips table data column for those ids to make sure they were populated:

```
sql/jsonb_metrics_query.sql
SELECT id, data FROM trips WHERE id IN (1,2,3);
```

Once you've verified each of the trips rows have metrics listed in their data columns, you're ready to proceed.

With these metrics stored as JSON data, imagine the types of queries you'd run on the data to gain insights. Let's start with the ride_details metric. Run the following query and use EXPLAIN. Without an index that covers the new data column, we expect to see a sequential scan on trips in the query plan. You may want to run \x again to toggle the result presentation.

sql/select_trips_data_json.sql
```
EXPLAIN SELECT * FROM trips WHERE data ? 'ride_details';
```

While this Seq Scan is OK for low row counts, as metrics are added to greater numbers of trips, you'd like to have confidence that the query will run reliably and predictably over time.

To do that, you'd like the query to be supported by an index. How can you index a jsonb column? To do that, let's create a GIN index for data. GIN indexes can be used with jsonb columns and cover nested data.

Run the following from psql to create the GIN index (giving it a specific name):

sql/create_index_gin.sql
```
CREATE INDEX trips_data_gin_idx ON trips USING GIN(data);
```

With the index created, run the same query again, using EXPLAIN to see the plan. With the index in place, this time you should see a *bitmap heap scan* and *bitmap index scan* that used the trips_data_gin_idx index that you just created.

Try querying the metrics data in different ways. Get the average number of bags in the trunk for all trips:

sql/avg_bags_in_trunk.sql
```
SELECT AVG((data->'ride_details'->'bags_in_trunk')::INTEGER)
FROM trips WHERE data ? 'ride_details';
```

Running the previous query gets the average figure. Prepending EXPLAIN again shows that the GIN index you added was used.

Besides the GIN index itself, are there other properties on the index worth knowing?

For B-Tree indexes, you've mostly used equality operations. Imagine that you want to efficiently dig into the data field to see what it contains. You want to check whether the list of keys contains a particular value. That type of operation is called a *containment* operation and uses the special symbol @>.

The PgAnalyze post, "Understanding Postgres GIN Indexes: The Good and the Bad,"[14] shows a containment query example we'll adapt to Rideshare.

This time you'll create a GIN index but use a different option, the jsonb_path_ops *operator class*. This may be your first time setting an operator class[15] when creating an index. Run the following from psql:

```
sql/create_gin_index_jsonb_path_ops.sql
CREATE INDEX trips_data_path_ops
ON trips USING GIN(data JSONB_PATH_OPS);
```

With this index added, containment queries can now be performed efficiently on trips.data. Query examples could be, "Which drivers offered a water bottle to riders?" or "Which trips had two or more bags in the trunk?"

Run the following queries from psql to find trips that match those conditions:

```
sql/query_json_operators.sql
-- Trips where water was offered
SELECT * FROM trips
WHERE data @> '{"ride_details":{"water_offered": true}}';

-- Trips w/ 2 bags in the trunk
SELECT * FROM trips
WHERE data @> '{"ride_details":{"bags_in_trunk": 2}}';
```

If you prepend EXPLAIN, verify that those queries are supported by the trips_data_path_ops index you've just added. As data and query volume increase, these queries will continue to run efficiently since they're supported by this index.

Next, you'd like to correlate these analytics with particular drivers and locations to gather some insights.

Combining Schemaless and Structured Data

 Combine schemaless and structured data with efficient queries like this in PostgreSQL, supported by indexes.

To do that, you'll use a B-Tree index with JSON data. B-Tree indexes can be used with JSON data by creating an expression, which you saw how to do earlier.

Create the following B-Tree expression index called trips_btree_expr on the data column:

---

14. https://pganalyze.com/blog/gin-index
15. https://www.postgresql.org/docs/current/indexes-opclass.html

```
sql/create_btree_index_json_expression.sql
CREATE INDEX trips_btree_expr ON trips USING BTREE(data)
WHERE (data->'ride_details'->'bags_in_trunk')::INT4 >= 2;
```

The index definition here is longer, and that's because the goal is for the index to match the query conditions exactly.

Let's drop the GIN index from earlier to make sure the intended index is picked.

```
DROP INDEX trips_data_gin_idx;
```

Let's use the query from earlier. Run the following statement, which has that query with EXPLAIN prepended. Verify the plan shows a bitmap index scan on trips_btree_expr:

```
sql/query_trips_data_json_expression.sql
EXPLAIN SELECT * FROM trips
WHERE (data->'ride_details'->'bags_in_trunk')::INT4 >= 2;
```

Nice. We see trips_btree_expr was used for the query. Running this query without EXPLAIN, we see that it returns the two trips rows with two or more bags in the trunk. We can visually inspect the data column on those result rows to confirm the values. What we've confirmed here is that both GIN and B-Tree indexes can be used with JSON data as index types to support queries.

The post, "Hidden Gems: ActiveRecord Store,"[16] shows how to use jsonb columns with the *Active Record Store* (store_accessor) for key value storage with Ruby on Rails.

One trade-off with Active Record Store is that it's limited to one level of depth. The metrics structure you used in this section has bags_in_trunk nested under ride_details, which is two levels of depth. For multiple levels of depth, use jsonb directly with Active Record.

How can we keep our JSON data well-maintained?

Maintaining Unstructured JSON Data

In the last section, you created unstructured data as JSON-formatted text. The flexibility afforded by not having to design your schema upfront meant you could add new types of metrics easily without worrying about their types or values.

While that flexibility is nice when starting, as things solidify over time, the trade-off is unstructured data is more difficult to maintain because it's unclear what data can go in and what types are associated with keys and values.

---

16. https://www.honeybadger.io/blog/rails-activerecord-store/

Wouldn't it be nice if we could balance both that flexibility and the ability to bring in some of the rigidity we've seen earlier with constraints to help describe and enforce good data in unstructured storage?

Staying Organized with Unstructured Data

 Add schema definitions later for your unstructured data as it solidifies. To do that, use tools like JSON Schema and the postgres-json-schema extension.

To help maintain JSON column data longer term, consider adding some schema definition elements to your JSON columns. How can we do that? One solution is the postgres-json-schema[17] extension. This extension supports adding a JSON Schema definition into your database. With that in place, you can then both describe the data and, crucially, *enforce* that definition.

For the enforcement part, you'll use one of your existing constraint friends: the flexible check constraint (see *The Versatile Check Constraint*).

Let's run through a brief hands-on example for Rideshare. If you've been working on the previous exercises, you've got a data column in your trips table and three data rows. If not, return to the earlier code snippet called code/sql /jsonb_trip_details_multi_insert.sql and go through that, adding the column and data.

From here onward, we'll assume you have got three trip records with JSON-formatted data in the trips.data column.

As you learned, constraints serve both as documentation and for enforcement. Let's set that up for the ride_details section that's stored within the data column in the trips table.

Here are the steps:

- Generate a JSON Schema compatible schema definition string from the data.

- Create a check constraint on trips with that schema definition and the data column.

- With the constraint in place, verify that data can still be inserted as expected, but inserts that violate the constraint are prevented.

How can we generate the JSON Schema? Use a tool to do that. A schema has been generated for the current trips.data column based on a sample row. Refer

---

17. https://github.com/gavinwahl/postgres-json-schema

to the Development Guides[18] repository that accompanies the book for more information.

Here's the general form from the postgres-json-schema documentation for how a constraint is added to a table called example, which is not the trips table we're using. This is shown here to help you learn the general format:

```
CREATE TABLE example (id serial PRIMARY KEY, data jsonb);
```

```
ALTER TABLE trips ADD CONSTRAINT data_is_valid CHECK (
  validate_json_schema('{"type": "object"}', data));
```

By referencing this section in the appendix, let's assume you've added all the ingredients. You've added the extension, the check constraint, and are now ready to test it on the existing table data.

Follow the usage steps in the Development Guides[19] repository, which are based on this example. Verify that data rows can still be inserted after the constraint is added. Verify that noncompliant data cannot be inserted.

Great! You've now added documentation for what's expected for the data in your JSON column. That documentation also enforces consistency for every write operation. This will really help your team maintain this data over time. They're able to see what's expected and avoid spending time solving bugs that are related to bad data.

In the next section, you'll explore another index type, the BRIN index. What is it and how is it useful?

Using BRIN Indexes

In this section, you'll work with *block ranges*. What are those?

> A block range is a group of pages that are physically adjacent in the table.[20]

Data in PostgreSQL is stored in *pages* that hold 8 KB (by default) *blocks*. A block *range* is a sequence of blocks.

A range of blocks has a special index type you can use. Use the *Block Range Index*, or BRIN type. What do index entries look like for BRIN indexes?

> A block range index entry points to a page (the atomic unit of how PostgreSQL stores data) and stores two values: the page's minimum value and the maximum value of the item to be indexed.[21]

---

18. https://github.com/andyatkinson/development_guides
19. https://github.com/andyatkinson/development_guides
20. https://www.postgresql.org/docs/current/brin-intro.html
21. https://www.crunchydata.com/blog/postgresql-brin-indexes-big-data-performance-with-minimal-storage

BRIN indexes can be a good fit for time ranges, where the physical layout of data in block ranges matches how the data is queried. The strength of this correlation between the physical ordering and query ordering informs how beneficial a BRIN index will be.

> For BRIN to be effective, you need a table where the physical layout and the ordering of the column of interest are strongly correlated.

Since BRIN indexes store page positions and since all rows are stored in pages, BRIN indexes help queries because they have enough information to know when to skip pages.

Since a BRIN index only stores page values, it takes up very little space. Given that BRIN indexes are small, they may be worth having as specialized indexes even alongside more generally useful B-Tree index equivalents for the same table.

The post, "When Does BRIN Win?"[22] shows queries with high and low *correlation*. The query uses an AVG() aggregate function across a large result set, and compares the query performance using a BRIN index and a B-Tree index.

The post, "Large Data Performance with Minimal Storage,"[23] calls AVG() on a large result set, comparing performance between a B-Tree index and a BRIN index. The BRIN index not only outperforms the B-Tree index, but does so while consuming very little space.

Let's create an example with Rideshare. Imagine a new model called TripPosition, captures GPS location points from drivers and riders as trips are happening.

You'll store these in a trip_positions table that you expect to be a high write volume, insert-only table. While you don't expect rows to be updated or deleted, they will be queried in high volume.

To simulate this, do some data load preparation. Insert TripPosition using a generated series, which you saw earlier, which ticks every second over several months. With this time range and frequency, this means you'll create over five million records. As seconds tick, the value is stored as a created_at timestamp. This means rows will be inserted chronologically from the beginning of the range to the end.

As you saw earlier, "high correlation" for a BRIN index to be effective means that for queries with results that are chronologically ordered, the row data insert order should match chronologically with the query.

---

22. https://www.crunchydata.com/blog/postgres-indexing-when-does-brin-win
23. https://medium.com/geekculture/postgres-brin-index-large-data-performance-with-minimal-storage-4db6b9f64ca4

Let's populate the data and find out. Run the following SQL from psql. This will take a while to run, so the statement_timeout is raised in a transaction.

sql/trip_positions_populate_correlation.sql
```
-- Set a seed
SELECT SETSEED(0.5);

BEGIN;

SET LOCAL statement_timeout = '60s';

INSERT INTO trip_positions (
  position, trip_id, created_at, updated_at)
  SELECT POINT('(37.769233' ||
      FLOOR(RANDOM() * 10 + 1)::TEXT ||
      ',-122.3890705)'),
  (SELECT MIN(id) FROM trips),
  seq,
  seq
  FROM GENERATE_SERIES(
    '2023-08-01 0:00'::TIMESTAMPTZ,
    '2023-10-01 0:00'::TIMESTAMPTZ,
    '1 second'::INTERVAL)
  AS t(seq);

COMMIT;
```

trip_positions is now populated with millions of rows. Run the following query in psql to count records by day, which groups hundreds of thousands of rows for a day, for the first five days of the month. Since there are no indexes on these fields, this will be slower to start.

sql/trip_positions_by_day.sql
```
SELECT
  DATE_PART('day', created_at) AS date,
  COUNT(*)
FROM trip_positions
WHERE created_at >= '2023-08-01' AND created_at < '2023-08-06'
GROUP BY 1
ORDER BY 1;
```

Prepend EXPLAIN (ANALYZE, BUFFERS) to the query. A *parallel seq scan* is used, launching two workers to crunch through the table in parallel. A high amount of buffers are accessed both in the shared memory and from the disk. We can lower the cost of this query with a well-placed index.

Since the WHERE clause filters on the created_at column, it should be indexed.

A B-Tree or BRIN index would work. As you saw earlier, the B-Tree and BRIN indexes can offer comparable performance, but the BRIN index consumes less space.

Create a BRIN index using the USING BRIN clause. To do that, run this statement from psql to add the index:

sql/trip_positions_create_index_brin.sql
```
CREATE INDEX trip_positions_created_at_brin
ON trip_positions USING BRIN (created_at);
```

This statement created a BRIN index named trip_positions_created_at_brin. Next, create a B-Tree index.

sql/trip_positions_create_index_btree.sql
```
CREATE INDEX trip_positions_created_at_btree
ON trip_positions (created_at);
```

This creates the trip_positions_created_at_btree index. Run the code/sql/trip_positions_by_day.sql query again.

With the indexes in place, the query runs faster and accesses fewer buffers. The query plan shows an *index-only scan* was used with the trip_positions_created_at_btree index. Try dropping that index. Run the query again with EXPLAIN and verify the BRIN index trip_positions_created_at_brin is now used.

Performance should be comparable between queries supported by each index type. Let's consider how much space each consumes. BRIN indexes store less data, so they take up less space.

Check the sizes of the indexes with the following statements. Add the B-Tree index back since you dropped it earlier. When that's added back, run these queries:

sql/trip_positions_index_sizes.sql
```
-- B-Tree
SELECT PG_SIZE_PRETTY(
  PG_RELATION_SIZE('trip_positions_created_at_btree'));

-- BRIN
SELECT PG_SIZE_PRETTY(
  PG_RELATION_SIZE('trip_positions_created_at_brin'));
```

For this data set size, the B-Tree index was around 113 MB while the BRIN index is much smaller, just 32 KB. That's 99.97 percent smaller!

You've now used BRIN indexes to efficiently query ranges of data, leveraging their benefits for query performance and for their small size. Both B-Tree and BRIN indexes supported the queries.

In the next section, we'll look at the hash type.

Hash Indexes over B-Tree?

Hash indexes are a less-used index type, as they offer only a single capability that's redundant with the default B-Tree type. Hash indexes support *only* equality comparisons, also supported by the B-Tree type. Besides the single operation, hash indexes have more limitations. They cannot be used for unique constraint enforcement while B-Tree types can. Given the limited features and the restrictions, when are hash indexes beneficial?

In the post, "PostgreSQL indexes: Hash vs. B-tree,"[24] the author runs benchmarks on PostgreSQL 15 with data that increases in size, and with increasing amounts of items stored. Both hash and B-Tree indexes are used and compared. The goal was to understand the tipping point where a hash index had an advantage.

Since hash indexes store computed hashes from source columns instead of the column value, they use less space overall. Items in the index are uniform in size, the size of the hash code. This means that the selectivity for the source item[25] that's been indexed does not affect the index size as it does for the B-Tree type. The advantages are less space consumption and a uniform size for entries.

With some advantages in mind, let's recap their restrictions:

- Equality comparisons (=) only!
- Can't enforce unique constraints[26]
- May be *much slower* to insert new entries

If you're indexing millions of items for fast retrieval, and the items indexed have large, variable size, and variable selectivity, hash indexes may offer an advantage. A big possible downside you'll need to test on your system is the write latency.

Besides measuring their relative size, measure their build time and their latency for DML operations relative to the B-Tree type. This assumes you've chosen one or the other, B-Tree or hash.

Combined with measuring their relative performance advantages for retrieval, with those other measurements you'll have a more complete picture. Finally,

---

24. https://evgeniydemin.medium.com/postgresql-indexes-hash-vs-b-tree-84b4f6aa6d61
25. https://thwack.solarwinds.com/groups/data-driven/b/blog/posts/an-introduction-to-b-tree-and-hash-indexes-in-postgresql
26. https://thwack.solarwinds.com/groups/data-driven/b/blog/posts/an-introduction-to-b-tree-and-hash-indexes-in-postgresql

consider that B-Tree indexes are enhanced in new PostgreSQL versions. For example, B-Tree index deduplication[27] was added in version 13. Index deduplication brings a possible reduction in index size, query performance improvements, and reduced DML overhead.[28]

The basics of creating a HASH type index for the name column in the vehicles table looks like this:

```
CREATE INDEX idx_name_hash ON vehicles USING HASH (name);
```

Hash Indexes

 As a rule of thumb, prefer the B-Tree type for indexes over the hash type, mainly due to limited operations supported by the hash type.

However, after reviewing their significant limitations, if you wish to determine whether advantages exist, conduct benchmarks with your data and queries.

While filtering down result sets using indexes is a common use case, what other use cases do B-Tree index types support?

Using Indexes for Sorting

Since B-Tree indexes are stored in a sorted order, they can be used to speed up ORDER BY operations. We'll use sorting and ordering interchangeably here. They can support queries that sort items either in the forward or backward direction.

B-Tree indexes are sorted in ascending order by default.[29]

To see this in action, let's work on an example for Rideshare.

The trips table has a completed_at column that's set when a trip is completed.

Run the following query from psql to order Trips by completion time, looking at the estimated query plan with EXPLAIN. If you've run the data generators, you should have at least 1000 Trips.

```
sql/explain_analyze_select_trips.sql
EXPLAIN SELECT * FROM trips
WHERE completed_at IS NULL
ORDER BY completed_at;
```

27. https://www.postgresql.org/docs/current/btree-implementation.html#BTREE-DEDUPLICATION
28. https://www.siriusopensource.com/en-us/blog/postgresql-new-features-version-13-index-deduplication
29. https://devcenter.heroku.com/articles/postgresql-indexes#b-trees-and-sorting

We know that this column allows nulls. Imagine that we'd like to pre-sort the items in descending order to match a query to sort the items this way. We'll add DESC to the index definition. How do we handle the null values? Do they go in front or at the back?

Ordering NULL Values with SQL or Arel

 NULL values are ordered in the front by default. To put them in the back, use NULLS LAST in SQL or write comparable ordering Arel shown in this section for Rails 6.1 or greater.

Let's put the rows that have null values for this column, which are allowed, in the back. If we're sorting in descending order, we want the first values that appear to be populated values, not null values.

We want to create this as an Active Record migration, so let's use Arel. In Arel, use the .nulls_last() method added in Rails 6.1.[30] Here's Active Record code that orders the trips in descending order and pushes rows with null values to the back:

```
Trip.where(completed_at: nil).
order(Trip.arel_table[:completed_at].desc.nulls_last)
```

Verify that NULLS LAST is visible in the generated SQL query using .to_sql(). To start with, when looking at the query plan, we see it's using a *sequential scan* on the trips table. There's no index that it picked that supports this query. Remember our earlier goal to have index conditions match query conditions for the index to be useful? How do we apply that here?

Taking inspiration from "B-Trees and Sorting"[31] referenced earlier, create an index on the trips.completed_at column that exists to support the ORDER BY clause.

As part of the index definition, configure NULL values for completed_at to be pushed to the back. Run this statement from psql to create the index:

```
sql/create_index_nulls_last.sql
CREATE INDEX trips_completed_at_index
ON trips(completed_at DESC NULLS LAST);
```

Run the query again as SQL or the Arel version. Verify that the sequential scan you saw earlier is now replaced with an *index scan* using the trips_completed_at_index that you just created. The query plan also shows a Sort node with Sort Key: completed_at.

---

30. https://www.bigbinary.com/blog/rails-6-1-adds-nulls-first-and-nulls-last-to-arel
31. https://devcenter.heroku.com/articles/postgresql-indexes#b-trees-and-sorting

Great! You've now used indexes to help support query result ordering.

In the next section, you'll shift gears and explore covering indexes. What are they and what are their benefits?

Using Covering Indexes

Covering indexes refer to the definition of the index, where the index entries provide all needed data for a query. These are a specialized type of index since index entries here support specific queries.

Since you've likely got hundreds or thousands of queries, why bother with specific indexes for specific queries? The reason is that like multicolumn, covering indexes offer some of the best performance possible when plans include index-only scan operations. All needed data is provided by the index.

PostgreSQL version 11 added the INCLUDE[32] keyword, which can be used to create covering indexes.

The INCLUDE keyword specifies columns that only supply data, called "payload" columns. Payload columns cannot be used for filtering like in WHERE clauses or JOIN conditions, but supply data for columns listed in the SELECT clause.

Sounds useful! Let's try it out. For a richer understanding, we'll also compare a INCLUDE style covering index to a multicolumn index that covers the needed fields.

For the multicolumn index, add first_name and last_name to the definition. Run these statements from psql:

```
sql/covering_index_multicolumn.sql
CREATE INDEX users_fname_lname_multi_idx
ON users (first_name, last_name);
```

The next query assumes you've run the data generators for Rideshare and that there are users with the first name "Elroy". If that's not the case, generate sample data or use a common first name value using the techniques you learned earlier (see *Replacement Values That Are Statistically Similar*).

Run the following query that uses EXPLAIN, and confirm the plan shows an index-only scan with the index users_fname_lname_multi_cov:

```
sql/covering_index_query.sql
EXPLAIN (ANALYZE) SELECT first_name, last_name
FROM users WHERE first_name = 'Elroy';
```

---

32. https://www.postgresql.org/docs/current/indexes-index-only-scans.html

Next up is the covering index using INCLUDE. Drop the multicolumn index users_fname_lname_multi_cov. Create the following single column index on first_name, but add the INCLUDE keyword listing last_name as a payload column:

```
sql/covering_index_include_payload.sql
CREATE INDEX users_fname_include_lname_incl
ON users (first_name)
INCLUDE (last_name);
```

Prepend EXPLAIN (ANALYZE, BUFFERS) to the prior query to see the query plan. You should still see an index-only scan with the new users_fname_include_lname_incl INCLUDING index. The SELECT portion lists both first_name and last_name. first_name is indexed normally, and last_name is in the INCLUDE payload area.

If you checked the sizes of these two indexes, you'd see they're about the same. Wait a minute. This is different from earlier comparisons of B-Tree and BRIN indexes, for example, that had very different sizes. Why is that? This makes sense since despite their different types, these indexes have similar content for their entries.

If there isn't a size advantage for INCLUDE covering indexes, what are the benefits over a multicolumn?

One difference is when enforcing uniqueness and "index economization," where you're trying to have a minimal set of indexes.

Imagine you'd like to enforce unique first names for users. To do that, you'd normally create a B-Tree index with a UNIQUE constraint on first_name.

With an INCLUDE covering index, a single index can serve both purposes. Do that by adding UNIQUE to the covering index definition that also has INCLUDE.

This saves having to create a second index for unique constraint enforcement and for covering purposes. As you learned earlier, from a write performance and space consumption perspective, the fewer indexes the better.

Modify the INCLUDE covering index users_fname_include_lname_incl from earlier adding the UNIQUE keyword.

You'll be prevented from adding it straightaway though because the users table has a lot of duplicate first names. Deleting the users will also fail because there are foreign key constraints linking the table rows to Trips and Trip Requests.

Since this is only an example, remove the original index, drop the constraints, and delete any user with a duplicate first name (which is most of the rows). Run through the following statements in psql.

Finally, at the end, create the index again with the UNIQUE keyword added.

```
sql/covering_index_include_style_with_unique.sql
-- Drop index, replacing it with UNIQUE
DROP INDEX users_fname_include_lname_incl;

-- Remove constraints for example, allows deletes
ALTER TABLE trips DROP CONSTRAINT fk_rails_e7560abc33;
ALTER TABLE trip_requests DROP CONSTRAINT fk_rails_c17a139554;

-- CTE to find duplicate first names, then
-- delete users with that first_name
WITH dupe_first_names AS (
  SELECT first_name, COUNT(*) FROM users
  GROUP BY first_name HAVING COUNT(*) > 1
)
DELETE FROM users
WHERE first_name IN (
  SELECT DISTINCT first_name FROM dupe_first_names
);

-- Create index again, adding UNIQUE
CREATE UNIQUE INDEX users_fname_include_lname_incl
ON users (first_name)
INCLUDE (last_name);
```

With the unique covering index added, the query from earlier continues to benefit from this index using a index-only scan, while also preventing duplicates!

Test it out. Imagine "Adela" exists. Try inserting a duplicate.

```
sql/covering_index_include_duplicate.sql
INSERT INTO users (
  first_name, last_name, email, type, created_at, updated_at
)
VALUES (
  'Adela', -- the duplicate
  'Lastname', 'email@example.com', 'Driver', NOW(), NOW()
);
```

You'll know it works properly if you see output like this:

```
ERROR:  duplicate key value violates unique constraint
    "users_fname_include_lname_incl"
DETAIL:  Key (first_name)=(Adela) already exists.
```

This index is twice as nice because it serves double duty.

Wrapping Up

You've learned a lot about index types, how to create them, when they're useful, and when they're not. You've learned how to optimize queries using a variety of index types and options that are available to you in PostgreSQL.

You saw how indexes help speed up queries and support ordering. Indexes also consume space and add latency. You became aware of those trade-offs to better inform your future designs. Indexes are only useful when they provide a benefit to queries.

Part of operating an efficient database is identifying "unused indexes" that can be removed. How do you identify them, and then how do you safely remove them? What other types of database maintenance operations are useful that help you achieve the best possible performance?

In the next chapter, you'll dive into common database maintenance challenges and learn how to solve them.

## CHAPTER 9

High-Impact Database Maintenance

In this chapter, you'll learn how to perform database maintenance operations to keep your database operations optimized. As an application developer, database maintenance may be something you have little or no experience with. On the other hand, if you regularly work with higher-scale PostgreSQL and self-host your instances, you may be familiar with many of these operations.

Do you need to worry about these operations if you use a PostgreSQL hosting provider? Typically, for cloud hosting providers, the maintenance operations described in this chapter are left up to users to run. Why is that? These operations require knowing about your specific data and query patterns. Usually, hosting providers don't have that level of access, so they rely on customers to inspect their own logs and metrics.

Maintenance operations are generally focused on improving the efficiency of storage, whether it be table data or index data. New write operations and queries become more efficient. The query execution planner can make the best choices possible.

Earlier, you learned that table rows you work with are made up of row versions (tuples) behind the scenes. Row versions are related to the Multiversion Concurrency Control (MVCC[1]) mechanism in PostgreSQL. Tuples that have been replaced and no longer have any references are considered *dead*. Dead tuples still exist in storage, though, until their space is reclaimed or until they've been removed.

Dead tuples are addressed automatically when Autovacuum runs, which is enabled by default. Autovacuum runs for a table when configurable thresholds are met. Maintenance is an important part of operating PostgreSQL, especially

---

1.   https://www.postgresql.org/docs/current/mvcc.html

at higher scale with heavy query volume, large-sized data, and when approaching the physical hardware limits of an instance.

What are some of the most important operations we'll cover in this chapter? The three important maintenance operations are VACUUM, ANALYZE, and REINDEX. We'll abbreviate this trio as VAR (see "Maintaining a PostgreSQL Database Health with ANALYZE, REINDEX, and VACUUM Commands"[2]). VAR is not a PostgreSQL acronym, but we're using it here to make it easier to memorize the first letter of each of these commands so that you can use them regularly.

Take a look at some of the terminology you'll work with in this chapter:

Maintenance Terminology

- Autovacuum—Automatic VACUUM operations, which are scheduled and running

- Visibility map—Tracks which row versions (tuples) are visible to transactions

- VACUUM—Marks space from dead tuples as reusable, updates visibility map

- VACUUM FULL—Reclaims space from dead tuples. Heavy exclusive locks; generally can't be run online

- ANALYZE—Updates table data statistics

- REINDEX—Rebuilds an index, can be performed CONCURRENTLY

Let's start out with a look at Autovacuum.

Basics of Autovacuum

Automatic Vacuum, or *Autovacuum*,[3] is a background scheduler that runs VACUUM workers for each table. The scheduler process runs by default when PostgreSQL starts.

Autovacuum thresholds are configurable and are considered conservative by default. Thresholds can be tuned using various parameters. When facing problems where Autovacuum can help, administrators often add more resources so that it runs more frequently.

---

2. https://andreigridnev.com/blog/2016-04-01-analyze-reindex-vacuum-in-postgresql/

3. https://www.postgresql.org/docs/current/routine-vacuuming.html

Autovacuum is conservative by default so that it runs on lower-powered servers and doesn't disrupt other operations. Adding more resources to Autovacuum can be surprising, but it makes sense when considering that heavily loaded systems should get a proportional increase in resource allocation to keep up.

If you're unfamiliar with Autovacuum, but are familiar with garbage-collected programming languages, Autovacuum can be thought of as the "garbage collection" process for PostgreSQL.

The orchestration process triggers a VACUUM worker to clean up the garbage for a table[4] when the threshold is met. Instead of de-allocated objects in a garbage-collected programming language, PostgreSQL Autovacuum workers find dead row versions in tables.

The dead tuples occupy space that could otherwise be reclaimed for new tuples (new row versions). When Autovacuum processes dead tuples, the space they used is marked for re-use and the *visibility map* (VM) is updated.

What's the VM? We only need to know the basics for now. The visibility map is a data structure that tracks information about *heap* (table) pages. The documentation describes it this way:[5]

> It keeps track of which data pages contain tuples that are visible to all transactions.

Refer to the PostgreSQL documentation for more information on Autovacuum and the visibility map. This section is intended mainly to introduce their names and basic functionality.

Let's explore row versions a bit more. The following query shows the row version, which is a hidden column from a normal query. The following query assumes the users table was populated and has a row with id = 1.

Run the following query to show the ctid column. The ctid is made up of two values. The first value is the *page number*, and the second value is the *tuple number*.[6]

sql/select_ctid_page_number_tuple_number.sql
```
SELECT ctid,id FROM users WHERE id = 1;
```

On a brand new database, this might return a value of (0,1) for ctid. This means the row version is in page number 0, and is tuple number 1. Where are we

---

4.   https://www.postgresql.org/docs/current/sql-vacuum.html

5.   https://www.postgresql.org/docs/current/storage-vm.html

6.   https://nidhig631.medium.com/ctid-field-in-postgresql-d26977de7b58

going with this? We're trying to understand more about row versions to build a mental model.

Try updating the same user by id. Run UPDATE users SET first_name = 'Jane' WHERE id = 1; from psql, then re-run the previous query to view the ctid.

The primary key id of course does not change because we're updating the first_name. However, in doing that, there's a new tuple. When we inspect the ctid again, we'll see that in the second portion of the ctid, the tuple number has changed.

The page number may or may not change, depending on whether the new tuple is in the same page as before or in a different page. Even updating the same row again with the same value produces a new tuple, likely still in the same page (unless the page has been filled).

You've now seen a bit more about tuples and learned about the hidden ctid field. You see how new tuples are created behind the scenes when rows are updated, and as tuples are abandoned, the space they occupy can be reclaimed by Autovacuum.

Autovacuum is tuned conservatively by default. Imagine that you want to add more resources to it. How would you go about doing that?

Tuning Autovacuum Parameters

Autovacuum is a scheduling process that runs VACUUM workers that process dead tuples. The workers are triggered based on configurable threshold values.

Generally speaking, as your workload increases, particularly update and delete operations for tables, you'll want to modify the Autovacuum thresholds so that it runs more.

Specifically, your goal is to make it run more frequently. When it does run, you also want it to run for a longer amount of time before putting itself to sleep.

You may also want it to run more jobs in parallel when you have a lot of tables since it schedules one job per table. You want to add more memory, and you'll want it to run parallel workers for partitioned tables, which is something you'll learn more about in an upcoming chapter.

With those changes in place, Autovacuum will use more CPU, memory, and disk resources, but that's OK because it will be proportional to your workload.

What happens if we don't scale it up? The risk is that performance and operations will suffer from greater amounts of bloat.

What's that? Bloat generally describes inefficient storage for live data. Bloat can worsen from high rates of UPDATE and DELETE statements that generate a lot of dead row versions (tuples). When dead row versions accumulate faster than Autovacuum runs, Autovacuum falls behind. In a severe case, the accumulation rate could exceed the rate Autovacuum runs, meaning it never catches up!

When Autovacuum is not keeping up, you'll see very long VACUUM run times listed in your postgresql.log. VACUUM run times are logged in the postgresql.log so you'll need to identify those events from searches or by using a log file processor that can help organize the information better.

Earlier, you learned about configurable thresholds. Let's try configuring thresholds to trigger Autovacuum.

The parameters autovacuum_vacuum_threshold and autovacuum_vacuum_scale_factor are related to the amount of dead tuples as a fraction of the total tuples. These values express a threshold that when exceeded, acts as triggering logic for a vacuum worker to run.

These values may be changed for all tables or on individual tables. Changing the value first for individual tables that are heavily updated is a good place to start.

Where do we start? The default scale factor value is 0.2. This means that when 20 percent of the table size is made up of dead tuples, VACUUM is triggered for that table.

A good place to start is by following a common recommendation to lower the autovacuum_scale_factor so that VACUUM runs when there are fewer dead tuples. A value of 0.01 (1 percent) or even less causes VACUUM to run earlier than it would have otherwise. Let's try making that change for Rideshare.

Run the following statement from psql:

```
sql/set_table_autovacuum_scale_factor.sql
ALTER TABLE trips SET (autovacuum_vacuum_scale_factor = 0.01);
```

This parameter can be changed as the owner user. You'll see ALTER TABLE printed out when it's applied successfully.

You've now changed autovacuum_vacuum_scale_factor for the trips table to kick in when dead tuples are 1 percent of the total, vs. 20 percent.

Let's try changing another parameter. The parameter autovacuum_vacuum_cost_limit[7] specifies a *cost* of work that Autovacuum completes before it stops running (and goes to sleep). Raising this value increases the cost before Autovacuum stops, which means the worker completes more work (higher cost) and runs longer before it sleeps.

Let's try out the vacuum_cost_limit parameter, which has a default value of 200. This parameter is used when VACUUM is run manually from psql. Try running VACUUM VERBOSE trips; from psql. The VERBOSE option shows more information about what's happening.

Change the value of vacuum_cost_limit to 2000 (ten times increase). Vacuum now completes ten times the amount of work before stopping. This is a change to try if your Autovacuum jobs are not cleaning up dead tuples at a fast enough rate. This parameter can be changed without restarting PostgreSQL, so you can experiment with different values to see the effect.

The corresponding autovacuum_vacuum_cost_limit for vacuum_cost_limit is for Autovacuum VACUUM jobs instead of manual ones.

You may also want to make global parameter changes. Try changing autovacuum_vacuum_cost_limit in your config file, which is a global change, then reloading the config file using pg_ctl reload (which assumes you've configured PGDATA. See Set PGDATA for pg_ctl, on page 406):

```
sh/postgresql_conf_parameter_change.sh
pg_ctl reload
server signaled
LOG:  received SIGHUP, reloading configuration files
LOG:  parameter "autovacuum_vacuum_cost_limit" changed to "2000"
```

Another parameter for versions earlier than 15 is autovacuum_vacuum_cost_delay. This parameter controls the length of time Autovacuum is paused. A lower value means Autovacuum is paused for shorter periods of time. In the table on page 207, the value is reduced from 20ms to 2ms. In PostgreSQL 15, the default value for this parameter became 2ms, so this parameter change isn't necessary on version 15 or newer.

The post, "Transaction ID Wraparound in Postgres,"[8] describes how that team lowered autovacuum_vacuum_cost_delay all the way to 0ms to get Vacuum to run more frequently.

---

7. https://postgresqlco.nf/doc/en/param/autovacuum_vacuum_cost_limit/
8. https://blog.sentry.io/2015/07/23/transaction-id-wraparound-in-postgres/

Parameter Name	Original Value	Tuned Value
autovacuum_vacuum_scale_factor	0.2	0.01
autovacuum_vacuum_cost_limit	200	2000
autovacuum_vacuum_cost_delay	20ms	2ms

Table 3—Autovacuum Database Parameters

You've now seen some ways to adjust Autovacuum so that it keeps up with your dead tuple accumulation rate.

In the next section, you'll move away from row versions and consider bloat in tables and indexes. How can that be addressed?

Rebuilding Indexes Without Downtime

Besides table data, indexes become bloated over time with entries to refer to dead tuples. To optimize your indexes, periodically rebuild the important ones.

Fortunately, PostgreSQL made it possible to rebuild indexes while they're being used concurrently, starting in version 12.

If you're on an earlier version of PostgreSQL, to get this functionality, the best bet is to upgrade to PostgreSQL 12 or newer. If upgrading is not an option, third-party tools like pg_repack[9] can be used to achieve similar results.

The post, "Using pg_repack to Rebuild Indexes,"[10] shows how to install and use it. This approach builds a replacement index in the background and then swaps the names between the original index and new index with a short exclusive lock.

In PostgreSQL 12, REINDEX gained support for the CONCURRENTLY option. This works similarly to how pg_repack does, but it's native to PostgreSQL. By being native, it continues to receive improvements in newer versions.

Let's try putting this into action. From psql, run the following command to reindex the index_trips_on_driver_id index. Use the VERBOSE option to show more information.

sql/reindex_concurrently_verbose.sql
```
REINDEX (VERBOSE) INDEX CONCURRENTLY index_trips_on_driver_id;
```

Providing a table name as an option to REINDEX performs a reindex for *all* indexes that are on the specified table. Try out the following example.

---

9. https://reorg.github.io/pg_repack/
10. https://andyatkinson.com/blog/2021/09/28/pg-repack

```
sql/reindex_table.sql
REINDEX (VERBOSE) TABLE CONCURRENTLY trips;
```

Great. You've now learned some basics with Autovacuum and how to tune it. You've seen how to manually rebuild indexes using native tools and third-party tools. Sometimes, you'll want to manually perform Vacuum operations. How do you do that?

Running Manual Vacuums

As you learned earlier, PostgreSQL stores data in pages that are 8 KB in size by default. The pages are not completely filled; space is left available to store new tuples from row modifications. Dead tuples take up space in those pages. PostgreSQL also considers unused free space part of what makes up bloat.[11]

When you want to make sure row visibility is updated and space from dead tuples is reclaimed, you can perform a manual VACUUM operation. Optionally, include the ANALYZE keyword to update table statistics at the same time. Try that out by running the following from psql:

```
sql/vacuum_table.sql
VACUUM (ANALYZE, VERBOSE) users;
```

New versions of PostgreSQL continue to add capabilities to Vacuum and Analyze. Version 11 added support for Vacuuming multiple tables at once. Version 12 added SKIP_LOCKED support, which skips locked tables (see "Postgres 12 Highlight—SKIP_LOCKED for VACUUM and ANALYZE"[12]).

Try out multiple tables and SKIP_LOCKED by running the following statement:

```
sql/vacuum_multiple_skip_locked.sql
VACUUM (SKIP_LOCKED) trip_requests, trips;
```

PostgreSQL tracks when Vacuum and Analyze are run, both when run from the automatic process and when they've been run manually.

The last_analyzed timestamp for users shows the time of the last manual vacuum and the last_auto_analyzed_at timestamp shows the last "automatic" analyze that was run from Autovacuum.

```
sql/last_analyzed_pg_stat_all_tables.sql
SELECT
  schemaname,
  relname,
```

---

11. https://www.postgresql.org/docs/current/glossary.html
12. https://paquier.xyz/postgresql-2/postgres-12-vacuum-skip-locked/

```
    last_autoanalyze,
    last_analyze
FROM pg_stat_all_tables
WHERE relname = 'vehicles';
```

Try running ANALYZE on the vehicles table listed in the previous query. Prior to running ANALYZE, the last_analyze timestamp may have been empty. After running ANALYZE vehicles; verify that last_analyze is now set.

What else is available related to Vacuum? Since PostgreSQL 13, parallel Vacuum workers can be configured (see "Parallel Vacuum in Upcoming PostgreSQL 13"[13]).

The default value for MAX_PARALLEL_MAINTENANCE_WORKERS is 2. Try increasing it to 4. Specify the PARALLEL option with a value of 4, and set the VERBOSE flag for more information. Up to four workers will be started.

sql/set_max_parallel_maintenance_workers.sql
```
SET MAX_PARALLEL_MAINTENANCE_WORKERS=4;

VACUUM (PARALLEL 4, VERBOSE) users;
```

We're exploring some of the ways to add more resources to maintenance operations. To learn more about the effects of bloat, it can be helpful to simulate it locally so that you have a test environment to use for learning.

How do we do that? Let's configure that in the next section.

Simulating Bloat and Understanding Impact

Since high estimated bloat levels aren't normal in local development or for new databases, we'll simulate high bloat locally so we can see the effect.

High bloat occurs for tables with a high amount of updates and deletes. Autovacuum can fall behind in processing the bloat. Check out the page "Bloat and Vacuum"[14] for a nice overview, and explore which of your application tables get the most updates. Find those tables using the query top_updated_tables.sql.[15]

Run the code/sql/insert_users_generate_series.sql SQL statement that you saw earlier, which creates a temp.users table with ten million rows. The fragment WITH (autovacuum_enabled = FALSE) is used to disable Autovacuum for the table.

After it's created, let's collect an estimate of the bloat percentage.

---

13. https://www.highgo.ca/2020/02/28/parallel-vacuum-in-upcoming-postgresql-13/
14. https://docs.crunchybridge.com/insights-metrics/bloat-and-vacuum#
15. https://github.com/andyatkinson/pg_scripts/blob/main/top_updated_tables.sql

Run the table_bloat.sql[16] script from psql, which can be found at https://github.com/ioguix/pgsql-bloat-estimation. Navigate to the SQL script, view the raw version, and copy and paste it into an editor. Add WHERE schemaname = 'temp' AND tblname = 'users' just before the ORDER BY to narrow down the results to the temp.users table you just made.

View the bloat_pct result row column, which shows an estimated bloat percentage. Since you haven't made many updates, this should start off as a low value, for example, less than 5 percent. This is mainly unused space left available in pages.

Next, simulate bloat by creating a lot of updates for temp.users. Run the following statement a few times, which creates up to one million updates, to increase the amount of dead tuples:

```
sql/bloat_simulate_user_updates.sql
UPDATE temp.users
SET first_name =
  CASE (seq % 2)
    WHEN 0 THEN 'Bill' || FLOOR(RANDOM() * 10)
    ELSE 'Jane' || FLOOR(RANDOM() * 10)
  END
FROM GENERATE_SERIES(1, 1_000_000) seq
WHERE id = seq;

-- Vacuum and Analyze the table
VACUUM (ANALYZE, VERBOSE) temp.users;
```

The statement has one update per row, matching id values up to one million. Each row gets a unique string that's either "Bill" or "Jane", based on id being even or odd.

After the update completes, check the bloat_pct column value. The estimated bloat percentage will start increasing.

The space used by the dead tuples can be marked for re-use by running the VACUUM command for the table. Remember that running VACUUM only (without FULL, discussed next) only marks the space available for re-use, but does *not* fully reclaim or free up the space.

To fully reclaim or free it up, we'd need to "rewrite" the table content behind the scenes. PostgreSQL provides the VACUUM FULL command to do that. This reclaims more space. Unfortunately, VACUUM FULL requires an exclusive table lock. The lock length is generally too long for this operation to be "online" if there's concurrent activity for the table.

---

16. https://github.com/ioguix/pgsql-bloat-estimation

With that said, you may be able to schedule a VACUUM FULL during a low activity period, or better yet, during a downtime window. Test how long it takes to run on a separate instance, although depending on how you create separate instances, you may not be able to fully retain the real bloat levels to test with. Otherwise, you'll be limited to maintenance operations that can be performed safely while "online."

What other options are there? The pg_repack tool you saw used for indexes can also be used to rebuild tables online (which includes the indexes). The post, "Using pg_repack to Rebuild PostgreSQL Database Objects Online,"[17] has examples. The post, "pg_squeeze—Shrinks Tables Better Than Vacuum,"[18] describes another tool called pg_squeeze that's an alternative way to rebuild (and shrink) tables.

You've now seen how to use the Vacuum, Analyze, and Reindex (VAR) commands to perform manual and automatic maintenance on your database. Regular maintenance helps keep performance optimal and predictable.

What other types of maintenance operations are available?

Removing Unused Indexes

As you've learned in earlier chapters, indexes are critical for query performance but should be added judiciously because they occupy space and add write latency. PostgreSQL tracks whether indexes are used in query plans, which you'll see for scan types like index scan or index-only scan.

The PostgreSQL Wiki has a dedicated page for "Index Maintenance"[19] that's worth reviewing. Equipped with scan information tracking, you're able to see which indexes were added but are *not* used (or were never used). Those are indexes you could remove to take up less space and reduce latency when indexed fields are modified.

Let's explore this further. Make sure tracking is enabled, which is the default. The following parameters should be set to on:

sql/show_track_activities.sql
```
SHOW track_activities;
SHOW track_counts;
```

---

17. https://www.percona.com/blog/pg_repack-rebuild-postgresql-database-objects-online
18. https://www.cybertec-postgresql.com/en/products/pg_squeeze
19. https://wiki.postgresql.org/wiki/Index_Maintenance

Besides write latency and space consumption, there are even more reasons to remove unused indexes.

- Unused indexes can prevent Heap Only Tuple updates, a higher performance update type that you'll want to aim for if possible.

- Unused indexes increase VACUUM run time.

- Unused indexes increase query planning time.

- Unused indexes slow down backup and restore operations.

What are *Heap Only Tuple* (HOT) updates?

HOT updates are a more efficient type of update only when updating non-indexed fields.[20]

Explore HOT updates further if you're looking to optimize your write performance, in particular, if your table is heavily updated for non-indexed fields. Besides scrutinizing the indexes on a table, you may also wish to lower the fillfactor to leave more space available for updates.[21]

Once you have run queries to find unused indexes, how can you safely remove them?

To safely add or drop indexes on a live system, use the CONCURRENTLY keyword.

If you're removing an index with an Active Record Migration, perform the index removal conditionally. This way, the statement only runs if the index is there. Review the following migration:

```ruby
ruby/remove_index_concurrently.rb
class RemoveIndexUsersEmail < ActiveRecord::Migration[7.1]
  disable_ddl_transaction!

  def change
    if index_exists?(:users, :email)
      remove_index(:users, :email, algorithm: :concurrently)
    end
  end
end
```

If the index name is different in production compared with your local database, use the name option in the migration.

Now that you've removed unused indexes, are there other types of index maintenance to perform?

---

20. https://www.postgresql.org/docs/current/storage-hot.html
21. https://www.cybertec-postgresql.com/en/what-is-fillfactor-and-how-does-it-affect-postgresql-performance/

Pruning Duplicate and Overlapping Indexes

The reason to remove an unused index is straightforward. What's less straightforward is when multiple indexes have overlap in their definitions. However, there are removal opportunities here, too, and removing them provides all the same benefits listed in the last section.

Let's get into specifics. Indexes cover one or more columns in their definition. As you've seen, the best index for queries might be a single-column or a multicolumn one. The column ordering is significant for queries. Then, we also have partial indexes! For these reasons, in a long-lived database, there can be plenty of overlap and redundant indexes on a table.

Further, PostgreSQL does not prevent you from creating straight-up duplicate indexes covering the exact same fields in the same order, as long as they have unique names. Besides well-meaning separate but redundant indexes, there can also be regular old mistakes where duplicate indexes are created with unique names but identical definitions.

Watch Out for Index Duplicates

 PostgreSQL does not prevent duplicate indexes

- Duplicate indexes cover the same fields and have different names. Remove one of them!

Let's look into this. Let's verify how PostgreSQL allows you to create an exact duplicate definition between two indexes by running the following statements:

```
sql/create_index_duplicates.sql
CREATE INDEX index_users_on_email2 ON temp.users (email);
CREATE INDEX index_users_on_email3 ON temp.users (email);
```

On a big table like temp.users, these indexes take up a lot of space and add write latency. One of them should be removed!

Indexes with column definitions that overlap might both have scans, but both indexes may not be strictly necessary.

Let's look at an example. One type of redundancy could be when a multicolumn and single-column index both have a column in common.

When a query filters on first_name, a multicolumn index covering first_name and last_name could be used. The single column and multicolumn index both have the same leading column of first_name. For a query on the first_name column, PostgreSQL can use any index that covers this column as the leading one.

You'll want to check for index scans on each of your indexes. You may need to reset counters. Use PgHero which detects and displays overlapping indexes. PgHero has a method, .duplicate_indexes(), that's used to compare covered columns and checks for overlaps.

PgHero also displays *duplicate indexes* with a message like "These indexes exist but aren't needed."

For example, a message like "users_first_name_idx (first_name) is covered by users_first_name_email_idx (first_name, email)" means that the single column index can be removed.

Since the multicolumn index has the same leading column "first_name" as the single column index, the single column index is redundant. Remove it, and remember to use the CONCURRENTLY keyword.

An Active Record Migration snippet is provided for you.

Great! You're now aware of redundant indexes that can be removed to avoid adding unnecessary write latency and space consumption to your system.

Let's focus on append-only tables next. Do they need indexes outside of indexes related to constraints?

Removing Indexes on Insert-Only Tables

For *append-only tables*, which are tables that only receive inserts but not updates or deletes, indexes may not be needed.

In Rideshare, trip_positions is this type of table, as it only receives inserts of new location points. Run the following query from psql to count DML operations for a table:

sql/check_table_dml_behavior.sql
```sql
-- Check number of inserts, updates, deletes
-- for `trip_positions` table
SELECT
  relname,
  n_tup_ins,
  n_tup_upd,
  n_tup_del
FROM pg_stat_user_tables
WHERE relname = 'trip_positions';
```

While PRIMARY KEY and UNIQUE constraints are needed for constraint enforcement, you may not need user-created indexes on append-only tables. If you do add indexes, make sure to track their scans.

For append-only tables, in past PostgreSQL versions, these tables were not Vacuumed. Since VACUUM didn't run, table statistics weren't updated, which could cause incorrect query planning estimates.

That oversight was fixed in PostgreSQL 13 which now updates statistics from Autovacuum even for append-only or insert-Only tables.[22] This change was mentioned in the "Row Estimates" episode of the Postgres.fm podcast.[23]

You've now seen how to perform maintenance jobs manually and learned how Autovacuum performs some maintenance based on thresholds. You even learned about index operations and index maintenance.

What if you wanted to schedule some manual maintenance operations beyond what Autovacuum schedules for you? How might you set that up?

Scheduling Jobs Using pg_cron

In this section, you'll use the pg_cron[24] extension to schedule jobs in your database. This extension has wide support on PostgreSQL hosting providers.

Since the owner user you normally work with is not a superuser, you'll connect to the rideshare_database as the superuser postgres to enable the extension. You'll also grant the USAGE privilege to the cron schema for the owner role so that the owner user can call functions from the extension. Owners can work with functions and objects within the rideshare_development database. Refer to the pg_cron section of db/README.md in Rideshare for the latest information.

Before diving into all of that, you'll need to set up pg_cron for macOS. While there is a Homebrew package for pg_cron, it's older, so you'll compile the latest version from source and make sure it's connected to your PostgreSQL installation. Refer to the appendix section pg_cron Installation, on page 405 for compilation instructions.

Once it's compiled, you'll need to complete more steps before using it:

- Add pg_cron to postgresql.conf as you've done earlier. Add it to the shared_preload_libraries. Refer to postgres.sample.conf in the postgresql directory of Rideshare for more information.

---

22. https://www.cybertec-postgresql.com/en/postgresql-autovacuum-insert-only-tables/
23. https://postgres.fm/episodes/row-estimates
24. https://github.com/citusdata/pg_cron

- Toward the bottom of postgresql.conf, specify cron.database_name = 'rideshare_development' so that the extension runs for that database.

- Restart PostgreSQL.

- Open psql as the postgres user, connect to rideshare_development, and run CREATE EXTENSION IF NOT EXISTS pg_cron;.

- Finally, run GRANT USAGE ON SCHEMA cron TO owner; while still connected as postgres.

With that permission granted, when owner connects to rideshare_development, that user should be able to call functions defined in the cron schema.

Let's try that out. Connect to the Rideshare database normally.

From there, let's schedule a job. To do that, you'll call the CRON.SCHEDULE() function provided by the extension.

You've decided to schedule a VACUUM (ANALYZE) job for the trips table in Rideshare. Let's have it run every ten minutes.[25] This kind of vacuuming shouldn't be needed in real applications, because Autovacuum should be leveraged per table to trigger it more frequently. However, this job is meant as a demonstration.

Run the following statement from psql:

```
sql/create_pg_cron_scheduled_job.sql
SELECT cron.schedule(
  'rideshare trips manual vacuum',
  '10 * * * *',
  'VACUUM (ANALYZE) rideshare.trips'
);
```

To view the job you've just scheduled, run:

```
sql/pg_cron_scheduled_job.sql
SELECT * FROM cron.job ORDER BY jobid;
```

Alright, now we wait ten minutes. Who are we kidding? We can't wait that long!

Let's alter the job to run *every minute*.[26] Get the job_id from the previous query, and supply it in the following one. For example, swap 1 with the job_id for your job.

---

25. https://crontab.guru/every-10-minutes
26. https://crontab.guru/every-1-minute

```
sql/pg_cron_alter_job_schedule.sql
-- Requires superuser
-- See: https://github.com/citusdata/pg_cron/\
--   issues/258#issuecomment-1852577347
--
-- psql -U postges -d rideshare_development
SELECT cron.alter_job(job_id:=1,schedule:='* * * * *');
```

At publication time, it wasn't possible for the job owner to alter a job they owned. To do that, use a workaround of altering the job id in a separate session while connected as the postgres superuser.[27]

Once altered using a superuser, after a minute has passed, you should then see job run details by querying cron.job_run_details (seeing only the jobs created by owner):

```
sql/pg_cron_job_run_details.sql
SELECT * FROM cron.job_run_details;
```

Besides cron.job_run_details, you'll also see activity in postgres.log:

```
sh/postgresql_log_pg_cron_jobs.sh
LOG:  cron job 6 starting: VACUUM (ANALYZE) rideshare.trips
```

Confirm the status is succeeded for job runs. Check the timestamps for manual ANALYZE and VACUUM jobs on trips with this query:

```
sql/last_vacuum_analyze_table.sql
SELECT schemaname, relname, last_analyze, last_vacuum
FROM pg_stat_all_tables
WHERE relname = 'trips';
```

Both should be set. This is great, but visibility for jobs and runs is limited to psql.

What if you'd like to expand the visibility of this information to more team members? Let's do that by extending the PgHero (see Introducing PgHero as a Performance Dashboard, on page 149) tool you worked with earlier.

The following PR adds a new Scheduled Jobs[28] screen to PgHero. This screen provides visibility into scheduled jobs and jobs that have run for any user that's accessing PgHero. This PR also serves as a demonstration of how you might use your Ruby programming skills to extend open source tools like PgHero further.

---

27. https://github.com/citusdata/pg_cron/issues/258#issuecomment-1852577347

28. https://github.com/andyatkinson/pghero/pull/3

Customize Open Source Tools Like PgHero

The beauty of open-source tools like PgHero is that they can be customized for your needs.

Does your team have a PgHero fork with interesting additions?

In this section, you've scheduled VACUUM (ANALYZE) jobs to run using pg_cron. You're able to monitor the progress within PostgreSQL, from the log file or from PgHero.

You've now applied a variety of maintenance techniques following the VAR acronym to help you remember Vacuum, Analyze, and Reindex operations.

In the next section, you'll explore maintenance tools that you could add to your development process.

Conducting Maintenance Tune-Ups

In earlier chapters, you saw active_record_doctor[29] and database_consistency[30] Ruby gems. These gems can be used to assist you in performing database maintenance. DatabaseConsistency has "Checkers" including a "RedundantIndexChecker" that can find redundant indexes.

The rails-pg-extras[31] gem can be used to find maintenance tasks. This gem checks for duplicate indexes, unused indexes, and bloat.

The gem also looks for null indexes, which are indexes that have a high proportion of NULL values. Null indexes could possibly be replaced by partial indexes that exclude NULL values. PostgreSQL 13 introduced index deduplication[32] that helps remove nulls from indexes.

Set up monitoring of key maintenance operations, like when Autovacuum runs, tables where it has not run, and parameter values, especially for heavily updated tables. Add resources to Autovacuum for heavily updated tables. Use the VAR acronym to remember the key maintenance operations. These operations ensure rows are visible, table stats are updated, and indexes have an acceptable amount of bloat.

With the techniques you learned in this chapter, you now have tools and tactics to help maintain optimal performance for your databases. Remember

---

29. https://github.com/gregnavis/active_record_doctor
30. https://github.com/djezzzl/database_consistency
31. https://github.com/pawurb/rails-pg-extras
32. https://www.cybertec-postgresql.com/en/b-tree-index-deduplication/

that these maintenance operations are up to you to perform. While they may not be directly related to performance, before working on performance optimizations, make sure tables and indexes are well maintained. Remember the VAR acronym.

As your application traffic scales up, reaching higher levels of concurrency, you'll face new operational challenges. In the next chapter, you'll dive into some of the challenges faced at high levels of concurrent activity. Read on to learn more.

## CHAPTER 10

Reaching Greater Concurrency

Imagine that the number of concurrent clients for your PostgreSQL instances has increased. Your platform is successful. While PostgreSQL works well without any tuning or auxiliary software, despite being generic and tuned for smaller hardware, at great levels of concurrency you'll likely run into some common issues.

As query volume increases, it's critical that queries run quickly and minimize their resource consumption.

Database connections are one of the limited server resources to safeguard. Connections are used each time the client application connects to PostgreSQL to run a SQL statement or command. You'll learn more about connections and learn how to use them more efficiently. The maximum number of concurrent client connections your server can handle will depend on the system resources available. If your client traffic exceeds the available resources, you'll need a way to continue to serve requests. How can you do that?

To achieve greater levels of concurrency, you'll add and configure auxiliary software to help support PostgreSQL. With your growing stack of tools, you'll be able to grow the capabilities of your platform and reach higher levels of scale.

Even if you aren't currently facing scaling-related issues, by developing awareness in advance, you'll identify scenarios where there's a possible benefit and be able to practice techniques using Rideshare and the performance database to cultivate your skills.

Let's explore some terminology you'll use in this chapter:

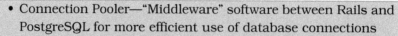

Concurrency Terminology

- Connection Pooler—"Middleware" software between Rails and PostgreSQL for more efficient use of database connections

- Client connections—For connection poolers, the connections between the Active Record client app and the pooler

- Server connections—The connections between the Pooler and PostgreSQL

- Timeouts—Configurable thresholds to control behavior when errors happen, to improve overall availability

You've started to explore database connections. What are they exactly?

Monitoring Database Connections

Your Ruby on Rails application is a client application that connects to PostgreSQL, sending TCP requests over the IP network (TCP/IP).[1]

psql is the command-line client application you've been using so far. pg_repack and pg_dump are other client programs. When these programs connect to PostgreSQL, they all require a database connection to connect. This is an object that's created on PostgreSQL and is observable. When you connect from Rideshare or when you connect to your database from your Rails application, you're using a database connection.

The total number of concurrent connections possible is limited by your server resources. Connections create new back-end processes, and the connection establishment process adds latency to your requests due to these factors:

- Negotiating SSL/TLS[2]
- Authentication

For OLTP transactions in high volume with short durations, we're eager to remove any latency possible from our database requests to improve the overall scalability of our instance.

What does the flow look like for a successful client server round trip from Active Record to PostgreSQL? Let's take a high-level spin through how this works.

---

1. https://www.postgresql.org/docs/current/runtime-config-connection.html#RUNTIME-CONFIG-TCP-SETTINGS
2. https://www.postgresql.org/docs/current/ssl-tcp.html

1. First, Active Record Ruby code generates a SQL query.

2. The postgresql adapter[3] ensures the SQL query text is compatible.

3. The pg[4] gem is used as a client interface from Ruby to PostgreSQL.

4. Active Record uses a Connection Pool,[5] which manages database connections to the server. They're opened and reused as new queries are sent and responses are received to minimize the startup costs of new connections. Settings are in config/database.yml.

5. With a connection from the pool, queries are sent from the client to the server.

6. PostgreSQL computes a result and sends it back to the client using the same connection. The connection on the server is left open, but idle.

An important note is that the Active Record client is responsible for closing the connection. If the connection is not closed, it will be left in an idle state until the idle_timeout is reached, when one's set. When one isn't set, idle connections are left around forever and cause problems.

Why keep idle connections around at all? Idle connections are kept around for new queries so that they can use an existing established connection and not pay the latency cost for every query. On the other hand, too many idle connections use up the limited number of connections that are available. We don't want a database running with a lot of opened but idle connections.

Idle Connections Goldilocks

 Just like Goldilocks, we want a number of idle database connections that's "just right." Not too many, not too few.

An idle connection can be performing work in a transaction, or it can be idle and not performing any work.

Most of the time, connections will be idle or active. You may also see connections in the idle in transaction[6] state. This state means a transaction was opened with BEGIN, but is not completing any work. These types of connections are errors and should be terminated. We'll see how to automate that later on.

---

3. https://guides.rubyonrails.org/configuring.html#configuring-a-database

4. https://github.com/ged/ruby-pg

5. https://api.rubyonrails.org/classes/ActiveRecord/ConnectionAdapters/ConnectionPool.html

6. https://www.postgresql.org/docs/current/monitoring-ps.html

Take a look at the following Active Record connection pool configuration and some of the settings values. The pool value is configured as pool: 5, which means up to five connections can be created. The idle_timeout value is the maximum allowed time a connection can be idle before it's canceled. The checkout_timeout is the maximum amount of time Active Record will wait to check out a connection before giving up.

```yml
yml/active_record_connection_pool.yml
default: &default
  adapter: postgresql
  pool: 5
  idle_timeout: 300s
  checkout_timeout: 5s
```

You've now seen what the flow looks like from Active Record sending queries and statements to PostgreSQL using database connections. You've seen a bit about how to configure the connection pool at the application level.

As these things are happening in your database, how can you peek inside and see what's going on?

Exploring Current Activity

To explore current activity, query the pg_stat_activity system view that you saw earlier (see *Getting Started with Observability*). Besides client queries in pg_stat_activity, you'll see your own current connection and any other running PostgreSQL background processes.

Filter on the application_name. Rails uses /bin/rails and a backend_type of client backend. Let's explore some real activity.

To do that, let's simulate application activity using Rideshare scripts, which will act as current activity using database connections. You'll start up the rails server and run a script that sends HTTP requests to the API.

Run each of the following commands from different terminal windows in the Rideshare directory:

```
bin/rails server
```

```
bin/rails simulate:app_activity
```

If you'd like to run the simulate:app_activity for a longer period of time since it can be run over and over, pass a higher value as an iteration count. For example you could pass ten or twenty or more to get the script to run for a longer period.

Run the following command to have it run ten times.

```
bin/rails simulate:app_activity[10]
```

In another terminal, load up psql. The following command uses \watch, which continuously runs the query, polling every two seconds by default until you stop it with Ctrl-c.

```
sql/list_connections_and_queries.sql
-- Use \watch to continually monitor results
SELECT
  pid,
  datname,
  usename,
  application_name,
  client_hostname,
  client_port,
  backend_start,
  query_start,
  query,
  state
FROM pg_stat_activity
WHERE pid != PG_BACKEND_PID()   -- exclude this query
AND datname = 'rideshare_development' -- specify app DB
AND state IS NOT NULL\watch
```

With the app activity simulation script running and continuously querying the pg_stat_activity system catalog, you're seeing a rudimentary live monitoring peek into your system as queries are running. You may not really see the connections get out of the idle state because the queries execute quickly, and in less than the two-second polling interval.

What are some of the fields we're seeing in this view? The documentation page "Monitoring Stats"[7] describes backend_start. This is set when the backend process was started. query_start is set on query start within the backend process. During the live simulation, you should see query_start changing values as queries run using the connection and backend process.

When the query is executing, the state is active. When the query is no longer executing, a state_change timestamp is recorded. For example, a connection that changes from active to idle gets a state_change set.

That completes our basic simulation of live activity.

Earlier, you learned that too many idle connections are bad. How can you avoid having too many of them?

---

7.   https://www.postgresql.org/docs/current/monitoring-stats.html

Managing Idle Connections

Let's explore a couple of ways to add upper bounds on idle connections.

The idle_timeout is an Active Record connection pool parameter you can set. By default it's 300 seconds (five minutes).

Besides this application (client) side parameter, Version 14 of PostgreSQL allows you to limit idle connections on the server using the idle_session_timeout parameter:[8]

> Terminate any session that has been idle (that is, waiting for a client query), but not within an open transaction, for longer than the specified amount of time.

When a statement exceeds the idle_session_timeout value, it's terminated. The benefit of terminating these types of statements is they don't tie up one of the limited database connections. You saw how to manually terminate connections using the pid value earlier in section *Getting Started with Observability.*

To automate the process of canceling those queries, set a value for idle_session_timeout for your system. The post, "Waiting for PostgreSQL 14—Add idle_session_timeout,"[9] shows different values and the effect.

When the timeout is exceeded, the query text is logged in postgresql.log, and the connection is terminated with the error FATAL: terminating connection due to idle-session timeout. In the second example, despite exceeding the idle_session_timeout, an open transaction (BEGIN) left in an idle state was not terminated. You'll see how to handle the open-transaction-but-idle scenario later on.

In the post, "How to Monitor PostgreSQL Connections," which you saw earlier, you learned that clients are responsible for closing connections.[10]

> It is worth mentioning that if the connection is not explicitly closed by the application, it will remain available, thereby consuming resources—even when the client has disconnected.

Thus, it's important to set these timeout parameters to avoid resources being consumed by idle transactions.

What else can you configure within Active Record?

---

8. https://postgresqlco.nf/doc/en/param/idle_session_timeout/
9. https://www.depesz.com/2021/01/12/waiting-for-postgresql-14-add-idle_session_timeout/
10. https://www.enterprisedb.com/postgres-tutorials/how-monitor-postgresql-connections

Setting Active Record Pool Size

The pool size should be set with care to not exceed the maximum number of connections PostgreSQL can handle. The max_connections on the server should reflect a safe maximum possible value. Active Record uses up to the pool size of connections, so fewer may be in use at any given time, and fewer should be used when activity is low.

The post, "Concurrency and Database Connections in Ruby with Active-Record,"[11] shows how to use an environment variable to control the value for pool, making it easier to change on the fly.

The post, "Finding and Killing Long Running Queries on PostgreSQL,"[12] shows how to find queries that started more than five minutes ago. Ignore the rows where state is idle. View the duration column to see how long they've been running.

Try running the following query from psql for your database:

```
sql/long_running_queries_duration.sql
SELECT
  pid,
  NOW() - pg_stat_activity.query_start AS duration,
  query,
  state
FROM pg_stat_activity
WHERE (
  NOW() - pg_stat_activity.query_start
) > INTERVAL '5 minutes'
AND state != 'idle';
```

For a query you'd like to terminate, find the pid from the previous results, and terminate the query using the system administration functions you saw in section Getting Started with Observability, on page 32.

Although you can manage these one by one, you'll want to use the available timeout parameters to automatically cancel queries that won't ever finish or won't finish in a reasonable amount of time. This will help you avoid problematic scenarios like running out of database connections when they're all tied up but idle.

What happens when database connections are used up?

---

11. https://devcenter.heroku.com/articles/concurrency-and-database-connections
12. https://medium.com/little-programming-joys/finding-and-killing-long-running-queries-on-postgres-7c4f0449e86d

Running Out of Connections

When all of the database connections are in use, PostgreSQL is not able to serve more requests. This is a severe problem that you'll want to avoid. What sorts of processes can use up connections?

Ruby on Rails applications that scale horizontally run more server processes. For multithreaded servers like Puma,[13] threads open database connections to perform work. Background job processing frameworks like Sidekiq[14] are commonly deployed next to Rails applications.

Puma and Sidekiq processes each have multiple execution threads, and each thread uses a connection.

When scaling up processes, carefully monitor the number of active client connections being opened to avoid exceeding the maximum allowed number. If that were to happen, you'd start seeing errors like FATAL: sorry, too many clients already.

The parameter max_connections[15] can be set to specify an upper bound. Changing this value requires a restart.

The default value PostgreSQL starts with, 100, is considered a low value for modern instances. You may wish to raise this to a higher value like 500. That might work, but explore alternatives such as more efficient use of your connections. Sizing database connections for instances is outside the scope of this section, but try using PGTune (https://pgtune.leopard.in.ua/) as a starting point for a good value.

Connection exhaustion is a severe problem that we want to avoid. Let's simulate it so we can see what happens.

Try changing the max_connections parameter for PostgreSQL, and then we'll deliberately use up all the connections. You'll run through these steps:

- Set max_connections to a low value of three.

- Open three psql clients to the server; each opens a connection and runs a long query.

- Open a fourth connection and verify that no new client connections are allowed.

---

13. https://github.com/puma/puma
14. https://github.com/mperham/sidekiq
15. https://postgresqlco.nf/doc/en/param/max_connections/

To start, run this statement in psql:

sql/show_max_connections.sql
```
-- default: 100
SHOW max_connections;
```

Let's lower the max_connections. Edit postgresql.conf and set the max_connections value to three. Besides that, edit the value of superuser_reserved_connections to be one less than the value of max_connections, which means it should be two. This is a requirement from PostgreSQL for this exercise. The commands are listed as follows. This assumes you've set PGDATA earlier (see *Set PGDATA for pg_ctl*).

sh/postgresql_conf_edit_max_connections.sh
```
# use `vim` or another text editor
vim /path/to/postgresql.conf

# set to low value
max_connections = 3
superuser_reserved_connections = 2

# restart PostgreSQL, required when changing `max_connections`
# Assumes you've set PGDATA earlier
pg_ctl restart
```

After lowering max_connections to three, when the fourth connection is opened, you should see an error. To simulate this, create a script exhaust_database_connection.sh like the following and run it from your terminal:

sh/exhaust_database_connections.sh
```
#!/bin/bash

#
# max_connections was set to `3`
#
query="SELECT PG_SLEEP(30)"

for number in {1..4}; do
  echo "Running query=${query} Number=${run}"
  psql $DATABASE_URL \
    -c "$query" & # separate processes
done
```

The fourth query should fail to run or even connect. No connections are available.

sh/exhaust_database_connections_output.sh
```
running query SELECT pg_sleep(30). times: 1
running query SELECT pg_sleep(30). times: 2
running query SELECT pg_sleep(30). times: 3
running query SELECT pg_sleep(30). times: 4
psql: error: connection to server on socket "/tmp/.s.PGSQL.5432" failed \
 FATAL:  sorry, too many clients already
```

Now that you have an idea of how this plays out, how can you prevent it from happening? You've got a few options.

- By scaling your server instance vertically, you'll be able to serve greater numbers of concurrent connections by raising your max_connections value (will require your own verification testing).

- Unrelated to max_connections, explore your idle connections and look for ways to reduce them. Your application may keep a large amount of idle connections open. Use a client side timeout value to set a max allowed time (idle_timeout) or consider lowering it.

- To close idle connections on the server (instead of the client), use a timeout like idle_session_timeout in PostgreSQL, setting a max allowed time.

Imagine that you'd like to investigate your idle connections to see whether they are legitimate.

To do that, run the following queries. Queries in an idle in transaction state that have been around for a while are bad because they're not performing work. They should probably be canceled.

sql/idle_transactions.sql
```
-- e.g.
-- count,state
-- 7,active
-- 3510,idle
SELECT COUNT(*), state
FROM pg_stat_activity
GROUP BY 2;

---https://dba.stackexchange.com/a/39758
SELECT * FROM pg_stat_activity
WHERE (state = 'idle in transaction');
```

As you study your server capacity, it will be helpful to think through which pieces of your stack use database connections. Here are some questions to consider:

- How many Ruby on Rails application instances are running (their process count)? How many threads are configured per process? Each thread may open a database connection.

- What is the connection pool size per process? Multiply the number of processes by the configured pool size.

- How many Sidekiq processes are running? How many threads per process? Sum the total number of threads to get an idea of the total possible concurrency.

Compare your theoretical maximum figure with how you configured max_connections earlier. Leave some headroom by leaving some connections available for administrative work like psql sessions or for other PostgreSQL clients.

You may not be able to scale vertically, or it may be cost-prohibitive.

When that's the case, is there anything else you can do to scale your capacity for greater numbers of concurrent clients?

Working with PgBouncer

The Active Record connection pool helps you efficiently manage connections and is built-in to Ruby on Rails. By default, you're using it, and it's very helpful. However, connections that are made directly between the application and the database server do have an upper bound. Even before hitting the upper bound, performance may degrade severely.

When you need to add more capacity, how can you do that? Don't worry, you've got options.

Dedicated connection pooling software exists to help you do that. This is extra software you can add to your stack. While a connection pooler brings additional operational complexity, it offers several benefits.

One of the biggest benefits is being able to expand beyond the physical limit of database connections that your instance could otherwise accommodate. Connection poolers can also more efficiently re-use physical connections by sitting in between your Ruby on Rails application instances and PostgreSQL.

In this section, you'll configure the open source connection pooler PgBouncer[16] to get familiar with connection pooling in general. You'll install and configure PgBouncer, placing it between Ruby on Rails and PostgreSQL.

Let's explore the benefits PgBouncer offers:

- Your client connections may now exceed the configured max_connections value.

- Connections can be held open, even if the database server is temporarily unavailable. Processing is delayed but not refused.

- A connection pooler re-uses connections more efficiently and offers various pool_modes with different trade-offs.

- Besides performance, connection poolers can help with maintenance and upgrades, by holding connections open during cutovers.

---

16. https://github.com/pgbouncer/pgbouncer

Let's install and configure PgBouncer on macOS. Install it with Homebrew[17] by running the following command:

```
sh/pgbouncer_install.sh
brew install pgbouncer
```

Run pgbouncer --version to verify the version is 1.21.0 or greater. This version added significant features, which we'll explore later. After PgBouncer is installed, you can manage it by using brew services. Run the following commands to inspect the pgbouncer process or restart it.

```
sh/pgbouncer_commands.sh
brew services info pgbouncer
brew services restart pgbouncer
```

PgBouncer runs on port 6432, which is exactly 1000 higher than the default PostgreSQL port 5432. A little nugget for your next PostgreSQL trivia night!

Use the owner user you set up with Rideshare earlier to connect. Add the following admin_users = owner section to make owner an admin user. Edit the .ini configuration file in your text editor. Find the file path by running brew info pgbouncer.

As always, consider backing up your file in version control so that you can roll back if needed. Rideshare also has a sample pgbouncer.sample.ini file in the postgresql directory. Open /usr/local/etc/pgbouncer.ini (verify your path) in your editor and make the following changes:

```
sh/pgbouncer_ini_config.sh
[databases]
rideshare_development = host=127.0.0.1 port=5432 dbname=rideshare_development

[pgbouncer]
 listen_port = 6432
 listen_addr = localhost
 auth_type = md5
 auth_file = /usr/local/etc/userlist.txt
 logfile = pgbouncer.log
 pidfile = pgbouncer.pid
 admin_users = owner
```

Since you're working locally, restart PgBouncer by running brew services restart pgbouncer. In production environments where you want an "online" restart, follow the guidance on PgBouncer usage,[18] which describes how to run multiple processes on the same port. Securely configuring PgBouncer installation is outside the scope of this section. Here, you're only running it locally.

---

17. https://brew.sh
18. https://www.pgbouncer.org/usage.html

With PgBouncer configured, you're ready to connect to the Rideshare database through it.

To do that, connect with psql like you normally have been doing except use port 6432, where PgBouncer runs. Use the same owner user to connect. Add another entry to ~/.pgpass for owner using the same password, but specify port 6432 (see .pgpass.sample in postgresql directory of Rideshare for an example).

```
sh/pgbouncer_psql_connection_string.sh
# Get the password for `owner` from ~/.pgpass
psql -U owner -d rideshare_development -p 6432
```

You should now be connected to the rideshare_development database, but you're connected through PgBouncer. Pretty cool!

PgBouncer acts transparently as a proxy. Explore PgBouncer a bit by running some commands. PgBouncer has its own set of commands that are different from psql.

To do that, disconnect from the Rideshare database, then connect to a special pgbouncer database using psql as follows:

```
sh/pgbouncer_connect_explore.sh
# Connect to pgbouncer database
psql -p 6432 -U owner pgbouncer

# Explore all commands
SHOW HELP;

# Try some commands
SHOW DATABASES;
SHOW CLIENTS;
```

If you run SHOW DATABASES;, one of the columns you'll see is pool_mode. What does that mean?

Choosing Your PgBouncer Pooling Mode

PgBouncer supports various "pool modes." The pool mode specifies how a server connection may be re-used by clients.

Pool modes are listed as follows, ordered from the most aggressive level to the most conservative level. A more aggressive pool mode re-uses connections earlier, potentially achieving higher levels of concurrency at the cost of reduced compatibility with client side features.

Features like advisory locks are not compatible with all pool modes. You're limited to session mode. Prepared statements were not compatible with PgBouncer until being added in version 1.21.0, a highly anticipated addition.

Prior to that version, when using Ruby on Rails, prepared statements were often disabled due to their incompatibility with PgBouncer. The default session pooling mode could be used, but that mode doesn't offer the connection reuse benefits the other modes offer. Pooling modes were discussed on the "Connection Poolers"[19] episode of Postgres.fm.

PgBouncer and Prepared Statements

- With version 1.21.0, statement and transaction pooling modes can now be used with prepared statements. Since prepared statements are enabled by default in Active Record, and since they can offer a performance advantage, this was a great addition!

The following pool mode descriptions are from PgBouncer documentation.

Mode	Description
session	The default mode. Server is released back to the pool when the client disconnects.
transaction	Server is released back to the pool when the transaction finishes.
statement	Server is released back to the pool when the query finishes. Transactions spanning multiple statements are disallowed in this mode.

Table 4—Pool Modes

Let's try out the transaction pool mode. Open up the configuration file again that you edited earlier. Add pool_mode=transaction to the [database] configuration and restart PgBouncer.

Use the max_prepared_statements[20] parameter in PgBouncer to set a maximum amount of prepared statements that are kept.

After enabling prepared statements with Rideshare (other incompatible features like query logs must be disabled), change the DATABASE_URL environment variable so it specifies the PgBouncer port 6432 instead of the PostgreSQL port 5432. This way, new Rails console sessions or the Rails server will use PgBouncer as a proxy for connections to PostgreSQL. Start up the Rails server and run the app activity simulation script from earlier:

---

19. https://postgres.fm/episodes/connection-poolers
20. https://www.pgbouncer.org/config.html

sh/pgbouncer_pool_mode_statement_prepared_statements.sh
```bash
#!/bin/bash
#
# Disable Query Logs if they're enabled
#
# Configure DATABASE_URL with password
# (can't read from ~/.pgpass), set port 6432
#
# Overwrite DATABASE_URL to use PgBouncer port
conn="postgres://owner:"
conn+="@localhost:6432/rideshare_development"
export DATABASE_URL="${conn}"

# Confirm prepared statements are initially empty
echo "List Prepared Statements results (empty to start):"
bin/rails runner "puts ActiveRecord::Base.connection.
  execute('SELECT * FROM pg_prepared_statements').values"

echo "Run a query to populate prepared statements:"
bin/rails runner "Trip.first"

# Check again
echo "List Prepared Statements results again:"
bin/rails runner "puts ActiveRecord::Base.connection.
  execute('SELECT * FROM pg_prepared_statements').values"
```

You've now installed and configured the PgBouncer connection pooler, enabling the transaction pool_mode. Restart PgBouncer if needed and run the previous script to observe how prepared statements are populated and stored. They can then be queried from Active Record. When you're done testing with PgBouncer, set DATABASE_URL back to the original value (which connects using port 5432).

With PgBouncer, you've now got a more efficient way to re-use database connections for Rideshare. With it, you're able to scale your concurrent activity beyond what would otherwise be possible. With prepared statements support, you may even see improved performance due to reduced CPU when parsing statements.

You've now seen some basics on how to scale your connections using a connection pooler like PgBouncer. Before putting this into production, you will want to perform testing with your Rails application to identify any incompatibilities with client or statement features. Check out the post, "PgBouncer is Useful, Important, and Fraught with Peril"[21] for a deeper dive on feature incompatibilities with PgBouncer. In fact, there are a lot of incompatibilities to be aware of.

---

21. https://jpcamara.com/2023/04/12/pgbouncer-is-useful.html

In transaction pooling mode, the post describes how operations like creating indexes concurrently happen outside of a transaction. The session pooling mode has wide compatibility, but both transaction and statement modes have less compatibility with advanced PostgreSQL features. If your application uses any of those incompatible features, you'll need to change to session pooling mode in order to use PgBouncer.

Besides PgBouncer, another open source connection pooler is PgCat, which is gaining popularity. Explore "PgCat: Nextgen PostgreSQL Pooler"[22] and the PostgreSQL wiki "Replication, Clustering, and Connection Pooling."[23]

With connection pooling covered, let's switch gears to how you might add more resiliency to your system.

At greater levels of concurrency, your queries may begin to have more errors. How do you add resiliency to your system to balance high query volume while minimizing errors?

Identifying Connection Errors and Problems

In this section, you'll use psql to analyze connections. Connections may be viewed in PgHero.[24]

Besides exhausting connections, you may run into other types of connection-related errors:

- "Transaction ID wraparound"
- Runaway or "zombie" queries that never finish

To minimize the effects of those errors, you'll add the following safeguards:

- A statement_timeout that sets a max allowed amount of time for statements to run

- A lock_timeout that sets a max allowed time a statement can wait to acquire a lock

- A idle_in_transaction_session_timeout[25] that sets a max allowed time for idle connections that have started a transaction, but have not committed, to run for before they're canceled

---

22. https://github.com/postgresml/pgcat
23. https://wiki.postgresql.org/wiki/Replication,_Clustering,_and_Connection_Pooling
24. https://github.com/ankane/pghero
25. https://www.postgresql.org/docs/current/runtime-config-client.html

These are all parameters that are probably unset in your system (if you aren't familiar with them already). You'll want to start out with good conservative values ("coarse-grained" values to start) and fine-tune the values by lowering them. The parameters are listed here, along with recommended tuned values (in milliseconds):

Parameter Name	Default	Tuned Value	Restart
idle_session_timeout (14+)	0	30000	false
idle_in_transaction_session_timeout	0	3000	false
statement_timeout	0	10000	false
lock_timeout	0	3000	false

Table 5—Database Concurrency Parameters

When considering idle_session_timeout[26] and idle_in_transaction_session_timeout, start by adjusting the second one. Hopefully, idle sessions in a transaction that hasn't finished are less common. Canceling them would be less disruptive compared with all types of idle sessions.

The recommended parameter values are based on the posts, "GOTO Postgres Configuration for RDS and Self-managed Postgres,"[27] and "My GOTO Postgres Configuration for Web Services,"[28] which are both great resources.

Gradually introduce changes, familiarizing yourself with the trade-offs. You will likely trade off more errors for improved resiliency. Start with higher values and observe the effects with logs or other tools. Try and keep the changes in version control and use *infrastructure as code* (IAC) systems so that they can be applied consistently across your PostgreSQL instances.

In this section, you looked at statement timeouts and lock timeouts. In the next section, you'll go into greater depth with safeguards related to locks.

More Lock Monitoring with pg_locks

In earlier chapters, you saw the basics of how the Autovacuum scheduler system works, scheduling workers to clean up tables. When Autovacuum runs a worker on a table, it uses a SHARE UPDATE EXCLUSIVE lock mode. This lock type is both an "exclusive" lock and a "shared" lock. How does that work?

Access for reads of the table is shared, while access for writes (like updates) is exclusive.

---

26. https://postgresqlco.nf/doc/en/param/idle_session_timeout/
27. https://tightlycoupled.io/goto-postgres-configuration-for-rds-and-self-managed-postgres/
28. https://tightlycoupled.io/my-goto-postgres-configuration-for-web-services/

In earlier chapters, you looked at how DDL operations use table locks. They are in effect while the change is made. In this section, you'll explore row-level locks from DML operations.

When an UPDATE occurs to a row, the row is locked during the update, taking a RowExclusiveLock.[29] This blocks other updates. However, concurrent reads of the row are possible. For further details, refer to https://pglocks.org, which breaks down all operations and their lock types.

SELECT...FOR UPDATE adds additional protection when selecting rows to be updated (see "Selecting for Share and Update in PostgreSQL"[30]). This statement acquires a ROW SHARE LOCK lock mode.

Taking an exclusive lock on rows means that even reads, like other SELECT statements, are blocked. This is the most restrictive and potentially harmful lock type. Concurrent readers or modification statements will be in a waiting state for the SELECT...FOR UPDATE transaction to COMMIT or ROLLBACK and be blocked until that happens.

How can you prevent excessive waiting (or "queueing") when conflicting statements are trying to acquire a lock that's in use? Earlier, you saw the lock_timeout parameter, which can be used to set a max allowed time for a statement to wait.

Another technique is to use the NOWAIT keyword, added to SELECT...FOR UPDATE statements. With this keyword, the statement won't wait if it can't acquire the lock immediately.[31]

FOR UPDATE is categorized as an "explicit" lock type, similar to how you might use the LOCK command to create an explicit lock on a resource. Here, you're explicitly locking the rows as the resource.

When using explicit locking, how can you monitor that locks being acquired don't block other queries?

Monitoring Row Locks

For general query logging from errors, try setting the log_min_error_statement[32] parameter. This logs queries to the postgresql.log file when they're blocked. Another more targeted option is the log_lock_waits parameter, which you'll see in an upcoming section.

---

29. https://pglocks.org/?pglock=RowExclusiveLock
30. https://shiroyasha.io/selecting-for-share-and-update-in-postgresql.html
31. https://www.postgresql.org/docs/current/sql-lock.html
32. https://www.postgresql.org/docs/current/runtime-config-logging.html

One gotcha to be aware of is mentioned in the post "Selecting for Share and Update in PostgreSQL."[33] When using SELECT...FOR UPDATE, referenced tables from foreign key columns will also be locked from SELECT...FOR UPDATE. This behavior is necessary to maintain referential integrity.

When that's too onerous, a weaker type of lock is SELECT...FOR SHARE. This lock type creates a shared lock on the rows being selected. A shared lock allows concurrent reads for the same rows.

A shared lock still prevents updates and deletes of the row, but as a weaker lock type, it provides greater read concurrency.

For a query running repeatedly, the SKIP LOCKED capability may be helpful. When the goal is to eventually process all rows, but locked rows can be skipped for later processing, this could be a good fit.

SKIP LOCKED is mentioned as being useful for a background processing or queueing system within PostgreSQL.

You've now seen various ways to create explicit locks, row-level locks, or temporarily skip processing for rows that are locked.

Imagine that you're currently facing some lock-related issues. Where would you start to debug those issues?

Finding Lock Conflicts

The Citus Data post, "PostgreSQL Rocks, Except When It Blocks: Understanding Locks,"[34] describes SQL operations and their lock types and conflicts.

For example, a SELECT never conflicts with a SELECT, so there is a green checkmark in the table cell indicating that these two operations don't conflict.

A SELECT will conflict with an ALTER TABLE since the ALTER TABLE requires an exclusive lock (which is hopefully brief).

Next, look at conflicts from CREATE INDEX. Scan the CREATE INDEX column, identifying SQL statements that conflict. Any DML operation will conflict with CREATE INDEX. For this reason, it's important to always use the CONCURRENTLY keyword when creating indexes on live systems so that other read and write operations can run at the same time.

How else can you analyze lock behavior?

---

33. https://shiroyasha.io/selecting-for-share-and-update-in-postgresql.html
34. https://www.citusdata.com/blog/2018/02/15/when-postgresql-blocks/

Using PgBadger for Lock Analysis

The PgBadger[35] log analysis tool you saw earlier can be used for lock analysis. As a refresher, make sure it's installed by running brew install pgbadger.

Call the pgbadger executable, passing in a single value that's the path to your postgresql.log file. The shape looks like this:

```
sh/pgbadger_log_analysis.sh
pgbadger /path/to/postgresql.log
```

PgBadger produces an HTML file named out.html by default. After processing the log file with PgBadger, open out.html in your browser to view it. Run man pgbadger to review the large list of optional arguments.

PgBadger Log-Processing Automation

 Check out the PgBadger automation script that finds your log file, processes it, and opens the output file in the repository, https://github.com/andyatkinson/pg_scripts, within the administration directory.

In your browser, navigate to the "Locks" tab to explore lock-related information processed from the log file.

If you're not getting statements logged, you'll want to set or lower the value for log_lock_waits[36] so that statements waiting on lock acquisition get logged.

If you're using SELECT...FOR UPDATE, consider checking whether any queries are being blocked by that operation.

In the next section, you'll explore a different type of lock, which is a client-side lock type you can use with Active Record. Read on to learn more.

Active Record Optimistic Locking

Locks are acquired either "optimistically" or "pessimistically." Pessimistic locking is what PostgreSQL uses most of the time in the default transaction isolation level (which is *read committed*). This means lockable resources like tables or rows are locked upfront.

Active Record supports an optimistic locking technique, which works differently. You'll work with it in this section.

With optimistic locking, resources are not locked upfront. Locks are said to be taken "late." What does that mean?

---

35. https://github.com/darold/pgbadger
36. https://postgresqlco.nf/doc/en/param/log_lock_waits/

This means that each process checks whether the object it's working with has already been modified separately. When a newer modification has lost the "race" due to an earlier concurrent process that modified the locked object, an ActiveRecord::StaleObjectError exception is raised. This usually means the client needs to retry.

To use this functionality, lockable resources need a version. With Active Record, you'll track the version in PostgreSQL using a new column. Add a lock_version column to tables for Active Record models that you want to lock. The column values are managed automatically by Active Record when objects are instantiated.

The Engine Yard post, "A Guide to Optimistic Locking,"[37] shows how to handle concurrent modifications. When locking is required and affects the user experience, consider rescuing lock errors and rendering an edit page showing the latest version of the object. Add a Rails Flash Message[38] that indicates an edit was not allowed and displays the latest version.

When locking does not affect the user experience, lock management may be best done using PostgreSQL capabilities. Use SELECT with either FOR UPDATE or FOR SHARE as shown earlier. Use FOR UPDATE when the goal is to select rows and prevent concurrent updates.

Is that the whole story? No. Brian, of Brian Likes Postgres,[39] points out PostgreSQL can also use optimistic locking in a way that's similar to Active Record.

Brian writes:

> While I think 99% of postgres shops use PostgreSQL with pessimistic locking, the SERIALIZABLE transaction isolation mode can be used for optimistic locking.[40]

Brian referenced the https://www.postgresql.org/files/developer/concurrency.pdf paper as a resource, recommending searching within it for "optimistic."

Brian: *PostgreSQL can do optimistic locking too.*

Andrew: *Oh really?*

Brian: *Yes, the SERIALIZABLE transaction isolation mode uses optimistic locking.*

Andrew: *Huh, interesting.*

Brian: *SERIALIZABLE can be used in pretty much the same way as the lock_version in Active Record.*

---

37. https://www.engineyard.com/blog/a-guide-to-optimistic-locking/
38. https://api.rubyonrails.org/classes/ActionDispatch/Flash.html
39. https://www.brianlikespostgres.com
40. https://www.brianlikespostgres.com

For some nice examples, review the post, "Transaction Isolation in Postgre-SQL,"[41] which shows each transaction isolation mode and example statements.

The last example shows the serializable isolation mode and how it can be used to prevent lost updates. The trade-off for that protection is that more update statements will fail, which means the client application needs to detect those failures and retry them.

Are there lighter-weight lock options with PostgreSQL?

Using Advisory Locks

PostgreSQL provides a weaker lock type called *advisory locks*.[42] This lock type is considered weaker because it's up to the application to create and enforce.

Ruby on Rails does make some use of advisory locks within the framework. One example is when Active Record migrations run. How does that work? An advisory lock is created during migrations to help limit the application of pending migrations to a single process. If two processes try that concurrently, an ActiveRecord::ConcurrentMigrationError exception is raised.

Advisory locks are useful but do come with trade-offs. The transaction or statement pooling modes with PgBouncer are not compatible with advisory locks. If you're using Transaction Pooling Mode with PgBouncer from Rails 6, advisory locks can be disabled by setting advisory_locks: false in config/database.yml.[43] You'll have to determine which features you'd like to have.

With the trade-offs being client incompatibilities, what are some other advantages of advisory locks?

> Advisory locks are faster, avoid table bloat, and are automatically cleaned up by the server at the end of the session.

Advisory locks can be at the session level or at the transaction level. The post, "Using PostgreSQL Advisory Locks to Avoid Race Conditions,"[44] compares a design that initially used SELECT...FOR UPDATE but was changed to use advisory locks. The with_advisory_lock[45] gem is used to create an advisory lock within a database transaction. The code creates a new unique sequence value instead of using a PostgreSQL Sequence object so that the sequence number can be

---

41. https://pgdash.io/blog/postgres-transactions.html
42. https://www.postgresql.org/docs/current/explicit-locking.html#ADVISORY-LOCKS
43. https://blog.saeloun.com/2019/09/09/rails-6-disable-advisory-locks.html
44. https://firehydrant.com/blog/using-advisory-locks-to-avoid-race-conditions-in-rails/
45. https://github.com/ClosureTree/with_advisory_lock

scoped to an application concept. This gave the application more control over concurrent creations and the design of the sequence number.

Let's wrap up!

Lock Up on Your Way Out

In this chapter, you've seen challenges that arise at greater levels of concurrency, whether they be from using limited database connection resources, or lock behavior with concurrent writes and reads.

You learned that concurrent activity can be scaled to greater levels beyond what's possible with physical connections by introducing connection pooling software. You explored connection pooling on the application level and using PgBouncer, configuring it for Rideshare. You saw how to integrate PgBouncer with a Ruby on Rails application to use the best features available while retaining as much client functionality as possible. To improve the resiliency of your system, you explored various timeout values that help limit the impact of errors on the overall availability of your system.

In the next chapter, you'll continue to focus on greater scalability. You'll shift your focus from PostgreSQL back to Rails code design and schema design. You'll work with common application features and see how to make them more scalable.

Part IV

Optimize and Scale

## CHAPTER 11

Scalability of Common Features

In this chapter, you'll work outside of Rideshare and analyze the schema design, indexes, and SQL queries for common application features.

First, you'll look at a popular gem for adding tags to items. Next, you'll look at various pagination techniques and their performance characteristics. These are features that are common to most Rails applications.

When you add Ruby gems as dependencies to your application, and they modify your database, you get benefits and possible downsides. The benefit is accelerated development, and for popular open source gems, solutions that were built and maintained with input from many developers.

The possible downsides are that the schema designs, indexes, or queries may be more general purpose than your specific needs. You'll know exactly what the tables, queries, and indexes look like if you get under the hood and take a look. That's what you'll work on now.

Consider how a gem might choose indexes for a table. There may be indexes to cover all kinds of query types beyond the specific queries you use from the gem. For that reason, you may have unused indexes that could be removed.

Review some of the indexing and pagination terminology you'll work with in this chapter.

Terminology

- Over indexing—Excessive indexes beyond ones used by queries
- Pagination—Fetching one page of results at a time
- Keyset pagination—Scalable pagination technique using indexed columns
- Database CURSOR—Database object useful for best pagination consistency

Let's dive into schema designs and index designs in the next section.

Analyzing Schema Designs from Gems

As you evaluate gems, create a process to explore the database aspects of the code. For an example, in this section, you'll work with the acts-as-taggable-on[1] gem.

This gem was not added to Rideshare. You could add this gem to your local copy, but you've decided to generate a new Rails application.

To do that, follow these steps, running commands from your terminal:

1. Generate a new Rails application with rails new. Use the --database=postgresql flag.

2. In the new application, add the acts-as-taggable-on gem to the Gemfile and run bundle install.

3. Create the new application database with bin/rails db:create.

4. Copy the migration files from the gem source to the application source by running bin/rails acts_as_taggable_on_engine:install:migrations.

5. Run bin/rails db:migrate to apply the migrations copied from the gem.

For a generated application called acts_as_taggable_test_app, the development database is acts_as_taggable_test_app_development. Connect to it from your terminal by running psql --dbname acts_as_taggable_test_app_development, or by using bin/rails dbconsole.

From here forward, we'll assume you're connected using psql or bin/rails dbconsole to the acts_as_taggable_test_app_development database.

Run "describe table" by typing \dt into psql. Explore the taggings and tags tables using the "describe" (\d) meta-command.

On the name column of the tags table, there is a single-column unique index that enforces a unique constraint. The name allows nulls. On the taggings table, there is a foreign key constraint from the tag_id column, referencing the tags.id primary key column.

The taggings table uses single table inheritance[2] (STI), which means there are "polymorphic" types referenced using the taggable_type and taggable_id columns.

---

1. https://github.com/mbleigh/acts-as-taggable-on
2. https://api.rubyonrails.org/classes/ActiveRecord/Inheritance.html

The taggings table defines uniqueness to include those two columns plus four others, for six total:

- tag_id
- taggable_id
- taggable_type
- context
- tagger_id
- tagger_type

One thing that stands out is the taggings table has a lot of indexes. The table has 11 B-Tree indexes, which are a mix of single and Multicolumn types. Some of these indexes may not be necessary. As you saw earlier, besides unused indexes, there can also be overlapping definitions and index redundancies.

Now that you know a little about the tables, indexes, and constraints for the tables from the gem, what do the queries look like?

Understanding Queries from Tagging Gem

To analyze queries from the gem, you'll need to add the gem to application models and do either manual or automated testing to generate activity.

Create a model for the tagging gem. Let's try working with manual testing. Generate a new Active Record model and open it up with your editor (any editor is fine; vim is displayed here).

```sh/rails_generate_resource_user.sh
bin/rails generate resource User name:string
```

```
vim app/models/user.rb
```

Add acts_as_taggable_on :tags to the User model.

Next, you'll need data. Run bin/rails console from your terminal. Run ActiveRecord::Base.logger = Logger.new(STDOUT) to enable SQL query logging.

Run this code in a Rails console and take note of the queries:

```ruby/acts_as_taggable_on_loading_tags.rb
irb(main):001:0> User.create!(name: "Andy")

TRANSACTION (0.1ms)  BEGIN
User Create (1.4ms)
  INSERT INTO "users" ("name", "created_at", "updated_at")
  VALUES ($1, $2, $3) RETURNING "id"
  [["name", "Andy"],
  ["created_at", "2023-01-20 17:04:28.354274"],
  ["updated_at", "2023-01-20 17:04:28.354274"]]
```

```
ActsAsTaggableOn::Tagging Load (2.6ms)
  SELECT "taggings".* FROM "taggings"
  WHERE "taggings"."taggable_id" = $1
  AND "taggings"."taggable_type" = $2
  [["taggable_id", 1],
   ["taggable_type", "User"]]
COMMIT
```

Let's explore some of the PostgreSQL details about queries that have been generated.

We see a transaction is opened with BEGIN. Within the transaction, an INSERT statement creates a new row in users table and queries the taggings table, which is polymorphic. All field data is selected from taggings with SELECT *. This query is unlikely to use an index-only scan because of the wide number of fields selected.

The following SQL is a cleaned-up version of the previous SELECT query. The parameters have been populated. Prepend EXPLAIN (ANALYZE, BUFFERS), running the query again and looking at the execution plan:

sql/select_from_tags_join_taggings.sql
```sql
SELECT * FROM tags
INNER JOIN taggings ON tags.id = taggings.tag_id
WHERE taggings.taggable_id = 1
AND taggings.taggable_type = 'User'
AND (
  taggings.context = 'tags' AND
  taggings.tagger_id IS NULL);
```

For tags and taggings tables, find out whether a sequential scan or index scan is used. Open psql --dbname acts_as_taggable_test_app_development and run the query with EXPLAIN (ANALYZE, BUFFERS), reading the execution plan. The query has multiple filters expressed as AND conditions:

- tagger_id IS NULL
- taggable_id = 1
- (taggable_type)::text = 'User'::text

The database columns evaluated with these filters are tagger_id, taggable_id, and taggable_type.

Since creating the database, adding tables, and adding indexes, VACUUM and ANALYZE may not have run. Run them by issuing the following command in psql:

sql/vacuum_analyze_tagging_gem_tables.sql
```sql
VACUUM (ANALYZE, VERBOSE) users, tags, taggings;
```

Remember that in local development, indexes that are used in production may not be used because PostgreSQL determines it's faster to perform a sequential scan.

One trick for local testing to try is to run SET enable_seqscan = OFF; in psql. This disables sequential scans when possible. Sequential scans may still be used, as you're not able to fully control the plan selection.

After disabling sequential scans, you may see indexes are used for the previous query. To restore the original value, run SET enable_seqscan = ON; to enable sequential scans.

Now that you've got a User, it's time to add tags. Open your terminal and run bin/rails console. Add a tag by running this code:

```
ruby/add_tags_to_user.rb
User.find_by(name: 'Andy').tag_list.add('author')
```

Use these techniques to explore the generated SQL queries. Within the queries, figure out which tables are accessed, which fields, and the indexes for the tables.

You've now seen the basics of adding tagging to a Rails app using a Ruby gem and how to explore the database design.

Next, you'll look at "pagination," another common need.

LIMIT and OFFSET Pagination

In Ruby on Rails applications that show pages of results, once there are more than ten or twenty items, it's common to move to a pagination approach that shows one page of results at a time. Typically, pagination queries are paired with user-facing UI controls that allow them to move forward or backward through pages.

Pagination refers to the process of fetching results for display, and there are various ways to do that. Pagination navigation elements may provide clickable numbered boxes, or may provide "endless pagination," continually adding more items onto the end.

The post, "Five Ways to Paginate in Postgres, from the Basic to the Exotic,"[3] presents different ways to perform pagination. The Ruby gems Kaminari[4] and Pagy[5] are popular ways to add pagination support to Active Record by using gems.

---

3. https://www.citusdata.com/blog/2016/03/30/five-ways-to-paginate/
4. https://github.com/kaminari/kaminari
5. https://github.com/ddnexus/pagy

The most common type of pagination is "limit and offset," which uses the LIMIT and OFFSET keywords. Limit and offset pagination is built-in to Active Record, using the .limit() and .offset() methods.

Let's try this out. Run bin/rails console in Rideshare. From there, run the following Active Record code:

ruby/active_record_limit_offset.rb
```
User.all.limit(10).offset(1)
```

While the LIMIT and OFFSET technique is common, it does have trade-offs. The "Five Ways" pagination post classifies the problems as "result inconsistency" and "offset inefficiency." What do those mean?

Result inconsistency refers to inconsistent results when navigating between pages. When concurrent changes happen while paginating, new items might either pop into pages when navigating backwards or shift the page items. This inconsistency may be tolerable depending on how critical it is to have discrete results.

Offset inefficiency might be more onerous. Normally, indexes are used to improve query performance. However, as the "Five Ways" post mentions, indexes can't be used for pagination because the queries aren't filtering. This can lead to full table scans (sequential scans) and poor performance.

Let's consider an example. Row counts keep growing with "soft deletes." Soft deletes are a common pattern used to hide rows and make it possible to recover them instead of fully deleting them from the database.

High amounts of soft-deleted records can worsen LIMIT and OFFSET style pagination because they contribute to more indexes being scanned and possibly more index write overhead.

Offset inefficiency may be contained well enough for low row counts where it's acceptable. When row counts are high, and if users don't paginate "deeply," the performance of this pagination technique may still be acceptable.

When row counts are high, and limit and offset style pagination isn't working well, you'll need another technique.

Let's find one. We'll dive into the database CURSOR object and see how we can use it for pagination.

Database CURSOR Pagination

PostgreSQL supports a CURSOR keyword, which creates a native database object. Native cursor objects are not supported by Ruby on Rails, so you may not have worked with them before.

Using a CURSOR object, statements may use the FETCH command to fetch items from the cursor. "Cursor pagination" is another style or type of pagination, although it's worth emphasizing that this section refers to the native CURSOR database object.

CURSOR objects are not supported in Active Record. Cursor pagination makes the application stateful and presents scalability challenges for multiple running application instances. "Stateless" web applications are preferred because they are easier to scale.

Client side state that's linked to server side CURSOR objects violates stateless design. CURSOR objects are worth exploring nonetheless, to broaden your understanding of pagination options. When pagination result consistency is most important and long transactions are tolerable, a database cursor offers the best consistency among the pagination options.

How does it work? First, CURSOR objects are declared, given a name, and used within a transaction. A CURSOR object persists as long as the transaction is open. One immediate risk you may notice is keeping long-lived transactions that could possibly block other operations.

Once a cursor has been declared and named, the FETCH command is used to fetch a set of items in a specified "direction."

Try creating a CURSOR object in a transaction, and keep it open. The following statements open a transaction, declare a cursor, then use FETCH to fetch 100 items in the forward direction. Finally, the transaction is closed by being committed, which removes the cursor.

Connect to the Rideshare database from psql and run the following statements individually.

```
sql/select_declare_cursor.sql
BEGIN;
DECLARE users_cursor CURSOR FOR SELECT * FROM users ORDER BY id ASC;
FETCH FORWARD 100 FROM users_cursor;
FETCH FORWARD 100 FROM users_cursor;
COMMIT;
```

The first batch id range is from 1 to 100. Running the same FETCH command again starts from where the last statement left off, meaning the next batch is from 101 to 200. Notice how the query orders the results by id in ascending order. You don't need to calculate any offsets yourself.

Since database cursors have transaction isolation, their consistency guarantee is stronger than any technique in this chapter.

The WITH HOLD type of cursor is not compatible with the transaction (or statement) pooling modes in PgBouncer (see "PgBouncer Features,"[6] although it is compatible with the "session" pooling mode).

WITHOUT HOLD,[7] however, *is* compatible with transaction pooling. This type of cursor can be used within a single transaction and is not kept open after the transaction closes.[8]

Although database cursors are not supported by Active Record directly and have limitations, they offer the best result consistency. How can you add database cursors to Rails?

The pagy-cursor[9] gem is an extension to Pagy that supports native CURSOR objects.

Additional cursor types are available, including the SCROLL type. The post "WITH HOLD Cursors and Transactions in PostgreSQL"[10] has more information on various cursor types.

Consider adopting database cursors when you're able to use transactions (check pooler compatibility), and want to prioritize consistent results.

With database cursors covered, let's discuss another pagination style called *keyset pagination*. Confusingly, keyset pagination is sometimes called "cursor style" pagination. However, keyset pagination here is a technique and doesn't use a database CURSOR object.

Improved Performance with Keyset Pagination

Keyset pagination has a very technical name but is a relatively straightforward concept. With keyset pagination, an indexed column is used both for filtering with a WHERE clause and for sorting with an ORDER BY clause.

---

6. https://www.pgbouncer.org/features.html
7. https://www.postgresql.org/docs/current/sql-declare.html
8. https://www.cybertec-postgresql.com/en/with-hold-cursors-and-transactions-in-postgresql/
9. https://github.com/Uysim/pagy-cursor
10. https://www.cybertec-postgresql.com/en/with-hold-cursors-and-transactions-in-postgresql/

Let's walk through retrieving a page of results. A query sets an order on the same column being filtered on and sets a max amount of records with a LIMIT clause. To fetch additional pages of results, new queries are sent that still filter and order on the same column but start from rows with a value that's one greater than the previous result's max value.

Because the column is indexed, both the filtering and ordering operations use an index scan, meaning their performance stays consistent as row counts increase.

While query performance is good, how does result set consistency compare to the other methods? Review this quote:[11]

> Keyset pagination is fast, and it is consistent too. Any insertions/deletions before the current page will leave the results unaffected.

What are the downsides of Keyset Pagination?

> The two downsides to this method are lack of random access and possible coupling between client and server.

Let's explore what "lack of random access" and "coupling between the client and server" mean.

For the lack of random access, let's use an example from Rideshare. Using the users table, use the keyset pagination technique with the primary key id column to fetch pages of results. Run the following query from psql and confirm that an index scan is performed using the primary key index:

```
sql/explain_select_users_keyset_pagination.sql
EXPLAIN SELECT * FROM users
ORDER BY id ASC
LIMIT 50;
```

If the first query starts from id value 1, and the sequence has no gaps, then by setting a LIMIT of 50, you'll get rows from 1 to 50. However, sequences can have gaps. For example, inserts can fail, and they "use up" a sequence value when that happens. This means that you may not get a full 50 results.

The second request should start from the next number after the max. For example, the next query could add WHERE id > 50 when 50 was the max item. The calculation of the next minimum value should be based on the previous max value. Hopping to a random specific page is not possible because each request needs to use the max value to calculate the next query's minimum value.

---

11. https://www.citusdata.com/blog/2016/03/30/five-ways-to-paginate/

The other downside discussed for keyset pagination is that there's a need to index on fields where filtering and ordering are happening. While it's true that there's a degree of "coupling" there between the client or UI and the server, having supportive indexes for these queries is a good practice for performance. You may already be creating specialized indexes to optimize individual queries. This downside is not limited to keyset pagination either. The Limit and Offset technique also requires indexes for good performance.

Let's compare limit and offset pagination against keyset pagination when working with large row counts with the users table.

From your terminal, run the script sh scripts/data_loaders.sh in Rideshare's root directory. This script loads ten million users and then analyzes the table.

With ten million users loaded, view the query execution plans for the following queries from psql:

```
sql/select_keyset_pagination_large_minimum_value.sql
EXPLAIN (ANALYZE, BUFFERS) SELECT * FROM users
ORDER BY id ASC
LIMIT 50
OFFSET 5000000;

EXPLAIN (ANALYZE, BUFFERS) SELECT * FROM users
WHERE id >= 5000000
ORDER BY id ASC
LIMIT 50;
```

Consider the details that are common to both. Each query selects all fields from the users table, shows 50 results, orders by the id column, and starts from the value of 5,000,000.

When looking at the query execution plans, both queries use an index scan on the primary key index. However, the limit and offset style version is much slower. Why?

In the limit and offset version, PostgreSQL scanned through 5,000,050 rows of the index, compared with the keyset pagination, where PostgreSQL scanned through just 50.

Besides the index scan, let's look at BUFFERS information. The limit and offset version read 117289 buffers, while the keyset pagination version read just 2.

Scanning fewer index entries and dramatically reducing the storage access (buffers) lowered the cost of the keyset pagination style query, making it much faster.

Wrapping Up

In this chapter, you explored common application features like adding tags and paginating results. You walked through some of the database design details for gem code, including the schema, indexes, and queries. You explored three pagination techniques, comparing their result set consistency and performance.

While you've learned many ways to improve the efficiency of queries that read data, what about the performance of queries that write data?

In the next chapter, you'll learn how to create more efficient data writes into PostgreSQL. You'll put various "bulk loading" techniques into action. Read on to learn more.

## CHAPTER 12

Working with Bulk Data

In this chapter, you will shift your focus from read operations to write operations. When working with high write queries per second, or high write operations like backfills, bulk ingestion, or data copying, try to perform work in batches as "bulk operations" since they operate on multiple rows at once.

Besides the multirow DML operations you'll explore in this chapter, you'll work with the PostgreSQL COPY command and foreign data wrappers (FDW).

\COPY Command

 COPY and \COPY are variants with different permission levels. The PostgreSQL Wiki page, https://wiki.postgresql.org/wiki/COPY, explains the differences. Run COPY with the postgres user which is a superuser. Run \COPY (with the leading backslash) with a nonsuperuser role. You'll use \COPY with the owner role you set up in Rideshare.

Ruby on Rails applications, like most web applications, typically have many more read operations than write operations.

Said another way, in SQL statement terms, this means most web applications have a greater number of SELECT statements compared with INSERT, UPDATE, and DELETE statements.

With more read operations than write operations, why worry about optimizing writes? The main reason to optimize writes is that writer instances in PostgreSQL can't be scaled horizontally. Adopting multirow write operations that are more efficient contributes to achieving greater scalability for your primary server instance.

While scaling your writer vertically adds more hardware resources, there's a max limit that can be reached for either hardware reasons or financial reasons.

Read queries aren't as difficult to scale since they can be scaled horizontally, which you'll work on in an upcoming chapter. In this chapter, let's focus on write performance.

You might be wondering what the factors are that make bulk operations more efficient? As you saw earlier, part of the answer is related to database connections, which have some overhead when they're established, adding latency to the statement. With bulk operations, you'll reduce the latency by operating on greater numbers of rows, with fewer statements, transactions, and connections.

Besides the bulk operation capabilities in PostgreSQL, you'll learn to use what's offered in Active Record and Ruby gems.

Let's explore the "thundering herd"[1] scenario. This is when there's a high volume of writes trying to run at the same time. Imagine that you're using the Sidekiq background processing framework, and it's temporarily offline. Jobs back up that would normally send writes to PostgreSQL at a steady rate.

When job processing starts working again, suddenly there's a huge volume of writes to process. Investing in efficient write operations could help your system survive thundering herds. Even under heavier load, when there's enough spare capacity, combined with more efficient operations, your server instance has a chance of surviving.

Some common types of write activity in web applications are:

- "Webhooks" that send requests and then write their status into the database
- User activity records or analytics
- Audits or tracked changes for primary objects
- Versioned records, with each version captured as a row
- Social media style metrics like views, likes, or favorites

Take a look at some of the terminology you'll work with in this chapter.

Bulk Data Terminology

- Upsert—Combined statement that either updates an existing row or inserts a new one
- \COPY Command—Efficient method for dumping and loading operations
- foreign data wrapper (FDW)—Connecting PostgreSQL to foreign data sources

---

1. https://en.wikipedia.org/wiki/Thundering_herd_problem

First up, you'll work with Active Record bulk operations. To get some interesting data, let's create a new Rake task.

Creating a Bulk Data Generator Rake Task

Earlier, in *Building a Performance-Testing Database*, you learned tactics to create a scrubbed copy of a large database.

Having a scrubbed copy of your production database is a great solution if you're able to set that up. A less complex alternative would be to use a small pre-production database and then populate it with large amounts of simulated data. Fortunately, you can do this using Active Record by way of the bulk insert methods.

Let's try out the .insert_all()[2] bulk insert method added to Active Record version 6. Rideshare has the following Rake task that inserts large batches of users with realistic-looking data supplied by the Faker[3] gem. Read this script and then run it.

ruby/fake_data_generator.rake
```ruby
require 'faker'

namespace :data_generators do
  desc "Generator Drivers"
  task drivers: :environment do |t, args|
    TOTAL = 20_000
    BATCH_SIZE = 10_000
    results = Benchmark.measure do
      TOTAL.times.to_a.in_groups_of(BATCH_SIZE).each do |group|
        batch = group.map do |i|
          first_name = Faker::Name.first_name
          last_name = Faker::Name.last_name
          Driver.new(
            first_name: first_name,
            last_name: last_name,
            email: "#{first_name}-#{last_name}-#{i}@email.com",
            password_digest: SecureRandom.hex
          )
        end.map do |d|
          d.attributes.symbolize_keys.slice(
            :first_name, :last_name,
            :email, :password, :type
          )
        end
```

---

2.   https://github.com/rails/rails/pull/35077
3.   https://github.com/faker-ruby/faker

```
      Driver.insert_all(batch)
      puts "Created #{batch.size} drivers."
    end
  end
  puts "VACUUM (ANALYZE) users"
  Driver.connection.execute("VACUUM (ANALYZE) users")
  puts results
  end
end
```

To run the script, cd to the root directory of Rideshare. From there, run the following command from your terminal:

```
bin/rails data_generators:drivers
```

When the script completes, it performs a VACUUM (ANALYZE) on the users table to make sure the VM[4] is updated and that statistics[5] are refreshed.

Let's review some of the technical details of the script:

- The TOTAL constant sets the max amount of records to load.

- BATCH_SIZE is a configurable batch size.

- The initial batch size is 10_000.

- For each batch, Driver objects are initialized in memory.

- From the objects, specific fields are sliced out. These are the nonnullable fields.

- The created_at and updated_at timestamp columns are set.

In this example, .insert_all() initializes Driver objects, which uses more memory. Alternatively, primitive types like arrays and hashes can be used. Validations on the Active Record instances are not run here. For example, the Driver model validates the drivers license number as a validation, and it's not run with this technique.

You've now seen how to perform inserts in batches using Active Record.

What does Active Record offer for reading large amounts of data?

Batching with Active Record

While this chapter focuses on write operations, it's worth briefly reviewing bulk operations for reads.

---

4. https://www.postgresql.org/docs/current/storage-vm.html
5. https://www.postgresql.org/docs/current/sql-analyze.html

Active Record supports .find_each(), .in_batches(), and .find_in_batches() that pull 1000 records at a time by default. This sets an upper bound on the amount of memory needed to initialize batches of objects. These methods do not improve your write efficiency, but they're part of the family of batch or bulk methods in Active Record.

Batches of rows are ordered by id in ascending order by default. .in_batches(), and .find_each() in Rails 6.1 can be ordered in reverse using an order: :desc option (see "Rails 6.1 Supports ORDER BY Clause for Batch Processing Methods"[6]).

Besides inserting and selecting data in batches, what other bulk operations are possible?

Handling Upsert Violations in Active Record

Active Record provides .update_all() to update multiple rows with the same value. To write less complex code with less branching, try combining updates and inserts into a single operation. This is called an *upsert*[7] operation, and it's supported in multiple ways between Active Record and PostgreSQL.

Following the .insert() and .insert_all() method naming conventions, Active Record added upsert() and the multirow variant .upsert_all(). By using .upsert_all() over .upsert(), you may write less code and get multirow efficiency.

PostgreSQL does not natively support an UPSERT keyword, although the SQL MERGE command added in PostgreSQL 15 is considered to be an upsert implementation. You'll cover this in an upcoming section, but focus on .upsert() methods in Active Record for now.

With .upsert_all(), when inserting or updating data, the data supplied may cause conflicts with database constraints. Constraint violations need to be handled, so you'll indicate how you'd like to handle conflicts (also called "conflict resolution") as part of the options you provide to a statement.

The post, "Rails: insert_all and upsert_all,"[8] shows how to use the unique_by option for these scenarios. When it's used, PostgreSQL adds an ON CONFLICT clause, which controls the behavior for constraint violations with multirow statements.

Active Record uses ON CONFLICT and UNIQUE constraints to identify conflicts. A conflict resolution clause is required. One option for conflict resolution is

---

6. https://www.bigbinary.com/blog/rails-6-1-supports-order-desc-for-find_each-find_in_batches-and-in_batches
7. https://wiki.postgresql.org/wiki/UPSERT
8. https://www.johnnunemaker.com/rails-insert_all-and-upsert_all/

DO NOTHING, which means that the insert or update will not raise a constraint violation error but will also not succeed.

An alternative is DO UPDATE, which means that some columns will be updated when constraint violations occur.

Besides these options, additional ones were added in Rails 7 to .upsert_all() (see "Rails 7 Adds New Options to upsert_all"[9]).

Let's dive into an example with Rideshare. Try calling .upsert() on the Vehicle class for a vehicle that exists that has the same name. The vehicle name must be unique according to the unique index definition. By passing a unique name, a new record will be inserted. By passing an existing name, no update will occur.

```ruby
# ruby/vehicle_upsert.rb
# Party Bus exists
attributes = {
  name:  "Party Bus (Upsert edition)"
}
Vehicle.upsert(
  attributes,
  returning: [:id],
  unique_by: [:name]
)
```

The RETURNING SQL keyword is used here in Active Record as the returning option. The id field is listed as the field to return from the statement.

.unique_by() specifies the column name (name in this case). When passing an existing name as an update, since the vehicle exists, id in the response is NULL (the response is nil).

Here are some additional options to review:

- update_only
- on_duplicate

update_only can be used to specify one or more columns that will be updated in the event of a conflict.

on_duplicate specifies a list of columns to be updated. It cannot be used at the same time as update_only. This behavior would be triggered when there are constraint violations.

Let's explore constraint violations in more detail.

---

9.   https://blog.kiprosh.com/rails-7-adds-new-options-to-upsert_all/

Handling Conflicts with ON CONFLICT

As you saw in the last section, the following conflict resolution modes are available:

- ON CONFLICT DO NOTHING
- ON CONFLICT DO UPDATE

Let's try them out. Create a people table in the temp schema as you've done earlier. Insert two rows. To do that, run these statements from psql:

sql/create_table_people.sql
```
CREATE SCHEMA IF NOT EXISTS temp;

CREATE TABLE temp.people (id BIGINT PRIMARY KEY, name TEXT);
INSERT INTO temp.people (id, name) VALUES (1, 'Jane');
INSERT INTO temp.people (id, name) VALUES (2, 'Bob');
```

The primary key constraint enforces unique id values. Inserting a row with a duplicate id fails. Verify this by running the following statement:

sql/insert_into_people_duplicate.sql
```
INSERT INTO temp.people (id, name) VALUES (1, 'Will Fail');
```

The id value is duplicated. How can you handle this?

First, try the INSERT again, specifying the DO NOTHING option. Query the people table afterward and verify the original row was not modified.

sql/on_conflict_do_nothing.sql
```
INSERT INTO temp.people (id, name)
VALUES (2, 'Bobby')
ON CONFLICT (id) DO NOTHING;
```

You should see INSERT 0 0, meaning no rows were modified.

When conflicts occur, PostgreSQL sets up a special table EXCLUDED.[10] Using EXCLUDED, you can access fields that were changing that had conflicts.

For example, EXCLUDED.name returns Bobby since id had a conflict, and you tried to change the name.

What about when you want to overwrite the name? Using EXCLUDED.name and a SET operation, you can do that. Run the following statement to overwrite the name:

---

10. https://www.postgresql.org/docs/current/sql-insert.html

```
sql/on_conflict_do_update.sql
INSERT INTO temp.people (id, name)
VALUES (2, 'Bobby')
ON CONFLICT (id) DO UPDATE
SET name = EXCLUDED.name;
```

INSERT 0 1 is returned. Normally, the second number is the number of rows that were inserted. Here, it's the number of rows that were updated.

Query the temp.people table and confirm that id 2 is Bobby.

By using an INSERT with DO UPDATE, you're performing an upsert since it updates existing rows.

Review this table that summarizes PostgreSQL and Active Record methods you've seen so far.

Operation	AR or PG	Version
.find_each()	AR	2.3
.in_batches()	AR	5.0
.insert_all()	AR	6.0
.upsert()	AR	6.0
.upsert_all()	AR	6.0
RETURNING	PG	8.2
MERGE	PG	15

Table 6—Bulk Operations in Active Record and PostgreSQL

In this section, you've worked with what's available in Active Record. What about capabilities with Ruby gems beyond what Active Record supports?

Beyond Active Record with activerecord-import

Prior to Rails 6, the activerecord-import[11] gem was arguably the "go-to solution" for bulk operations. The activerecord-import gem was added to Rideshare, where you can experiment with it.

With Active Record supporting bulk operations like .insert_all() and .update_all(), the need for the gem has lessened.

However, activerecord-import has capabilities beyond Active Record. One of the features is an .import() method.

---

11. https://github.com/zdennis/activerecord-import

The .import() method accepts an array of objects of varying types, including Active Record instances or Ruby types like Hash and String. Validations can be performed by setting validate to true.

Try this example out from bin/rails console in Rideshare:

```ruby
# ruby/activerecord_import.rb
# import from Hashes
vehicles = [
  {name: "Monster Truck", status: 'draft'},
  {name: "Jetski", status: 'draft'}
]
Vehicle.import(vehicles, validate: false)

# import from object instances
vehicles = [
  Vehicle.new(name: "Monster Truck", status: 'draft'),
  Vehicle.new(name: "Jetski", status: 'draft')
]
Vehicle.import(vehicles, validate: true)
```

Columns and arrays may be passed separately. This could be useful for building an importer.

With Active Record bulk methods, a single INSERT statement is used to insert all items at once. With activerecord-import, a batch_size option controls the number of items in a statement, which means multiple multi-item statements can be generated.

This means you can split up multiple INSERT statements for more fine-grained control. Active Record model callbacks are not called with this approach.

Try out this batch_size[12] option.

Set a batch_size to 3 for six Vehicle instances. You should see two INSERT statements, each containing three vehicles. Run Vehicle.destroy_all if you'd like to clear out the table first.

From your terminal, run bin/rails console and run this Ruby code:

```ruby
# ruby/activerecord_import_batch_inserts.rb
# Log SQL statements in Rails console
ActiveRecord::Base.logger = Logger.new(STDOUT)

# Set up 6 Vehicle instances
vehicles = [
  Vehicle.new(name: "Lucid Air", status: VehicleStatus::DRAFT),
  Vehicle.new(name: "Bugatti Veyron", status: VehicleStatus::DRAFT),
  Vehicle.new(name: "Ferrari LaFerrari", status: VehicleStatus::DRAFT),
```

---

12. https://github.com/zdennis/activerecord-import#batching

```
  Vehicle.new(name: "Porsche 911 GT2 RS", status: VehicleStatus::DRAFT),
  Vehicle.new(name: "Toyota GR Supra", status: VehicleStatus::DRAFT),
  Vehicle.new(name: "McLaren Senna", status: VehicleStatus::DRAFT)
]
columns = [:name]

# batch_size of 3, should generate 2 INSERT statements,
# each statement with 3 vehicles
Vehicle.import(columns, vehicles, validate: false, batch_size: 3)
```

You should see two logged INSERT statements in the SQL log from Rails console, and multiple vehicles in the VALUES portion.

A trade-off with this approach is that counter cache columns aren't updated.[13] You'll need to update those manually. Remember that after bulk operations, it's a good idea to update table statistics by running the ANALYZE command for the table.

Now that you've started to perform multirow inserts, what other types of multirow statements are available?

Performing SQL Multirow Operations

In an earlier chapter, you used the ROW_NUMBER() Window Function to label results and help identify duplicate rows. Once you found the duplicate rows, you removed them so that you could add a new constraint. These operations were wrapped in a multirow delete statement.

Similar to the multirow deletions you worked on, let's try a multirow update to see how that works.

Create a table of list items and generate ten rows with the same list_id. Number the rows sequentially with no gaps from one to ten.

Run these statements from psql, using the temp schema:

sql/list_items_create_and_generate.sql
```
-- temp schema
CREATE SCHEMA IF NOT EXISTS temp;

-- create list_items table
CREATE TABLE temp.list_items (
  id SERIAL PRIMARY KEY,
  list_id INTEGER,
  position INTEGER,
  CONSTRAINT unique_pos UNIQUE (position)
);
```

---

13. https://github.com/zdennis/activerecord-import#counter-cache

```
-- generate 10 rows, `id` and `position` numbered 1-10
INSERT INTO temp.list_items (list_id, position)
SELECT 1, GENERATE_SERIES(1, 10, 1);
```

This does rely on some specific properties to work. The primary key id is populated from a Sequence used by the Serial type. Since they're new rows, they're ordered from one to ten with no gaps. The position column value is also one to ten with no gaps, but it's populated from the GENERATE_SERIES() function. The values end up being the same between the id column and the position column.

Given that setup, imagine that you wanted to swap the position values between the first and second rows. You could do that with two UPDATE statements, one that swaps the first row and one for the second.

However, the position has a UNIQUE constraint on it, so you couldn't temporarily duplicate the position values. You could use three UPDATE statements, which would reassign one of the values to an invalid position like -1, which would free up the valid position values to use.

The following statements perform those three moves in a transaction. Run them from psql:

sql/list_items_swap_multiple_updates.sql
```
-- Depends on: list_items_create_and_generate.sql

BEGIN; -- perform work in a transaction

-- make position 1 available, to list item 2
UPDATE temp.list_items SET position = -1 WHERE id = 1;

-- set list item 2, to position 1, now that it's available
UPDATE temp.list_items SET position = 1 WHERE id = 2;

-- set list item 1, to position 2
UPDATE temp.list_items SET position = 2 WHERE id = 1;

END;
```

While this solution does work, it uses three statements. This operation could be efficient and run as a single statement.

Review this statement, which uses hard-coded id values as described earlier. In a real statement, you'd dynamically populate the VALUES clause.

Try running this statement from psql:

sql/list_items_swap_single_update.sql
```
-- Dependency on temp.list_items
-- Created from:list_items_create_and_generate.sql

-- use UPDATE... FROM syntax
-- https://stackoverflow.com/a/18799497
```

```
-- This fails!
UPDATE temp.list_items AS li SET
  position = li2.position
FROM (VALUES
  (2, 1),
  (1, 2)
) AS li2(id, position)
WHERE li2.id = li.id;
```

This statement fails due to the unique constraint on the position column since it duplicates existing values.

How can you work around the unique constraint so that you can perform this statement?

To do that, you'll use a trick to defer the enforcement of the constraint until the transaction commits. Fortunately, unique constraints are one of the constraint types that support deferred enforcement.[14]

From psql, try opening a transaction and making the unique constraint that you set up earlier (named unique_pos in the temp schema) deferred. Do this by running SET CONSTRAINTS temp.unique_pos DEFERRED; inside a transaction:

sql/defer_unique_constraint_1.sql
```
BEGIN;

SET CONSTRAINTS temp.unique_pos DEFERRED;
--ERROR:  constraint "unique_pos" is not deferrable

ROLLBACK;
```

You'll see the error constraint "unique_pos" is not deferrable, which means the constraint is not configured as deferrable.

To fix this, drop the constraint and create it again as "deferrable."

Run these statements to do that:

sql/defer_unique_constraint_2.sql
```
-- Drop the existing constraint
ALTER TABLE temp.list_items
DROP CONSTRAINT unique_pos;

-- Create it again, as DEFERRABLE
ALTER TABLE temp.list_items
ADD CONSTRAINT unique_pos
UNIQUE (position) DEFERRABLE;
```

With the constraint optionally deferrable, you're ready to run the multirow statement from earlier.

---

14. https://emmer.dev/blog/deferrable-constraints-in-postgresql/

Enable deferred constraint enforcement inside the transaction again, then run the multirow update from psql:

sql/list_items_swap_single_update_transaction_deferred.sql
```sql
BEGIN;

SET CONSTRAINTS temp.unique_pos DEFERRED;

UPDATE temp.list_items AS li
SET
  position = li2.position
FROM (VALUES
  (2, 1),
  (1, 2)
) AS li2(id, position)
WHERE li2.id = li.id;

COMMIT;
```

List id 1 should now have position 2, and id 2 should now have position 1.

sql/list_items_swap_final_results.sql
```sql
SELECT id, position
FROM temp.list_items
ORDER BY position ASC
LIMIT 5;
--  id | position
-- ----+----------
--   2 |        1
--   1 |        2
--   3 |        3
--   4 |        4
--   5 |        5
-- (5 rows)
```

In this section, you updated multiple rows for the same table with a single statement. The table had a unique constraint that was selectively deferred until the transaction was committed.

You've now seen some tactics for how to perform multirow inserts, updates, and deletes. You've used conflict resolution control with the ON CONFLICT clause.

Earlier, the SQL MERGE command added in PostgreSQL 15 was mentioned. How does that work?

Upserts with SQL MERGE

PostgreSQL 15 added support for SQL MERGE,[15] which is a new command that you'll explore in this section.

---

15. https://www.postgresql.org/docs/current/sql-merge.html

MERGE supports two clauses:

- WHEN MATCHED THEN
- WHEN NOT MATCHED THEN

These clauses describe how to handle matches and no matches. Let's look at an example.

Using the same temp.people table you created earlier with Jane and Bob as rows, write a SQL statement like this:

```
sql/merge_when_matched_then.sql
MERGE INTO temp.people p
  USING ( VALUES(2, 'Jill') ) people_data
  ON people_data.column1 = p.id
WHEN NOT MATCHED THEN
  INSERT VALUES(people_data.column1, people_data.column2)
WHEN MATCHED THEN
  UPDATE SET name = people_data.column2;
```

Let's review the details. In this statement, the VALUES data is aliased as people_data and refers to an id value of 2. Since it matches, the WHEN MATCHED THEN branch is selected, which sets the name to Jill.

You should see MERGE 1. The name Bob was overwritten and is now Jill.

Now, try a name that doesn't exist, like VALUES(3, 'Brad').

This time the WHEN NOT MATCHED THEN branch is selected, which performs an INSERT. The result is still MERGE 1 but there are now three people in the table, Jane, Jill, and Brad.

You've now seen how to perform an upsert with the SQL MERGE command.

In the next section, you will work with bulk operations using pg_dump and pg_restore.

Working with pg_dump and pg_restore

Row data from PostgreSQL tables can be dumped to a file using the pg_dump client program.

The same dump file can be restored using pg_restore. pg_dump supports a couple of options, including dumping into a text file as INSERT statements. This technique is useful when copying rows to another database, where having the rows in an intermediate file is helpful to review or possibly modify the statements. What other options are there?[16]

> Dumps can be output in script or archive file formats.

When using this technique, you're performing bulk inserts. The usual caveats apply for bulk loads. Consider disabling Autovacuum for the table receiving new rows. Consider the impact that replication will have when that's used, and all of those new rows. If you're unsure about the impact, test the process out first using a separate database instance.

When copying rows this way between databases, the table definitions must match exactly on both sides.

Try this out by performing a dump and restore for a single table.[17]

Dump the users table from Rideshare. The .dump file will be compressed using the --format=c option. The data can be restored from the file with pg_restore. The .dump file won't be readable as it will no longer be plain text.

Run the following pg_dump command from your terminal:

```
sh/pg_dump_users_table.sh
# Use `postgres` superuser, must have password set
# May need to prepend: `sudo -u postgres` to command
pg_dump \
  --username postgres \
  --format=c \
  --host localhost \
  --table rideshare.users \
  rideshare_development > users_table.dump
```

Now, try restoring the row data from the file. To make it easier, restore the rows into a new database. Run the following statements as a superuser. First, you'll create the temp_restore database. You'll then connect to it and create the rideshare schema, and then the Rideshare tables.

```
sql/create_temp_restore.sql
-- Run as superuser
CREATE DATABASE temp_restore;

\c temp_restore

CREATE SCHEMA rideshare;
```

---

16. https://www.postgresql.org/docs/current/app-pgdump.html
17. https://dev.to/andyatkinson/dump-and-load-a-postgresql-table-p0o

Exit to your terminal. From there, run pg_restore as a superuser. This command restores the rideshare schema users table from the dump file into the temp_restore database:

```
sh/pg_restore_users_table.sh
pg_restore \
  --username postgres \
  --dbname temp_restore \
  users_table.dump
```

Once this finishes, try connecting to it. Exit and then run psql --dbname temp_restore to connect and make sure that the rideshare.users table exists. The table should have the same row count as the source table in the rideshare_development database.

You have now seen how to dump table rows to a file and restore them to another database.

Another way to move data around besides INSERT statements is to use the \COPY command. You'll explore that next.

Populating Table Data with \COPY

PostgreSQL supports bulk loading data from CSV files. This can be very efficient. The CSV file can contain millions of rows, which can be loaded quickly using the \COPY command.

These are some use cases:

- Consuming a large public data set, distributed as CSV files

- Ingesting data from another PostgreSQL system or different database system, using intermediate CSV files

- Creating an Extract Transform Load (ETL) pipeline, using CSV files as intermediaries

Try dumping data from Rideshare while connected to the rideshare_development database. Connect normally using the owner role. Use the client version of the COPY command, which starts with a backslash. Before running these commands, you may want to reset it to the smaller size. To do that, run bin/rails db:reset && bin/rails data_generators:generate_all from the Rideshare directory.

If RIDESHARE_DB_PASSWORD is not set, run export RIDESHARE_DB_PASSWORD="HSnDDgFty W9fyFl", replacing the password with the one you've set in earlier in ~/.pgpass for owner. Once those are set, you'll be ready to dump data.

To do that, run the following statement from psql:

sql/copy_to_users_table.sql
```
-- \COPY command
\COPY rideshare.users TO '/tmp/users_dump.csv'
```

You should see COPY 20210 or similar, meaning 20210 rows were copied into the file.

Run du -h /tmp/users_dump.csv to check the size, which is around 2.5 MB.

The \COPY command can also be used to dump a filtered set (from a query) of rows.[18]

Let's try that. The following query dumps half the rows ordered randomly (see "Split Table in (PostgreSQL) Randomly 50/50"[19]).

To work around syntax issues with \COPY in psql and multiline queries, the query is first placed into a view, which is then read inside the COPY...TO statement.

sql/copy_command_with_query.sql
```
-- https://stackoverflow.com/a/42405094/126688
-- Reminder to drop view, credit: https://www.brianlikespostgres.com
--
CREATE VIEW v1 AS (
  SELECT *
  FROM users
  ORDER BY RANDOM()
  LIMIT (SELECT COUNT(*)/2 FROM users)
);

\COPY (SELECT * FROM v1) TO '/tmp/users_dump_half.csv';

DROP VIEW IF EXISTS v1;
```

This time, you'll see that \COPY prints COPY 10105, which is exactly half of 20210. du -h /tmp/users_dump_half.csv shows the file is now about 1.5 MB in size.

As an engineer with database access and SQL skills, you can use this technique to provide data rows to team members as CSV data when appropriate. Make sure not to share sensitive information through using insecure methods.

The Awesome Public Data Sets[20] project has a "Transportation" category of data, which is worth looking at.

---

18. https://hevodata.com/learn/postgres-export-to-csv/#m1
19. https://stackoverflow.com/a/52175450
20. https://github.com/awesomedata/awesome-public-datasets

In the uber-tlc-foil-response repo, the file uber-trip-data/uber-raw-data-aug14.csv clocks in at 36 MB with around 830K rows. This data represents Uber pickups in the New York City area from August 2014. The data model has similarities to Rideshare, where trips are linked to a trip request and riders specify a start location. Download the CSV file data from GitHub.

On macOS, copy it from ~/Downloads into the /tmp directory.

sh/mv_uber_data_file.sh
```
mv ~/Downloads/uber-raw-data-aug14.csv \
  /tmp/uber-raw-data-aug14.csv
```

Create the trip_pickups table using the same temp_restore database you created earlier. Make the table UNLOGGED since WAL protection isn't needed, and you want writes to be faster.

Run these statements as a superuser from psql:

sql/create_table_trip_pickups.sql
```
-- use the temp_restore database created earlier

\c temp_restore

CREATE UNLOGGED TABLE trip_pickups (
  time TIMESTAMP WITHOUT TIME ZONE,
  lat NUMERIC(15,10),
  lon NUMERIC(15,10),
  base_code VARCHAR(10)
);
```

Make sure you can access the file. Run the following statement:

sql/select_pg_stat_file.sql
```
-- Download:
-- https://github.com/fivethirtyeight/uber-tlc-foil-response
-- /uber-trip-data/uber-raw-data-aug14.csv

-- Placed file in /tmp dir:
SELECT PG_STAT_FILE('/tmp/uber-raw-data-aug14.csv');
```

Use COPY FROM instead of COPY TO since you're loading from a file:

sql/copy_command_copy_from.sql
```
\c temp_restore

COPY trip_pickups
FROM '/tmp/uber-raw-data-aug14.csv'
CSV HEADER;
```

This should return COPY 829275 or similar, meaning 829275 rows were created. This was very fast, taking only a few seconds.

As discussed in "Populating a Database," combining COPY and CREATE TABLE in the same transaction can be even faster.[21]

> COPY is fastest when used within the same transaction as an earlier CREATE TABLE or TRUNCATE command.

Let's try that out. Create a transaction that creates the table, performs a COPY FROM command, and COMMITs the transaction at once. Place these SQL commands in a file called copy_command_trip_pickups.sql:

sql/copy_command_trip_pickups.sql
```
-- Use temp_restore database
\c temp_restore

DROP TABLE trip_pickups;

BEGIN;

CREATE UNLOGGED TABLE trip_pickups (
  time TIMESTAMP WITHOUT TIME ZONE,
  lat NUMERIC(15,10),
  lon NUMERIC(15,10),
  base_code VARCHAR(10)
) WITH (autovacuum_enabled = FALSE);

COPY trip_pickups
FROM '/tmp/uber-raw-data-aug14.csv'
CSV HEADER;

COMMIT;
```

Run these statements from the file by using psql as follows:

sh/psql_bulk_load.sh
```
psql \
  --dbname temp_restore \
  --file copy_command_trip_pickups.sql
```

Verify that you see similar output:

sh/copy_command_output.sh
```
You are now connected to database "temp_restore" as user "andy".
DROP TABLE
BEGIN
CREATE TABLE
COPY 829275
COMMIT
```

You've now seen how to load and dump large amounts of data to and from PostgreSQL using CSV files.

---

21. https://www.postgresql.org/docs/current/populate.html

Next, you'll cover another trick with CSV files.

Did you know CSV files can be used like read-only database tables? Read on to learn how.

Creating a File Foreign Data Wrapper (FDW)

PostgreSQL makes it possible to connect to foreign data sources using functionality called *foreign data wrappers* (FDW).

The file foreign data wrapper module[22] (file_fdw) can be used to work with a CSV file as if it were a read-only table. When you have a large amount of data represented in a file, this can be a nice way to query it and work with it without needing to import it.

Let's try this out.

To create a table, you'll need a source CSV file. The PostgreSQL documentation has an example you'll use here. Use the postgresql.log from your PostgreSQL installation, but first, you'll need to enable the CSV logging format.

To do that, edit your postgresql.conf by changing the log_destination to csvlog.

In PostgreSQL 15, JSON was added as log format (log_destination = jsonlog), which might be more useful in general, but you'll use CSV here.

Change the values for log_destination and logging_collector as shown here, and then restart PostgreSQL:

```
sh/postgresql_log_csvlog.sh
# add 'csvlog' to postgresql.conf
log_destination = 'stderr,csvlog'

# set this value in postgresql.conf
logging_collector = on

# restart PostgreSQL
pg_ctl restart -D /path/to/data/dir
```

Once restarted, verify that logs are written as CSV files in the log directory. Copy one of the files into a /tmp directory with an absolute path to make it easier to work with.

After copying has been completed, from psql, run the SELECT PG_STAT_FILE() function with the previous file path to make sure the file is accessible.

In the following commands, connect to the temp_restore database you set up earlier as a superuser.

---

22. https://www.postgresql.org/docs/current/file-fdw.html

Next, enable the file_fdw extension. Create a SERVER[23] object called file_server by running the following statement:

sql/create_server.sql
```
\c temp_restore

CREATE EXTENSION IF NOT EXISTS file_fdw;

CREATE SERVER file_server
FOREIGN DATA WRAPPER file_fdw;
```

With the SERVER created and the CSV file accessible, you're ready to create the table.

Run the following statement, which creates the pglog table using CREATE FOREIGN TABLE. It uses the file_server SERVER object you just set up.

sql/create_foreign_table_pglog.sql
```
SELECT PG_STAT_FILE('/tmp/postgresql-2023-09-25_131154.csv');

CREATE FOREIGN TABLE pglog (
  log_time TIMESTAMP(3) WITH TIME ZONE,
  user_name TEXT,
  database_name TEXT,
  process_id INTEGER,
  connection_from TEXT,
  session_id TEXT,
  session_line_num BIGINT,
  command_tag TEXT,
  session_start_time TIMESTAMP WITH TIME ZONE,
  virtual_transaction_id TEXT,
  transaction_id BIGINT,
  error_severity TEXT,
  sql_state_code TEXT,
  message TEXT,
  detail TEXT,
  hint TEXT,
  internal_query TEXT,
  internal_query_pos INTEGER,
  context TEXT,
  query TEXT,
  query_pos INTEGER,
  location TEXT,
  application_name TEXT,
  backend_type TEXT,
  leader_pid INTEGER,
  query_id BIGINT
) SERVER file_server
OPTIONS ( FILENAME '/tmp/postgresql-2023-09-25_131154.csv', FORMAT 'csv' );
```

---

23. https://www.postgresql.org/docs/current/sql-createserver.html

With the table created, you're ready to query it.

Run this query to list ten recent queries:

```
sql/query_pglog.sql
SELECT
  log_time,
  message,
  detail,
  query,
  query_pos,
  query_id
FROM pglog
WHERE query IS NOT NULL
LIMIT 10;
```

With this in place, you can now explore your query activity from the database by using SQL.

This technique could be used to build a query log analysis solution. The file_fdw extension can be used with any CSV file. You could also try configuring a table with the Uber data files you set up earlier to explore the data.

Wrapping Up

In this chapter, you worked with bulk data access methods in a variety of ways, both writing and reading data using Active Record and PostgreSQL. You performed bulk inserts, updates, and upsert operations. You learned to use conflict resolution and worked with the SQL MERGE command.

You performed bulk loads of CSV data, wrote data out as INSERT statements, and turned a CSV file into a read-only database table.

In the next chapter, you'll take things to another level. You'll move beyond a single PostgreSQL instance and begin to work with multiple instances. You'll see how to put multiple instances to use to serve greater levels of traffic from your Rails application.

## CHAPTER 13

Scaling with Replication and Sharding

In earlier chapters, you ran PostgreSQL on your local server running the Rideshare databases.

PostgreSQL is a single primary database, meaning just one server receives writes. What happens when your needs expand beyond the capabilities of a single server? What if your primary database fails and you need to bring a new server in quickly? What if you'd like to run multiple copies of your database structure that different customers use on different servers so that their server resources and storage are isolated? How can that be achieved?

In this chapter, you'll tackle the underpinnings needed to unlock these use cases and more. To get there, you'll move beyond a single PostgreSQL instance and set up multiple instances working together.

While server instances have an upper limit on hardware resources, another practical limitation is cost. What if your platform needs to support a few large customers, but the majority of the customers are small and need few resources? This scenario is common and creates cost-efficiency challenges. You may be in a situation where you need to "overprovision" your main server to accommodate the large customers.

Additional instances can help you meet demand from greater numbers of clients. They can also give you options to split up copies of databases on multiple servers, sizing the needs with the resources more proportionally and yielding greater cost efficiency.

Multiple Instances Use Cases

With multiple instances, you'll be able to adopt new capabilities:

- Hot and warm standbys
- High availability and failover
- Read and write splitting
- Horizontal sharding

To support these use cases, you'll need your current server to transform into a primary instance that creates a stream of changes. This stream of changes is replicated to one or more secondary servers that receive and apply them. A second server (or instance) that receives changes runs in a read-only mode. Secondary instances are horizontally scalable, which means you can add more of them. You'll explore that further in upcoming sections. To achieve this, you'll set up multiple types of native replication in PostgreSQL with various instances.

PostgreSQL offers two types of replication:

- Physical replication
- Logical replication

You'll configure both in this chapter.

To get started, what is *physical replication*? Physical replication, a type of "streaming replication," creates a "byte-level physical copy" of a PostgreSQL cluster.

Remember that in PostgreSQL, a "cluster" is the collection of all databases on the instance. From a replication perspective, this means that with physical replication, users are not able to configure individual databases to replicate. Physical replicas receive changes from all databases.

Physical replication is categorized as streaming replication because changes are streamed to a second instance asynchronously by default. This means that when transactions are committed on the primary instance, they're sent to one or more secondary instances that are configured to receive replication.

Once you've set up a primary and replica pair, what can you do with it? With that pair in place, you can begin to enable more use cases, like having a hot standby (more on this shortly) ready for promotion if needed and read and write splitting. In this chapter, you'll mainly focus on using the pair for read and write splitting within the context of Active Record multiple databases support.

Since we're focusing on database skills, most of the chapter is spent configuring replication with lots of focus on PostgreSQL configuration. With that knowledge and configuration in place, you'll be poised to layer the Active Record multiple databases configuration on top.

You've seen hot standby mentioned and might be wondering what it is. A hot standby can be part of a basic *disaster recovery* (DR) and *high availability* (HA) configuration. If a primary instance fails because the replica instance with physical replication is receiving a full set of all changes, the replica can *take over* the role of the primary and act as the new primary.

When this happens, it's called "promotion." Since the replica instance is mostly caught up with the stream of changes, at the time promotion happens, that's minimal to zero data loss from the primary (depending on activity level).

The promotion can be configured to happen automatically, which is called an *automatic failover*. Configuring automatic failover involves greater amounts of operational complexity in exchange for greater uptime and availability. While automatic promotion and failover concepts are being mentioned here, they are outside the scope of this chapter. The purpose in mentioning them here is to list them as very important use cases that can leverage live replication.

Let's start setting up replication. Since you've only got one computer, how can we set up multiple PostgreSQL instances?

To do that, you'll run PostgreSQL instances within Docker[1] containers. You'll set up multiple containers that serve in primary and replica roles. The containers can connect with each other using the same network, although they run on different ports.

Is Replication Necessary?

 Configuring and maintaining replication adds additional complexity but can bring benefits to restore time and availability.

Consider how costly downtime is for your organization. How long would it take to bring in a new instance using a backup of your data? How much data loss are you willing to accept?

Before diving into that, let's take a peek at some of the terminology you'll work with.

---

1. https://github.com/docker

Replication and Sharding Terminology

- Replica—Secondary server instance that receives changes and runs in a "read-only" mode

- Recovery mode—This is the read-only mode a replica runs in

- Physical replication—Byte-for-byte copy of a cluster, usually receiving changes asynchronously (configurable)

- Logical replication—Replication type with configurable databases, tables, and operations. Does *not* replicate DDL

- Read and write splitting—Distributing the load from reads and writes across multiple instances

- Cluster—A collection of databases

- Instance—A PostgreSQL server

- Replication lag—The latency from when changes occur on the primary until they're available on a replica

To help determine whether read and write splitting would provide benefits, let's categorize different types of statements.

How is that done?

Categorizing Query Workloads

Your database is performing different categories of work. There's work from your client Rails application as SQL queries writing and reading data, structural changes being applied, work being performed automatically in the background in PostgreSQL, and work being performed manually by administrators. That's a lot of activity happening at the same time.

Let's focus on the work from the client Rails application. Specifically, let's look at the table rows being created, updated, deleted, and queried.

You've already learned what DDL and DML are. INSERT, UPDATE, and DELETE are DML, and SELECT statements are classified as *Data Query Language* (DQL).

Earlier, you learned that web applications tend to have many more reads (DQL) than writes (DML).

What if you could separate the reads or DQL statements and perform that work on a separate instance? That's the basic idea behind read and write splitting.

Once you've configured a second instance running in a read-only mode, that instance can serve most of your read queries, with some caveats. When a read replica absorbs load that would have otherwise been on the primary instance, the primary instance can now serve more requests.

Is Read and Write Splitting Necessary?

Separating reads to a new instance adds operational complexity.

Consider deferring this until you've measured the impact of read queries on your primary instance and have the budget and skills needed, as part of a long-term investment, to conduct read and write splitting.

Further, the number of read replicas can be expanded horizontally. As seen in the last chapter, read queries can be distributed outside the application at the infrastructure level using connection pooling software like PgCat. Read the PgCat documentation on "Load Balancing of Read Queries"[2] for more information.

Alternatively, that routing logic can live within the application. Read queries can be sent to replica instances using Active Record configuration. That's what you'll be working on in upcoming sections.

How do we get started?

Enabling Physical Replication

Since you'll need multiple instances to work with, you'll set up PostgreSQL instances in Docker containers. These containers run PostgreSQL as their main process. You'll use one container (db01) to act as a primary instance and then set up additional containers as replica instances. This is a long chapter, but if you stick with it, you'll configure both physical and logical replication, providing a foundation to build on top of.

Database Configuration

There's a lot of database configuration needed to set up replication. As a Rails developer, this might be way outside the typical work that you do.

Just remember, you've learned a lot so far. This chapter may be more challenging or more "foreign," but stick with it. You're expanding your knowledge and skills bit by bit.

You've got this!

---

2. https://github.com/postgresml/pgcat#load-balancing-of-read-queries

Here's an overview of the steps you'll be working through. The instructions were developed using Docker on macOS Sonoma 14.1 and PostgreSQL 16.1.

1. Run a Docker PostgreSQL container as the primary instance.

2. Run a second container as a replica instance.

3. Enable Write Ahead Log (WAL) replication on the primary. Create a replication user and a replication slot.

4. Permit access to the replication user using the pg_hba.conf file on the primary.

5. Empty out the data directory on the replica so that it can be replaced with the data directory from the primary.

6. Run pg_basebackup on the replica, specifying the replication user and replication slot.

7. Restart the replica, which now runs in a read-only mode, receiving changes.

8. Verify that replication is working.

Shell Scripts Automation

 Much of the configuration in this chapter has been automated with runnable shell scripts that you can find in the docker directory in Rideshare on GitHub.

That's a lot of steps! If you haven't already installed Docker on macOS, stop and do that now. Navigate to https://docs.docker.com/desktop/install/mac-install/ and follow all of the steps. Start up Docker Desktop before proceeding.

With Docker installed, you're ready to add containers.

Here's a preview of the containers you'll be creating and connecting to as this chapter unfolds. Initially, you'll focus just on db01 and db02.

Container name	Role	Port	User
db01	primary	54321	postgres
db02	replica (physical)	54322	postgres
db03	replica (logical)	54323	postgres

You'll run shell scripts that execute docker run to boot PostgreSQL containers. The shell scripts are in Rideshare in the docker directory.

Most of the scripts are copied into this chapter, although you may need to refer to the downloadable source code or GitHub. In this chapter, you'll work in your terminal, generally from the docker directory in Rideshare. You'll be encouraged to run scripts from your checkout of the repository since they'll be tested and maintained there after the book has been published.

Let's start running commands. To allow the containers to work together, create a shared docker network.[3] Make sure Docker is running. Run the following command in your terminal:

```
docker/sh/network_create.sh
# Remove it first, if it exists
# docker network rm rideshare-net
#
docker network create rideshare-net
```

PostgreSQL runs on the standard port 5432 on each container. The scripts map a port on your local machine to the port inside the container. Each port number is increased by one to make them more memorable, but the outside port could be any value.

- Port 54321 is used for db01.

- Port 54322 is used for the replica instance.

- The rideshare-net Docker network is used by both containers, allowing them to reference hosts like db01.

- A persistent volume (specified with the --volume option) is set up as docker/postgres-docker. Subdirectories within that directory are mapped to the db01 and db02 PostgreSQL data directories (/var/lib/postgresql/data).

You'll access the containers generally using the postgres/postgres superuser credentials. Besides that user, you'll set up a replication user on db01 that is used to authenticate from other instances.

Open up your terminal and the Rideshare project. From there, cd into the docker directory.

From the Rideshare directory, cd into the docker directory, as shown here. From there, run the shell script as follows:

```
cd docker

sh run_db_db01_primary.sh
```

---

3.   https://docs.docker.com/engine/reference/commandline/network_create/

Here is the script:

```
docker/sh/run_db_db01_primary.sh
#!/bin/bash
#
# Run from Rideshare dir
# Use bind dir: ./postgres-docker/db01
# network: "rideshare-net"
docker run \
  --name db01 \
  --volume ${PWD}/postgres-docker/db01:/var/lib/postgresql \
  --publish 54321:5432 \
  --env POSTGRES_USER=postgres \
  --env POSTGRES_PASSWORD=postgres \
  --net=rideshare-net \
  --detach postgres:16.1
```

After running sh run_db_db01_primary.sh, you should see the container listed when running docker ps or see it listed in Docker Desktop. Make sure it's running before proceeding.

With db01 running, it will serve as your primary instance.

Let's connect to db01. The following connection string connects to the postgres database running on db01 using port 54321. This is the published port that maps to the internal 5432 port in the container.

```
sh/db01_connect.sh
# Local mapped port 54321 to 5432
# DB: postgres
# Username/password: postgres/postgres
psql postgres://postgres:postgres@localhost:54321/postgres
```

You should see a prompt like this:

```
psql (16.1)
Type "help" for help.

postgres@localhost:54321 postgres#
```

Type \q to quit. An alternative way to connect is like this:

```
docker exec --user postgres -it db01 psql
```

Type \q to exit.

Let's start modifying the configuration on db01. You'll need to know where it's located. To find that out, connect again to db01 using psql with one of the previous methods, and from there, run this:

```
sql/show_config_file.sql
-- Connected as `postgres`
-- Connect as `owner`, which was granted `pg_read_all_data`
SHOW config_file;
```

By default, the path is /var/lib/postgresql/data/postgresql.conf. PostgreSQL containers set up the environment variable PGDATA that points to this directory, which is easier to access. Verify that with this one-liner in your terminal: docker exec db01 env | grep PGDATA.

Since there's no text editor on the container, to modify the configuration file you'll use a workaround. You'll download the file to your local machine where you edit it and save your changes, then you'll upload it again to the container.

To do that, use docker cp to download the file from the container to your local OS.

You will follow a bunch of steps in this section. To make the steps easier to run, they have all been placed into the following file. The file is not intended to be run with one command, but is intended for readers to run each step individually.

You'll edit the configuration file and set a value for the wal_level setting in postgresql.conf. Then you'll put the file back on db01. The next section explains why this value was chosen.

Run through the following steps from your terminal:

```
docker/sh/db01_postgresql_conf.sh
# copy from container to local filesystem
docker cp db01:/var/lib/postgresql/data/postgresql.conf .

# create a backup of the file
cp postgresql.conf postgresql.backup.conf

# edit the config, using your own editor (replace vim if needed)
vim postgresql.conf

# Change wal_level to logical as follows:
# Find the "wal_level" value which is commented out
#
# wal_level = logical

# Once edited and saved, copy it back to db01
docker cp postgresql.conf db01:/var/lib/postgresql/data/.

# For wal_level, need to restart the container:
docker restart db01

# Confirm wal_level was set to logical
docker exec --user postgres -it db01 psql -c "SHOW wal_level"
```

Let's review the steps. After downloading postgresql.conf from the container, a backup of the file was made. Use the backup file to start over if needed.

You found the wal_level setting and enabled it, setting the value as follows: wal_level = logical.

After restarting the container, you confirmed using psql that wal_level was, in fact, changed to logical.

Since you're configuring physical replication in this section, you might be wondering why wal_level was set to logical.

The logical value covers both physical and logical replication.[4] Since you'll be working with logical replication later in this chapter, this was chosen to minimize the changes needed.

Choosing a wal_level Value

The wal_level value of logical creates additional logs that are needed for logical replication. You're doing that here because you'll also work with logical replication later.

When working in your databases in production, choose a different wal_level if you don't plan to use logical replication.

You're making great progress! You've configured a container as a primary instance and set the wal_level. Next up, you'll configure a user for replication.

Creating a Replication User on the Primary

For replication to work, you'll need a PostgreSQL user on db01. Remember that users in PostgreSQL are ROLE objects that have the LOGIN privilege. Besides LOGIN, the replication user gets the REPLICATION privilege granted.

You'll create the user on db01, then use the credentials for that user to initialize the replication process from replica instances.

Let's configure db02 to act as a replica. The replication user must already exist on the primary instance. You'll use the credentials on the replica to connect. Besides the credentials, you'll grab the IP address of the replica.

To permit access to 'db01', use the PostgreSQL Host-Based Authentication (HBA) file. This file is on the primary instance[5] and gives access to the replication user, requiring their password, and from specific IP addresses that are permitted.

---

4. https://www.postgresql.org/docs/current/runtime-config-wal.html
5. https://www.postgresql.org/docs/current/auth-trust.html

Let's create the replication user now. As discussed earlier, the user called replication_user will be created, but using a script. This makes the creation more repeatable if needed. The password for the replication user also needs to be distributed to the replica instances.

The replication user gets a generated password that's part of their creation process and is also copied into a special .pgpass file that's copied to the db02 replica instance. This way, the password is accessible there for password-based authentication from db02 to db01.

This process is automated using the following shell script. Read through the steps in the script, but don't attempt to run them individually or copy and paste the script. Instead, cd into the docker directory in Rideshare in your terminal, and run the script from there.

Before doing that, though, let's check some preconditions. Let's start up db02. The script expects db02 to be running so the .pgpass file that gets populated can be copied there.

Use the same process that you used earlier with db01.

From the docker directory in Rideshare, run

```
cd docker
```

```
sh run_db_db02_replica.sh
```

The script content is copied here:

```
docker/sh/run_db_db02_replica.sh
#!/bin/bash
#
# Run from Rideshare dir
# Use bind dir: ./postgres-docker/db02
# network: "rideshare-net"
docker run \
  --name db02 \
  --volume ${PWD}/postgres-docker/db02:/var/lib/postgresql/data \
  --publish 54322:5432 \
  --env POSTGRES_USER=postgres \
  --env POSTGRES_PASSWORD=postgres \
  --net=rideshare-net \
  --detach postgres:16.1
```

Run docker ps from your terminal and verify that db01 and db02 are running (or use Docker Desktop).

With db01 and db02 running, you're ready to proceed with the script that creates the replication_user user.

Here's a preview of the steps in the script:

1. Generates a password, assigning it to an environment variable

2. Creates the file replication_user.sql with CREATE USER SQL commands to create the replication user, giving it the generated password. The SQL file is copied to db01 so it can be run there.

3. The generated password is placed in a .pgpass file. The .pgpass file is then copied to db02 (which is already running). That will allow replication_user to connect from db02 to db01 using password authentication.

Don't manually type out the script, but here are the steps for review. Keep in mind there may be newer iterations to the script on GitHub.

docker/sh/db01_create_replication_user.sh

```bash
#!/bin/bash
#
# Purpose:
# - Generate password, and place in .pgpass
# - Create replication_user using generated password, on db01
# - Copy .pgpass to db02
#
# The .pgpass password is used to authenticate replication_user,
# when they run pg_basebackup
#
# Precondition: Make sure db01 and db02 are running
#
running_containers=$(docker ps --format "{{.Names}}")
if echo "$running_containers" | grep -q "db01"; then
  echo "db01 is running...continuing"
else
  echo "db01 is not running"
  echo "Exiting."
  exit 1
fi

if echo "$running_containers" | grep -q "db02"; then
  echo "db02 is running...continuing"
else
  echo "db02 is not running"
  echo "Exiting."
  exit 1
fi

# Password for replication_user
export REP_USER_PASSWORD=$(openssl rand -hex 12)
echo "Create REP_USER_PASSWORD for replication_user"
echo $REP_USER_PASSWORD

# "rm replication_user.sql" for a clean starting point
# CREATE USER statement as SQL file
```

```
# Set password to DB_PASSWORD value
rm -f replication_user.sql
echo "CREATE USER replication_user
WITH ENCRYPTED PASSWORD '$REP_USER_PASSWORD'
REPLICATION LOGIN;
GRANT SELECT ON ALL TABLES IN SCHEMA public
TO replication_user;
ALTER DEFAULT PRIVILEGES IN SCHEMA public
GRANT SELECT ON TABLES TO replication_user;" >> replication_user.sql

rm -f .pgpass
echo "*:*:*:replication_user:$REP_USER_PASSWORD" >> .pgpass

# Copy replication_user.sql to db01
docker cp replication_user.sql db01:.

echo "Copy .pgpass, chown, chmod it for db02"
# Copy .pgpass to db02 postgres home dir
docker cp .pgpass db02:/var/lib/postgresql/.
docker exec --user root -it db02 \
  chown postgres:root /var/lib/postgresql/.pgpass
docker exec --user root -it db02 \
  chmod 0600 /var/lib/postgresql/.pgpass

# Create replication_user on db01
docker exec -it db01 \
  psql -U postgres \
  -f /replication_user.sql
```

Now that you've read it, run it from Rideshare. cd to the docker and run:

```
cd docker
```

```
sh db01_create_replication_user.sh
```

You should see output like this:

```
db01 is running...continuing
db02 is running...continuing
Create REP_USER_PASSWORD for replication_user
a3bbee7ec73598536290239b
Successfully copied 2.05kB to db01:.
Successfully copied 2.05kB to db02:/var/lib/postgresql/.
CREATE ROLE
```

Resetting

If you need to reset this, there's a helper script for that.

From the docker directory, run: sh teardown_docker.sh to tear everything down.

The next step is to make sure that replication_user can connect from db02 to db01.

Read on to learn more.

Allowing Access for the Replication User

In this section, you'll configure access from the host and password authentication for the user you've just created.

For host access, you'll configure the pg_hba.conf file that runs on the db01 instance. Rideshare has a sample HBA file you can reference in the postgresql directory. This file has a very specific format and can be tricky to work with if you're brand new to it.

Refer to official documentation "The pg_hba.conf File"[6] for greater depth.

As you did before with the PostgreSQL config file, you might be wondering where the HBA file is located. Let's find out. Run the following from your terminal:

```
sql/show_hba_file.sh
docker exec --user postgres -it db01 \
psql -c "SHOW hba_file"
```

By default, in Docker PostgreSQL it's /var/lib/postgresql/data/pg_hba.conf. You'll use that path in a bit.

While you could manually customize this file, it can be tedious and error prone. Fortunately, Rideshare includes a script that replaces the file content with slimmed-down, generated content that you'll use to get going instead.

One piece of custom data you need is the IP address of the db02 replica instance. Besides that value, you'll allow connections to the replication pseudo-database for replication_user using the md5 password authentication mechanism. You'll connect using the generated password value for replication_user, which is read from the ~/.pgpass on the container.

Let's look at how to get the IP address first. Run docker ps in your terminal. Confirm db02 is running. Run the following command:

```
docker/sh/ip_address.sh
# Get the IP address of the db02 container
docker inspect -f \
  '{{range .NetworkSettings.Networks}}{{.IPAddress}}{{end}}' \
  db02
```

You should get an IP address (v4) like 172.18.0.3. Normally, you'd copy and paste that value yourself, however, this step has been automated by being included in a script that fetches the value and places it into generated file content.

---

6. https://www.postgresql.org/docs/current/auth-pg-hba-conf.html

Here's an example of what that line looks like:

sh/pg_hba_conf_replication_user.sh

```
# TYPE  DATABASE        USER              ADDRESS           METHOD
host    replication     replication_user 172.18.0.3/32      md5
```

Let's run the script. Navigate to the docker directory in Rideshare, and run:

```
sh pg_hba_reset.sh
```

The script creates a local pg_hba.conf file populated with the necessary values, then uploads it to db01.

After the file is uploaded, reload the db01 configuration which picks up any changes made to the HBA file:

```
docker exec --user postgres -it db01 \
 psql -c "SELECT pg_reload_conf();"
```

Print out the contents of the file on db01 and verify the line is present for replication_user with an IP address like 172.18.0.3/32:

```
docker exec --user postgres -it db01 \
  cat /var/lib/postgresql/data/pg_hba.conf
```

If the config looks good, you're ready to test out connectivity and authentication. Connectivity is covered by the HBA file changes you've just made, and authentication is covered using the ~/.pgpass file that was uploaded earlier, which has the password for replication_user. Using that file, scripts authenticate without needing to supply the password explicitly since it comes from the file.

Run the following commands:

```
docker exec --user postgres -it db02 /bin/bash
```

```
psql postgres://replication_user:@db01/postgres
```

Replication User Credentials

In the connection string we saw earlier, no password was supplied, but password authentication is required. How does that work? The password comes from the ~/.pgpass file which the postgres user can read. This approach keeps the password out of code.

To verify the password is truly required, try using a bogus password instead by placing it after the colon after replication_user. You should see an error message like password authentication failed.

Excellent! Access from db02 is permitted to db01. replication_user can authenticate using their password. You know that pg_hba.conf is configured properly, which is a big deal because *knowing is half the battle.*[7]

HBA Password Options

You're using md5 here for pg_hba.conf instead of trust for replication_user. While md5 is OK for this demonstration, the recommended method is scram-sha-256 for improved security.

Refer to https://www.postgresql.org/docs/current/auth-password.html for more information.

While this was a long section, verifying connectivity and authentication will help save you headaches later as you kick off replication.

You're ready to proceed with configuring replication.

Configuring the Replica Instance

With everything you've accomplished so far, you're ready to start up replication. If you've never set up physical replication on a secondary instance, the first step might be surprising.

The first step in the process is to completely remove the data directory on the replica using the dangerous rm command. Huh?! The data directory for db02 replica is then replaced with the content of the db01 data directory.

Why? As you learned earlier, physical replication is a byte-for-byte copy of the entire cluster. What you're doing is replacing the data directory for db02 with a copy of the data directory content from db01. Once that's done initially, replication keeps changes in sync from db01 to db02, using the WAL stream.

While you might think of using a command like cp to copy and paste the data directory, there's an official program to do that with lots of options.

The first step you'll perform is to create a *base backup*. To do that, use the built-in CLI program pg_basebackup.[8]

Once pg_basebackup captures the initial backup, you'll restart the db02 container (which restarts PostgreSQL). The db02 instance is now receiving a live stream of changes from db01 and running in a read-only mode.

---

7.   https://www.youtube.com/watch?v=pele5vptVgc

8.   https://www.postgresql.org/docs/current/app-pgbasebackup.html

With Docker PostgreSQL, since there's only one process that's running, stopping the PostgreSQL process also stops the Docker container and vice versa.

Data Directory Replacement in Docker

 Replacing the data directory for PostgreSQL in Docker is tricky. Follow these steps closely.

You may need an extra cup of coffee for this section! Be extra vigilant anytime you're running rm -rf!

If you make it all the way to the bottom, you'll unlock a cheat code and find a surprise.

Removing the data directory on the running container is odd because it will kill the container within a few moments. This is not ideal.

For this process to work, you'll remove the data directory content *and then immediately* run pg_basebackup. *You must do this quickly* or the container will stop. The best way to do this is to copy both commands at once, the rm -rf and the pg_basebackup command.

In the script run_pg_basebackup.sh, the commands use && so they run as one (with backslashes to split over multiple lines). Copy both to your clipboard at once. When you paste in the terminal for db02 and press "return", that ensures that pg_basebackup runs immediately after the rm -rf command.

pg_basebackup runs as replication_user, and you've confirmed earlier that replication_user can access their password from the ~/.pgpass file. The chmod and chown commands ran earlier on ~/.pgpass in preparation for access. Because that file's in place, you won't need to (and shouldn't) supply a password to the pg_basebackup command.

Before creating the base backup, you'll need to make one more change on the primary instance. You'll create a *replication slot* there that will be referenced in the base backup configuration. Let's do that now.

Creating the Replication Slot

Replication is described using a replication slot object created on the primary instance. cd to the docker directory in Rideshare.

From there, run the following command to create the rideshare_slot replication slot on db01:

```
cd docker
sh db01_create_replication_slot.sh
```

If that ran correctly, you'll see output like this, showing the slot named rideshare_slot was created:

```
 pg_create_physical_replication_slot
- - - - - - - - - - - - - - - - - - - - - - - - - - - - - - - - - - - - - -
 (rideshare_slot,)
```

If the slot already exists, there's a comment in db01_create_replication_slot.sh showing how to drop it. If you're starting over, you may wish to drop the slot.

With the replication slot created, you're ready to use it in your pg_basebackup configuration, as mentioned earlier.

Remember the warnings from the last section on how to run rm -rf and pg_basebackup as one command. Let's run through the expected preconditions one more time.

Make sure db01 and db02 are running. The rideshare_slot replication slot must exist since pg_basebackup references it. pg_basebackup runs using the replication_slot user, which grabs their password from the ~/.pgpass file that they can access.

The following .sh file shows the commands needed, which you'll run individually. The file isn't intended to be a runnable script.

Run each of these commands individually, but stop at the rm -rf command.

From there, copy rm -rf and pg_basebackup together and paste them as one into the db02 container terminal.

```
docker/sh/run_pg_basebackup.sh
# Connect to db02 as "postgres". Why?
# postgres - kicks off replication
# replication_user - authenticates for replication
# against db01
docker exec --user postgres -it db02 /bin/bash

# ############# WARNING #############
#
# Copy the "rm" and "pg_basebackup" commands
# together as one, and paste them together
#
# pg_basebackup run immediately, before container stops
#
# This expects "rideshare_slot" to exist
# ################################
rm -rf /var/lib/postgresql/data/* && \

pg_basebackup --host db01 \
  --username replication_user \
  --pgdata /var/lib/postgresql/data \
  --verbose \
```

```
  --progress \
  --wal-method stream \
  --write-recovery-conf \
  --slot=rideshare_slot

# Restart container
# (or `docker start` if stopped and needing to connect)
docker start db02

# Review live logs
docker logs -f db02
```

If the command on db02 ran successfully, you'll see output in the terminal like this:

```
pg_basebackup: initiating base backup, waiting for checkpoint to complete
pg_basebackup: checkpoint completed
pg_basebackup: write-ahead log start point: 0/2000028 on timeline 1
pg_basebackup: starting background WAL receiver
23105/23105 kB (100%), 1/1 tablespace
pg_basebackup: write-ahead log end point: 0/2000100
pg_basebackup: waiting for background process to finish streaming ...
pg_basebackup: syncing data to disk ...
pg_basebackup: renaming backup_manifest.tmp to backup_manifest
pg_basebackup: base backup completed
```

Great! The pg_basebackup command used the --write-recovery-conf option, which created a standby.signal file in the data directory on db02.

With that file present, when db02 starts (by you running docker start db02), it entered *standby mode*. The log file from db02 should show entering standby mode and that it's running in a read-only mode.

Let's confirm that. Run docker logs -f db02 to tail the logs (after it's started), and look for entries like these:

```
2023-11-30 03:01:29.968 UTC [30] LOG:  entering standby mode
2023-11-30 03:01:29.974 UTC [1] LOG:  database system is ready to \
  accept read-only connections
2023-11-30 03:01:29.980 UTC [31] LOG:  started streaming WAL from primary\
  at 0/3000000 on timeline 1
```

Great! You made it! You've now unlocked the cheat code that was hinted at earlier. Let's also relax a bit with a fun video.

Check out the educational, slightly humorous-although-not-really "Dev Deletes Entire Production Database, Chaos Ensues."[9] Although this video relates to a catastrophic event of accidentally deleting the data directory, it might be

---

9.   https://www.youtube.com/watch?v=tLdRBsuvVKc

fun to take a break away from reading and typing. The video is quite educational and you'll see many familiar commands.

The video shows the same process of running `rm -rf` and `pg_basebackup` and how disastrous that is when it's run in the wrong location.

For the "cheat code," you should know that most of the steps you completed manually have been automated in shell scripts available in Rideshare. They weren't revealed earlier (although you might have found them in the `docker` directory) since you were learning the steps. If you simply ran the scripts to start, you wouldn't learn what the individual commands do.

Now that you know the steps and how to quickly reset the docker instances, take a look at these scripts that you can use to easily "tear down" and "reset" the db01 and db02 instances.

```
cd docker
sh teardown_docker.sh
sh reset_docker_instances.sh
```

These scripts bring you right up to where you'd kick off the base backup process. To do that, once they've run, connect to db02 and copy and paste the `rm -rf` and `pg_basebackup` command again to initialize replication for db02. Start db02. You can continue to run this series of commands to tear down and reset the configurations for db01 and db02 to practice configuring physical replication.

From this point forward, we'll assume physical replication is up and running and that you have a good understanding of these steps.

Now that it's running in read-only mode, let's verify that's true by seeing what happens when we send write statements to db02.

Run `docker exec --user postgres -it db02 psql` to connect. Try running this CREATE TABLE statement, which should fail:

```
CREATE TABLE riders (id INT);
```

This should produce:

```
ERROR:  cannot execute CREATE TABLE in a read-only transaction
```

Great, that was expected.

Let's verify replication is working from db01 to db02. Open up psql sessions for db01 and db02 by running each of these commands in different terminals:

```
docker exec --user postgres -it db01 psql
docker exec --user postgres -it db02 psql
```

From db01 psql, try SQL like:

```
CREATE TABLE riders (id INT);
```

From db02, run the "describe table" meta-command, \dt. The riders table should appear on db02 almost instantly.

Try inserting some rows into riders on db01. Verify the rows show up on the db02 instance. They should appear nearly instantly. After that, try deleting some. Here are some statements to conduct those verifications:

```
-- From psql on db01:
INSERT INTO riders (id) VALUES (1);

-- From psql on db02
-- SELECT * FROM riders;

DELETE FROM riders WHERE id = 1;
```

Great! Your configured physical replication works as expected between your primary db01 instance and your db02 replica instance. You made sure replication was working for inserts and deletes and observed that they propagated nearly instantly.

With your replication pair ready to go, you're ready to layer on application side usage.

Since we're working with Ruby on Rails and Active Record, how would you configure access to read replicas for read-only queries from Active Record?

Active Record Multiple Databases Background

Starting in Rails 6, Active Record added a feature called *multiple databases*. This feature provides native support for connecting to multiple databases from Active Record, which can then be used in various ways.

As a brief intro, with multiple databases, Rails applications have different databases, on the same instance or different instances, that they can route requests to. They would do that to help with performance, reliability, and scalability.

One of the use cases this unlocks is read and write splitting, which sends most of the read-only queries to the read replica instance.

While this functionality is not new and existed before Rails 6, developers needed to use third-party gems like MultiDB[10] to connect to multiple databases. With native support in Active Record, the bar to adopting this

---

10. https://github.com/OutOfOrder/multidb

functionality has been lowered. The functionality is now better tested and documented due to greater numbers of engineers working on it and applications using it.

Native support brought official Active Record API documentation, Rails Guides coverage, and may spark more coverage at conferences and in blog posts. By making the support for this native, new releases of Ruby on Rails can continue to enhance it.

This has already been happening. For example, Rails 6.1 expanded on multiple databases launched in 6.0, adding *horizontal sharding.*[11]

Horizontal sharding is a form of "application-level sharding," where the application is responsible for routing traffic to shards. In horizontal sharding, each shard has the same tables and the same schema design but unique data to the shard. Where data would have been combined before, it's now distributed among the shards in distinct data sets.

While the databases may run on the same instance, typically, they'd run on different instances to distribute their load.

What types of applications might use this? Multitenant applications that combine data from different customers, or "tenants," may wish to separate large tenants from shared environments to their own dedicated environment.

Before exploring this solution further, let's discuss what a tenant is. AWS has the following definition:[12]

> A tenant is the most fundamental construct of a SaaS environment.

The tenant is a customer within your system. Now that we've defined what a tenant is, what is a multitenant system?

> The software provided in this model is referred to as a multi-tenant SaaS system because each of the tenants of the service are consuming a single, shared system that supports the needs of these tenants through a unified experience.

While the databases could run on the same server instance, by using separate instances, a shard can be scaled independently. For example, in a multitenant system, with a tenant as a shard, their shard may have many server resources to better handle higher query volume, heavier data growth, and have their data isolated. While the tenant data may have started in a shared system, by splitting out the tenant to a dedicated shard, the original instance would

11. https://guides.rubyonrails.org/active_record_multiple_databases.html#horizontal-sharding

12. https://docs.aws.amazon.com/wellarchitected/latest/saas-lens/silo-pool-and-bridge-models.html

reclaim resources for other tenants. The large tenant's dedicated shard could then be scaled up with more resources.

How can we put multiple databases into action?

Configuring Active Record Multiple Databases

Let's configure the basics of Active Record Rails 6 multiple databases for read and write splitting. This requires the streaming replication you just set up in earlier sections. You've already solved the initial database operational challenges by enabling live replication between the instances. You set up the replica to receive changes, but you haven't yet configured the application to connect to multiple databases. Let's do that now!

Rideshare is currently configured for a single database. To change that, you will first need to edit config/database.yml, setting up connections to each of db01 and db02.

From the "Multiple Databases with Active Record"[13] page, config/database.yml is changed from a "two-tier" YAML configuration to a "three-tier" configuration. New, unique names are given to the primary and replica instances to identify them.

Since you're working locally, change the development environment section.

You've set up db01 as the primary instance earlier, but it doesn't contain the Rideshare database.

The rideshare_development databases aren't on the db01 Docker container instance. The data lives in your localhost database.

Let's copy the localhost rideshare_development database to the db01 instance. Once that's copied, replication will kick in and copy all the data from db01 to db02.

Let's get started. In rideshare_development, where you ran data generators, there are around 20K rows in the users table.

Run the following commands to dump the table data into a file, then restore it into the db01 instance. Run docker ps as you did earlier to confirm that db01 and db02 are running before trying to copy data to them. Neither instance should have a database named rideshare_development at this point. If they do, you'll need to remove it first.

---

13. https://guides.rubyonrails.org/active_record_multiple_databases.html#generators-and-migrations

Run the following commands to configure db01 instance with the necessary roles and privileges. This copies the configuration you set up already for your local Rideshare PostgreSQL instance.

With the roles, schema, and privileges created on db01, you're ready to restore the data. Run the commands individually to do that.

sh/dump_rideshare_local_to_db01.sh
```
# Copy Rideshare db/setup.sh to db01
# including all the supporting SQL files
docker exec -it db01 mkdir db
docker cp db db01:.

# Run "sh db/setup.sh" on db01, which should provision an empty
# rideshare_development database on the db01 instance
# On db01, the file is at "/setup.sh" in the root dir
# Preconditions:
# - env var DB_URL is set
# - env var RIDESHARE_DB_PASSWORD is set
#
# These should be set locally *first*
# so that they can be supplied to the container
#
docker exec \
  --env DB_URL="$DB_URL" \
  --env RIDESHARE_DB_PASSWORD="$RIDESHARE_DB_PASSWORD" \
  db01 sh -c "/setup.sh"

# Once created, we won't migrate there, since we'll be copying
# tables using pg_dump

# Connect to db01 and confirm:
# - schema "rideshare" exists (\dn)
# - database "rideshare_development" exists
# - database is empty (has no tables)
docker exec --user postgres -it db01 \
  psql -d rideshare_development

# Dump the local rideshare_development database into a file
pg_dump -U postgres \
  -h localhost rideshare_development > rideshare_dump.sql

# Check the size
# Should be around 3MB with generated data
du -h rideshare_dump.sql

# Restore rideshare_development from the file
# to db01
# Warning: this might take a few moments!
PGPASSWORD=postgres psql -U postgres \
  -h localhost \
  -p 54321 \
  -d rideshare_development < rideshare_dump.sql
```

```
# Connect again and confirm the tables and row data
# have been loaded
# NOTE: connect as "owner"
#
docker exec --user postgres -it db01 \
  psql -U owner -d rideshare_development

# SELECT COUNT(*) FROM users; -- 20210
```

Once each of these commands has run, db01 now contains the data from rideshare_development that was populated locally. Since you configured physical replication earlier, the schema, tables, and row data have all been copied to the db02 instance.

Verify that by connecting to db02 and comparing the counts from tables to db01:

```
docker exec --user postgres -it db02 \
  psql -U owner -d rideshare_development
```

Great! db02 has a full copy of the data, thanks to the physical replication you set up earlier.

You're now ready to configure db01 and db02 in Active Record. Let's give db01 the configuration name of rideshare, and db02 the configuration name of rideshare_replica. You'll set this configuration in the app/models/application_record.rb model in Rideshare. This configuration exists already but is commented out. Uncomment that section in the model class.

This is the skeleton structure for config/database.yml for rideshare and rideshare_replica:

```
yml/db_config_primary_replica.yml
development:
  rideshare:
    database: rideshare_development
    url: <%= ENV['DATABASE_URL_PRIMARY'] %>
    ...
  rideshare_replica:
    database: rideshare_development
    url: <%= ENV['DATABASE_URL_REPLICA'] %>
    ...
    replica: true
    database_tasks: false
```

Copy the contents of config/database-multiple.sample.yml from Rideshare, overwriting the existing config/database.yml.

Another change was that options replica: true and database_tasks: false were added to the rideshare_replica configuration,[14] which is intended for physical replication (which propagates DDL like tables and indexes).

Safety Tips for Database Configurations

 Rails Guides have recommendations for good practices to follow. Use replica: true for the replica configuration, which prevents migrations from running. Use database_tasks: false to disable even more things, including schema management, migrations, and seeds. Use a read-only user with PostgreSQL for the replica to prevent mistaken writes.

To set this up, replace the postgres/postgres credentials used in these examples. Refer to Rideshare database provisioning scripts for a read-only user configuration example.

The file references two new environment variables that point to the db01 and db02 instances. These variables are defined in the .env in Rideshare.

Using the environment variables set in .env, Active Record should pick them up courtesy of dotenv[15] when you run Rails commands like dbconsole (or db).

Run bin/rails db from the root directory of Rideshare in your terminal.

Since you're not specifying the primary or replica, Active Record picks the first configuration. This means that instead of connecting to rideshare_development on localhost, the command connects to db01.

Again, you're connecting here as owner without supplying a password since it's expected to be in ~/.pgpass. Make sure the file has an entry for the local mapped port to db01.

Try connecting to each of the primary and replica by supplying the --database option as follows:

```
bin/rails db --database rideshare
bin/rails db --database rideshare_replica
```

Great! You have now configured Active Record to connect to each database instance.

How can you use these new configurations to split up your write and read workload? Read on to learn more.

---

14. https://guides.rubyonrails.org/active_record_multiple_databases.html#connecting-to-databases-without-managing-schema-and-migrations
15. https://github.com/bkeepers/dotenv

Multiple Roles with Active Record Models

You have come a long way! With the writing and reading roles configured, we are coming to the end of the scope of this chapter. However, in a sense, for application developers, this is where the fun part comes in. You've done all the heavy lifting to get PostgreSQL instances configured and connected to Ruby on Rails. Now, you can decide where to go from here and how to use them.

Let's look at some basics.

From your terminal, run bin/rails console. Let's try running queries using the reader role. This is the structure:

```ruby
# ruby/active_record_connected_to.rb
ActiveRecord::Base.connected_to(role: :reading) do
  # all code in this block will be connected to the reading role
end
```

With that structure in mind, try running something like this:

```ruby
ActiveRecord::Base.connected_to(role: :reading) do
  User.first
end
```

The block uses the role: :reading option, which is defined in ApplicationRecord. Swap out reading for writing and try both.

The prevent_writes option can be passed in set to true to prevent writes. This makes sense as a default for the reading role. Setting this option to true inside a connection with the writer role returns a ActiveRecord::ReadOnlyError error. Give that a try.

With the new reading role in place, any Active Record query code that is tolerant of *replication lag* can be run there. As you begin to roll this out in your project, you may wish to manually move query code over to the replica instance.

Rideshare could be converted now to pepper in more places to run queries on the replica instance. That will be left as an exercise for the reader in their local copies of Rideshare.

As you begin migrating more and more query code, you may find that it's a lot of work.

What if there was a way to automatically run query code on the replica instance?

Using Automatic Role Switching

Instead of manually switching all Active Record queries, it's possible to automatically send them to the replica. The Active Record feature automatic role switching,[16] which runs as a middleware from Rails 6.0 onward, provides that functionality.

How does it work? Automatic role switching identifies incoming HTTP requests by their verb. HTTP requests that are GET and HEAD requests are always read-only types. This means that Active Record can send queries for those requests to the reading role. Other HTTP request verbs (POST, PUT, DELETE, or PATCH) always go to the writer role.

Automatic role switching has some caveats to be aware of. For requests related to individual resources, Active Record checks the creation time (using the created_at column) and, by default, sends all requests to the writer for resources created within the last two seconds. This is a configurable delay value that can be customized by changing Rails.application.config.active_record.database_selector.

Use the following generator to create a starter file for automatic role switching:

```
bin/rails g active_record:multi_db
```

Explore the file and documentation to learn about options. Another scenario where replication lag is discussed is the concept of "read your own writes." In this scenario, even GET and HEAD requests go to the writer role when the delay is within two seconds.

To customize connection switching, create a class that inherits from Database Selector::Resolver and overrides the methods. Refer to "Activating Automatic Role Switching"[17] for details. Unfortunately, Rideshare has not been set up for automatic role switching, but all the starter ingredients are in place for readers to take this on as an exercise.

You've now seen some basics on how to use Active Record with primary and replica instance configurations for various use cases. You configured a writer and reader role and worked with these connections from Active Record models.

In the next section, you'll dive back into the PostgreSQL side and take a deeper look at replication slots.

---

16. https://guides.rubyonrails.org/active_record_multiple_databases.html#activating-automatic-role-switching
17. https://guides.rubyonrails.org/active_record_multiple_databases.html

Replication Slots and the Write Ahead Log (WAL)

Earlier, you set up the rideshare_slot replication slot to enable physical replication. That slot had the slot_type value of physical. The script that initialized the base backup on the replica instance referenced the slot by name.

Both physical and logical replication types use replication slots.

As you've seen in earlier chapters, system views provide visibility into PostgreSQL internals. Replication slots can be explored by querying the pg_replication_slots view.

Let's take a look. Run SELECT * FROM pg_replication_slots; on db01 psql to view created slots. Replication slots have an active status Boolean that's true when the slot is being used.

The maximum number of slots is configured as ten by default, although that number can be raised.

Why might you add slots? As your read query workload increases, you may wish to add more replica instances. Read replicas can serve other purposes like ad hoc querying, data exports, or act as "warm" standbys. Warm standbys actively receive replication but aren't used for queries from the application. A unique replication slot must be created for each replica and have a name that's unique to the cluster.

Replicas are "hot" when they receive replication and are used for queries. For Rideshare, you've configured db02 as a "hot" replica.

With either a hot or a warm replica, they can be "promoted" in the event that the primary instance fails. Since failover is beyond the scope of this chapter, refer to the Failover PostgreSQL documentation, which covers "High Availability, Load Balancing, and Replication"[18] for more information.

Ruby on Rails does not natively support distributing reads across multiple replicas as of Rails 7.1, although this may be added in future versions.

What if you'd like to run multiple read replicas and distribute the read query workload there? To do that, use a third-party Ruby gem like distribute_reads.[19]

---

18. https://www.postgresql.org/docs/current/warm-standby-failover.html
19. https://github.com/ankane/distribute_reads

The connection pooler PgCat[20] provides the ability to distribute reads to multiple instances. Read more about this in the post "Adopting PgCat: A Nextgen Postgres Proxy"[21] on the Instacart Engineering blog.

Once you've set up your replication slots, how can you make sure replication is working? To do that, monitor the replication lag by running a query like the following on the db01 primary instance:

```
docker exec --user postgres -it db01 psql
```

sql/monitor_replication_lag.sql
```
-- Monitor replication lag
SELECT
  redo_lsn,
  slot_name,
  restart_lsn,
  ROUND((redo_lsn-restart_lsn) / 1024 / 1024 / 1024, 2) AS GB_behind
FROM PG_CONTROL_CHECKPOINT(), PG_REPLICATION_SLOTS;
```

For each replication slot, check out the gb_behind column in the results to see whether there's pending content to replicate. Replication lag should generally be very fast—under a second. This will depend on a variety of factors though.

Now that you've covered some of the details of replication slots and replication lag, let's explore more ways to use the replica instance.

Earlier, you learned about application-level sharding, which involves splitting your database into two or more writeable databases. How does that work in Active Record?

Sharding at the Application Level

Sharding is an overloaded and confusing term and isn't a capability that's natively supported in PostgreSQL. Generally, the term means to expand your database beyond a single instance, which can be achieved in several ways.

The term can be confused with *table partitioning*, which is something different in PostgreSQL that you'll look at in the next chapter. Let's look at the "Shard (database architecture)" definition from Wikipedia.[22]

Let's explore two types of application-level sharding in Active Record:

- Distinct schemas (also called "functional sharding")
- Same schema (called "horizontal sharding" in Active Record)

---

20. https://www.instacart.com/company/how-its-made/adopting-pgcat-a-nextgen-postgres-proxy/
21. https://www.instacart.com/company/how-its-made/adopting-pgcat-a-nextgen-postgres-proxy/
22. https://en.wikipedia.org/wiki/Shard_(database_architecture)

How Does Wikipedia Define a Shard?

A database shard, or simply a shard, is a horizontal partition of data in a database or search engine. Each shard is held on a separate database server instance to spread the system load across the instances.

Active Record added native sharding support to Rails in version 6.1.

You'll focus more on horizontal sharding in upcoming sections. This sharding type refers to running copies of your database (same schema), which are shards, across multiple server instances.

Each database has the exact same schema definition with horizontal sharding, which means they have the same tables, indexes, and other objects. What are the benefits of that? By distributing copies of the schema across different server instances, requests can be routed to different shards, and the load from the entire set of requests can be distributed across one or more of the server instances, each serving a shard.

Application level sharding means the client application has the responsibility of routing requests to shards. Since PostgreSQL is not a distributed database with multiple-writer primary instances, the framework can establish connections to split work among multiple databases that become part of the overall database architecture.

This is an amazing functionality to have natively in the framework when needed.

Before diving into horizontal sharding, let's look at distinct schema sharding, or "functional" sharding, and what support Active Record offers for that.

Migrating Multiple Database Schemas

You may have only used Active Record migrations to evolve the design of one database. Imagine if your Rails application worked with multiple databases and you could use Active Record migrations to evolve the designs of multiple databases at once.

Let's consider a hypothetical example for Rideshare to make this more concrete. First, we'll need to imagine a new design within Rideshare. Imagine that the company behind Rideshare wishes to grow the business by expanding into a new business line area beyond the transportation of people.

They want to continue to leverage the vast amount of on-demand cars, drivers, and customers that have been acquired.

To do that, the business decides to launch grocery delivery. This will be a new source of revenue for the company and will leverage existing assets, helping reduce time to market.

To reduce time to market, the team decides to build within the existing Ruby on Rails codebase but create a separate database called deliveries.

Let's assume deliveries has tables that correspond to Active Record models like Delivery, DeliveryItem, and Store. Deliveries include items that are picked from a store.

Rideshare models can be mixed in, too. Once a delivery is created by a customer, a trip request between the store's location and the customer's location is created. By leveraging the Rideshare models, there will be less new code to create, although existing code may need to be generalized.

Imagine the following steps are used to provision the deliveries database:

1. Create a deliveries database. Run createdb deliveries_development.

2. Add the deliveries database configuration to the Rails app.

3. Create a directory for deliveries migration files. mkdir db/deliveries_migrate.

4. Generate migrations using bin/rails g migration, using the --database option with deliveries as the value.

5. For each migration, its file is stored in the db/migrate/deliveries_migrate directory.

Active Record allows you to relocate the original migrations to their own directory or leave them where they are. The deliveries migrations get their own new directory.

Imagine that deliveries becomes very popular. Just like Rideshare, the deliveries database can be split into a primary and replica pair. Using the same mechanisms you worked with earlier, you can take advantage of read and write splitting for Deliveries as a second database that's all part of the same Rideshare codebase.

Active Record multiple databases provides powerful and flexible functionality!

With distinct-schema sharding covered, let's dive into the same-schema type of sharding introduced earlier.

This type of sharding is supported natively in Active Record and is called horizontal sharding. How does it work?

Using Horizontal Sharding for Multitenancy

Horizontal sharding was added to Active Record multiple databases in 6.1.[23]

Horizontal sharding is a general mechanism to run copies of a same-schema database on more instances. What are some use cases?

One compelling use case for horizontal sharding is for multitenant architectures. For Software as a Service (SaaS) platforms with hundreds of customers, some customers may have exceptional query volume or data growth. When those customers are in a database on an instance that's shared by many customers, they can create a "noisy neighbor" problem, where the resources they consume degrade the performance for others.

To address that, organizations may migrate the data for that customer out of the multicustomer database and into a single-customer database, running on a different instance. In that configuration, the single-customer database instance can be scaled up to meet their needs, which benefits them and other customers. The load associated with the single-customer instance is now separated, so it doesn't negatively affect the availability and performance for customers on the shared database instance.

In that scenario, the server instance that's been separated can be called a "shard." The separated database is a shard because the rows that would have otherwise been in the same table on the same instance are now in a new database on a new instance.

The use of "horizontal" in horizontal sharding refers to rows, which are horizontal in a table. These are distinct from "columns," which can be thought of as vertical in a table. (As an aside: *vertical sharding* is also a concept, but not part of Active Record.)

Imagine that you're exploring this for your platform. What would it take to get there?

To get there, your team would need to provision a new instance, create the same schema on that instance (and begin deploying schema changes), and then migrate the data out of the original database into the new one. With that in place, the application would then need to route requests to the correct database.

Achieving horizontal sharding is time-intensive. How does a business justify this expenditure? Horizontal sharding can yield much greater cost efficiency,

---

23. https://rubyonrails.org/2020/12/9/Rails-6-1-0-release

meaning after a "payback period" on the initial investment, infrastructure can operate at a lower cost.

Duplicating infrastructure for duplicated Ruby on Rails application deployments is costly. By limiting duplication to database server instances, other infrastructure that powers the application, like web servers, background processing workers, or other databases, can be shared. By separating a noisy neighbor, the shared customer database gets better performance with the same resources, and the single customer may be charged more appropriately for their infrastructure, which reflects their heavier usage and needs.

Imagine that you'd like to set this up for Rideshare. You've got two PostgreSQL instances, each with identical database definitions. One database instance serves all customers but one, while the other serves a single especially large "noisy neighbor" customer.

To correctly route writes and reads, Active Record needs a way to map requests to particular databases.

Fortunately, you can implement this using Active Record. How does that work?

Using Subdomain-Based Routing

Active Record allows you to work with multiple database instances and route write and read traffic to the correct database.

However, as the application designer, you are responsible for implementing a routing design. You've got options. One technique involves using the HTTP request.subdomain[24] for routing. Imagine that you've created subdomains multi and singlecompany and would like to route requests from those subdomains to the multi-customer and single-customer databases.

The post, "Horizontal Sharding in a Multi-tenant App with Rails 6.1,"[25] shows one way to do that. The post shows how a Tenant model can hold the subdomain information and the shard.

The post uses the term "tenant", which you can think of as the customer, account, or client. The application describes having both a "global" context and a "tenant-specific" context. The context is a configuration, and each context has a primary and replica database.

What are the mechanisms within Active Record to achieve this?

---

24. https://api.rubyonrails.org/classes/ActionDispatch/Http/URL.html#method-i-subdomain
25. https://www.freshworks.com/horizontal-sharding-in-a-multi-tenant-app-with-rails-61-blog

Active Record provides an ActiveSupport::CurrentAttributes API that can be used to keep per-request state information like Current.shard.

How might this work? When a new customer is added to the platform, they're assigned to either the multitenant shard or their own shard. From that point forward, their context or configuration is queried to perform the routing. This does mean there will be additional latency involved in routing requests.

Besides database shards having different compute resources allocated, they might have different database infrastructure.

The multitenant shard might need connection pooling using PgBouncer due to a greater overall number of client connections.

The single-customer shard may not need connection pooling beyond what Active Record provides. Using connection pooler software might be skipped when not strictly necessary to reduce complexity or cost.

Let's look at a shard configuration example. This configuration shows a shard and a role used in a block. A before_action identifies the shard. The shard is loaded and set as Current.shard.

The example here shows the basics of what this might look like. The example also combines shard information with reader and writing role configuration you saw earlier:

```ruby
# ruby/current_shard.rb
# 1. identify `singlecompany` subdomain based on requests from:
# `singlecompany.myapp.com`
#
# 2. Set: (shard = Tenant.find_by(subdomain: 'singlecompany').shard)
#
# 3. In `before_action`, set: `Current.shard`
#
# ```
# before_action do
#   shard = Tenant.find_by(subdomain: 'singlecompany').shard
#
#   Current.shard = shard
# end
# ```
ApplicationRecord.connected_to(shard: Current.shard, role: :writing) do
  # perform write requests here
  # or use `role: :reading`
end
```

Subdomain routing isn't the only way to do routing. Shards could also be numbered. The benefit of a numbers approach is that it's disconnected from any company-specific details like whether a customer belongs to a multi-customer or single-customer database. Instead, all customers could be given a shard number or identifier.

HTTP request components from a URL could also be used for routing. When primary key integer values are available in the URL, "even" values could go to one shard and "odd" values to another.

By using one of these routing mechanisms, you're able to manually select a shard to use.

Going beyond manual shard switching, Active Record even supports automatic shard switching. The mechanism is similar to what you saw earlier with automatic role switching.

How does it work?

Switching Shards Automatically

Let's look at the basics of automatic shard switching.

To switch automatically, Active Record uses a ShardSelector class. A shard selector runs as a middleware and maps a HTTP request to a shard.

To set this up, you'll need a ShardSelector and a Resolver class. Following is an example Resolver class for the shard selector, with a lock parameter value.

The lock parameter indicates whether the shard can be changed within the block where it's used or not.

The Resolver class processes the request host to identify a tenant and then finds the shard for that tenant.

```ruby
ruby/database_shard_resolver.rb
Rails.application.configure do
  config.active_record.shard_selector = { lock: true }

  config.active_record.shard_resolver = ->(request) {
    Tenant.find_by!(host: request.host).shard
  }
end
```

You're just getting some basic information here. You've got all the pieces needed to begin building these into your copy of Rideshare.

While Rideshare is a great way to practice and develop your skills with these technologies, consider the trade-offs involved before implementing these in your applications.

One of the trade-offs to achieve greater write scalability using distinct-schema sharding involves relocating tables out of existing databases into new databases. If you're considering that for your own applications, this will be a considerable undertaking, and it's worth surveying the PostgreSQL landscape more broadly.

Citus Data, part of Microsoft, supports multiple paradigms for PostgreSQL-based sharding offered as open source software (see "Citus 11.1 Open Source Release"[26]). Citus isn't covered in this chapter because it moves to a multi-primary paradigm for PostgreSQL, which opens up many new operational challenges. The emphasis here is how to leverage the extensive capabilities within Active Record, such as application-level sharding and multiple database support.

However, Citus is a popular sharding option, and given how significant sharding is as a database architectural investment, it's worth exploring various alternatives. To get a broader picture that includes Citus among the options without a Ruby on Rails focus, check out the post, "Understanding Partitioning and Sharding in Postgres and Citus."[27]

Citus Open Source Sharding

In this chapter, you've worked with sharding at the application level using native capabilities in Active Record.

Citus continues to launch more open source PostgreSQL-based sharding options that are worth a look.

Let's get back to Active Record. A downside of splitting up tables into multiple databases is that data that could be joined before can no longer be joined. This is because data can't be joined across databases. Is that a showstopper?

No. Fortunately, Active Record provides a workaround.

In new versions of Active Record, cross-database joins can be simulated. When data is selected with Active Record from multiple databases, the data is combined at the application level. How does that work?

Simulating Joins Across Databases

Rails 7.0 made it possible to simulate cross-database joins (see "Rails 7—Associations Across Databases with disable_joins"[28]). To do this, data is fetched

---

26. https://www.postgresql.org/about/news/announcing-citus-111-open-source-release-2511/

27. https://www.citusdata.com/blog/2023/08/04/understanding-partitioning-and-sharding-in-postgres-and-citus/

28. https://blog.kiprosh.com/rails7-association-across-databases-with-disable-joins/

from multiple databases as individual queries, an then combined in memory within the client Rails application.

Let's look at the basics of how this works. First, you'll need to add some configuration to the relationships in your models.

To change associations to reflect tables that have been split into distinct databases, use the disable_joins option on the associations. This option was introduced in Rails 7.0. Using this option means that the relationship can no longer be traversed using a direct join. Since most associations support joins, you'd use this option selectively just for associations where it's needed.

Let's use the deliveries example from before to explore how this could work. Imagine that the Trip model (trips table) and the Delivery model (deliveries table) are tables in different databases, but we'd like to join data together from each table.

Since the tables have column values in common, those columns can be leveraged by multiple queries that can simulate a join.

First, set disable_joins: true on each side of the association.

The model configuration would look like this:

```ruby/disable_joins.rb
class Trip < ApplicationRecord
  has_many :deliveries, disable_joins: true
end

class Delivery < DeliveriesRecord
  belongs_to :trip, disable_joins: true
end
```

With the associations configured, when the associations are traversed, Active Record issues separate queries to each database. The results are combined as an ActiveRecord::Relation.

This approach has various trade-offs to be aware of. When working with multiple client requests, there will be additional latency compared with a single request to a single database.

Processing the results and combining these may use more CPU and memory on the application instances compared with a join operation that would have happened on the database server.

There's another trade-off with this design: operations like ordering rows can no longer happen in the database and will need to happen in memory. The performance from in-memory sorts and memory allocation should be monitored closely when using this technique. Lazily loading the schema cache (see "Rails 7 Now Lazy Loads Schema Cache"[29]) from each database may perform poorly.

What are the benefits then? The benefit to this approach is that developers can continue working with the same ActiveRecord::Relation objects they're used to, while Active Record takes care of the technical details with connections to multiple databases behind the scenes.

With these caveats in mind, being able to relocate a table into a new database, running on a separate instance, while retaining the Rails developer ergonomics of an ActiveRecord::Relation is pretty slick.

In the next section, we'll shift away from Active Record and return to replication in PostgreSQL.

Earlier, you set up physical replication and set the wal_log setting to logical, which supports both physical and logical replication.

The instructions said that logical replication would be covered later. That time is now.

Creating a Replica Using Logical Replication

In this section, you'll go back to the roots of this chapter and muck around with the PostgreSQL configuration. Instead of configuring physical replication, you'll set up "logical" replication. Fortunately, you'll re-use much of what you did before, so it will be less work.

What is logical replication? Logical replication is different in that it's a configurable type of replication. With logical replication, you can choose specific databases, specific tables, and even specific DML operations within those tables to replicate. For example, you'll configure replication to send only INSERT operations.

Logical replication has a big trade-off, though. Only DML operations (as of PostgreSQL 16) are replicated. This means you'll need to create duplicates of all the tables and other objects. Ongoing DDL changes will need to be created on the replica using some other mechanism. Despite that trade-off, logical replication unlocks several interesting use cases and is a popular feature.

With logical replication, you'll work with a concept you haven't seen yet: a *publication*. Once that's created, you create a corresponding *subscription* object that references the publication but on the replica side.

---

29. https://blog.saeloun.com/2022/04/20/rails-7-lazy-loads-schema-cache.html

As a Rails developer, you may notice similarities between publications and subscriptions in PostgreSQL and other publish/subscribe systems or ActiveSupport::Notifications.[30]

To keep your replica changes separate from db02, let's configure a new instance, db03. This will be the third PostgreSQL instance you've configured, in total, but you'll re-use the existing db01 as the publisher. The instructions in this section are based on the PostgreSQL documentation, "Logical Replication Quick Setup."[31]

On the db01 primary instance, you'll create two publications. Call the first one all_tables_all_ops_pub and specify ALL TABLES.[32] This means all DML operations from all tables are replicated. This is nearly the same as physical replication. What about a more dialed-down variation?

You'll create a second publication called my_pub_inserts_only, which configures WITH (PUBLISH = 'INSERT'); to publish only INSERT statements.

Each table that you intend to replicate needs to exist on the replica instance. You'll need to create it manually. Each table also needs something called a replica identity. What's that?

The *replica identity*[33] uniquely identifies a row. Typically, it's the primary key for a table since the primary key is guaranteed to be unique. What happens when there's no primary key? In those cases, the replica identity can be any unique table element like a UNIQUE constraint.

Let's get started. Connect to db01 and run SHOW wal_level; to confirm that it's still set to logical. From there, create the two publications:

```
sql/db01_create_publication.sql
-- Connect to Primary
-- docker exec --user postgres -it db01 psql

SHOW wal_level; -- confirm it's 'logical'

-- Create Publication
CREATE PUBLICATION all_tables_all_ops_pub FOR ALL TABLES;

-- Second publication: all tables, but inserts only
CREATE PUBLICATION my_pub_inserts_only FOR ALL TABLES
WITH (PUBLISH = 'INSERT');

-- View Publications
SELECT * FROM pg_publication;
```

---

30. https://api.rubyonrails.org/classes/ActiveSupport/Notifications.html
31. https://www.postgresql.org/docs/current/logical-replication-quick-setup.html
32. https://www.postgresql.org/docs/current/logical-replication-publication.html
33. https://www.postgresql.org/docs/current/sql-altertable.html#SQL-ALTERTABLE-REPLICA-IDENTITY

Query pg_publication to review the publications.

Now, you're ready to set up the receiver. Instead of starting up db03 directly like the others, use a script in the Rideshare docker directory to start it. The preparation script starts it up so it's ready to receive files. Then the original .pgpass file created earlier is copied to db03.

From your terminal, cd into docker, then run this command:

```
cd docker

sh db03_create_subscription_prepare.sh
```

This command configures db03, including the ~/.pgpass file needed for the postgres user to access the password for replication_user. You'll notice some instructions in the output.

The script fetches the IP address for db03 and asks you to modify the existing pg_hba.conf file. You'll need to manually intervene here with your text editor. Add the line that's printed out to the existing pg_hba.conf file immediately after the line before it that has the IP address for db02.

Once that's done, upload the file to db01 and reload the HBA configuration. You'll connect to the postgres database, and the script expects that it will be empty. If the public.riders table is still on db01, go there now and drop it.

With that configuration in place, run through the following steps individually from the docker directory in your terminal:

```
sql/db03_create_subscription.sh
# Preconditions:
# - db01: wal_level = logical
#    - docker exec --user postgres -it db01 psql -c "SHOW wal_level"
# - db03 is running
# - db01 permits access from IP address of db03:
#    - See: ./db03_create_subscription_prepare.sh
# - db01 has publication "my_pub_inserts_only"

# Connect to db03 as "postgres"
docker exec --user postgres -it db03 /bin/bash

# To remove the subscription from /bin/bash db03 if needed:
# This also removes "my_sub" replication slot on db01
# psql -U postgres -c "DROP SUBSCRIPTION my_sub"

# Generate snippet and send to psql
echo "CREATE SUBSCRIPTION my_sub
CONNECTION 'dbname=postgres host=db01 user=replication_user'
PUBLICATION my_pub_inserts_only;" | psql

# View subscriptions
psql -c "SELECT * FROM pg_subscription;"
```

The subscription configures a CONNECTION, using a well-known connection string[34] format, for db01. The PUBLICATION name is referenced within it.

Let's recap what you've done so far:

- Added two publications to db01

- Permitted access from db03 for replication_user to db01 via a modified pg_hba.conf file

- Added the .pgpass credentials file for replication_user to db03, so replication_user can connect

- Created a subscription on db03 that references the my_pub_inserts_only publication

Phew! You should now have a publication and subscription that are working together. Let's do some verifications.

Query your subscriptions using the pg_subscription system view or by running the \dRs+ meta-command from psql on db03.

To monitor everything, run the following four commands in four different terminal windows:

- Monitor db01 logs by running docker logs -f db01
- Monitor db03 logs by running docker logs -f db03
- Open a psql connection on db01: docker exec --user postgres -it db01 psql
- Open a psql connection on db03: docker exec --user postgres -it db03 psql

Make sure you've restarted db03. When you do that, monitor the logs and look for logical replication apply worker for subscription "my_sub" has started. If you have db02 running from earlier, you can run docker stop db02 to stop it since it's no longer needed.

Let's kick the tires and make sure this is working!

Run the following in psql on both db01 and db03. The statements create a neighbors table that has a primary key acting as the replica identity.

```sql
sql/neighbors_create_table.sql
CREATE TABLE neighbors (
  id BIGINT GENERATED ALWAYS AS IDENTITY PRIMARY KEY,
  name TEXT
);
```

---

34. https://www.postgresql.org/docs/current/libpq-connect.html#LIBPQ-CONNSTRING

With the table created on both db01 and db03, insert rows into neighbors on db01:

sql/neighbors_insert_rows.sql
```
INSERT INTO neighbors (name) VALUES ('Mike');
INSERT INTO neighbors (name) VALUES ('Elizabeth');
```

Make sure replication is working. Monitor logs with docker logs -f db01 and look for something like this:

```
2023-12-01 05:02:43.044 UTC [74] STATEMENT:  START_REPLICATION SLOT \
  "pg_16400_sync_16397_7307483758791823399" \
  LOGICAL 0/157D740 (proto_version '4', origin 'any',
  publication_names '"my_pub_inserts_only"')
```

Instantly, after inserting rows in neighbors on db01, you'll see them show up on db03. Nice. What about deletes? Run this from psql on db01:

```
DELETE FROM neighbors WHERE name = 'Mike';
```

Since the publication only publishes inserts, Mike is gone on db01, but when you query neighbors on db03, Mike is still there.

If you run into issues, look for table "neighbors" has finished in the logs for db03. Stop db02. If needed, drop and recreate the subscription again. The script has instructions on how to drop the subscriptions that are commented out.

Hopefully, you'll then be able to see inserts replicated as expected, and deletes ignored.

Excellent! You've now added logical replication to your box of tools to go along with physical replication. You configured a publication and subscription using logical replication to replicate specific operations.

You've now configured a primary instance and multiple types of replicas.

While the primary can serve both writes and reads, the replica instances can only serve reads.

This means that each instance can be customized for its role using database parameters. Does PostgreSQL support different parameter values on replicas?

Customizing Replication Database Parameters

PostgreSQL has hundreds of tunable parameters for all sorts of purposes. In this section, you'll look at just one parameter related to replication. Because PostgreSQL allows primary and replica instances to have distinct parameter values, you can customize parameters on replicas to better serve their role.[35]

---

35. https://www.postgresql.org/docs/current/runtime-config-replication.html

When might this be helpful? When long queries run on a replica, they can get canceled due to accessing row versions that cause a conflict with versions on the primary.

This can happen when VACUUM runs on the primary, triggered by the accumulation of dead tuples and having met a threshold. When VACUUM is running, if the reader instance is querying the rows that have dead tuples being processed or an active transaction is referencing them, this causes a conflict between VACUUM and the replica.

When that conflict happens, PostgreSQL cancels the replica query due to the conflict. The cancellation can cause users to experience problems and errors.

The cancellation looks like this in the log:

```
ERROR: canceling statement due to conflict with recovery
```

Is there a way to avoid that? One solution is to use the hot_standby_feedback parameter. Setting this parameter to on on the replica makes the primary instance aware of long-running queries. That can help avoid cancellations due to conflicts. Note that this setting applies only to replicas that use physical replication.

The trade-off with this is that the replica may have more stale data (see "PostgreSQL ERROR: Canceling Statement Due to Conflict with Recovery"[36] for more information).

This is merely one example to demonstrate that each instance in a primary and replica pairing can have different parameter values.

With that, let's wrap up this huge chapter!

Wrapping Up

This was a big chapter! You learned how to move beyond a single database instance, putting multiple instances to work. You can now leverage multiple instances working together to solve bigger challenges related to scale and growth for your databases and Rails applications.

You learned how to use the read and write splitting tactic by configuring primary and replica instances with Active Record. You explored the basics of horizontal sharding in Active Record. Besides running the same schema across multiple instances, you saw how distinct-schema databases could be evolved using the same Active Record migrations mechanism you're used to.

---

36. https://stackoverflow.com/a/21686285

By scaling beyond a single PostgreSQL instance, you're able to use the same administration skills you've cultivated at greater concurrency, query volume, and data sizes.

Despite the increased scale, you can continue to use native features in PostgreSQL and Active Record to maintain your development velocity. This helps minimize your operational complexity by squeezing more performance out of your existing technology stack.

You used Active Record to manually switch between writer and reader roles and between shards. You even saw how to enable automatic switching, which helps you put changes into production faster, with less manual work. You saw how you can continue to use Active Record relations, even after relocating tables into new databases. Those new databases can run on separate instances, and data can be joined across databases in the application using Active Record.

In the next chapter, you'll continue the theme of putting advanced PostgreSQL capabilities into action to meet demanding requirements.

You'll focus on how to increase the scalability of your write operations but within the scope of a single primary instance.

To do that, you'll learn about native table partitioning in PostgreSQL and then put it into action for Rideshare. Read on to get started!

## CHAPTER 14

Boosting Performance with Partitioning

In this chapter, you'll work with native PostgreSQL *table partitioning*. You'll learn what it is, what it isn't, when to use it, and how to apply it to a simulated use case using Rideshare.

Let's talk about what it is. Partitioning is sometimes confused for sharding, which you saw in the last chapter as application-level sharding (see Sharding at the Application Level, on page 310) and horizontal sharding. You saw how a workload could be distributed to multiple instances in various ways. Sharding can be thought of as a way to split up your workload into multiple instances or to break up a database by relocating a set of tables.

Partitioning is similar to sharding in that it's also related to splitting things up. However, instead of workloads or databases, with table partitioning in PostgreSQL, you're focused on a single table.

The table you're focused on is within a single database and on a single instance. For that reason, partitioning helps the scalability of queries for a single table or related tables, helps with instance scalability by lowering the costs of queries related to that table, and helps out with maintenance operations on that table. However, partitioning does not help with scalability across multiple instances.

When is partitioning useful? Partitioning can provide three benefits, which we'll cover in this chapter. These benefits aren't guaranteed, though, and you'll need to do testing with your own database queries, schema, indexes, and usage patterns to determine how beneficial they are. What are the benefits we'll look at?

- Creating a low-impact data archival mechanism
- Enabling more reliable and predictable table modifications for huge tables
- Improving some types of query performance for scoping queries to individual partitions

The data archival and query performance benefits require lengthier explanations and will be covered in their own sections later on in this chapter.

To start, let's focus on how partitioning makes table modifications easier. What does that mean?

As tables grow into, for example, hundreds of gigabytes or even terabytes in size, adding database objects to them like indexes or constraints becomes much slower and can be unpredictable, challenging, or nearly impossible, depending on other concurrent access and query patterns.

When performing changes like adding indexes, due to the table size, those operations take up a lot of server instance resources like CPU, memory, and IO. These resources are shared with other concurrent operations, so big tables have higher needs that can take away resources from other operations.

How does splitting up a table help? By splitting up a large table into smaller tables, we can somewhat restore the behavior of modifications to smaller tables, which are less resource-intensive by comparison.

With less resource-intensive operations, these kinds of changes can become more reliable and predictable, allowing you and your team to focus elsewhere. The benefits from table partitioning are not guaranteed, though, and will depend on many factors.

While table partitioning is a powerful capability, it only makes sense to take on when tables are very large. This is because it does add a runtime component and adds operational complexity. Before taking those things on, you'll want to be reasonably assured that you'll receive the benefits of smaller partitioned tables.

How will you know when you've reached that point?

Structure of Partitioned Tables

You've learned that partitioned tables are like regular tables but split into smaller pieces. How do they coordinate with each other? Partitioned tables have a "parent" and "child" relationship. Children are the "partitions" of a parent table. The parent table doesn't store data but primarily exists to describe the partitioning definition, which is used for routing rows and other purposes. This type of relationship has similarities to a base class and child class inheritance from object-oriented programming.

The parent table can be thought of as a virtual table that has definitions for the table structure, indexes, and constraints but doesn't store any data. Data is stored in the child tables or "partitions" of the parent. The parent and child tables must have identical table definitions.

The partition definition on the parent is used to route rows to the correct child table or partition. This routing happens for all DML operations, including inserts, updates, deletes, and merges.

If you don't have huge tables now or haven't experienced challenges working with them, you might be wondering about common symptoms that could indicate places where table partitioning would help.

Sometimes teams will notice that adding constraints or indexes gets to be very slow and can even be canceled due to timing out or contention with other operations. Replication of row changes (logical replication is supported since PostgreSQL 13) can become slow.

Why's that? As you learned earlier on page 97, modifying a table requires an exclusive lock. For large tables, the length of time the table is locked is greater due to the greater number of rows. This means that table locks that otherwise might be fine on small tables can be very disruptive and increase risk when they're on equivalent but larger tables.

Table partitioning can help ease this operational burden by better managing the large size. Partitioning doesn't help directly, but it makes working with smaller tables that fit your instance size better, easier, and more predictable.

If you're considering table partitioning and already have a huge table, can you directly split the table up? Unfortunately, as of PostgreSQL 16, that's not possible with any kind of ALTER statement or direct modification. How is it possible then to split up large tables into smaller chunks, outside of taking a downtime period?

To achieve that, you'll use a technique that creates a new partitioned table structure entirely. Once that's created, you'll migrate every row from the former unpartitioned table structure that you wish to keep into the new table structure by creating a copy of each row.

This will be a big job! Before getting started, you'll have several decisions to make about how to design your partitioning structure.

For example, you could decide that you'd like to have ten 100 GB tables. Or you might want 100 10 GB tables. The latter configuration could work better on a smaller PostgreSQL instance with less memory.

Designing a partitioning structure involves analyzing the access patterns, including how data is ingested and queried and the amount of server resources available for the table and database. Besides all of that, you'll also need to decide on a partitioning constraint design that divides up the rows into partitions.

Migrating to a Partitioned Table

 Migrating data from an unpartitioned table to a partitioned table is a significant undertaking.

You'll practice the technique using a Rideshare example based on a real-world project to get more familiar with the steps.

Fortunately, in recent versions of PostgreSQL, and thanks to open source tools, the process is more accessible than it was in the past, even for Rails developers who aren't database specialists.

We'll explore some of those enhanced capabilities and tools in upcoming sections. Before doing that, let's see what's available for partitioning within Ruby on Rails. Read on to learn more.

Ruby on Rails Partitioning Support

Active Record does not currently support native table partitioning (as of version 7.1) with PostgreSQL or any other relational database. However, since table partitioning creates a table that *mostly* appears like a traditional table, using table partitioning with Ruby on Rails works just fine.

With that being said, partitioned tables do have differences from traditional tables, which are worth learning.

To perform a data migration to a partitioned table, first you'll want to work from the Rails application code in a development branch where the partitioned table is in use but where you haven't migrated any data. You could configure this in your CI with an extra shell script to migrate your existing database only on the branch.

That way, you can run your test suite for the application and identify any incompatibilities between the partitioned table and the Active Record code that interacts with it.

What are some of those possible incompatibilities? Partitioned tables have different requirements for their primary keys. They also require some different maintenance steps that regular tables do not.

You'll work on both of those items in upcoming sections in this chapter within Rideshare.

Before diving in, there's still a bit more to learn about PostgreSQL table partitioning. Let's explore different styles of partitioning. After all, there wasn't always native support in PostgreSQL. The native style is newer and is called declarative partitioning. What does that mean?

Choose Declarative Partitioning

Declarative partitioning is a newer style of partitioning that's been built-in to PostgreSQL since version 10.

Prior to PostgreSQL 10, partitioned tables could be created by hand using an inheritance structure. Database administrations (DBA) created functions, triggers, additional constraints, and other database objects to set up partitioned tables. They likely used the built-in procedural language, which means they created and maintained a lot of database procedural language code. This meant that table partitioning was limited to programmers with strong database skills, who were comfortable working with that code, likely with less sophisticated developer tooling, and requiring deep familiarity with PostgreSQL. Because of all of these things, partitioning was arguably inaccessible to application developers or back-end engineers prior to the introduction of native partitioning.

And even since launching native partitioning in PostgreSQL version 10, many significant enhancements have been made to it that make partitioned tables more like regular tables. This includes constraints and logical replication (since version 13) and more.

Similar to how SQL is a declarative paradigm, with an intentional separation between the SQL query text the programmer writes and how the query planner determines and executes a plan, declarative partitioning in PostgreSQL means that the user "declares" their partitioning structure, and PostgreSQL handles the routing details internally.

This declarative approach abstracts away many of those technical details required before to effectively route row changes. Arguably, this has made partitioning more straightforward by comparison, which in turn has made it accessible for the first time to application developers and back-end engineers. This is quite exciting because table partitioning is a broadly useful technique but has arguably been underutilized by application-centric engineers.

Besides lowering the technical complexity, which is a huge win since table partitioning is native to PostgreSQL, the quality of the documentation increased greatly by being first-party documentation within the source code.

In each major version of PostgreSQL, there's been a steady stream of improvements made to declarative partitioning.

What are some details that PostgreSQL handles with native partitioning? PostgreSQL routes rows from inserts, updates, and deletes into the correct partition. Constraints and replication are also handled.

Take a look at some of the partitioning terminology you'll use in this chapter. You will learn how to use three available partitioning types: RANGE, LIST, and HASH. You will learn about the pgslice CLI program, and how to use it to perform a data migration for an append-only table.

Partitioning Terminology

- Online migrations—Performed simultaneously with other client activity

- Offline migrations—Performed when PostgreSQL is disconnected from web application traffic

- RANGE—Used normally for time-based data: daily, weekly, monthly, but also works for other data types

- LIST—Numerical data values that have significance, like customer_id, but also supports other types

- HASH (11+)—Fixed set of partitions based on the remainder from a modulo operation for row routing

- Append only—Table receives only INSERT operations, not UPDATE or DELETE operations

- pgslice—CLI Ruby tool that helps programmers perform partitioned table migrations

- Composite Primary Key (CPK)—Primary key definition on more than one column

Since a migration to a partitioned table is a significant investment, how do we know when it's worth it?

Deciding When to Partition

You might be wondering when to partition. You may also be wondering whether table partitioning is truly required or is more of a nice-to-have. Let's take a look.

Let's start with a high-side extreme. PostgreSQL does set limits on most things, including a maximum table size.

At publication time, the maximum table size is 32 TB.[1]

This means that when inserts or other DML operations are sent to a table that exceeds 32 TB, they'll fail. While that's the hard upper limit in PostgreSQL, you'll likely hit issues well before that, depending on the size of your instance and your concurrent activity.

If hitting that limit sounds unrealistic, consider that there are real-world stories where that happened and caused downtime. Derk van Veen of Adyen[2] showed how their team was forced to partition a table that grew to 32 TB. In the recommendations portion of the presentation, Derk recommended partitioning well before reaching that limit so that partitioning isn't performed under emergency circumstances.

Alright, so you might have big tables, but they're still much smaller than 32 TB. What size might be a reasonable minimum size where benefits are possible? While there aren't hard rules, there are helpful "rules of thumb" to consider as guidance.

Let's look at an example. Imagine your primary instance has 384 GB of memory available.

The PostgreSQL document "Table Partitioning"[3] has a rule of thumb based on the server instance memory and table size, about when to partition:

> The size of the table should exceed the physical memory of the database server.

To follow this guideline, you'd partition any table that exceeds 384 GB.

What other rules of thumb are there? The Postgres.fm episode "Transaction ID Wraparound Prevention"[4] covers partitioning and recommends a less complicated rule of thumb.

They recommend partitioning when a table exceeds 100 GB in size.

Does this mean as soon as a table size hits 100 GB, we should immediately partition it? No. Brian explains a bit more:[5]

---

1. https://www.postgresql.org/docs/current/limits.html
2. https://www.adyen.com/knowledge-hub/introduction-to-table-partioning
3. https://www.postgresql.org/docs/current/ddl-partitioning.html
4. https://www.youtube.com/watch?v=dAYbJfW1bLM
5. https://www.brianlikespostgres.com

> **Brian:**   *I think the PostgreSQL Documentation is saying, "don't worry about the table if it fits in memory."*
>
> **Andrew:**   *Are users missing out on benefits by deferring table partitioning?*
>
> **Brian:**   *Partitioning could add complexity for no real benefit.*
>
> **Brian:**   *I recommend adopting table partitioning only when currently experiencing or about to experience a problem where partitioning helps.*

Brian even suggests one of those common problems that teams face. We haven't covered it much, so we'll briefly introduce it.

A team might have some data tables where the data is only needed temporarily. To keep the tables from growing forever, they might periodically delete data from those tables. While this is logical and common, unfortunately, deleting large batches of rows from large tables frequently causes operational problems in PostgreSQL that can surprise teams. We'll explore this scenario in more depth later on and see how migrating to a partitioned table provides a better design for regularly archiving large amounts of data.

With guidelines and rules of thumb, while they are helpful as a starting point, ultimately you'll need to make the call as to what's best for your system. To do that, you'll need to perform some analysis and planning work. This work will be worthwhile because you'll want a significant project like a table partitioning migration to be well supported.

With that understanding of when to consider table partitioning and some of the factors that influence the decision, let's shift our focus to the types of partitioning that are available. Selecting the partitioning type is a crucial step in the process.

Which types are available for your use case, and which one is best? Let's consider a Rideshare use case that would benefit from table partitioning, then begin working on how we'd migrate the data.

Estimating Growth of Time-Oriented Data

PostgreSQL Declarative Partitioning offers several partitioning types to choose from. The types are related to both how you'll divide up and store the data and also, equally important, how you'll access the data. Besides how you'll divide up the data being stored, consider how it will grow over time.

You're now ready to jump into a concrete example.

Take a look at the trip_positions table in Rideshare. In the main branch, this is a regular PostgreSQL table that's not partitioned. In upcoming sections, you'll explore whether it makes sense to partition this table.

As discussed earlier, take a look at the data types being stored, how frequently rows are inserted, and what your growth projections are for the table. For trip positions, the data is time-oriented (or "temporal") data, meaning it's inserted with a correlation to time. Data rows represent a geo point from a point in time.

Out of dozens of tables, a web application might have a few that capture time-oriented data and grow quickly. Rows in these tables could represent an event, log entry, or capture a location tracking point. The trip_positions table tracks latitude and longitude coordinate pairs from trips being completed. Since trips are the main service that Rideshare offers, and since each trip has hundreds or thousands of geo points based on the length of the trip, you can imagine how this would be a high-growth table.

Analyzing Trip Positions Table Rows

 In Rideshare, locations are tracked for drivers who are providing trips to riders. The mobile devices that drivers are using send the position coordinates to the Rideshare API, which then stores them as rows in this table.

Keeping in mind Rideshare is fictional, estimating hypothetical growth is a real-world task that can help inform your designs. Let's do some investigation of the growth pattern that's expected for the trip_positions table.

Imagine that trip positions are sent every ten seconds by the mobile app. In every minute, there are six intervals of ten seconds, so we'd expect around six records per minute to be inserted.

Assume the average trip length is 30 minutes. This means there are 180 records per trip (30 * 6).

Let's estimate the data from one driver, then extrapolate that to greater numbers of drivers. Let's assume drivers complete two 30-minute trips in an hour. For one driver, in a one-hour period, we'd expect to receive 360 trip positions (180*2).

If Rideshare had 100 drivers on the platform, each providing two trips per hour, working an average shift length of eight hours, then we'd expect to see 288_000 trip position records per day. That figure was calculated by multiplying 100 drivers working eight hours, where 360 trip position records are captured each hour.

Let's scale up our estimates from 100 drivers to 1000 drivers.

Imagine that Rideshare has expanded internationally. At 1000 drivers on the platform, we'd expect to receive 2.88 million trip_positions records being inserted per day. This was calculated by multiplying 2880 trip positions points in an eight-hour period worked, multiplied by 1000 drivers.

PostgreSQL is certainly capable of receiving three million records per day, although clearly, this will be a high-growth table at the level of 1000 drivers working full shifts on the platform per day.

Using a partitioned table structure will benefit that type of ingestion rate because data could be stored in smaller increments, broken up by day, week, or month. The resulting tables storing only a day's worth, week's worth, or month's worth of data will be much smaller compared to one monolithic table storing all records.

One strategy there would be to create a partition for each day. With a daily partition, there would be roughly up to three million rows in each partition, based on current projections. This design could, of course, accommodate fewer rows, but it is also scalable to accommodate a greater number of rows.

If a day's worth of records is queried, a daily partition structure could bring significant performance improvements over a single large table. Why's that?

That's because even if the entire day's worth of records are scanned, as a partitioned table, only the single-day partition needs to be scanned since it contains all rows for the day. This means even sequential scans can be fast enough on partitioned tables based on their row count.

However, you aren't limited to sequential scans. Partitioned tables can be indexed just like unpartitioned tables. There's a difference though: PostgreSQL duplicates the index defined at the parent level on each child partition. While this means there are a lot more indexes compared with an unpartitioned table, since there's one per partition, the index entries correspond only to the records in that partition.

This means a per-partition index will be smaller and add less latency from index maintenance compared with an alternative where there's a single index on a big unpartitioned table that's involved in more maintenance from DML operations.

By splitting up rows into separate partitions for each day, old data can more easily be removed through an archival process.

What would that look like?

Use Partitioning to Help with Archiving

When is partitioning useful? Partitioning can provide three benefits, which we'll cover in this chapter. These benefits aren't guaranteed, though, and you'll need to test your own database queries, schema, indexes, and usage patterns to determine how beneficial they are. What are the benefits we will look at?

Commonly, time-oriented data isn't needed in the main database after some time has passed. We could consider the trip positions data mentioned earlier. Outside of the original trip or maybe a reporting period afterward where the rider needs a receipt or the driver needs to get paid based on their work performed, how long would the geo data really be needed?

By removing older unneeded data, which we'll refer to as "archival," you'll get a number of performance benefits. The problem is that for unpartitioned tables, deleting large batches of rows from a single table that's concurrently accessed is fraught.

By placing time-oriented data into partitions, you'll get a number of benefits.

There will be fewer partitions to scan to find rows, fewer index entry maintenance operations due to greater isolation, fewer VACUUM operations, and more.

Let's look at the archival process. Imagine you wanted to remove unneeded data. For trip positions, we'll imagine that data older than 90 days can be removed, or "archived." Archival means the data can live on in another form, such as being dumped to a file that's stored in a low-cost location. The data does not need to be completely removed organization-wide; it's just removed from PostgreSQL in this process.

Let's look at a common way to do this for unpartitioned tables with the following pg_dump command.

Deleting rows using a DELETE statement for rows older than 90 days could look like this:

sql/delete_trip_positions.sql
```
DELETE FROM trip_positions
WHERE created_at < (NOW() - INTERVAL '90 days');
```

This is OK, and it works, but there are issues with this kind of statement. Even if you haven't experienced the issues firsthand with a variation of this in your database, based on what you've seen in earlier chapters, you know that DELETE operations cause bloat, which causes knock-on issues.

Let's look at some of the issues with this DELETE statement approach. First, this statement may become slow. To make it fast, you may need an index covering the deleted_at column, which is used in the WHERE clause of the query. If the index isn't needed for other queries, then it's a special index just for this DELETE statement. Since indexes consume space and add latency, we generally want to avoid them unless they're beneficial.

The bigger issue is that running DELETE operations on large batches of rows suddenly creates a large amount of table bloat.

Since a lot of former row versions now are no longer needed, there's a big spike of dead tuples. VACUUM should kick in and clean these up, but at a considerable resource utilization cost.

Let's look at alternative approaches to large bulk deletes.

We haven't yet considered that the records could be soft deleted instead. What would that look like? Is that better?

Soft deletes, from a bloat perspective, aren't better. They're UPDATE operations that set a column like deleted_at from NULL to the current time so that the row can be hidden from the application. Besides deletes that cause bloat, we also know updates cause bloat. Soft deletes aren't really different in that they also create a spike of bloat to be cleaned up by Autovacuum.

Another idea might be to TRUNCATE the table. The benefit of TRUNCATE is that it doesn't cause bloat. The problem is that this approach isn't viable because it deletes *all* rows, and you're trying to perform a filtered operation that only removes specific rows based on a filter condition.

Besides not being filterable, TRUNCATE also won't run with foreign keys in place without either removing them first or using CASCADE. That option is more dangerous because you could end up deleting many more rows than you intended. That's not going to work!

What if we flipped things around? We could create a new table and then copy only the rows we wish to keep into it. This avoids the bloat problem but means that all of the constraints, indexes, sequences, and other objects need to be copied forward to the new table. As you saw earlier (see Speeding Up Inserts for Clone and Replace, on page 55), copying all of the table objects is a considerable amount of effort.

Among the other solutions, in lieu of high-volume deletes, this approach of copying into a new restricted table is the best option from a bloat management perspective. In this design, the old table with the unneeded rows is abandoned.

There's still no getting around increased operational load, though, as the rows being copied increase load considerably, and that load would grow with each subsequent operation if the growth rate for the table perpetually increased. If pursuing this option, closely monitor the impact of additional IO and WAL replication.

While this copy-then-abandon approach avoids introducing bloat, it still requires a lot of engineering work. Given there's no way around considerable engineering investment, what if there was an alternative that didn't involve so much intensive operational impact?

With all of those solutions in mind, we've set the stage for table partitioning to shine.

The option we'll look at here would be to use the RANGE type for a new partitioned table.

The big win over large-scale deletes is to leverage an operation type that's available *only* for partitioned tables. What we'll do is perform a DETACH operation, which detaches a child partition from the parent structure.

How is that less intensive? PostgreSQL supports running a DETACH PARTITION command (and the opposite command, ATTACH PARTITION) using our friend, the CONCURRENTLY keyword, added in PostgreSQL 14. This means these operations run alongside other queries, accessing the table without disrupting them.

If your delete operation covers a day's worth of data, perfect, you're all set. Instead of deleting rows, you'll run a DETACH CONCURRENTLY on the partition that corresponds to that day.

Partition detachment is fast, nonblocking, and doesn't cause table bloat. What happens when it's detached? A detached partition becomes a regular PostgreSQL table. Since a detached table is no longer connected, any archival method works, and an archival process doesn't block any other concurrent access.

Hopefully, you've been convinced that table partitioning offers worthwhile benefits that will help you more effectively manage high-volume data growth tables by creating a nonblocking archival process.

With all of that in place, let's move forward with a RANGE partitioned variant of the trip positions table.

In the next section, you'll move into the specifics of implementing declarative partitioning.

Let's get started.

Choosing Your Partition Column

Wow, you've covered a lot of background. While the depth and breadth of background might seem overkill, there is a purpose. Table partitioning is a significant undertaking. You'll want ample evidence that the investment of time and additional operational complexity will be worthwhile.

With that said, you're ready to dive into the table partitioning details. Although you haven't yet seen the other two types offered by PostgreSQL, you'll implement RANGE partitioning here and then cover the other types more briefly afterward.

Next, with the partitioning type selected, you'll choose a column to partition the data by.

For trip positions, use the created_at timestamp column. The value of created_at will be used on the fly by PostgreSQL to route inserted rows into the correct child partition.

As discussed earlier, we won't (and can't) convert the existing table. Instead, we'll create a new partitioned table and then migrate the data to it.

Since you want to avoid taking any downtime, you'll copy all the rows you want to keep from the old table into the new table. Once all the rows are copied over, there will be a short cutover period. From that point onward, the application will begin writing rows and reading them exclusively with the partitioned table.

Let's review the high-level plan:

- Create a new parent table using the RANGE partitioning type on the created_at column.

- Create child partitions of the table, then attach them.

- Copy all rows from the current unpartitioned table into the new partitioned table.

- Restart web servers or forcibly repopulate the schema cache due to schema differences.

After the data migration has been performed, you'll be able to archive old data. What's the rough plan for the archival part?

- You've decided to archive data that is older than three months.

- For partitions that have data older than three months, DETACH them and use the CONCURRENTLY option.

- For detached partitions, archive their data to a dump file or CSV file using pg_dump.

- Once the data is safely archived into the file, run a DROP command on the table, as it's no longer needed. Alternatively, the table could be truncated, which leaves the structure intact but without data rows.

Between those two lists, that's a lot of steps! This will be a lot of work. Fortunately, you'll use a tool to help you out. What is it?

Range Partitioning with pgslice

Table partitioning can be implemented without using a library and purely by writing SQL DDL to configure the partitions. With that said, there can be a lot of steps involved in a migration, and those steps can be tedious to run, especially if you've been running them on multiple instances. For that reason, there are open source and commercial tools that help programmers create and manage partitioned tables and perform data migrations.

To lessen the manual steps needed, you'll perform a data migration using the pgslice[6] CLI program. You'll dive into it for the remainder of this chapter.

pgslice has some nice approaches for online zero-downtime data migrations. These beneficial approaches are built into how it works. The tool is written in Ruby, which means that Ruby developers can open up the source code to read and modify if needed.

By running as a client program, you won't be limited by what's available on your PostgreSQL server instance or need to configure your instances with a dependency. You'll use pgslice to connect to your local PostgreSQL instance, any CI or pre-production instances, and finally, your production instances.

How does it work? pgslice is like an assistant that provides a pre-baked set of steps that create a cookie cutter partitioned table configuration, and help you perform an online data migration of your row data into the new location.

pgslice has nice features like building in "rollback" mechanisms for steps. You'll still be responsible for making some of the choices mentioned, and executing the program, but once it's running, you'll benefit from conventions that it offers.

The pgslice gem was added to Rideshare, so you can use it from there. To run it, call the bin/pgslice binstub in the project from your terminal. You'll invoke the main command with subcommands.

---

6. https://github.com/ankane/pgslice

What are the subcommands that pgslice supports? They're listed in order as follows:

- prep
- add_partitions
- analyze
- fill
- swap

You'll work with each command in upcoming sections. The intention is to run each subcommand in order because each step uses conventions that expect the previous step to have run.

pgslice is not the only way to perform a partitioned table creation and data migration. Are there trade-offs with pgslice?

pgslice has limitations, like only supporting the RANGE partitioning type. It's designed for data row migrations from "append only" tables. If there are UPDATE or DELETE operations to rows that occur during your migration process, you'll be on your own to bring those changes forward to your destination table. You'll need to do that manually using some other approach outside of pgslice. For that reason, it's best to use pgslice only for append-only tables.

With the benefits and trade-offs covered, let's continue with the implementation.

Data Migration Preparation for Rideshare

Imagine you've decided to migrate all the rows in the current rideshare.trip_positions table into a partitioned structure by month. The hypothetical example you looked at earlier considered a daily partition design, but we'll use a month here for fewer partitions.

This means there will be one partition that corresponds to each calendar month of the year. You don't need a partition for every month of all time, only for the months where you have data.

Use the pgslice --dry-run option as you start, to explore the SQL statements it generates.

To use pgslice, set up a PGSLICE_URL environment variable that has a connection string for the Rideshare database. This variable was added to the .env file in Rideshare. The value is listed as follows. Note that you'll be using the owner role so that the new table structure ownership is configured as owner.

```
export PGSLICE_URL=postgres://owner:@localhost:5432/rideshare_development
```

In pgslice, use schema-qualified tables for commands, like rideshare.trip_positions.

As you've done throughout using DATABASE_URL, now that you've set PGSLICE_URL, verify you can correctly use it to connect by running the following command from your terminal. You may need to cat .env from Rideshare and then export the variable.

```
psql $PGSLICE_URL
```

Once you've done that, you're connected to Rideshare in an equivalent way. Running \dn and \dt shows the expected schema and tables. If you have debris from earlier examples and exercises and wish to start over cleanly, run the following steps:

```
sh db/teardown.sh
sh db/setup.sh
bin/rails db:migrate
bin/rails data_generators:generate_all
```

We'll assume that your database has been reset and the trip_positions table is populated.

The first pgslice command to look at is the prep command.

This command creates a copy of the original table, appending _intermediate to the original name for the new table name. For Rideshare trip_positions, for example, the intermediate table is called trip_positions_intermediate.

Run the following pgslice command from your terminal, which has the dry-run enabled:

```
bin/pgslice prep rideshare.trip_positions created_at month --dry-run
```

Let's review the parts. The created_at column was specified as the partition column.

The month option was used, which figures out the current month and the start and end dates and then creates *non-overlapping* month-based partitions. Finally, --dry-run was used, which does not perform the steps but prints out the SQL statements of the steps that it *would* perform.

Non-overlapping Partitions

 It's critical to create non-overlapping partition constraints. This way, PostgreSQL knows how to route rows into the correct partitions.

After running the prep command with the dry run option, you should see SQL similar to this:

```sql
sql/pgslice_prep.sql
BEGIN;

CREATE TABLE "rideshare"."trip_positions_intermediate"
(LIKE "rideshare"."trip_positions"
  INCLUDING DEFAULTS
  INCLUDING CONSTRAINTS
  INCLUDING STORAGE
  INCLUDING COMMENTS
  INCLUDING STATISTICS
  INCLUDING GENERATED
  INCLUDING COMPRESSION)
PARTITION BY RANGE ("created_at");

ALTER TABLE "rideshare"."trip_positions_intermediate"
ADD FOREIGN KEY (trip_id) REFERENCES trips(id);

COMMENT ON TABLE "rideshare"."trip_positions_intermediate"
IS 'column:created_at,period:month,cast:date,version:3';

COMMIT;
```

When you're happy with the commands you see, run pgslice without the --dry-run option. This will create the table.

As you read through the SQL statements, try to identify some of the design details that pgslice uses that you've seen in earlier chapters or sections.

Notice that the parent table uses the CREATE TABLE LIKE format (with the LIKE keyword), and that a database comment was added. You'll also see that the intermediate table does not have a primary key defined on it. We'll discuss that more later on.

You worked with CREATE TABLE LIKE back in section Speeding Up Inserts for Clone and Replace, on page 55, and database comments in section Tracking Columns with Sensitive Information, on page 46. The comment here is not only meta-data, as it was back in that section, but is required for internal use within the pgslice implementation.

You'll also see that objects like defaults and constraints are explicitly copied forward from the original table, as you did earlier in the Performance database chapter.

Although you have the intermediate table, there are not yet any child partitions attached to it. We'll do that next.

To do that, use the pgslice add_partitions command. Run the following command from your terminal:

```sh/pgslice_add_partitions.sh
bin/pgslice add_partitions rideshare.trip_positions \
  --intermediate --past 3 --future 3
```

This command adds three months' worth of partitions to the past, before the current month, and three months' worth of future month partitions. The add_partitions command used the CREATE TABLE...PARTITION OF keywords.

Including the current month and the six other partitions, you should now have seven partitions in total. The partitions can be described from psql by running \d+ trip_positions_intermediate, where the "+" is added to list partitions on the bottom.

You may also describe an individual partition in the same way as a regular table by running \d trip_positions_202309, replacing the partition name with one that you have.

On the partition, you'll see there is a primary key defined on the id column. You now have the table and partitions of the table but no data rows.

How do we fill up the partitions with data?

Online Data Migration

pgslice is designed for online (or "zero downtime") migrations. As you learned earlier, this means you don't need to stop PostgreSQL or disconnect clients from accessing the table while you migrate data. Since row copying happens while PostgreSQL is running, concurrent requests continue to be served. While this is a great benefit, this approach comes with trade-offs like increased operational risk due to the increased load placed on the server during the row copying.

pgslice has commands to copy data rows from the original table into the intermediate table you just created. This approach can be called "nondestructive" because it doesn't modify the original data. With nondestructive approaches, we're able to roll back the process if needed, reverting to the original table. This is valuable because it provides an escape hatch if something goes wrong.

With that, you're ready to start copying.

The generated SQL statements SELECT from the original table and INSERT into the intermediate table. PostgreSQL inspects the created_at partition column to determine which partition to place the row into.

The fill command uses some additional good practices for bulk operations. Work is performed in batches and can be slowed down (also called "throttled") or paused. Pauses help with index maintenance happening in the background, creating extra IO and giving replication an opportunity to catch up.

pgslice uses a range of id column values to create a batch. The following example copies 10,000 rows from trip_positions to trip_positions_intermediate. The id range is from 1 to 10000. Since there are fewer than 10,000 rows in this table, they're all copied in one batch.

Here's what the batch looks like:

```
sql/pgslice_fill.sql
-- bin/pgslice fill rideshare.trip_positions --dry-run
-- Uses INSERT INTO ... SELECT pattern to copy rows

/* 1 of 1 */
INSERT INTO "rideshare"."trip_positions_intermediate"
  ("id", "position", "trip_id", "created_at", "updated_at")
  SELECT "id", "position", "trip_id", "created_at", "updated_at"
  FROM "rideshare"."trip_positions"
  WHERE "id" > 1 AND "id" <= 10000
  AND "created_at" >= '2023-06-01'::date
  AND "created_at" < '2024-01-01'::date
```

Run the fill with the optional --dry-run (remove it to perform the real fill) by running the following command in your terminal:

```
bin/pgslice fill rideshare.trip_positions --dry-run
```

Once you've run the fill subcommand, the rows from the original table are now copied into trip_positions_intermediate for the last 90 days.

You wouldn't be able to copy rows older than 90 days because no partition exists that would match. The data still exists in the original table. If you found you needed older data, you could use the pgslice program to generate more partitions for the past.

pgslice fill performs a large number of INSERT statements. As you learned earlier, whenever you've performed a write operation with a large number of rows, it's helpful to update the table statistics using the ANALYZE command. pgslice does not perform a VACUUM on partitions. You may wish to do that to ensure the visibility map[7] is updated.

Let's continue working with pgslice and migrating the trip positions data in the next section.

---

7.   https://www.postgresql.org/docs/current/storage-vm.html

Row Copying Operational Tips

Let's review. You've copied the data over. When running Rideshare locally, you can take your time to work on each step. However, in a production context, you'd want to rehearse these steps and run them with minimal gaps of time in between each step.

Before you send live queries to the new intermediate table, you'll want to analyze each partition that you're working with. Fortunately, pgslice can be used here to generate an ANALYZE command for every partition. The full command includes ANALYZE with the VERBOSE option.

To generate those statements from pgslice, run the analyze subcommand as follows:

```
sh/pgslice_analyze.sh
bin/pgslice analyze rideshare.trip_positions
```

If that ran successfully, you'll see a lot of INFO log entries showing that each partition was analyzed. You're now ready to cut over to the new table. However, it still has the intermediate name which won't match up with what the Active Record model expects. We'll need to rename the table.

Fortunately, pgslice has you covered here. Use the pgslice swap subcommand to swap around the table names. Run the following in your terminal, with the optional dry-run to preview the statements:

```
bin/pgslice swap rideshare.trip_positions --dry-run
```

We see there's a short lock timeout set of five seconds for a transaction. Inside that transaction, the original table name gets a _retired suffix. This frees up the original table name so that the intermediate table can now be renamed to take it over. Those operations are done inside a transaction so that it succeeds or fails as one unit.

Remove the dry-run option and run it.

Great! You've now run through the main steps on your local development system to migrate your trip positions data into a partitioned table.

Prior to running this in production, you'll want to practice these steps locally, in CI, and in pre-production environments.

Despite all of that rehearsal, in production, things can still go wrong. Fortunately pgslice has an unswap command that will revert the table renames. Use this if things go really wrong, and you need to swap back to the original table.

After the swap completes, the partitioned table is now the live table.

One More Fill

From the moment you started the first fill until the moment the swap transaction commits, there may have been more inserts that weren't copied over.

How do we get those rows? pgslice recommends running a second fill that adds the --swapped option.

This option means that pgslice can copy over any missing rows, even after the tables are renamed, so that you don't miss any data.

Remember pgslice doesn't support tables that have received updates or deletes (or updates from SQL MERGE) in the time period between the fill and the swap. If you have that type of pattern and want to use pgslice, you'll need to handle those updates or deletes separately or use a different tool. You could manually identify those changes and bring them forward. You could temporarily take a downtime for that table so no updates or deletes were possible while the copying happened. Another option would be to make the table read-only during the copy process, which would be a partial downtime or unavailability.

With all of that said, great, you did it! While the conversion process may go smoothly on your local server, you might have a different experience in production.

What kinds of gotchas might you run into?

Partitioning Gotcha: Primary Key Definition

As you learned earlier, Active Record creates a schema cache (see Avoiding Schema Cache Errors, on page 109), tracking schema information like columns, types, and more. The original primary key definition for trip_positions had a primary key defined on the id column.

For partitioned tables, a primary key cannot be enforced across all partitions. pgslice creates a new primary key on the id column in each child partition but does not add a primary key to the parent.

Is a primary key needed on the parent? Trying to add the single column id primary key to the parent is not possible. That's because partitioned tables require the partition key column to be included in the primary key definition. Remember that we're using the created_at column for our partition key.

Another option is to create a *Composite Primary Key* (CPK), which is a primary key that has multiple columns. The CPK would include id and created_at for trip_positions, added to the parent table. By creating each partition initially without a primary key at all, we're able to add one. Creating this CPK on the parent table will be synced from the parent to the children:

sql/add_trip_positions_primary_key.sql
```
-- Composite Primary Key (CPK)
-- on (id, created_at)
ALTER TABLE trip_positions
ADD PRIMARY KEY (id, created_at);
```

Unfortunately, pgslice, by default, adds the primary key to all child partitions, which means it's incompatible.

To solve that, one strategy would be to drop the id primary key from child partitions. To do that, they must be dropped from all children first. With those removed, you're able to define a new CPK on id and created_at at the parent level that will automatically propagate to children. Note that performing this does require a significant lock period since all partitions are modified.

Imagine that you're performing this offline. First, run a DROP CONSTRAINT for all children. Example partitions like trip_positions_202306 are used in this example:

sql/drop_primary_key_child_partitions.sql
```
-- \d trip_positions

-- Run DROP for *each* child partition table
ALTER TABLE trip_positions_202309
DROP CONSTRAINT trip_positions_202309_pkey;

ALTER TABLE trip_positions_202310
DROP CONSTRAINT trip_positions_202310_pkey;

-- Repeat for all partitions
```

If you have a large set of partitions, you'll want to generate these statements or create a script that performs these drops.

With all existing id primary key constraints dropped on children, add the CPK using the statement from earlier. Once added, the same CPK will exist on the parent and all children.

What does this have to do with the schema cache? If you modify the definition of the table that is cached in the schema cache by Active Record, it will be stale and cause application errors until it's repopulated.

If you face schema cache inconsistencies, the least complex way to resolve them is to accept some number of errors while you restart the application. If that's not an acceptable solution, you may also manually[8] clear the Active Record schema cache.

---

8. https://api.rubyonrails.org/classes/ActiveRecord/ConnectionAdapters/SchemaCache.html#method-i-clear-21

Partitioning Gotcha: Logical Replication Replica Identity

As you saw in the last chapter, when logical replication is used, rows are identified using a replica identity. The primary key normally acts as the replica identity.

Another reason to use a CPK strategy on the parent table is that subscribers expect to identify table rows uniquely using their replica identity. When using pgslice without a parent table primary key, double-check that logical replication will work OK; otherwise you'll need to add a primary key definition to the parent.

Another gotcha you may run into is within your Rails application test suite. Any test code that inserts data into the database as part of an integration-style test may create data that falls outside the ranges of partitions you've configured.

When that happens, tests should be updated to use "relative" dates based on the current time, or more partitions will need to be added so that they exist for data to be inserted into.

Finally, you'll want to consider automating parts of your system.

How does that work?

Automate Partition Creation and Monitoring

Learning the importance of monitoring the hard way
by: Andrew Atkinson, Software Engineer

It was a normal summer evening. We were outside our house with neighbors. The adults were chatting, and the kids were playing together.

Suddenly, I got an alert on my phone. Hm, maybe it's not urgent. I'll check the stack trace.

My heart sank. I knew immediately what the problem was, and that it was my fault. That incomplete ticket for monitoring here came to bite.

Despite conducting thorough pre-release testing, which is always a good idea, things can still go wrong.

The system being described in this story used monthly partitions. We'd reached the end of the development cycle and monitoring was one of the last tickets to get picked up.

The intention was to monitor for required partitions in months *in advance*. That way, if a missing partition was found, developers would have plenty of time to debug and fix the issue. Unfortunately, that ticket was never completed.

Despite thorough testing and manual post-deploy verifications, something changed over time, causing the future partition cron to fail. Fortunately, the problem was noticed first on smaller databases, but writes for that table were failing. We quickly created partitions manually to fix the issue and to buy time to investigate what had changed in the automated processes.

How does pgslice help here? pgslice recommends creating a cron job that runs on a schedule to create partitions. An example cron job might look like this:

```
sh/pgslice_add_partitions_cron_entry.sh
# Set PGSLICE_URL on cron host
#
# At time: "00:00", on the first day of month
# Link: https://crontab.guru/#0_0_1_*_*
#
0 0 1 * * bin/pgslice add_partitions rideshare.trip_positions \
  --future 3 \
  --url $PGSLICE_URL
```

Besides automated tests, manually run any commands that are run from cron hosts to make sure they run without permission or ownership errors. This command depends on PGSLICE_URL being set and that bin/pgslice runs on the cron host.

To schedule cron jobs with Ruby, use a Ruby gem like whenever.[9] bin/pgslice add_partitions can be run multiple times and only creates partitions that don't exist (idempotent).

With the verified job in place, you're most of the way there. However, it's still strongly recommended to monitor for future partitions, and alert when they don't exist. Catch issues before they become emergencies to avoid having your name show up in a story like mine!

Next, let's take a look at how to retire old partitions once they're no longer needed.

Retiring Unneeded Partitions

Over time, as old partitions are no longer needed in PostgreSQL, you'll be able to archive the data and remove the partitions.

Get the partition name and then call DETACH using the CONCURRENTLY keyword to avoid interrupting any concurrently executing queries.

---

9. https://github.com/javan/whenever

This example shows a SQL statement to detach the partition named trip_positions_202209:

sql/detach_partition_concurrently.sql
```
ALTER TABLE trip_positions
DETACH PARTITION trip_positions_202311 CONCURRENTLY;
```

As you saw earlier, a detached partition becomes a regular PostgreSQL table. The detached partition may be reattached later, as long as the schema definition does not change, or the partition can be emptied (using TRUNCATE) or dropped entirely.

Try reattaching it so that you're familiar with how to do that. You'll need to provide the original non-overlapping bounds when reattaching. The partition below trip_positions_202311 should get the bounds FOR VALUES FROM ('2023-11-01 00:00:00') TO ('2023-12-01 00:00:00').

sql/attach_partition.sql
```
ALTER TABLE trip_positions
ATTACH PARTITION trip_positions_202311
FOR VALUES FROM ('2023-11-01 00:00:00') TO ('2023-12-01 00:00:00');
```

You've now added it back.

However, we would like to proceed with testing the archival process. Let's detach the trip_positions_202309 partition so that we can archive the data in it. Since these partition names are dynamically generated based on when you ran these commands, change the partition name to one on your system.

For the archival process, we'll use the pg_dump command.

Run the following pg_dump command on the trip_positions_202309 partition. The -Fc option creates a compressed binary representation of the table data.

sh/pg_dump_trip_positions_partition.sh
```
pg_dump -c -Fc \
  --table rideshare.trip_positions_202309 \
  $PGSLICE_URL > trip_positions_202309.dump
```

From that file, pg_restore can be called to perform the reverse action and restore the row data from the file.

Notice that PGSLICE_URL is used to connect to the database, and the --table option is used to specify the schema-qualified partition name rideshare.trip_positions_202309.

Besides the compressed binary format, other plain text formats like CSV can be used. These formats may interoperate better with heterogeneous database types if you wish to use the files as an intermediate representation of data to copy elsewhere.

Once the data has been saved to a file and the file has been stored in a backup storage location, the partition holding the data can be dropped. To do that, run this DROP command from psql:

sql/drop_table_partition.sql

```
DROP TABLE trip_positions_202309;
```

You've now seen how to archive row data into a file and then drop the associated partition.

Before moving on, it's worth testing the restore process using the intermediate file. Try restoring the data from the trip_positions_202209.dump file. To do that, run the following pg_restore command from your terminal:

sh/pg_restore_dump_file.sh

```
pg_restore -Fc trip_positions_202309.dump |
  --dbname rideshare_development
```

Great. Let's verify the data is there. Open up the rideshare_development database. Run psql $PGSLICE_URL and the following SQL statement:

```
SELECT * FROM trip_positions_202309 LIMIT 5;
```

You should see that the table exists and that there are data rows. Excellent!

Let's recap what you've done. You've dumped the data from an unneeded partition and then safely detached the partition in a nonblocking way. From the dumped data intermediate file, you verified that the data can be restored into a table successfully. By placing the file into a backed-up and secure location, you can keep the data for as long as needed outside your database.

With these pieces, the next step would be to automate a process that detaches old partitions, archives the data to a file, and then drops the partitions. An automated archival mechanism like this will help control the growth of your database and provide a more scalable design for a high-growth table.

With the RANGE partitioning type well covered, let's explore more partitioning types that are available.

Use LIST Partitioning for Known Divisions

Besides time-oriented data, where you'd partition on a timestamp column, you may wish to partition on integer or numeric type columns. Note that the RANGE type is not limited to timestamp types either and could be used on integer types.

Imagine that you had integer data that wasn't time-oriented.

For that type of data, you may want to use the LIST type.

Let's consider an example. Imagine that you run a Software as a Service (SaaS) platform and want to segment a large table that has data from a mix of customers. Each row has a customer_id foreign key column that's connected to a customer. The table contains data from both active and inactive customers.

By using the customer_id foreign key column as the partition column with LIST partitioning, the table data can be partitioned by customer_id.

Why might you want to do that? For one reason, you could consider an archival process for customer data that's related to customers who are no longer active on the platform.

Another benefit would be performance benefits for queries that can be scoped to a customer. How does that work?

With partitioned tables, as long as queries for those tables include the customer_id column in their WHERE clause, the PostgreSQL planner can identify a single partition where this customer data is located. That's called *partition pruning*, and you'll see more on that later.

LIST and RANGE partitioning can even be combined into a composite partitioning strategy, layering two types together.

While LIST partitioning is a great strategy when you have a known identifier, what about when you'd like to break up a big table but don't have a clear column to partition on? What are your options there?

Use HASH Partitioning for a Fixed Amount of Buckets

PostgreSQL Version 11 added a third type of declarative partitioning called HASH.[10] If RANGE or LIST types don't work well for your use case, consider the HASH type.

Imagine that you've got a table sized around 500 GB that you'd like to split up. By splitting it up ten ways, you'll end up with ten 50-GB tables as partitions. The 50 GB tables may be easier to manage and faster to query, especially when the data being queried lives in a single partition, and queries can be issued that include partition identifiers.

To create three partitions, use the MODULUS operator with the primary key id value to route row DML operations into a partition.

---

10. https://hevodata.com/learn/postgresql-partitions/

Let's set this up. The following SQL statements create a HASH partitioned table and show the three partitions. Change the MODULUS clause from 3 to 10 if you'd like.

sql/hash_partitioned_trips_table.sql

```
CREATE SCHEMA IF NOT EXISTS temp;

CREATE TABLE temp.trips_test (id serial) PARTITION BY HASH (id);

CREATE TABLE temp.trips_test_0
PARTITION OF temp.trips_test
FOR VALUES WITH (MODULUS 3, REMAINDER 0);

CREATE TABLE temp.trips_test_1
PARTITION OF temp.trips_test
FOR VALUES WITH (MODULUS 3, REMAINDER 1);

CREATE TABLE temp.trips_test_2
PARTITION OF temp.trips_test
FOR VALUES WITH (MODULUS 3, REMAINDER 2);

\d+ temp.trips_test
```

When deciding how many partitions to create, strike a balance between the final table size you're after and the total number of partitions. Note that with greater numbers of partitions, query planning time will increase. You'll need to experiment to see the impact on planning time if you're considering very large amounts of partitions.

You'll want to leverage the parallelization of worker jobs, which can run in parallel across partitions. Ideally, your result partitions will be considerably smaller than the 100 GB guideline or smaller than the size of the memory available on your instance. Remember that shared buffers are tuned from 25 to 40 percent of the available system memory, so you won't have access to all of the available memory.

Since you can't change the HASH partitions structure later, plan a little headroom for the resulting partition size based on the growth you'd expect.

What happens if you want to change the structure later? That would be another new partitioning migration from the current structure to the new one.

While the primary focus of this chapter has not been on the benefits of partitioning, performance benefits could be huge for your system. It will really depend on your queries and partition design.

What other performance benefits from partitioning are there?

Performance Benefits from Partitioning

Partition pruning[11] is the mechanism PostgreSQL uses to determine which partitions can be ignored by the query planner based on partition constraints. When the planner can exclude partitions, this improves query performance because fewer partitions need to be evaluated.

To use this, make sure enable_partition_pruning is set to on. Run SHOW enable_partition_pruning; from psql and turn it on if it's not:

```
sql/set_enable_partition_pruning.sql
SET enable_partition_pruning = ON;
```

Enabling partition pruning is straightforward. The more challenging part will be making sure your queries include the partition key column for all queries.

The partition key column should appear in the WHERE clause so that the query planner knows which partition contains the row.

Besides query performance benefits, partitioned tables have benefits for background work.

Earlier, you learned how Autovacuum schedules one VACUUM worker per table to clean up dead row versions. In PostgreSQL 15, multiple vacuum workers can run in parallel across multiple partitions of a table.[12]

> In PostgreSQL 15, the vacuum process has been optimized to make it more efficient and faster to vacuum large tables. It includes improvements such as the ability to vacuum multiple partitions of the same table in parallel, vacuum indexes concurrently, and skip vacuuming indexes unaffected by an update.

Partitioned tables can improve query performance, although partitioned tables with unmodified queries could also worsen performance. Make sure to add partition information to your queries.

Add Partition Key Column to Queries

 When querying partitioned tables, it's critical that the partition key column is included in the query text. Whether it's customer_id, created_at, or something else, PostgreSQL needs this information so that it can identify which partition contains the row and which partitions can be excluded.

Besides parallelizing Vacuum jobs and limiting the partitions to scan, index maintenance can be faster with partitioned tables. How does that work?

---

11. https://www.postgresql.org/docs/current/ddl-partitioning.html#DDL-PARTITION-PRUNING
12. https://www.percona.com/blog/postgresql-vacuuming-to-optimize-database-performance-and-reclaim-space

When indexes are defined on the parent, the definition is propagated to all children, so that each child partition gets their own copy of the index that corresponds to their own rows.

The index for a partition covers the rows only in that partition and not globally across partitions. This means that when building an index initially and when keeping index entries updated, those operations are faster because they're restricted to fewer rows, compared with being on an equivalent larger unpartitioned table.

In earlier versions of PostgreSQL, indexes had to be created on each child partition manually. From Version 11, indexes created on the parent table are automatically propagated to all child partitions. Besides indexes, foreign key constraints have also been used with partitioned tables since Version 11.[13]

Partitioned tables have some additional parameters to consider that aren't enabled by default.

The parameters enable_partitionwise_join and enable_partitionwise_aggregate are useful when your queries join partitions together or perform aggregations on partitions. Setting these parameters to on may improve query performance, with the trade-off of slower query planning time.[14]

The post, "Improving Database Performance Using Partitioning,"[15] shows example partition structures and queries and then visualizes how these settings work.

When creating indexes on partitioned tables, there are caveats to be aware of. Creating indexes CONCURRENTLY on the parent table is not supported as of PostgreSQL 16. To work around this limitation, use CREATE INDEX CONCURRENTLY to create the index manually on each child partition. Once that's done, run CREATE INDEX on the parent.[16]

Because the parent doesn't contain data rows and because the indexes were created on all children prior to this statement, this technique avoids locking on children for index creation and minimizes the lock duration when creating the corresponding index on the parent.

To explore more performance benefits with partitioned tables, refer to the "Query Performance Benefits" section of the Partitioning documentation.[17]

---

13. https://pgdash.io/blog/partition-postgres-11.html
14. https://pganalyze.com/blog/5mins-postgres-partition-wise-joins-aggregates-query-performance
15. https://www.postgresql.fastware.com/postgresql-insider-prf-prt-mec
16. https://stackoverflow.com/a/70958260
17. https://www.postgresql.org/docs/current/ddl-partitioning.html

> **Consider pg_partman**
>
> pg_partman runs as a PostgreSQL extension and is an alternative to pgslice that's worth considering if you're investigating table partitioning.

While this chapter focused exclusively on pgslice, a more advanced partitioning tool called pg_partman[18] is worth a look. pg_partman runs differently in that it runs as a PostgreSQL extension within PostgreSQL. The benefit of pgslice is that it's a Ruby client program, which means it might be easier to customize if needed.

However, the pg_partman extension is broadly available on PostgreSQL hosting providers. pg_cron, which you saw earlier (see Scheduling Jobs Using pg_cron, on page 215), can be used for automation. pg_partman has guides covering various ways to transition into the partitioned structure that are beyond the more limited options with pgslice.

That's it!

Let's Split

It's time to reflect on what you've accomplished in this chapter and then look toward the next one.

You learned all about declarative table partitioning in PostgreSQL—what, when, and how to use it. You worked through a concrete use case using Rideshare trip positions data and migrated it into a partitioned table structure using the pgslice tool.

With sufficient planning and testing, for an append-only table, pgslice helps you achieve zero downtime online data migration. With a partition table in place, you're well-positioned to archive unneeded data from your database as a nonblocking operation.

You briefly looked at other partitioning types, filling out your basic knowledge of all three supported types. You explored the benefits of table partitioning from data archival to maintenance operations to query performance.

In the next chapter, you'll continue to put advanced PostgreSQL techniques into action using examples from Rideshare. You'll bring bits and pieces from many things you've learned throughout to adapt PostgreSQL to all sorts of use cases you may not have considered. See you there!

---

18. https://github.com/pgpartman/pg_partman

Part V

Advanced Usages

## CHAPTER 15

Advanced Uses and What's Next

You made it to the last chapter! Over the course of this book, hopefully you've grown your knowledge and skills with PostgreSQL and Ruby on Rails.

Is that the end of the story? No! Innovation in PostgreSQL and Ruby on Rails continues year after year, building on decades of contributions from thousands of contributors.

Dozens of new companies are launching now and building on top of PostgreSQL. It's not surprising when you think about it. Database software must be reliable, support backward compatibility, and offer resilience capabilities, good performance, and scalability. PostgreSQL does all that and takes things further with great extensibility. The extensibility of PostgreSQL has been embraced by the community of extension creators and database product developers who continue to widen the capabilities of PostgreSQL beyond what's offered in the core.

PostgreSQL can be thought of as a data platform[1] with capabilities well beyond basic SQL and OLTP. In this chapter, you'll learn how to use PostgreSQL for advanced capabilities like analytics, search, or message queues. While PostgreSQL is a general-purpose database, it can offer a competitive feature set and performance to specialized or dedicated databases without their associated monetary cost or the complexity involved in synchronizing data between multiple databases.

To achieve that, you'll need to tap into features you've worked with in earlier chapters, new ones you haven't yet seen, and dip into the wide array of PostgreSQL extensions and Ruby gems.

---

1.   https://www.contributor.fyi/tembo

Besides performance improvements to core PostgreSQL software, modern hardware has improved greatly in performance in the last decade. Solid State Disk (SSD) advancements in speeding up random access, which is often what we're doing when using a database, makes using relational databases like PostgreSQL viable for some types of work where it wasn't before.

With that in mind, let's analyze where things came from and what's possible today. In the 2010s, before these advancements in software and hardware performance, organizations turned to specialized databases or "heterogeneous" database types. They used these databases in areas where relational databases had struggled. While specialized databases can offer unique and compelling features or performance for specialized work, running additional databases carries more operational complexity.

Each database needs to be provisioned, patched, upgraded, and debugged when things go wrong. When these databases use different paradigms, whether it's multinode distributed databases, key value stores, or search focused, learning to use them well is not trivial.

Even when these specialized databases are hosted by a provider, there are still fundamental challenges for the user. Hosting companies often don't have access to data directly, and ask customers to provide logs and metrics information for troubleshooting. This implies your team members all have access, know where to find this information, and know how to take action on any recommendations the hosting provider has.

Besides all of the technical and operational challenges, there's another fundamental data consistency challenge. Data stored in PostgreSQL, replicated to specialized databases and possibly existing in other forms, needs to be consistent. This means all inserts, updates, and deletes need to be propagated correctly. Without some shared concept of a transaction, this is a significant technical challenge. Your team may explore distributed transactions and the saga pattern,[2] which involves greater operational complexity.

Organizations running this heterogeneous mix of databases dedicate *significant* engineering time toward addressing all of these challenges. In extreme cases, these challenges can negatively impact the business by leaving open security holes from poorly maintained software, unresolved performance issues that negatively impact the customer experience, and a platform that's more difficult to work with, slowing down product development.

---

2.   https://microservices.io/patterns/data/saga.html

Why You Shouldn't Operate a Database Zoo

The phenomenon of using many databases at once is so common that terms like "database zoo" and "database sprawl" have sprung up to describe it.

What do database zoos look like? In a database zoo, you might find Elasticsearch or OpenSearch for searching document text. Redis is probably running for storing small bits of text as a key value (KV) store, like background job data, cache data, or session identifiers.

MongoDB[3] might be used to store schemaless data in a JSON-compatible format. Kafka[4] might be used as a message queue, publishing events from other systems to connected subscribers.

Running one or more of these databases means that your team members need access to the logs and metrics they produce. Your team will want to follow best practices by configuring least-privilege access and customizing these databases using tunable parameters. Your team needs to perform major version upgrades, debug performance problems and errors, and identify compatible client software for administration tasks or application connectivity.

Although specialized databases offer benefits, the downsides mentioned so far can be thought of as their "carrying costs."[5] Besides the financial cost of using these databases, there's the "opportunity cost"[6] associated with developers and engineers investing time to troubleshoot a variety of database technologies vs. fewer.

This discussion would not be complete without considering databases outside of the OLTP realm.

Most organizations have an entirely separate OLAP database and possibly a team of data engineers maintaining complicated synchronization processes from PostgreSQL. Once data is copied into analytical databases, it might be used for machine learning data models, forecasting, or other types of decision-making.

These databases are data warehouses,[7] data lakes,[8] or even "data lakehouses,"[9] which seems like a made-up term (but it's not!)

---

3.   https://www.mongodb.com

4.   https://kafka.apache.org

5.   https://en.wikipedia.org/wiki/Carrying_cost

6.   https://en.wikipedia.org/wiki/Opportunity_cost

7.   https://cloud.google.com/learn/what-is-a-data-warehouse

8.   https://cloud.google.com/learn/what-is-a-data-lake

9.   https://cloud.google.com/discover/what-is-a-data-lakehouse

Given these needs for OLTP and OLAP, what if there was a less complex alternative? What options are there?

Why You Should Just Use PostgreSQL

In the post, "Just Use Postgres for Everything,"[10] the author proposes a tongue-in-cheek retort to modern database sprawl and complexity: Just Use Postgres.

The author provides short descriptions of how to use PostgreSQL to take on more work. Instead of Redis, MongoDB, Kafka, or Elasticsearch, the author proposes ways to achieve similar capabilities using PostgreSQL.

This chapter expands on the spirit of that post, focusing on a couple of specific PostgreSQL implementations that might be alternatives to using specialized databases. With the focus on Ruby on Rails here, we'll look at implementations in Ruby on Rails and Active Record.

For specific uses, PostgreSQL can be customized with hundreds of tunable parameters and extensions, turning it from a general purpose database into something closer to a specialized database. Combined with targeted schema design with capabilities like table partitioning, efficient index design, and dedicated instances, PostgreSQL can offer competitive performance and functionality.

If you're already using PostgreSQL and considering expanding the use cases it provides, you'll want to leverage parameters and extensions to "squeeze"[11] as much performance and functionality out of it as possible. If you're not starting from scratch, you may be faced with an online data migration from a specialized database. Refer to the tactics of online migrations and backfilling on page 110 and working with bulk data on page 272 as you investigate a data migration.

In the upcoming sections, you'll explore several use cases that can be solved using PostgreSQL:

- Basic business analytics
- Pattern matching in document search
- Full-text search, fuzzy search, and keyword search in documents
- Alternatives to Redis for background jobs and caching
- Vector similarity search

Let's dive in!

---

10. https://www.amazingcto.com/postgres-for-everything/
11. https://blog.danslimmon.com/2023/08/11/squeeze-the-hell-out-of-the-system-you-have/

Basic Analytics with PostgreSQL

When your organization runs a lot of long queries for analytics, it's a good idea to keep those separated from the short OLTP style queries on the same instance.

How can we achieve that? For startups and small companies with less complex needs and server space capacity, Blazer[12] is a basic analytics tool worth considering.

Once deployed, Blazer provides a dashboard where team members can create and share SQL queries. Blazer ships as a Ruby gem in your Ruby on Rails application or can be run separately using Docker. Stored SQL queries can accept named parameters that your team configures. Since Blazer is open source, there's no licensing cost, and you're free to deploy it how you'd like.

Since queries running with Blazer add operational load, you may want to separate it. You've got some options. You can configure a read replica instance that's attached to your current primary database where you run Blazer queries. Or, you can use a separate primary PostgreSQL instance with a second deployment of your Rails application or one that's configured to receive DML changes using logical replication (as you learned about on page 319) for the databases and tables you want to report on.

Since Blazer has tables and database objects itself, using logical replication on a separate instance is nice because the instance still supports writes[13] where those Blazer tables can live.

Another common need organizations have is to search across document text as part of a product feature offering. While many organizations reach for dedicated search databases, they may be able to use PostgreSQL instead. How would that work?

Pattern Match Searching

PostgreSQL supports a lot of search types, and we'll dive into them in this section. Pattern matching using LIKE and ILIKE is supported along with regular expressions.

These are useful when the user who's searching knows exactly what to search for. Let's consider an example.

---

12. https://github.com/ankane/blazer
13. https://www.crunchydata.com/blog/data-to-go-postgres-logical-replication

Imagine a search for the first name of "Jane" within Rideshare users. That search could be a LIKE query. Match on the string Jane%, which has the name Jane and the wildcard character % on the right side.

Jane may not be a common value in your data. If you run data generators in Rideshare, you'll have at least 20K users. If needed, populate users by running bin/rails data_generators:generate_all, then psql $DATABASE_URL -c 'ANALYZE users'. Use what you learned earlier on page 43 to find the most common values for user first names. Replace Jane with a common first name from your data.

Run this query from psql:

sql/select_like_example.sql
```
SELECT first_name FROM users
WHERE first_name LIKE 'Jane%'
LIMIT 5;
```

Running that query (or one of *your* common first names) found some similar names:

```
first_name
------------
 Janessa
 Janey
 Janel
 Janelle
 Jane
```

As covered in "Fuzzy Text Search and Case-insensitive ICU Collations in Postgres," LIKE and ILIKE support the % symbol, which matches zero or more characters. The _ (underscore) character can be used instead to match exactly one character. *Collations*[14] are how text types are sorted and compared.

In "5 mins of Postgres E23: Fuzzy Text Search & Case-insensitive ICU Collations in Postgres,"[15] we see how the text_pattern_ops operator class can be used with a B-Tree index to speed up text matching queries.

You learned about operator classes earlier on page 182 where you used them with GIN indexes.

Remember that operator classes are chosen for the column type that's indexed (see "Operator Classes and Operator Families"[16]).

Why set an operator class here?

---

14. https://www.postgresql.org/docs/current/collation.html
15. https://www.youtube.com/watch?v=7xXIvWMogPw
16. https://www.postgresql.org/docs/current/indexes-opclass.html

The difference from the default operator classes is that the values are compared strictly character by character rather than according to the locale-specific collation rules.

If pattern matching is sufficient but query performance is poor, improve the query performance with a well-placed index. Let's try creating an index with a specific operator class for this query.

Use the operator class values text_pattern_ops for text column types and varchar_pattern_ops for varchar types. Run this statement to create the index:

```
sql/create_index_varchar_pattern_ops.sql
-- Use `varchar_pattern_ops` Operator Class
CREATE INDEX idx_users_first_name_vpo
ON users(first_name VARCHAR_PATTERN_OPS);
```

Try the query again, prepending EXPLAIN (ANALYZE), confirming that the query plan lists the idx_users_first_name_vpo index.

Besides the % operator, matching using regular expressions is supported in PostgreSQL using the SIMILAR TO keywords or the tilde operator (~).

After you've confirmed the index was used, drop it by running DROP INDEX idx_users_first_name_vpo;.

Exact matches or pattern matches are great when they find relevant results and when users know exactly what to search for.

What about when users do *not* know exactly what to search for? Does PostgreSQL allow users to provide a "fuzzy" input, as text that's close but not exactly correct, and still find relevant matches?

Implementing Full-Text Search (FTS)

In this section, you'll go beyond the exact matching you worked with in the last section and explore PostgreSQL full-text search (FTS) capabilities. You'll adapt content from the post, "Full-Text Search in Milliseconds with Rails and PostgreSQL."[17]

Let's consider common objections right up front. How does the performance of full-text search in PostgreSQL compare to dedicated search databases like Elasticsearch?

The Supabase post, "Postgres Full-Text Search vs. the Rest,"[18] compares the performance using benchmarks between PostgreSQL and Elasticsearch.

---

17. https://pganalyze.com/blog/full-text-search-ruby-rails-postgres
18. https://supabase.com/blog/postgres-full-text-search-vs-the-rest

The post, "Full-text Search Engine with PostgreSQL (part 2): Postgres vs. Elasticsearch,"[19] explores this and provides benchmarks. The data set being used includes more than 100K rows to search through. In those benchmarks, the post concludes by advising that PostgreSQL provides comparable performance to Elasticsearch for up to 100K rows!

In the post, "Postgres Full-text Search Is Good Enough!"[20] the author shows how PostgreSQL FTS works well for many types of searches.

What is Elasticsearch (or the fork OpenSearch)? Elasticsearch is a specialized search database that uses a distributed multinode paradigm. This means that the load from indexing and querying is distributed horizontally across nodes. Elasticsearch is backed by Lucene[21] and stores JSON documents in its indexes using HTTP as an interface both for ingestion and querying.

As a powerful specialized search database, it's also quite complex to operate for large-sized data and query volume. With multiple nodes to manage, operators need to determine whether to scale horizontally or vertically, factoring in write and read performance, reliability, and cost efficiency.

If PostgreSQL can provide comparable performance for user searches, the less-complex single-primary paradigm offers compelling advantages in being easier to operate and having the benefits of transactions available.

Let's shift our focus now to full-text search features in general, and specifically the ones that PostgreSQL supports. If you're evaluating PostgreSQL for full-text search, study which features and capabilities you'll need, or consider starting out with PostgreSQL to keep your operations less complex if you aren't sure what your search needs are.

Besides the basic pattern matching that you saw earlier, PostgreSQL supports a lot of search capabilities:

- Wildcard searches
- Handling misspellings
- Fuzzy matching
- Non-English accented characters
- *Stemming, normalization, stopwords, lexemes,* and language dictionaries
- Column weighting and ranking for relevancy
- Search results highlighting within results

---

19. https://xata.io/blog/postgres-full-text-search-postgres-vs-elasticsearch
20. http://rachbelaid.com/postgres-full-text-search-is-good-enough
21. https://lucene.apache.org

If you're not well-versed in search terminology, you may be seeing terms here for the first time.

Before diving into the details of the support in PostgreSQL, let's look at search domain terminology to help prepare for upcoming sections. The definitions here are simplified. Use official PostgreSQL documentation or the Glossary[22] for authoritative definitions.

Search Terminology

- Document—Input text to be searched

- Stopwords—Very common words with low search value, filtered out for ranking

- Dictionary—Contains useful words like stopwords, synonyms

- Normalization—Converting words into a base form

- Lexeme—Normalized words

- Lemmas, Lemmatization—The base parts after normalization

- N-Gram—Combinations of letters from a word as a smaller fragment; two are a bigram, three are a trigram, "n" is an n-gram

- Ranking—Prioritizing one item over another

- Levenshtein Distance—Algorithm for measuring the distance between letters

- Soundex—Algorithm for how similar two words sound to each other

- ICU Collations—"International Components for Unicode" describes how text types are sorted and compared

With that, let's dive into fuzzy searching in PostgreSQL.

Fuzzy Searching with tsvector

Looking for a match with an inexact input string or sequence is a form of *fuzzy* searching. Fuzzy searching means that what's being searched isn't known precisely. The user has supplied "approximately correct" text as search

---

22. https://www.postgresql.org/docs/current/glossary.html

input, or possibly mistaken text, but still expects to get relevant search results back. Who can blame them, really? Modern search engines excel at taking approximate input and producing relevant search results.

Since these terms are familiar, let's briefly discuss full-text search. Full-text search refers to the document text that is being searched. For Google or website search engines, this could be metadata from the site, or content within that site, that forms the document text to be searched. A user might perform a fuzzy search for website titles, descriptions, or for content on the pages, in order to find relevant web pages.

Fuzzy Search vs. Full-Text Search

Fuzzy searching refers to what the user is typing. They can find results without typing the exact sequence of characters to match.

Full-text search refers to the text that is being searched. Usually, it implies advanced text processing capabilities.

What other kinds of fuzzy searches are there? Some other examples are misspellings, pluralization errors, "creative" spellings, or incorrect verb conjugations. PostgreSQL can help with all of those and more. Another search capability is searching "homonyms," which are words that sound the same but are spelled differently.

By using PostgreSQL FTS plus a few common extensions, you can leverage these powerful search capabilities in your Rails app.

How do you get started? First, there are new PostgreSQL concepts to learn. The first concept is the tsvector[23] data type. The tsvector data type takes text as input, which is text to process for searching, then creates a tsvector object from that text.

Text is said to be "vectorized" when the TO_TSVECTOR()[24] function processes it, producing a tsvector result. Both the tsvector type and processing functions are included in the core distribution of PostgreSQL.

Try running the following example from psql:

```
sql/select_to_tsvector.sql
SELECT TO_TSVECTOR('english',
  'PostgreSQL Full Text Search with Ruby on Rails');
```

---

23. https://www.postgresql.org/docs/current/datatype-textsearch.html
24. https://www.postgresql.org/docs/current/textsearch-controls.html

That produces a result like this, showing what the vectorized text looks like:

```
                          to_tsvector
----------------------------------------------------------------
 'full':2 'postgresql':1 'rail':8 'rubi':6 'search':4 'text':3
```

The text being searched is referred to as the "document." The tsvector works with unique tokens, called *lexemes*. Each lexeme has a position in the document. Notice the word full has the position 2.

This process of transforming the document text into lexemes with integer positions is called normalization. This normalization process uses language grammar from a language like English to transform the words into "lexemes." For example, "Rails" is transformed into "Rail" (singular), which is recognized in the English dictionary. The lexeme is produced based on rules without knowledge of what Ruby on Rails is.

Common words that occur in almost all documents, like "the" or "a," are called "stopwords."[25] Stopwords are removed in the normalization process when a tsvector is created.

Once there's a processed tsvector for document text, you're ready to query it. How is that done? To query a tsvector, use a special function TO_TSQUERY()[26] (or several others) to transform query text into a tsquery type.

> to_tsquery normalizes each token into a lexeme

Let's try another example. The following query compares the input text with the tsvector from the document. The @@ operator checks for "existence" within the tsvector. The command returns true when a match exists in the document.

Run this in psql:

```sql
sql/search_tsvector_with_tsquery.sql
-- Search 'rail' within the (vectorized) document
SELECT
  TO_TSVECTOR(
    'english',
    'PostgreSQL Full Text Search with Ruby on Rails'
  ) @@ TO_TSQUERY('english', 'rail');
```

This returned true. What does that mean?

- The text being searched is turned into a tsquery using the TO_TSQUERY() function
- The text input is "rail"
- "rail" exists in the vectorized document text (the tsvector)

---

25. https://www.postgresql.org/docs/current/textsearch-dictionaries.html#TEXTSEARCH-STOPWORDS
26. https://www.postgresql.org/docs/current/textsearch-controls.html#TEXTSEARCH-PARSING-QUERIES

Let's review some of the search terminology you've seen and some that's upcoming:

Glossary of Search Terminology

- tsvector—A PostgreSQL type, composed of vectorized text
- tsquery—Query type for working with tsvector data
- Weight—Using the function SETWEIGHT() to bias search results
- TS_RANK()—Function to rank a result that's more relevant over others

Now that you have got tsvector and tsquery types, let's explore the SETWEIGHT() function for weighting columns. For weight values, the functions use English language letters A, B, C, and so on to prioritize one column over another. Weights are then supplied to a *ranking function* (TS_RANK()[27]) function. Besides built-in ranking functions, PostgreSQL supports custom ranking functions.

Let's look at the built-in TS_RANK() function. This function takes weight values that have been set, a tsvector, and the search query as arguments.

Weighting and Ranking

Text being searched can be "weighted" and "ranked."

Weighting in PostgreSQL refers more to the words, or sections, or table columns.

Ranking uses the weights as input and tries to find the most relevant search results for a query.

Let's try this out in Rideshare.

Imagine the hiring process for drivers on the Rideshare platform. Drivers send in their resumes and work experience. By searching through all of that text, recruiters or hiring managers can find the best-qualified candidates. Finding candidates likely involves automatic and manual screening.

The system combines and processes all of the text associated with a driver. A benefit of this being done within PostgreSQL is that relational driver data like their city, vehicles, and rides they've provided are all available. The search data can live right next to the relational data.

Imagine that this text has been processed and turned into tsvector objects that are now queryable using tsquery objects. As you begin querying this information, you'll want to make sure that searches run quickly, even when there are a

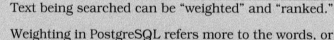

---

27. https://www.postgresql.org/docs/current/textsearch-controls.html#TEXTSEARCH-RANKING

lot of drivers on the platform. To achieve that, you'll need to index the processed text.

What does that look like? Do tsvector objects need to be stored in a column for indexing? No. Check out this discussion for a couple of options related to efficient retrieval of transformed text.[28]

> *Brian:* *tsvector text can be indexed without being stored in a new column.*
>
> *Andrew:* *Oh really?*
>
> *Brian:* *Using a PostgreSQL index on an expression (also called a "functional index"), the TO_TSVECTOR() function can be part of the index definition.*
>
> *Andrew:* *That makes sense. Is there a benefit to that approach?*
>
> *Brian:* *The benefit of the functional index over the new column is that it requires less space.*
>
> *Brian:* *Remember that the index definition does need to match the query exactly to be picked by the planner.*

Let's explore both approaches. First up is the approach that places the tsvector into a new column.

Prior to version 12 of PostgreSQL, developers created a new column to store processed tsvector objects. Since the source text could change, they might have kept the new column updated using a database trigger function. While that works, there's a newer option that's less work.

From PostgreSQL 12, a stored *generated column* (you saw those earlier in section Storing Transformations in Generated Columns, on page 85) can be used to store the processed text.

Let's create a generated column to store the persisted tsvector data. The benefit of the generated column over a regular column is that it's automatically updated, meaning the tsvector is recomputed whenever the source column changes. No separate trigger function is required.

Keep in mind that the persisted tsvector stored generated column uses more space. The space consumption and write latency trade-offs for the indexed tsvector are likely worthwhile for the benefits of improved query performance. Test on your system to verify.

How can these PostgreSQL capabilities be integrated into Ruby on Rails? To do that, you'll work with the pg_search[29] gem.

---

28. https://www.postgresql.org/docs/current/textsearch-tables.html
29. https://github.com/Casecommons/pg_search

Here's what you'll do as an exercise:

1. Add a new *stored generated column* called searchable_full_name to the users table.

2. Concatenate the first and last names together in this column, and transform the consolidated text into a tsvector.

3. Using the existing pg_search gem in Rideshare, configure the user model to use the searchable_full_name column.

4. Populate ten million users in the table.

5. After querying the column without an index, add a GIN to searchable_full_name and confirm the index is used and speeds up the query.

First up, you will need to cd into your Rideshare directory and run bin/rails g migration AddUsersSearchableFullName to generate a new migration.

Use the following .change() method implementation:

```ruby
# ruby/migration_add_searchable_tsvector_generated_column.rb
class AddSearchableFullNameToUsers < ActiveRecord::Migration[7.1]
  def change
    safety_assured do # executing in non-prod
      execute <<-SQL
        ALTER TABLE users
        ADD COLUMN searchable_full_name TSVECTOR GENERATED ALWAYS AS (
          SETWEIGHT(TO_TSVECTOR('english', COALESCE(first_name, '')), 'A') ||
          SETWEIGHT(TO_TSVECTOR('english', COALESCE(last_name,'')), 'B')
        ) STORED;
      SQL
    end
  end
end
```

After pasting that in (it's from an old migration) and running bin/rails db:migrate, you've now added the new stored generated column.

Let's review what it does:

- safety_assured {} from Strong Migrations (you saw this earlier on page 100) is used because Strong Migrations can't validate plain SQL migrations.

- Adds the searchable_full_name column to users using the options TSVECTOR GENERATED ALWAYS AS

TSVECTOR is the type for the column. The keywords GENERATED ALWAYS AS call back to the IDENTITY column options you saw earlier when using identity columns as primary keys.

Next up is the consolidation of first_name and last_name:

- First and last names are concatenated using the || operator.
- The COALESCE function reads their value, or returns an empty string.
- Both first_name and last_name are turned into tsvector objects.
- Each is given weights, where first_name gets an A, and last_name gets a B.

Finally, we see the STORED option, which means it's a stored generated column.

Open up the User model in your editor. Find the pg_search configuration.

Look for this block. This block sets individual weights for the first_name and last_name columns:

```
against: {
  first_name: 'A', # highest weight
  last_name: 'B'
}
```

Try it out:

```
User.search_by_full_name("Andrew").first
```

That's great, but it's not using the new column you've just added. Let's remove the current against configuration (comment it out or delete it). Change the value portion for against as follows, specifying the new column. Set the following configuration on your User model:

```
against: :searchable_full_name
using: {
  tsearch: {
    dictionary: 'english',
    tsvector_column: 'searchable_full_name'
  }
}
```

With the configuration in place, run the query again from bin/rails console and try dumping the SQL:

```
print User.search_by_full_name("Andrew").to_sql
```

This is the SQL, which has been reformatted to fit.

```
SELECT "users".*
FROM "users" INNER JOIN (
  SELECT "users"."id" AS pg_search_id,
  (ts_rank(("users"."searchable_full_name"),
  (to_tsquery('english', ''' ' || 'Andrew' || ' '''')), 0)) AS rank
  FROM "users"
  WHERE (("users"."searchable_full_name") @@ (
    to_tsquery('english', ''' ' || 'Andrew' || ' ''''))))
    AS pg_search_7dfb4cf67742cb0660305e
    ON "users"."id" = pg_search_7dfb4cf67742cb0660305e.pg_search_id
    ORDER BY pg_search_7dfb4cf67742cb0660305e.rank DESC, "users"."id" ASC
```

Running this query from psql for the 20K users included from the data generators, the query runs quickly (in under 30ms) using a sequential scan of users.

Let's increase the data and see how this performs. Create ten million users in Rideshare by running the sh scripts/bulk_load.sh script from the db directory. This script raises the statement timeout to two minutes and then bulk loads the rows.

Loading Ten Million Rows

 Remember that this requires gigabytes of space, so make sure you're OK with that before running this.

Let's see what performance looks like for the same query, with ten million users instead of 20K. Run the same query, prepending EXPLAIN (ANALYZE), and look at the time.

Locally, this ran much slower, in around two to five seconds, using a parallel sequential scan of users. Can we improve the performance using an index? Yes.

For the tsvector type, let's add a GIN index that covers the searchable_full_name column. After adding the index, run the query again. While you'd normally add the index using a migration, with ten million rows, the statement may exceed the timeout.

Here's the migration approach:

`ruby/migration_add_index_searchable_gin.rb`
```ruby
class AddIndexSearchableFullNameToUsers < ActiveRecord::Migration[7.1]
  disable_ddl_transaction!

  def change
    add_index :users, :searchable_full_name,
      using: :gin, # GIN index
      algorithm: :concurrently
  end
end
```

An alternative is to add the index using SQL inside psql and inside a transaction where the statement_timeout is raised to two minutes to allow for enough time to add the index. Open psql and run the following:

```
BEGIN;
SET LOCAL statement_timeout = '120s';
CREATE INDEX index_users_on_searchable_full_name
ON rideshare.users
USING GIN (searchable_full_name);
COMMIT;
```

Wow! With the index in place, the query is back to around 30–40ms, which is much faster. The query plan shows that a bitmap index scan on index_users_on_searchable_full_name is used.

You've now seen the basics of working with the tsvector type, and how to efficiently index columns with that type and query them. tsvector is one of the built-in types available without adding extensions.

If we add extensions into the mix, PostgreSQL has even more fuzzy search capabilities. Let's look at those in the next section.

Expanding FTS with Extensions

In this section, you'll expand your knowledge of full-text search capabilities in PostgreSQL from extensions. The extensions are widely supported by major hosting providers.

First, you will work with fuzzystrmatch,[30] which adds more types of text matching support. Next, you'll add soundex, which provides a SOUNDEX() function that is useful for finding homonyms.

You'll also use the Levenshtein Distance (LD) function to compare two words and find how similar they are based on their letters in common. Having more letters in common produces a shorter LD.

To enable these extensions, connect to Rideshare as owner. The search search_path should be set to rideshare. Verify that:

```
owner@localhost:5432 rideshare_development# SHOW search_path;
 search_path
-------------
 rideshare
```

---

30. https://www.postgresql.org/docs/current/fuzzystrmatch.html

From there, run the following CREATE EXTENSION statements:

```
sql/create_extension_fuzzystrmatch_pg_trgm_unaccent.sql
CREATE EXTENSION fuzzystrmatch;
CREATE EXTENSION pg_trgm;
CREATE EXTENSION unaccent;
```

After that, run the \dx meta-command to *describe extensions*, verifying each is listed.

Check Your PostgreSQL User

Although it's possible to create an extension using WITH SCHEMA, if you're being prompted to do that here, double-check that you're connected as the owner user. owner should have access to create extensions in the rideshare schema, without needing to specify the schema name.

With the extensions installed, you're ready to use them. In the following example, the soundex code is fetched for variations of the name "Sara" and "Sarah." These names sound identical when spoken but have different spellings. The "h" in the second variation is silent. Soundex codes are composed of four characters. Since these words sound identical, we'd expect them to have identical codes. Let's check:

```
sql/select_soundex.sql
SELECT SOUNDEX('Sarah'), SOUNDEX('Sara');
--  soundex | soundex
-- ---------+---------
--  S600    | S600

SELECT DIFFERENCE('Sarah', 'Sara');
```

They have the same code, which is S600 for both. How can you use this? The soundex codes can be calculated for words in a document that you want to search on. This is another way to find words that are similar. Once the codes are calculated, use the DIFFERENCE() function passing in both strings to identify words with a low distance value.

The Levenshtein Distance (LD) is another way to find similar strings. Identical strings have a distance of 0. The LD between "Sara" and "Sarah" is 1, which is considered to be a low value. The distance between "Sara and "Andrew" is 5, which is a greater distance and means these words aren't similar.

```
sql/select_levenshtein.sql
SELECT LEVENSHTEIN('Sarah', 'Sara');
--  levenshtein
-- -------------
--            1
```

PostgreSQL offers more functions in this area. Check out LEVENSHTEIN_LESS_ EQUAL() and others in the documentation.[31]

Once you start to use these comparison functions, and as your text sizes grow, you'll want your queries to be fast and reliable. How can you achieve that?

Optimizing FTS with Specialized Indexes

Let's continue to work with the soundex codes you learned about in the last section, but consider how queries could be made fast when accessing those values. As you've seen in early examples with *expression indexes* (see Transform Values with an Expression Index, on page 181), the index definition can transform input text as index entries. This means the soundex code can be calculated and stored in the index as an entry.

The following statement requires the fuzzystrmatch extension mentioned earlier to be enabled. Run the following statement from psql to create the index:

```
sql/create_index_first_name_soundex.sql
CREATE INDEX idx_users_first_name_soundex
ON users(SOUNDEX(first_name));
```

Run the following query with EXPLAIN to verify the index is used:

```
sql/select_first_name_by_soundex.sql
EXPLAIN (ANALYZE, BUFFERS)
SELECT * FROM users
WHERE SOUNDEX(first_name) = SOUNDEX('Sara');
```

You should see the index idx_users_first_name_soundex listed in the query plan. With this index in place, even for ten million users, finding users with a similar soundex code runs in less than 10ms. Very fast!

Let's explore more techniques for searching text in PostgreSQL.

In the next section, you'll learn about trigrams and how to use them.

Using Trigrams with FTS

In this section, you'll work with *trigrams*, which are another way to search text. To do that, you'll use the pg_trgm[32] extension mentioned (and enabled) earlier.

If you're not familiar with trigrams, let's cover what they are.

---

31. https://www.postgresql.org/docs/current/fuzzystrmatch.html#FUZZYSTRMATCH-LEVENSHTEIN
32. https://www.postgresql.org/docs/current/pgtrgm.html

Words are made up of sequences of letters. These sequences are called *n-grams*[33] in the field of Natural Language Processing (NLP). N-grams are sequences without a specified length. An n-gram with a length of one is a *unigram*, two is a *bigram*, and three is (drumroll, please) a *trigram*.

When two words have many overlapping trigrams, they tend to be very similar. Consider the example of misspellings. A misspelled word will usually be very similar to the target word, sometimes off by a single letter. If you split up the misspelled word and target word into letter sequences, grouped them, and compared them, they'd have similar groupings of n-grams.

In PostgreSQL, while we have functions to create trigrams from words, in order to access them quickly for comparison purposes, we'll want to index the trigram data.

Using the same technique as earlier with the tsvector type, create a GIN or GiST index type covering your trigram columns. You learned about the GiST index type to help support an EXCLUSION constraint way back in the data integrity chapter (see Preventing Overlaps with an Exclusion Constraint, on page 78).

You also learned about GIN indexes back in the indexes chapter (see Using GIN Indexes with JSON, on page 182). For more information, refer to the post, "Postgres GIN Index in Rails."[34]

The post, "Optimizing Postgres Text Search with Trigrams,"[35] shows how to use a GiST index for a fast trigram search.

Let's try it out! Try searching the Rideshare database for users named Andrew using the % operator. With Rideshare data generation, and at least 20K users, there's a good chance you've got users named Andrew. However, as you did before, consult the top values using the statistics PostgreSQL collects, and replace Andrew for another name that's common in your generated data.

Run the following query from psql:

```
sql/select_first_name_similarity_filter_and_sort.sql
EXPLAIN (ANALYZE, BUFFERS)
SELECT
  DISTINCT(first_name),
  SIMILARITY(first_name, 'Andrew') AS score
FROM users
WHERE first_name % 'Andrew'
ORDER BY score DESC;
```

---

33. https://en.wikipedia.org/wiki/N-gram
34. https://blog.kiprosh.com/postgres-gin-index-in-rails/
35. https://alexklibisz.com/2022/02/18/optimizing-postgres-trigram-search

Without an index, the query run time might be 5–10 seconds. This is slow! Either a Seq Scan or parallel sequential scan shows up in the query plan. We can do better. By now, hopefully you're thinking about the solution already: a well-placed index that supports the query.

Although both GIN and GiST index types work with trigrams, only the GiST type supports both filter and order operations. Let's use the GiST type.

Create a GiST index and specify the gist_trgm_ops operator class. Create one covering the first_name column. Set a siglen value, which is the "signature length" precision value. Higher values for signature length are more precise, but the index consumes more space.

Run this statement from psql:

```
sql/create_gist_index_gist_trgm_ops_siglen.sql
BEGIN;

SET LOCAL statement_timeout = '600s';

CREATE INDEX users_first_name_trgm_gist_idx ON users
USING GIST(first_name GIST_TRGM_OPS(SIGLEN=64));

COMMIT;
```

Add these ten million users to what you loaded before by running bin/rails data_generators:generate_all.

That way, there'll be realistic looking fake names compared with the bulk load script which generates less realistic names like "fname9544382". With more than ten million users, building the index will take several minutes or more.

As you have done before, you will need to raise the statement_timeout within the transaction to extend it beyond the short value set in config/database.yml. The transaction uses SET LOCAL to do that and raises the value to ten minutes. If the index isn't created within ten minutes on your system, raise the value further and try again.

Once the index is in place, run the query again. We're hoping to see a much-improved query performance time and no sequential scan.

What are the results? The query plan now shows a bitmap index scan was used with the users_first_name_trgm_gist_idx index, which is the one you've just created.

Instead of the 5–10-second runtime from before without an index, after re-running a few times and the query being warmed up, it runs in less than one millisecond. Wow! An enormous speedup. This example is a great demonstration of the importance of well-placed indexes.

For more on this topic, check out the post, "String Similarity Search and Fast LIKE Operator Using pg_trgm."[36] That post has example queries and performance benchmarks that are worth reading.

Since Rideshare has names of people, it's important to preserve accents in their names. Querying "Esme" should find a person named "Esmé", even though the e was provided as search input but didn't include the accent over the letter.

Can PostgreSQL handle accented characters?

Expanding FTS with Mixed Accents and Collations

PostgreSQL supports accented characters in document text and search queries using the unaccent extension. You enabled this extension earlier. Let's try out the TS_LEXIZE() function from the extension.

Run the following query from psql, passing in Esmé, which has an accent on the second "e":

```
sql/select_ts_lexize.sql
SELECT TS_LEXIZE('unaccent','Esmé');
-- ts_lexize
-- -----------
-- {Esme}
```

This function removes the accent. Results from this function can be turned into a tsvector. This example creates a tsvector after removing accents, and then the tsvector is searched with input text. The @@ operator is used, which returns a Boolean value when text matches.

```
sql/select_to_tsvector_unaccent_to_tsquery.sql
SELECT TO_TSVECTOR('english', UNACCENT('Esmé')) @@ TO_TSQUERY('english','Esme');
-- ?column?
-- ----------
-- t
```

Without the UNACCENT() function, passing in the name with accents like Esmé would not have matched Esme. Consider building support for mixed use of accents into your system for document text and search text.

The last topic on text searching covered here is *collations*.[37] What are they? *International Components for Unicode* (ICU) collations were added to PostgreSQL 10 and have received improvements in newer versions. A COLLATION is a database object that's useful for text searching.

---

36. https://mazeez.dev/posts/pg-trgm-similarity-search-and-fast-like
37. https://www.postgresql.org/docs/current/collation.html

How's it used? Collations can be used for case-insensitive searches. Let's compare an approach using collations to the example you worked with earlier using the citext extension (see citext on page 83).

In that example, citext was used as the column type to store the original casing if the text that was passed in. However, the passed-in text was treated as case insensitive for matching purposes.

ICU collations can achieve similar results to citext without requiring the extension. Let's try that out.

Run the following statement in psql to create the COLLATION object named english_ci.

```
sql/create_collation_english_ci.sql
CREATE COLLATION english_ci (
  PROVIDER = icu,
  LOCALE = 'en-US-u-ks-level2',
  DETERMINISTIC = FALSE
);
```

With the collation created, as you did with citext, use the collation as the column type. Run the following statements individually from psql.

```
sql/alter_table_add_column_collate.sql
ALTER TABLE users ADD COLUMN first_name_ci TEXT COLLATE english_ci;

\d users; -- confirm first_name_ci exists, text type, uses english_ci COLLATION

-- Set first_name to Audrey for MIN(id)
-- Backfill first_name_ci to the same value (capitalized)
UPDATE users
SET
  first_name = 'Audrey',
  first_name_ci = 'Audrey'
WHERE id = (SELECT MIN(id) FROM users);

-- Users contains two rows with "Audrey" first name,
-- but case doesn't match `first_name`
SELECT id, first_name
FROM users
WHERE first_name = 'audrey';

-- Searching on `first_name_ci` is case insensitive,
-- two matches returned
SELECT id, first_name
FROM users
WHERE first_name_ci = 'audrey';
```

Let's review what's happening here. After you added the column, you set a capitalized value for first_name and first_name_ci of "Audrey".

Searching the first_name column for "audrey" in lowercase doesn't find any matches. Searching the first_name_ci column in lowercase does find "Audrey"!

No separate extension was needed for case-insensitive search.

This wraps up searching in text using keywords, fuzzy inputs, and trigrams. Is that the whole story for text search in PostgreSQL?

Nope. Recently, *vector similarity searching* burst onto the scene, leveraging Large Language Models available from popular AI API services. This kind of searching offers very fast and robust matching of "meaning" within large amounts of text.

How do we use that in PostgreSQL?

Storing and Searching Vector Embeddings

Large Language Models (LLM) developed by companies like OpenAI have grown tremendously in 2023.

API services accept text input and produce "embeddings" from the text. Embeddings are "numerical representations of text." These numerical representations are then stored in PostgreSQL and can be indexed for high-performance search queries. The advantage of this approach, just like with tsvector objects, is that the processed search objects are stored right alongside your relational data.

What's the flow like for this integration? The API service is said to embed the text, and then returns a vector (or list) data structure. Vectors are lists like the Array type in Ruby. The vector has one or more floating point numbers. The quantity of floating point numbers is described as the "dimensionality" for the embedding. Greater numbers of dimensions are called "higher dimensionality." Dimensions from the popular OpenAI API at publication time might be between 1000 and 2000 values.

To benefit from this semantic search, organizations pre-compute vector embeddings for the text they want to make available for searching. Then, when the user is searching, their search inputs are embedded for comparison to pre-computed embeddings. When matches are found, associated relational data can be fetched.

A popular choice for storing embeddings in PostgreSQL is the extension pgvector.[38] This extension offers a vector data type for columns, various similarity search functions, and various types of indexes that are used for fast

---

38. https://github.com/pgvector/pgvector

retrieval. With the combination of the types, functions, and indexes, PostgreSQL is competitive with specialized vector search databases.

The pgvector extension provides nearest neighbor search functionality using a variety of algorithms.

The algorithms are L2 (also called Euclidian Distance), inner product, and cosine distance. Each of the distance functions compares vectors using special operators. You'll use operators like <-> (Euclidian Distance) in SQL, <#> (negative inner product), or <=> (cosine distance).

The original index type for pgvector was *IVFFlat*. In version 0.5.0, HNSW[39] was added as a new index type. The HNSW index type offers improved search performance with the trade-off of being slower to create.

Whether searching for similar keywords or when using vector similarity search, PostgreSQL is a great place to store both your original text and processed and indexed text for fast searching.

That concludes the coverage of using PostgreSQL for keyword and semantic searching.

What other types of work can PostgreSQL take on?

Session Persistence and Rails Cache Without Redis

For storing small bits of text, Redis has been a popular key value (KV) store for more than a decade, often deployed alongside PostgreSQL in order to leverage the high performance for read and write operations.

Redis is often deployed to store cache data, session identifiers, or background job data. Sidekiq[40] is the most popular background processing framework for Ruby on Rails and uses Redis exclusively for persistence.

Redis is not a SQL database, which means it loses many of the benefits of SQL databases like types, referential integrity, transactions, and more. Redis has different commands like SADD[41] and LPUSH[42] that are straightforward to learn, but are unique to Redis.

As fast SSD storage devices have offered greater capacity at lower price points, PostgreSQL has benefitted by being capable of faster storage access. With

---

39. https://github.com/pgvector/pgvector#hnsw
40. https://github.com/mperham/sidekiq
41. https://redis.io/commands/sadd/
42. https://redis.io/commands/lpush/

greater amounts of memory for servers and faster SSD storage, are the performance benefits of Redis necessary? If PostgreSQL offers comparable performance, it could be one less database system to run in your stack.

As you saw in "Just Use Postgres for Everything,"[43] the author suggests PostgreSQL can take over the work that's performed by Redis. Let's take a look at how we might do that for some use cases in a Rails application.

In PostgreSQL, to get the maximum possible write rate for table access, you saw earlier on page 112 that tables can be UNLOGGED and Autovacuum can be disabled. Losing the protection of the WAL is a significant loss. What type of data might support losing that protection?

For cache data, which is secondary data created from primary data, crash protection benefits may be worth losing in exchange for faster write performance. If secondary cache data was lost, performance would be poor until the cache store was restored, but then it would be automatically restored as caches were repopulated.

Inserts in UNLOGGED tables can be 90 percent faster compared to traditional LOGGED tables. Since unlogged tables don't have crash protection from the Write-Ahead Log (WAL), an unplanned restart runs a TRUNCATE when the recovery process starts.[44] Without the WAL, there's no replication either.

Where does cache data come from in Rails?

The Rails.cache[45] entries that normally go into Redis or another cache store could go into a PostgreSQL unlogged table. Consider running a separate PostgreSQL instance used as a cache store. You'll need only a single primary instance since replication isn't possible. You're equipped to set up a new instance and connect the Rails app to it using Active Record multiple databases.

At publication time, a newly announced project called rails/solid_cache[46] was announced that offers support for relational databases as the cache store.

To replace Redis, we need to consider more use cases. Redis has a feature that allows keys to automatically expire. To use this feature in Redis, you set an expiration time as the Time-To-Live (TTL) value, creating keys, for example, by using the SETNX Redis command with a TTL value. Redis handles automatically removing expired keys.

---

43. https://www.amazingcto.com/postgres-for-everything/
44. https://pganalyze.com/blog/5mins-postgres-unlogged-tables
45. https://guides.rubyonrails.org/caching_with_rails.html
46. https://github.com/rails/solid_cache

Unfortunately, PostgreSQL doesn't offer something like this. Do we have options? While there's no official type or support, we can roll our own approximation of expiring keys in PostgreSQL using a couple of different tactics.

Imagine a table called cache_entries that stores items for a period of time and then removes expired items automatically. cache_entries might have a created_at timestamp showing when a row was added. An expires_at timestamp column might be set by the client. A cron job could run periodically, look for expired rows, and then remove them.

An alternative to a cron job polling the table takes inspiration from this Stack Overflow post.[47] In this case, a PL/pgSQL function and a trigger function are used.

Let's try that out. Create a cache_entries table as shown from psql. Copy and paste the function and trigger function into psql.

Try creating rows with a created_at value for the current time and a second row for one created four minutes ago. After waiting one minute, try inserting another row. You should now see only two rows because the middle row, some:cache:value:456, was removed for being older than five minutes.

sql/cache_entries_removal_function_and_trigger.sql
```
-- Table features:
-- Unlogged, identity primary key, Autovacuum disabled
CREATE UNLOGGED TABLE cache_entries (
  id BIGINT GENERATED ALWAYS AS IDENTITY PRIMARY KEY,
  content TEXT,
  created_at TIMESTAMPTZ
) WITH (autovacuum_enabled = FALSE);

-- Function returns trigger, using PLPGSQL, TX control
CREATE FUNCTION cache_entries_delete_old()
RETURNS TRIGGER LANGUAGE PLPGSQL AS $$
BEGIN
  DELETE FROM cache_entries
  WHERE created_at < NOW() - INTERVAL '5 minutes';
  RETURN NEW;
END;
$$;

-- Trigger
CREATE TRIGGER cache_entries_delete_old_trigger
AFTER INSERT ON cache_entries
EXECUTE PROCEDURE cache_entries_delete_old();
```

---

47. https://stackoverflow.com/a/26063344

```
-- Current time, should not be deleted
INSERT INTO cache_entries (content, created_at)
VALUES ('some:cache:value:123', NOW());

-- Insert a value from 4 minutes ago, run `SELECT COUNT(*)` on cache_entries
-- confirm it's 2
INSERT INTO cache_entries (content, created_at)
VALUES ('some:cache:value:456', NOW() - INTERVAL '4  minutes');

SELECT * FROM cache_entries;

-- Wait 1 minute, try inserting a new row:
-- Confirm the count is 2, and "some:cache:value:456" was removed
INSERT INTO cache_entries (content, created_at)
VALUES ('some:cache:value:789', NOW());
```

Cache Entries Duration

 This trigger-based design has an assumption built-in. The assumption is that there are a steady amount of DML operations happening for the table, so entries older than five minutes will be promptly found and removed. Without steady activity, entries would live longer.

Let's consider one more design for a cache_entries table. In this design, you'll use RANGE partitioning, which you worked with earlier on page 341. Partition ranges could reflect the time range you wish to have entries available. When a range has aged out, the partition for that old time period can be detached concurrently and then dropped, creating a very minimal operational impact.

Imagine that partitions have a time range of 24 hours. In that design, the partition for the previous day would be detached and dropped. Detaching is a faster, nonblocking alternative to deleting rows, which doesn't cause bloat.

Throttling Without Redis

 Redis has been used for persistence related to rate-limiting requests. At publication time, a new project, Pecorino (https://github.com/cheddar-me/pecorino), was available and provides throttling but is designed for PostgreSQL.

Another reason that Redis is commonly deployed with Rails applications is the use of Sidekiq.

To replace Redis from a Rails app, we'd need an alternative background processing framework that works with PostgreSQL. Are there options?

Background Jobs Without Sidekiq

Background jobs are an important part of Ruby on Rails applications for actions like sending emails or SMS messages, updating caches, or creating reports. Actions should always be pushed to the background when possible, outside of the web request, to be processed as background jobs.

To reflect that importance to Ruby on Rails, the Active Job[48] framework was added in version 4.2. With native background jobs support, part of the goal was to consolidate different libraries into a unified API.

Sidekiq grew to become the most popular background job framework for Ruby on Rails,[49] and has been used to great success for more than a decade. However, these days we may wish to bring that workload into PostgreSQL to gain some advantages like working with transactions in the same instance.

What alternatives to Sidekiq exist for background job processing that use PostgreSQL for persistence?

The GoodJob framework is one such alternative that's distributed as a Ruby gem and works exclusively with PostgreSQL. GoodJob is a "Multithreaded, Postgres-based, Active Job Backend for Ruby on Rails."[50] GoodJob requires Rails Version 6+ and PostgreSQL 10+ because it uses some newer PostgreSQL features like advisory locks and the LISTEN and NOTIFY[51] commands. You worked with advisory locks earlier (see Using Advisory Locks, on page 242). GoodJob uses advisory locks to lock jobs while they are performed.

You haven't yet seen LISTEN and NOTIFY. What are those?

LISTEN and NOTIFY are generic mechanisms to send notifications to channels with an optional payload. Clients may LISTEN to channels by name, then when a NOTIFY happens for that channel name, listening clients are notified. How are these used in GoodJob?

PostgreSQL LISTEN and NOTIFY are used as interprocess communication to signal when new background jobs are enqueued and as part of polling a table for new records. Message payloads are sent as JSON-formatted text.

Let's configure the basics of GoodJob for Rideshare to get an idea of how it uses PostgreSQL.

---

48. https://guides.rubyonrails.org/active_job_basics.html
49. https://rails-hosting.com/2022/#configuration
50. https://github.com/bensheldon/good_job
51. https://www.postgresql.org/docs/current/sql-notify.html

Follow the instructions at https://github.com/bensheldon/good_job to add the good_job gem to your Rideshare Gemfile. Run the good_job:install generator, which adds a migration that adds the GoodJob tables. The tables are:

- good_jobs
- good_job_processes
- good_job_settings

Configure GoodJob to be the Active Job queue adapter by changing config/application.rb to be:

```
config.active_job.queue_adapter = :good_job
```

Let's look at the database objects that were created. GoodJob uses a jsonb column for settings and serialized values. Eight indexes are added, including single column, multicolumn, and partial indexes (you saw those earlier on page 177).

With installation complete, let's try out a test job. Generate a job by running bin/rails g job hello_world in your terminal. This creates a HelloWorldJob Ruby class in app/jobs.

Launch bin/rails console. Enable SQL logging by running ActiveRecord::Base.logger = Logger.new(STDOUT).

Manually enqueue the job by running HelloWorldJob.perform_later(). Let's look at the generated SQL. The SQL query text is shown here, and it's been formatted to focus on the PostgreSQL statements:

```ruby/background_job_perform_later_good_job.rb
irb(main):008:0> HelloWorldJob.perform_later
TRANSACTION (0.1ms)  BEGIN
GoodJob::Execution Create (4.9ms)  INSERT INTO "good_jobs" ...
  TRANSACTION (1.1ms)  COMMIT

NOTIFY good_job, '{"queue_name":"default"}'
```

The log shows that the job was inserted into the good_jobs table, and then NOTIFY was called about the job added to the default queue. Nice!

To process the job, GoodJob uses the LISTEN command. Let's try that out.

Start up the job processor from your terminal by running this:

```sh/good_job_start.sh
bundle exec good_job start
```

Example output looks like this:

```
sh/good_job_logs.sh
[GoodJob] [86964] [GoodJob::Scheduler(queues=* max_threads=5)-thread-2] \
    Executed GoodJob 5c44e910-576b-47bc-b1eb-ccf2ef10b471
```

Are there more concepts in GoodJob that you've seen in earlier chapters?

GoodJob uses keyset pagination (you saw this earlier in Improved Performance with Keyset Pagination, on page 254) to efficiently select jobs to be processed.

That concludes the basics of GoodJob. You've now explored an alternative to Sidekiq that would allow you to replace that usage of Redis by switching to a background jobs tool that uses PostgreSQL. At publication time, Solid Queue was announced, which offers a "DB-based Queuing Back-end for Active Job."[52]

Next, you'll look at another use case that's commonly handled outside of PostgreSQL but could be handled within it.

Different analytical data stores are often deployed alongside PostgreSQL where important analytics queries run. The historical way to keep the two databases in sync was to use batch processing. Batch processing involved copying very large quantities of rows at once from PostgreSQL, perhaps using a pipeline approach or an intermediate CSV file and then doing a very large insert into a separate analytical database.

Batch processing starts out with straightforward requirements and runs reliably. Over time, as data volume increases and queries and requirements shift, it can become complex and unpredictable. Queries for reading and writing slow down, conflicts can occur with live and dead tuples, there needs to be a way to handle updates and deletes, and keeping a schema in sync across heterogeneous databases is challenging.

A more modern alternative is to stream changes as events from PostgreSQL as a data source. You saw the foundations of this earlier when you set up logical replication (see Creating a Replica Using Logical Replication, on page 319). For database engines that don't natively work with PostgreSQL, though, how might they receive changes in a textual format that's not tied to PostgreSQL?

Using Change Data Capture (CDC) and wal2json

In this section, you'll expand on the logical replication configuration you set up earlier into a specific use case for sending data to disparate database engines.

---

52. https://dev.37signals.com/introducing-solid-queue/

As you learned earlier, logical replication can be used to replicate row changes (insert, update, and delete) for specific databases and tables.

By default, changes are sent using an encoded format. You created a PUBLICATION on the publisher side, which created a replication slot object that described the replication details. On the subscriber side, you created a SUBSCRIPTION object that linked to the PUBLICATION. A replication slot is created for each database.

> Each slot streams a sequence of changes from a single database.[53]

Logical replication relies on the Write Ahead Log (WAL) as the data source, which has an internal, nonreadable representation of the changes.

While the log is machine-readable, the encoded format can be decoded using different human-readable formats. How does that work?

To accomplish that, PostgreSQL allows users to select an *output plugin*. An output plugin can be used to turn the WAL stream into JSON-formatted text changes. With that JSON representation of events, the text is readable by humans and by heterogenous database systems that want to ingest it.

Let's look at an example. JSON is a popular format for data interchange that Ruby on Rails developers are used to working with. Let's transform the WAL changes into JSON. How do we do that? Let's use the wal2json[54] extension.

A use case for this would be to build a *Change Data Capture* (CDC) system. CDC is a software design pattern[55] for data interchange that can be implemented using wal2json. PostgreSQL acts as the data source.

The post, "Change Data Capture in Postgres: How to Use Logical Decoding and wal2json,"[56] shows how to build a CDC system using PostgreSQL. The post shows examples of DML changes from PostgreSQL that are turned into JSON-formatted text events under a change key. Clients parse those events using any compatible client JSON parser. At that point, clients are aware of all insert, update, and delete changes happening in PostgreSQL, even if the client is a completely different database.

When working with logical replication and replication slots, there are pitfalls to be aware of. Review the "Caution" section[57] from "Logical Decoding Concepts."

---

53. https://www.postgresql.org/docs/current/logicaldecoding-explanation.html
54. https://github.com/eulerto/wal2json
55. https://en.wikipedia.org/wiki/Change_data_capture
56. https://techcommunity.microsoft.com/t5/azure-database-for-postgresql/change-data-capture-in-postgres-how-to-use-logical-decoding-and/ba-p/1396421
57. https://www.postgresql.org/docs/current/logicaldecoding-explanation.html

Beware of Unused Replication Slots

- Make sure all replication slots are consumed
- If PostgreSQL restarts, changes may appear in the stream again. Consumers should handle duplicates.

As you put logical replication into production, monitor replication slots to make sure they're active. Check their idle state. Query the pg_replication_slots table. Make sure the stream of changes has a consumer defined. A slot may have only one output plugin. pg_recvlogical is used to create the slot and then perform the logical decoding process.

In this section, you learned how logical replication can be used to build a CDC system. This system transforms WAL stream changes from PostgreSQL into JSON-formatted text events.

Before wrapping up, since logical replication is so flexible and powerful, let's look at one more use case for it.

Zero Downtime Cutovers and Upgrades

In this last section, let's briefly cover one more use case for logical replication.

Most organizations that run PostgreSQL for an extended period of time will upgrade to the major version. Changing PostgreSQL instances without minimal downtime is tricky. Logical replication can help. How does that work?

Imagine that you wanted to perform an upgrade to a new major version of PostgreSQL without taking your current database offline.

Unfortunately, there's not a native mechanism to do that. However, using Logical replication can be part of a solution to achieve a zero downtime upgrade.

First, set up a new PostgreSQL instance with the target major version that you wish to upgrade to. You won't be upgrading the original instance, but you'll *cut over* to a new one. To do that, you'll need to load all of the cluster information on the new instance, including the schema, roles, tables, and other database objects. Since logical replication doesn't replicate DDL, you'll be responsible for creating tables, indexes, and other DDL manually or using another mechanism.

Once the schema is fully in sync on the new instance, logical replication can be configured to replicate DML changes to the new server instance, even when it's running a different major version.

Besides minimizing the cutover window, this approach unlocks the ability to test a live replica instance on the new target version with the same data. That sort of live testing can greatly raise confidence that the "upgrade" will be successful.

Various resources help describe this process and provide additional tools for it. The Instacart post, "Zero-Downtime PostgreSQL Cutovers,"[58] describes their cutover process. The tool pg_easy_replicate[59] is a CLI orchestrator written in Ruby that helps you achieve zero downtime cutovers by following a series of steps.

Closing Remarks

You've arrived at the closing remarks for the book. We've covered a *lot* of ground with PostgreSQL and Ruby on Rails.

Writing this book has truly been an honor and a privilege. Many people have provided encouragement over the months of writing with technical reviews and suggestions that helped improve the quality. I'm deeply grateful for their help. I hope this team effort has provided you with a lot of new knowledge, skills, and enthusiasm for how to leverage these technologies to their fullest potential. I'd love to hear about what you're building.

Where do things stand now with PostgreSQL and Ruby on Rails?

There may be no better time in history than now, to develop PostgreSQL-powered Rails applications. These are mature technologies, refined over decades. They are reliable, predictable, and both have enormous, vibrant, international open source communities.

PostgreSQL and Ruby on Rails help you move quickly. These technologies can scale with the size of your team, from being a small operation to becoming a huge corporation. Your team will do that using a beloved open source programming language and database technology.

Thank you so much for reading this book.

Please reach out by email, on social media, or find me at conferences and say hello.

I hope this book has helped you build high-performance PostgreSQL web applications with Ruby on Rails!

---

58. https://www.instacart.com/company/how-its-made/zero-downtime-postgresql-cutovers/
59. https://github.com/shayonj/pg_easy_replicate

The Administrator's Field Guide

Problem: Slow queries reducing performance

- Learn how to read query execution plans. Reading Query Execution Plans, on page 152

- Identify costly queries using pg_stat_statements. Capture Query Statistics in Your Database, on page 146

- Add missing indexes. Finding Missing Indexes, on page 153

- Optimize indexes. Chapter 8, Optimized Indexes for Fast Retrieval, on page 167

- Match query filters to index definitions. Understanding Index Column Ordering, on page 175

- Get IO insights from the pg_stat_io[1] view.

Problem: Queries getting blocked

- Enable log_lock_waits[2] to log waiting queries

- Learn which lock types are acquired by statements. https://pglocks.org

- Vacuum heavily updated[3] tables more. Chapter 9, High-Impact Database Maintenance, on page 201

- Limit the use of explicit locks. More Lock Monitoring with pg_locks, on page 237

---

1. https://www.postgresql.org/docs/current/monitoring-stats.html#MONITORING-PG-STAT-IO-VIEW
2. https://www.postgresql.org/docs/current/runtime-config-logging.html
3. https://github.com/andyatkinson/pg_scripts/blob/main/top_updated_tables.sql

Problem: High latency for writes

- Reduce index entries with partial indexes. Filtering Rows with Partial Indexes, on page 177

- Prune unused indexes and perform index maintenance. Chapter 9, High-Impact Database Maintenance, on page 201

- Increase HOT updates. Removing Unused Indexes, on page 211

Problem: Application bugs from invalid data

- Prevent invalid data by adding constraints like FOREIGN KEY and NOT NULL. Chapter 4, Data Correctness and Consistency, on page 67

- Consider migrating unstructured, schemaless data into columns with data types.[4]

- Add validation checks for JSON data with a schema definition and check constraint. Maintaining Unstructured JSON Data, on page 188

- Add EXCLUSION constraints to prevent overlapping data. Preventing Overlaps with an Exclusion Constraint, on page 78

Problem: Excessively high connections

- Reduce allowed time and quantity of idle connections. Monitoring Database Connections, on page 222

- Increase resiliency by setting timeouts like idle_timeout, statement_timeout, and lock_timeout. Identifying Connection Errors and Problems, on page 236

- Read "Deep Dive into Database Timeouts in Rails."[5]

- Use connection pooling. Working with PgBouncer, on page 231

Problem: Schema design choices added latency

- Use partitioned tables for large tables where only recent data is accessed. Chapter 14, Boosting Performance with Partitioning, on page 327

---

4. https://www.postgresql.org/docs/current/datatype.html
5. https://engineering.grab.com/deep-dive-into-database-timeouts-in-rails

- Automate the detachment and archival of unneeded data to save space, storage costs, and to improve performance. Use Partitioning to Help with Archiving, on page 337

- Prefer sortable, space-minimizing integer types for primary keys and foreign keys over UUID.

- When UUID is required, use version 7 or greater with a time segment.

Problem: Missing out on good practices

- Read "Don't Do This"[6] on the wiki.

- Adopt SQL MERGE for upserts. Significant Casing and Unique Constraints, on page 83

- Prefer IDENTITY and GENERATED ALWAYS over SERIAL or BIGSERIAL for Sequences.

- Follow a *secure schema usage pattern*.[7]

- Revoke access to the public schema when it's not needed.

- Create a scrubbed performance database as a playground test environment. Chapter 3, Building a Performance-Testing Database, on page 39

Problem: Scaling beyond a single instance

Increased Operational Complexity

 These strategies increase operational complexity.

Make sure your system will receive benefits before proceeding.

- Separate a cohesive set of high-write tables to their own database and instance (Application-level sharding). Chapter 13, Scaling with Replication and Sharding, on page 281

- Run same-schema copies of your database on separate instances using horizontal sharding.[8] Using Horizontal Sharding for Multitenancy, on page 313

---

6.   https://wiki.postgresql.org/wiki/Don%27t_Do_This

7.   https://www.postgresql.org/docs/current/ddl-schemas.html#DDL-SCHEMAS-PATTERNS

8.   https://guides.rubyonrails.org/active_record_multiple_databases.html#horizontal-sharding

Problem: Limiting your use of PostgreSQL to OLTP

- Perform Full Text Search. Implementing Full-Text Search (FTS), on page 367 and Vector Similarity Search. Storing and Searching Vector Embeddings, on page 384

- Create a cache store. Session Persistence and Rails Cache Without Redis, on page 385

- Create a message queue and run background jobs. Background Jobs Without Sidekiq, on page 389

- Perform basic analytics. Basic Analytics with PostgreSQL, on page 365

Problem: Old versions and old practices

- Upgrade patch versions and minor versions.

- Perform zero downtime major version cutovers using Logical Replication. Zero Downtime Cutovers and Upgrades, on page 393

- Read Release Notes, News, and explore Community Events on PostgreSQL.org.[9]

---

9.   https://www.postgresql.org

Why psql?

Although there are many great Graphical User Interface (GUI) clients for PostgreSQL, readers exclusively use psql here. Why is that?

psql is the official open source client maintained by PostgreSQL without any licensing limitations. You can run the client connected to your local database or to a remote database with low latency. Skills you develop with it will be valuable for years since the program has longevity.

By using psql, you'll join a community of administrators, operators, and power users that use it every day and customize it. The more you use it, the better you'll commit meta-commands to memory, learn to use variables, and find other useful tricks.

There's a wealth of self-help and documentation for psql. Where can we find it?

Run man psql to explore the manual page for psql. For example, after running man psql, type /--dbname to jump to the dbname section and read the description.

There's also a built-in help system. Run the \? meta-command to explore it.

Type \help to view built-in documentation, then add specific statements or commands.

For example, type \help ALTER TABLE. psql supports tab completion, so typing "ALT" will fill out "ALTER". From there, you can hit tab again and see lots of options for altering different types of things. Start to practice using the built-in help as a reference for statements and commands.

On a remote host, a tmux[1] (or screen[2]) session can contain a psql session that you can detach from. When is that useful? With this approach, you can start a long-running statement from psql within tmux or screen, detach, then do something else while the statement keeps running. You can even disconnect from the host entirely and come back later. When you reconnect, you'll reattach to the existing session and check out the status of the long-running task. To learn more about that workflow and tmux, check out "tmux 2 Productive Mouse-Free Development."[3]

Meta-Commands

A reference for relevant psql meta-commands:

Meta-Command	Description
\l	List databases. This is the letter "l" and not the number 1.
\d	Describe table
\dn+	Describe schemas (namespaces)
\dt	Describe all tables
\dv	Describe views
\d+	Describe definition when used with a view
\x	Toggle expanded display
\! clear	Clear the screen
\set	Set a psql variable (see following section)
\e	Edit queries in EDITOR
\df	Describe functions
\dx	Describe extensions
\di *	Describe indexes that match pattern, e.g. \di index_users*
\dRs+	Describe subscriptions

Setting psql variables

Setting a psql variable, for example: \set foo 1, sets foo. foo can then be included in statements. For example, in SELECT :foo; there's a colon before the variable. Note that \set in psql is different from the SQL SET[4] command. Try creating some variables in psql to get the hang of that.

---

1. https://github.com/tmux/tmux
2. https://linuxize.com/post/how-to-use-linux-screen/
3. https://pragprog.com/titles/bhtmux2/tmux-2/
4. https://www.postgresql.org/docs/current/sql-set.html

The meta-commands you run in psql perform SQL queries[5] behind the scenes. You can see them by setting this variable:

```
\set ECHO_HIDDEN on
```

Once set, run any meta-command to see the SQL query printed out.

---

5.   https://twitter.com/PostgresqlStan/status/1652003347338067968

Getting Help

Online Resources

- High Performance PostgreSQL for Rails forum: https://devtalk.com/books/high-performance-postgresql-for-rails

- Rideshare repository: https://github.com/andyatkinson/rideshare

- Development Guides repository: https://github.com/andyatkinson/development_guides

Documentation and Guides

- Active Record and PostgreSQL: https://guides.rubyonrails.org/active_record_postgresql.html
- Rails API Documentation: https://api.rubyonrails.org/
- Rails Guides: https://guides.rubyonrails.org/
- PostgreSQL Glossary: https://www.postgresql.org/docs/current/glossary.html
- PostgreSQL Documentation: https://www.postgresql.org/docs/
- PostgreSQL Modules and Extensions: https://www.postgresql.org/docs/current/contrib.html

High-quality third-party documentation:

- pgMustard EXPLAIN Glossary: https://www.pgmustard.com/docs/explain

Communities of Practice

These are communities where you can receive and provide help for PostgreSQL and Ruby on Rails.

- Postgres Slack: https://postgresteam.slack.com
- PostgreSQL User Groups: https://www.postgresql.org/community/user-groups/
- Ruby on Rails forum: https://discuss.rubyonrails.org/

News

- Planet PostgreSQL: https://planet.postgresql.org

Jobs

- Ruby on Rails: https://jobs.rubyonrails.org/
- pgsql-jobs: https://www.postgresql.org/list/pgsql-jobs/

Source Code

- Ruby on Rails: https://github.com/rails/rails
- PostgreSQL: https://git.postgresql.org/gitweb/?p=postgresql.git

PostgreSQL source code is mirrored to GitHub.

DBA Tools

- postgres_dba:[1] "The missing set of useful tools for Postgres DBAs and all engineers"

- lol_dba:[2] Helpful tools like identifying missing indexes

- pg_scripts:[3] A personal collection of PostgreSQL queries and scripts from around the Internet

Managing .pgpass files

.pgpass files need correct permissions and ownership.

For the OS user andy in the staff group, with a file in the home directory /Users/andy/.pgpass, run the following commands:

```
chmod 0600 ~/.pgpass
chown andy:staff ~/.pgpass
```

PostgreSQL Installation Methods

For Rideshare on macOS, the recommended PostgreSQL installation method is Postgres.app.[4]

Homebrew is a popular alternative. For Homebrew, you'll need to configure more things to match the configuration of Postgres.app.

---

1. https://github.com/NikolayS/postgres_dba
2. https://github.com/plentz/lol_dba
3. https://github.com/andyatkinson/pg_scripts
4. https://github.com/PostgresApp/PostgresApp

Add a postgres/postgres superuser by running createuser -s postgres --pwprompt with postgres as the password.

For Postgres.app, the default database is named after the OS user.

For Homebrew, create that database if it doesn't exist by running createdb -O andy andy, replacing andy with your OS username.

Finding PostgreSQL Installation Paths

If you've installed PostgreSQL using Postgres.app, verify which pg_config shows:

/Applications/Postgres.app/Contents/Versions/latest/bin/pg_config

pg_config --includedir shows:

/Applications/Postgres.app/Contents/Versions/16/include

These paths can be helpful if you're compiling extensions.

pg_cron Installation

The pg_cron[5] extension is used with PgHero to show Scheduled Jobs. While there was a pg_cron Homebrew package available at publication time, it was connected to the older PostgreSQL 14 version.

For an updated version, compile pg_cron on macOS. Follow the instructions on the README. Compiling from source involves running make and make install. If you encounter problems during compilation, refer to the "Issues"[6] page.

When pg_cron is compiled and configured in PostgreSQL, the PostgreSQL log shows the pg_cron scheduler has started:

2022-12-28 13:31:45.361 CST [84234] LOG: pg_cron scheduler started

In exercises, you'll configure pg_cron to use the rideshare_development database. See section Scheduling Jobs Using pg_cron, on page 215 for more.

pg_hint_plan Installation

```
git clone git@github.com:ossc-db/pg_hint_plan.git
cd pg_hint_plan
make && make install
```

Refer to the pg_hint_plan section of the Development Guides repo https://github.com/andyatkinson/development_guides for more information.

---

5. https://github.com/citusdata/pg_cron
6. https://github.com/citusdata/pg_cron/issues

postgres-json-schema

```
git clone git@github.com:gavinwahl/postgres-json-schema.git
cd postgres-json-schema
make install
```

From psql connected to Rideshare, run:

```
psql -U postgres -d rideshare_development
CREATE EXTENSION "postgres-json-schema" WITH SCHEMA rideshare;
```

Set PGDATA for pg_ctl

```
export PGDATA="$(psql -U postgres \
  -c 'SHOW data_directory' \
  --tuples-only | sed 's/^[ \t]*//')"
echo "Set PGDATA: $PGDATA"
```

With PGDATA set properly, running commands like pg_ctl reload no longer requires passing the path as an argument.

Index

Thank you!

We hope you enjoyed this book and that you're already thinking about what you want to learn next. To help make that decision easier, we're offering you this gift.

Head on over to https://pragprog.com right now, and use the coupon code BUYANOTHER2024 to save 30% on your next ebook. Offer is void where prohibited or restricted. This offer does not apply to any edition of *The Pragmatic Programmer* ebook.

And if you'd like to share your own expertise with the world, why not propose a writing idea to us? After all, many of our best authors started off as our readers, just like you. With up to a 50% royalty, world-class editorial services, and a name you trust, there's nothing to lose. Visit https://pragprog.com/become-an-author/ today to learn more and to get started.

Thank you for your continued support. We hope to hear from you again soon!

The Pragmatic Bookshelf

Text Processing with JavaScript

You might think of regular expressions as the holy grail of text processing, but are you sure you aren't just shoehorning them in where standard built-in solutions already exist and would work better? JavaScript itself provides programmers with excellent methods for text manipulation, and knowing how and when to use them will help you write more efficient and performant code. From extracting data from APIs to calculating word counts and everything in between, discover how to pick the right tool for the job and make the absolute most of it every single time.

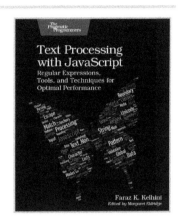

Faraz K. Kelhini
(240 pages) ISBN: 9798888650332. $51.95
https://pragprog.com/book/fkjavascript

Modern Asynchronous JavaScript

JavaScript today must interact with data-intensive APIs and networks. The solution is a program that can work *asynchronously* instead of finishing tasks in order. In modern JavaScript, instead of callbacks you'll use promises to improve your application's performance and responsiveness. JavaScript features introduced in ES2020, ES2021, and ESNext like Promise.allSettled(), Promise.any(), and top-level await help you develop small, fast, low-profile applications. With the AbortController API, cancel a pending async request before it has completed. *Modern Asynchronous JavaScript* gives you an arsenal of tools to build programs that always respond to user requests, recover quickly from difficult conditions, and deliver maximum performance.

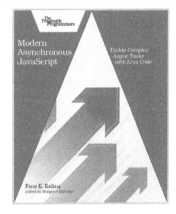

Faraz K. Kelhini
(77 pages) ISBN: 9781680509045. $14.99
https://pragprog.com/book/fkajs

Rust Brain Teasers

The Rust programming language is consistent and does its best to avoid surprising the programmer. Like all languages, though, Rust still has its quirks. But these quirks present a teaching opportunity. In this book, you'll work through a series of brain teasers that will challenge your understanding of Rust. By understanding the gaps in your knowledge, you can become better at what you do and avoid mistakes. Many of the teasers in this book come from the author's own experience creating software. Others derive from commonly asked questions in the Rust community. Regardless of their origin, these brain teasers are fun, and let's face it: who doesn't love a good puzzle, right?

Herbert Wolverson
(138 pages) ISBN: 9781680509175. $18.95
https://pragprog.com/book/hwrustbrain

Pandas Brain Teasers

This book contains 25 short programs that will challenge your understanding of Pandas. Like any big project, the Pandas developers had to make some design decisions that at times seem surprising. This book uses those quirks as a teaching opportunity. By understanding the gaps in your knowledge, you'll become better at what you do. Some of the teasers are from the author's experience shipping bugs to production, and some from others doing the same. Teasers and puzzles are fun, and learning how to solve them can teach you to avoid programming mistakes and maybe even impress your colleagues and future employers.

Miki Tebeka
(110 pages) ISBN: 9781680509014. $18.95
https://pragprog.com/book/d-pandas

Numerical Brain Teasers

Challenge your brain with math! Using nothing more than basic arithmetic and logic, you'll be thrilled as answers slot into place. Whether purely for fun or to test your knowledge, you'll sharpen your problem-solving skills and flex your mental muscles. All you need is logical thought, a little patience, and a clear mind. There are no gotchas here. These puzzles are the perfect introduction to or refresher for math concepts you may have only just learned or long since forgotten. Get ready to have more fun with numbers than you've ever had before.

Erica Sadun
(186 pages) ISBN: 9781680509748. $18.95
https://pragprog.com/book/esbrain

Go Brain Teasers

This book contains 25 short programs that will challenge your understanding of Go. Like any big project, the Go developers had to make some design decisions that at times seem surprising. This book uses those quirks as a teaching opportunity. By understanding the gaps in your knowledge, you'll become better at what you do. Some of the teasers are from the author's experience shipping bugs to production, and some from others doing the same. Teasers and puzzles are fun, and learning how to solve them can teach you to avoid programming mistakes and maybe even impress your colleagues and future employers.

Miki Tebeka
(110 pages) ISBN: 9781680508994. $18.95
https://pragprog.com/book/d-gobrain

Hands-on Rust

Rust is an exciting new programming language combining the power of C with memory safety, fearless concurrency, and productivity boosters—and what better way to learn than by making games. Each chapter in this book presents hands-on, practical projects ranging from "Hello, World" to building a full dungeon crawler game. With this book, you'll learn game development skills applicable to other engines, including Unity and Unreal.

Herbert Wolverson
(342 pages) ISBN: 9781680508161. $47.95
https://pragprog.com/book/hwrust

Programming WebAssembly with Rust

WebAssembly fulfills the long-awaited promise of web technologies: fast code, type-safe at compile time, execution in the browser, on embedded devices, or anywhere else. Rust delivers the power of C in a language that strictly enforces type safety. Combine both languages and you can write for the web like never before! Learn how to integrate with JavaScript, run code on platforms other than the browser, and take a step into IoT. Discover the easy way to build cross-platform applications without sacrificing power, and change the way you write code for the web.

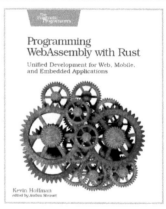

Kevin Hoffman
(238 pages) ISBN: 9781680506365. $45.95
https://pragprog.com/book/khrust

Rails 5 Test Prescriptions

Does your Rails code suffer from bloat, brittleness, or inaccuracy? Cure these problems with the regular application of test-driven development. You'll use Rails 5.2, Minitest 5, and RSpec 3.7, as well as popular testing libraries such as factory_bot and Cucumber. Updates include Rails 5.2 system tests and Webpack integration. Do what the doctor ordered to make your applications feel all better. Side effects may include better code, fewer bugs, and happier developers.

Noel Rappin

(404 pages) ISBN: 9781680502503. $47.95

https://pragprog.com/book/nrtest3

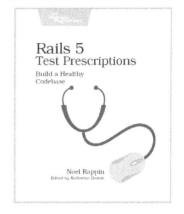

Learn to Program, Third Edition

It's easier to learn how to program a computer than it has ever been before. Now everyone can learn to write programs for themselves—no previous experience is necessary. Chris Pine takes a thorough, but lighthearted approach that teaches you the fundamentals of computer programming, with a minimum of fuss or bother. Whether you are interested in a new hobby or a new career, this book is your doorway into the world of programming.

Chris Pine

(230 pages) ISBN: 9781680508178. $45.95

https://pragprog.com/book/ltp3

The Pragmatic Bookshelf

The Pragmatic Bookshelf features books written by professional developers for professional developers. The titles continue the well-known Pragmatic Programmer style and continue to garner awards and rave reviews. As development gets more and more difficult, the Pragmatic Programmers will be there with more titles and products to help you stay on top of your game.

Visit Us Online

This Book's Home Page
https://pragprog.com/book/aapsql
Source code from this book, errata, and other resources. Come give us feedback, too!

Keep Up-to-Date
https://pragprog.com
Join our announcement mailing list (low volume) or follow us on Twitter @pragprog for new titles, sales, coupons, hot tips, and more.

New and Noteworthy
https://pragprog.com/news
Check out the latest Pragmatic developments, new titles, and other offerings.

Save on the ebook

Save on the ebook versions of this title. Owning the paper version of this book entitles you to purchase the electronic versions at a terrific discount.

PDFs are great for carrying around on your laptop—they are hyperlinked, have color, and are fully searchable. Most titles are also available for the iPhone and iPod touch, Amazon Kindle, and other popular e-book readers.

Send a copy of your receipt to support@pragprog.com and we'll provide you with a discount coupon.

Contact Us

Online Orders:	*https://pragprog.com/catalog*
Customer Service:	*support@pragprog.com*
International Rights:	*translations@pragprog.com*
Academic Use:	*academic@pragprog.com*
Write for Us:	*http://write-for-us.pragprog.com*